HAZLITT
SELECTED ESSAYS

HAZLITT
SELECTED ESSAYS

EDITED BY

GEORGE SAMPSON

Cambridge:
at the University Press
1954

PUBLISHED BY
THE SYNDICS OF THE CAMBRIDGE UNIVERSITY PRESS

London Office: Bentley House, N.W. 1
American Branch: New York

Agents for Canada, India, and Pakistan: Macmillan

First Edition 1917
Reprinted 1920
1924
1926 (*twice*)
1928
1937
1940
1950
1954

Printed in Great Britain at the University Press Cambridge
(Brooke Crutchley, University Printer)

PREFACE

IN preparing this selection from Hazlitt's many essays I have had in view the possible needs of students in Training Colleges, candidates for the Board of Education's Certificate examination, pupils in the highest forms of schools, and even those general readers who may care to have certain fine prose pieces "extra-illustrated," as it were, by appropriate annotation. My actual teaching experience with the second of these groups has shown me that one can take nothing for granted in the students' general knowledge. I have found that even the simplest allusions need elucidation and the simplest foreign phrases translation. If therefore some of the notes seem unnecessary, readers should remember that what is unnecessary to them may be useful to others.

The choice of essays will be found to embody a departure from the usual procedure in the case of Hazlitt, who is generally represented in students' editions by *Characters of Shakespear's Plays*. The present selection ranges through the whole of Hazlitt's essays from *The Round Table* to the posthumous pieces. The first four essays show him as the Boswell of Lamb and the candid friend of Wordsworth and Coleridge. The next three are an extension of this group, forming a pleasant parallel to Lamb's *Detached Thoughts on Books and Reading* and his delightful essays on the old actors. The next three show a very attractive and original Hazlitt—Hazlitt the enthusiastic critic or "gustator" of fine pictures. The last three show us Hazlitt savouring things of the world, rejoicing in the multitude of sporting crowds and in the solitude of lonely wanderings. If it be urged that political essays have been excluded, the answer must be that there is no essay of Hazlitt that is not political. Whether his subject be Poussin or pugilism, it is odd if he cannot get in a few thrusts at apostate poets and government tools.

The notes, I fear, will lie open to the charge of being, like Falstaff's waist, "out of all reasonable compass." But then Hazlitt is the most allusive of essayists, and to extend his snatches of quotation and expand his tantalising allusions is a pleasure as well as a duty. If the notes, beyond their immediate utility, tempt certain adventurers along some hinted paths of future reading, they will have accomplished the editor's chief intention. Says old Fuller in the preface to his *History of the Worthies of England*:

> I confess the subject is but dull in itself, to tell the time and place of men's births, and deaths, their names, with the names and number of their books, and therefore this bare sceleton of *Time*, *Place*, and *Person*, must be fleshed with some pleasant passages. To this intent I have purposely interlaced (not as meat, but as condiment) many delightful stories, that so the Reader if he do not arise (which I hope and desire) *Religiosor* or *Doctior*, with more Piety or Learning, at least he may depart *Jucundior* with more pleasure and lawful delight.

It is the first and best defence of the garrulous commentator—or at least of one such commentator's intention.

The introduction is necessarily more than a recital of personal facts, for Hazlitt was the child of his time. One can read Lamb without caring what century he was born in; but one will enjoy Hazlitt the more for knowing why his vigorous utterance is so often a challenge or a condemnation.

Some of Hazlitt's books have been constantly reprinted since the first issue; but much of his work was overlooked and almost unknown until the appearance of the Collected Works (12 vols., 1902–1904, Index vol. 1906), edited by A. R. Waller and Arnold Glover. To the notes of these editors I am indebted for the identification of many quotations.

GEORGE SAMPSON

BARNES

October, 1916

CONTENTS

INTRODUCTION

A GENERAL SKETCH OF HAZLITT'S LIFE AND WRITINGS

Early in the year 1778 there lived at Maidstone, in the county of Kent, a very excellent Dissenting minister named William Hazlitt. He represented a union of the three kingdoms, for he was born at Shronell, in Tipperary, educated at Glasgow (where Adam Smith was then a professor), and appointed to minister in England. The Pastor was about forty-one. His wife, Grace Loftus of Wisbech, nine years his junior, was said to have been a beauty and to have resembled the younger Pitt—we must reconcile the statements as we can. What is certain is that she was an excellent wife and mother. There were two surviving children, John, then nearly eleven, and Margaret, six-and-a-half. The little family lived in amity, and in such happiness as may be enjoyed by people of strict and lofty principle inhabiting a lax and Laodicean world.

Parentage and Birth

The times were troubled. George III, in natural intelligence a very limited monarch, and in purpose largely shaped and directed by his very German mother, was steadily labouring to substitute for constitutional government in England the sort of personal rule we shall find compendiously described in Macaulay's essay on Frederic. He had been partially successful, and one consequence of his personal kingship was then pursuing its course. The war against the American colonists was nearly three years old, and what may be called its crucial point was reached almost at the very moment we are now considering; for in February 1778 France signed a treaty with the Americans and threw her sea power into the scale against England. The war was popular in the worst sense. It was popular with the mob, who like to enjoy a cheap and extensive victory, and have therefore no objection to the bullying of a small power by a greater, when the greater is their own. The American war had seemed to promise this spectacle; and so its tragic failure had made the crowd both angry with disappointment and eager for reprisals.

But there was a minority. There were some, like Burke and Chatham, who from the beginning of trouble had urged a policy of magnanimity upon a court and government to which magnanimity was a thing incomprehensible. The reverses had caused some wavering in this party. It was felt by many that there could be no drawing back after the intervention of France; on the other hand it was urged that every additional moment of civil war made peace more remote and costly. Among the sincere and consistent pro-Americans was the Rev. William Hazlitt of Maidstone; and to his zeal on the unpopular side we must doubtless attribute the disunion that presently appeared in his congregation.

At this moment the little family in the Rose Yard manse received an addition; for on the 10th of April, 1778, into a world of foreign war, colonial revolution and domestic discord, was born a boy, William Hazlitt, the future essayist, critic and revolutionist. Wordsworth was then eight, Scott six, Coleridge five and Lamb three. A day or two before Hazlitt's birth, the great Chatham, rewarded by his sovereign for a life of patriotic labour with the title "trumpet of sedition," had fallen, a dying man, on the floor of the House of Lords. Within a few weeks, two even greater than Chatham passed over—Voltaire in May, Rousseau in July. The old heroes were falling, but, across the Channel, new champions were preparing for the coming combat. Mirabeau was then twenty-nine, Robespierre twenty and Danton eighteen. Far away in his Mediterranean island, a small boy, Napoleon Buonaparte, nearly nine, was eagerly looking forward to the military school whither he was to go in the following year.

The disagreement among the congregation at the Earl Street Meeting House in Maidstone became acute; and to avoid creating a schism, the Minister resigned his charge in 1780, and sought a new sphere of labour at Bandon, County Cork, in the island of his birth. Here he was even more unhappy, for his feelings as well as his principles were outraged by the ill-treatment to which American prisoners were subjected. The indignant Pastor called public attention to these outrages, and so we shall not be surprised to learn that he soon found it necessary to leave not merely Ireland but the British Islands. Across the western waters lay a refuge for sturdy independents. In January 1783 preliminaries of peace were signed, and a new republic entered the assembly of nations. Three months later, when the child William was a little short of five, the Hazlitt family set sail for America. They reached New York on May 26th, and proceeded on a two days' waggon journey to Philadelphia.

Ireland and America

The Pastor found no settled employment, and the family migrated often—from Philadelphia back to New York, thence to Boston, thence to Weymouth, thence to New Dorchester. The Pastor himself travelled further still. Over a wide area from Maine to Maryland he preached and lectured, contributing much to that spread of Unitarianism in America for which his more famous acquaintance Dr Priestley afterwards got most of the credit. There was near Weymouth a pleasant old nonagenarian named Gay, who had held that one ministerial charge for nearly seventy years. Him it was thought that Hazlitt might succeed; but the old gentleman clung to life and pulpit so immovably that Hazlitt resolved to return to England. He set sail in the October of 1786, and arrived in December. Almost immediately the sempiternal Gay died. The Hazlitt family remained in America for nearly another year—till July 1787, in fact, when they left Boston for England, reaching it the next month. William was then a little over nine.

We must be grateful to the vital obstinacy of the Rev. Ebenezer Gay. Had he been cut off prematurely in the early nineties the Hazlitts would probably have settled for life in New England, and William would have been the first of American essayists. But he would not have been the Hazlitt that we know. Hazlitt without the strong stimulus of European art, literature and politics would have been merely the pallid simulacrum of our Hazlitt. In the country of Jonathan Edwards he would have become probably a theologian, and almost certainly a metaphysician, unread, and perhaps unreadable, in either capacity. As it was, America did a little for him. It counted for something that the champion of popular government had spent his early impressionable years in the first of modern Republics, one of a family self-exiled from the iniquities of European kingdoms. Naturally there is little to record of the boy's life during this transatlantic period, though it happens that his earliest surviving composition is a letter, in which, at the age of nine, he reaches the melancholy conclusion that the discovery of America was a mistake, and that the country should have been left to the aboriginal inhabitants[1].

The first London lodging of the family was in Walworth,—
London and Wem
not the sordid and swarming Walworth of to-day, but the semi-rural Walworth of Mr Wemmick. There, the flowers, cates and cream of the Montpelier Tea Gardens, once a Paradise of pleasure, and now utterly submerged beneath a dingy tide of brick, so stamped themselves on the boy's mind, that all his later joy in these "suburb delights" took their colour from the gorgeous summer hues of that first garden of his innocence[2]. Later in the year 1787 the Pastor got a settled charge at Wem in Shropshire, and here for several years the growing boy remained, going to school, studying with his father, and learning French with the girls of a neighbouring family. These children he visited when they returned to Liverpool, and there he first encountered one abiding love and pleasure of his life—the theatre. Kemble and Dignum and Suett, players celebrated in many an essay later, swam like new planets into his astonished vision. He was then twelve or thirteen, and most of

[1] The authority for details of the American sojourn is a diary kept by Margaret, the essayist's sister.

[2] See *Table Talk*, "Why Distant Objects Please."

those few years had been passed far from the pleasures of cities. The Nonconformists of a century ago did not all anathematize the theatre. We hear of theatrical visits at Wem, and the reverend Pastor spoke with frequent admiration of one famous player—the Mrs Pritchard whom we know from Boswell.

It seems to have been assumed that William was to follow his father into the ministry, and so in 1793 he was duly entered as a student at the Hackney Theological College. The curriculum there, as far as his letters show, was in the best sense liberal. The classics agreeably mitigated the austerities of theology, and Hazlitt seems to have been a diligent student, though he managed astutely to substitute some cherished speculations on the political nature of man for the graver feats of exegesis expected from him. But his real education was received outside the Hackney walls. His brother John, now twenty-six, was established in London as a painter and miniaturist. The young theologian of Hackney of course paid many visits to the studio in Rathbone Place, and there encountered not only the frank-speaking and free-thinking men who gather in the rooms of young painters, but visions of the world of art, with all its happy industry and its association with beauty. The hands that should have been employed in penning theses became busy with the brushes. It was canvas, not sermon-paper that the boy longed to be filling, and so a crowning disappointment was preparing for the good old man in Shropshire. William heard the call, not of Samuel, but of Giotto. A wistful passage written many years later throws some light on the perturbations of this period. It is long, but it is so significant that it must be quoted at length:

Theology and Art

The greatest misfortune that can happen among relations is a different way of bringing up, so as to set one another's opinions and characters in an entirely new point of view. This often lets in an unwelcome day-light on the subject, and breeds schisms, coldness and incurable heart-burnings in families. I have sometimes thought whether the progress of society and march of knowledge does not do harm in this respect, by loosening the ties of domestic attachment, and preventing those who are most interested in, and anxious to think well of one another, from feeling a cordial sympathy and approbation of each other's sentiments, manners, views, &c., than it does good by any real advantage to the community at large. The son, for instance, is brought up to the church, and nothing can exceed the pride and pleasure the father takes in him, while all goes on well in this favourite direction. His notions change, and he imbibes a taste for the Fine Arts. From this moment there is an end of anything like the same unreserved communication between them. The young man may talk with enthusiasm of his "Rembrandts, Correggios, and stuff": it is all *Hebrew* to the elder; and whatever satisfaction he may feel in hearing of his son's progress, or good wishes for his success, he is never reconciled to the new pursuit, he still hankers after the first object that he had set his mind upon. Again, the grandfather is a Calvinist, who never gets the better of his disappointment at his son's going over to the Unitarian side of the question. The matter rests here, till the grandson, some years after, in the fashion of the day and "infinite agitation of men's wit," comes to doubt certain points in the creed in which he has been brought up, and the affair is all abroad again. Here are three generations made uncomfortable and in a manner set at variance, by a veering point of theology, and the officious meddling biblical critics! (*Table Talk*, "On the Knowledge of Character.)

A year after his entry into the Hackney College, Hazlitt turned his back for ever upon ministry and theology, and retired to Wem, where he passed the next few years, ostensibly doing nothing, but actually busy with reading, painting, walking, brooding and struggling to express himself in words. A volume entitled *An Essay on the Principles of Human Action*, etc. (published in 1805) occupied his busy mind and tasked his unready pen; but he had the infinite leisure of youth, and his slow progress troubled him little. It is of this and the succeeding period that he writes in the following passage:

> For many years of my life I did nothing but think. I had nothing else to do but solve some knotty point, or dip in some abstruse author, or look at the sky, or wander by the pebbled sea-side—
>
> > To see the children sporting on the shore,
> > And hear the mighty waters rolling evermore.
>
> I cared for nothing, I wanted nothing. I took my time to consider whatever occurred to me, and was in no hurry to give a sophistical answer to a question—there was no printer's devil waiting for me. I used to write a page or two perhaps in half a year; and remember laughing heartily at the celebrated experimentalist Nicholson, who told me that in twenty years he had written as much as would make three hundred octavo volumes. If I was not a great author, I could read with ever fresh delight, "never ending, still beginning," and had no occasion to write a criticism when I had done. If I could not paint like Claude, I could admire "the witchery of the soft blue sky" as I walked out, and was satisfied with the pleasure it gave me. If I was dull, it gave me little concern: if I was lively, I indulged my spirits. I wished well to the world, and believed as favourably of it as I could. I was like a stranger in a foreign land, at which I looked with wonder, curiosity and delight, without expecting to be an object of attention in return. I had no relation to the state, no duty to perform, no ties to bind me to others: I had neither friend nor mistress, wife or child. I lived in a world of contemplation, and not of action. (*Table Talk*, "On Living to Oneself.")

There were epochs in his young life marked by the days of delight when he first discovered certain treasures of great literature —the sentiment of Rousseau, the grandeur of Burke, the majesty of Milton. A sort of furious intensity characterised all he did from the days of childhood, when he fell ill through the excited exhaustion of his first studies in Latin, to the later time of manhood, when he drenched his body with the energy of his racquet-playing,

Hazlitt's Seeding Time

and inflamed his mind with the fierceness of his political fervour. Few men have hated so vigorously; few have enjoyed so gloriously; and for his much love much will be forgiven him. As the man, so the youth; and we discern him dimly in these days of adolescence, hot with pent-up and unknown powers, eager, yet baffled and inarticulate, lonely, yet happy with books and brushes, out of sympathy with his excellent father, and thinking himself steadily into a belief that he had a gift for philosophy. There are many melancholy and companionless youths who cherish the same delusion. Cheerfulness comes breaking in with the responsibilities of manhood. Meanwhile, in the great world beyond Wem, a new generation was springing up. In 1798, Hazlitt's wonder-year, when he himself was twenty, Byron was ten, Shelley six and Keats three.

And now there came to Hazlitt the revelation that opened his heart and mind and taught him to know himself. **His First Acquaintance with Poets** In 1798 he met Coleridge. The ever delightful essay in which he describes this meeting stands first in the present volume and makes any further account worse than unnecessary. The many who date an epoch in their own lives from a first reading of *Biographia* and *Lyrical Ballads* will always feel a peculiar affection for this essay, which wonderfully recaptures the thrill of youth, and mingles with its rapture so much mature and humorous wisdom. From the extent of our own vast debt to the mere printed pages of poetry and criticism we can measure the ecstasy with which young Hazlitt made his first acquaintance with poets and drank in the utterances of their own living lips. With the boy in *Comus* he could say:

> How charming is divine philosophy!
> Not harsh, and crabbèd as dull fools suppose,
> But musical as is Apollo's lute,
> And a perpetual feast of nectar'd sweets
> Where no crude surfeit reigns.

It is Coleridge who is the hero of the story, as he always will be to ardent youth,—Coleridge "in the dayspring of his fancies with hope like a fiery pillar before him." At that date it was gloriously apparent that the head of Coleridge was in the heavens; it was less obvious that his feet were in the mire of a road down to ignoble sloth and moral suicide. Coleridge was still Mirandola, not yet Micawber. Wordsworth is less attractive to the youthful mind. He seems gaunt, frigid and set, as if he had never been young. We have to turn often to those delightful early books of *The Prelude* to remind ourselves of Wordsworth's fiery, volcanic, youth.

To Hazlitt the wisdom of these poets had the weight of those **Pictures and Paris** few years' seniority that mean so much to the boy of twenty. He kindled his zeal anew at the altar fire of their genius. He felt that he must do something instantly. The talk of Coleridge turned his mind again towards philosophy, and made that unfinished and apparently interminable *Essay on the Principles of Human Action* a reproach to him. This he began anew, though as a sort of parergon, for he now solemnly chose painting, and especially portraiture, as his life work. He went to his brother in London where, in the same palpitating year, a new revelation awaited him,—the glory of great art made manifest in the Titians, Rembrandts, Rubens and Vandycks of the Orleans collection then on exhibition in Pall Mall and the Lyceum. More than ever inflamed, he tramped the country, to paint if he could, and certainly to see the pictures in great collections. Startled flunkeys tried in vain to check the excited young man who would insist on penetrating to the picture galleries of noble connoisseurs. Hazlitt wanted to see pictures, and, in his own wild way, almost fought to see them. So impressive was he in this artistic phase, that one trusting merchant in Liverpool was moved to offer him a hundred guineas for copies of certain pictures in the Louvre. It is scarcely necessary to say that he accepted. To Hazlitt Paris was simply Paradise writ small. Everything was propitious. The year was 1802 and Paris was at its greatest. The first phase of the war had been concluded by the Peace of Amiens. France was enjoying the only real emotions of tranquillity she had known since the first blows had fallen on the gates of the Bastille. There was an air of liberty new-gained yet well-established. Napoleon had just been declared First Consul for life and the Louvre was overflowing with the spoils of his Italian triumph. The city was crowded with visitors. English ladies and gentlemen flocked eagerly to see the land and people they had been tenacious in fighting, and listened, in Court and Salon, to stories of the Revolution related by Marshals of France who had been poor citizens or private soldiers at the time of the great upheaval.

In Paris, then, from October 1802 to January 1803, Hazlitt lived and worked, poor, cold and hungry, but intensely happy. He did not see Napoleon, nor did he penetrate to the distinguished circles of rank and fashion; but he breathed the charged electrical atmosphere, and rejoiced. He returned to England duly certified as the copyist of some ten or dozen pictures specified in a document signed by M. le Directeur Général du Musée Central des Arts, and epically dated "le 12 Pluviose, an 11." It was at this time that he made the acquaintance of one who was to prove his truest friend, one who spoke well of him when many spoke ill, who helped him in material need, and closed his eyes when peace came at last to his tempestuous spirit. There were many to whom Charles Lamb in various ways did good; there were few to whom his genial and wholesome influence was more beneficial than to Hazlitt; and Hazlitt knew it. Sometime friends of our author are often enough pilloried, not to say crucified, in his vengeful paragraphs; but it is impossible to read his references to Lamb without discerning unaltered admiration and something like affection. Hazlitt became one of the intimates who met at Lamb's weekly gatherings. He quarrelled, in time, with all of them, even with Lamb himself, though in this instance the enmity was neither long nor bitter. Like most shy and over-sensitive natures, Hazlitt was easily irritated, and much that was thought ill-temper was often no more than anger with himself for his own lack of social ease and smoothness. Moreover, there would sometimes arise in discussion, as we shall see, questions of principle about which he could make no compromise. Extremes meet. During the great eruption, both Burke and Hazlitt became socially explosive and impossible, the one with detestation for the Revolution, the other with admiration for it.

The business of portrait painting cannot be said to have prospered. What Hazlitt could do in this line

Farewell to Painting may be seen in the familiar portrait of Lamb attired as a Venetian senator, now in the National Portrait Gallery and frequently reproduced as a frontispiece. Hazlitt was probably as anxious to make it like a Titian as like Lamb. The mouth and chin resemble the strong profile of Hancock's drawing, but the whole picture is rather inexpressive and might be anyone but Elia. With Wordsworth and Coleridge he was even less successful. Of the Coleridge Southey writes, "you look as if you were on your trial, and had certainly stolen the horse; but then you did it cleverly." The Wordsworth was described as "at the gallows, deeply affected by his deserved fate, yet determined to die like a man." The portrait of his father, into the painting of which went so many happy hours—hours of reconciliation, no doubt—gained the distinction of a place in the Royal Academy Exhibition of 1806. It is pleasantly mentioned in the first essay on *The Pleasure of Painting*, and in a later piece, *On Sitting for One's Picture* (*Plain Speaker*). The Museum at Maidstone has four of his portraits and copies. The horrible medium he used for his colour has so blackened with age that the pictures are almost buried and might as well not exist. As time went on, Hazlitt began reluctantly to realise that painting was not his real work. Titian or Rembrandt he could not be, and less he disdained to be. But his labour had not been wasted. Painting cultivated in him the seeing eye, and made him one of the soundest among our early writers on art. Sir Joshua taught in his *Discourses* the principles that he happily forgot in his studio. Hazlitt did not write like a painter; he painted like a critic. He enjoyed certain pictures immensely, and his enjoy-ment was the begetter both of his copies and his criticisms. There are no sublimities of rapture or flights of virtuosity in his writings on art. To him a portrait by Titian was neither a moral tract nor a study in values; it was something to be relished, like a novel by Scott or a comedy by Vanbrugh or a good meal at an inn after a long day's march. He liked pictures in a hearty

cheerful fashion and his readers catch the wholesome infection.
As for himself, his painting gave him, if not a livelihood, at least
a lively joy which he never forgot. It was twenty years after
his early painting days that he wrote this passage:

> Yet I dream sometimes; I dream of the Louvre—*Intus et in cute*.
> I dreamt I was there a few weeks ago, and that the old scene returned
> —that I looked for my favourite pictures, and found them gone or
> erased. The dream of my youth came upon me; a glory and a vision
> unutterable, that comes no more but in darkness and in sleep: my
> heart rose up, and I fell on my knees, and lifted up my voice and wept,
> and I awoke. (*Plain Speaker*, "On Dreams.")

The prevailing interest in the Lamb circle was literature.
Moving among authors, Hazlitt naturally became
eager to turn certain written words of his own into
print. He managed to persuade some hopeful
bookseller to publish that perennial *Essay on the Principles of
Human Action* in 1805, and he issued next year, apparently at
his own risk, a pamphlet, now very rare, entitled *Free Thoughts
on Public Affairs*. It is difficult to prove that anyone bought a
copy of either; but at least he had appeared as a real printed
author, and went on cheerfully to perform two pieces of hack
work, the first an abridgement into one volume of the original
seven occupied by *The Light of Nature Pursued*, a leisurely philosophical miscellany written by Abraham Tucker; the second a
compilation called *The Eloquence of the British Senate*, exhibiting
the oratory of famous statesmen in specimens and their lives in
brief biographical sketches. With characteristic economy Hazlitt
used certain of these sketches again in later works. One, indeed,
the acidulated *Character of Pitt*, crops up with unfailing regularity
in so many volumes as almost to baffle enumeration. These two
works appeared in 1807, the year that saw also the publication of
Hazlitt's *Reply to Malthus*, the clergyman who had issued in 1798
a gloomy prognostication of human lot, based on the fact, clear
to him, that population was increasing in geometrical progression,
while subsistence was increasing only at the comparatively
beggarly arithmetical rate. The emphatic style of the preface to
Tucker and the bold, penetrating criticism of the Malthusian
theories indicate the coming of the real Hazlitt, whose pen was
thereafter busy for many years in many papers. Nothing came
amiss to him, from parliamentary reporting to operatic criticism.
He became, in fact, a professional man of letters, and was to
experience very fully the intermittent joys and the unfailing
chagrins of that precarious calling.

Soon after his debut as an author, Hazlitt married. In his
early London days he had made the acquaintance
of John Stoddart, an ardent Revolutionist who,
like certain others, lived to abjure his first principles
and to become a stiff champion of Legitimate Monarchy. A
knighthood and a colonial judgeship were his reward. Stoddart's

(margin notes:) Beginnings of Authorship

(margin notes:) Hazlitt's Marriages

sister Sarah had a small property at Winterslow on the road from Andover to Salisbury across the Plain. At the age of thirty-three she combined a strong inclination for matrimony in the abstract with an almost complete indifference to any bridegroom in particular. From the letters of Mary Lamb we hear of several suitors, but in the end Hazlitt was the lucky (or unlucky) man. Sarah was older than Hazlitt who, with Shakespeare's example and precepts before him, should have known better. The wooing was short, and the ceremony was performed on Mayday in 1808 at St Andrew's, Holborn. The rest of the matrimonial story had better be told at once, and then dismissed. Hazlitt married in haste and repented at leisure. The two were quite unsuited to each other. The lady found marriage in the concrete with an untidy and all-pervading man much less agreeable than marriage in the contemplative with an abstract idea of husband. She had no domestic gifts, and no sense of her deficiency. Hazlitt's own eager preoccupation with writing and painting as things-in-themselves added nothing to the household harmony and very little to the household economy. There seems to have been no violent disagreement,—nothing but a steady growth of antipathy. By 1819 they were living apart. There was no Divorce Court in England till 1857; but in Scotland, dissentient parties could be separated almost as expeditiously as eloping couples were united. To Scotland, therefore, came the inharmonious but still friendly pair, and there in 1823 they were divorced. Hazlitt ventured matrimony a second time. He was too hasty to be warned in the first case by Shakespeare, and a dozen years too early to be warned in the second by Mr Weller. He married a widow, Mrs Bridgwater, in 1824, and spent a leisurely honeymoon in travelling through France, Switzerland and Italy, combining business with pleasure by recording his impressions in some very readable sketches contributed to *The Morning Chronicle* in 1824, and collected as a volume in 1826. This second marriage was of very doubtful validity in England. Whether this weighed on the conscience of the second Mrs Hazlitt, or whether the position of being married to a man whose first wife was still living and quite friendly with him was too embarrassing for her, we do not know; but in any case the union was brief. The lady's first husband had held the rank of Lieutenant-Colonel, and she appears, by the fleeting testimony of Haydon and Leigh Hunt, to have been a woman of much personal dignity, with whom Hazlitt would have to mend his rather Bohemian (not to say Boeotian) habits. The usual story of their final separation in Switzerland at the end of the honeymoon must be received with caution. We do not really know how, when, or where they parted. The second Mrs Hazlitt disappears from the story as mysteriously as she enters it.

One other kindred incident may have its necessary mention in this place. In 1820 Hazlitt went to live (apart from his first wife) in Southampton Buildings, Chancery Lane, where a certain Mr and Mrs Walker had lodgings to let. Here he became infatuated with their daughter Sarah, and devoted a disagreeable book, half dialogue, half correspondence, to the incident.

Now revert. This digression into the backwaters of matrimony left the main stream of Hazlitt's story in the first **Winterslow** proud days of authorship. Almost the sole benefit he derived from his union with Sarah Stoddart was the discovery of Winterslow. Thither he went after his marriage; and when in later years he wanted a lodge in the wilderness, it was to Winterslow that he turned—not then, of course, to the "small property" of Sarah Stoddart, but to the Pheasant Inn or Winterslow Hut as it is more generally known to us. Here much of his best work was written and many of his happiest hours were spent. A passage from one essay may be quoted as an illustration of what may be called his Winterslow frame of mind:

If the reader is not already apprised of it, he will please to take notice that I write this at Winterslow. My style there is apt to be redundant and excursive. At other times it may be cramped, dry, abrupt; but here it flows like a river and overspreads its banks. I have not to seek for thoughts or hunt for images: they come of themselves, I inhale them with the breeze, and the silent groves are vocal with a thousand recollections—

> And visions, as poetic eyes avow,
> Hang on each leaf and cling to every bough.

Here I came fifteen years ago, a willing exile; and as I trod the lengthened greensward by the low wood-side, repeated the old line,

> My mind to me a kingdom is!

I found it so then, before, and since; and shall I faint, now that I have poured out the spirit of that mind to the world, and treated many subjects with truth, with freedom, and power, because I have been followed with one cry of abuse ever since *for not being a government-tool*?....

I look out of my window and see that a shower has just fallen: the fields look green after it, and a rosy cloud hangs over the brow of the hill; a lily expands its petals in the moisture, dressed in its lovely green and white; a shepherd boy has just brought some pieces of turf with daisies and grass for his mistress to make a bed for her sky-lark, not doomed to dip his wings in the dappled dawn—my cloudy thoughts draw off, the storm of angry politics has blown over—Mr Blackwood, I am yours—Mr Croker, my service to you—Mr T. Moore, I am alive and well—Really, it is wonderful how little the worse I am for fifteen years' wear and tear, how I come upon my legs again on the ground of truth and nature, and "look abroad into universality," forgetting that there is any such person as myself in the world. (*Plain Speaker*, "Whether Genius is conscious of its Powers.")

The allusions in this passage lead us naturally to some consideration of Hazlitt's political principles and the **Hazlitt and the French Revolution** bitter antagonism in which they involved him. Hazlitt was in a special sense the child of Revolution

He was cradled in strife, and passed his earliest years in the
new transatlantic Republic. He was eleven when the Bastille
fell, and began his career at Hackney College in the year of
the Terror. Coleridge and Wordsworth, the poetical apostles of
Revolution, first taught him to know himself, and so confirmed
him in his liberal faith that he went to the First Consul's capital
as ardent for France and freedom as any Frenchman of them all.
Even his career of authorship began with a baptism of fire, for
upon his first visible publications shone "the sun of Austerlitz."
The tragedy of Hazlitt is that in a changing world, a world of
honest conversion and of profitable recantation, he kept his first
principles fiercely unaltered. And really, seen from the angle of
the present time, those principles are nothing terrible. Let us
endeavour to view the whole matter as he saw it.

The picturesque reading of young people seems to create in
them an impression that the French Revolution and the Reign of
Terror are the same thing. To such readers the French Revolution
is little more than the continuous decapitation of elegant aristocrats
amid howls of execration from a stage mob of *tricoteuses* and *sans-
culottes*. In the unhappy history of mankind there have been
many reigns of terror with no compensatory revolutions; if the
ten months of Terror could be blotted out from French history,
the great achievements of the Revolution would remain unaltered.
The immediate beginning of that great upheaval was an attempt
to erect a workable constitution in the place of a centralised
autocracy that had hopelessly broken down. That the constitutionalists were able to extort submission from what had
seemed the most impregnable monarchy of Europe was hailed by
all free spirits as a triumph of liberty. The subsequent troubles
had their rise in the secret treachery of the French Court, and
especially its collusion with the armies of Prussia and Austria,
which presumed to dictate to France whether or not she should
reform her government. In July 1791 Austria summoned the
princes of Europe to unite against the Revolution. Hostile
German troops, aided both secretly and openly by the Court and
nobles, threatened the frontiers. The September massacres of
1792 were the answer of France to a German invasion; and
henceforward slaughter in the name of War or in the name of
Justice was to be the history of some terrible years. Hazlitt
puts the matter briefly:

It has been usual (as men remember their prejudices better than
the truth) to hold up the Coalition of the Allied Powers as having
for its end and justification the repressing the horrors of the French
Revolution; whereas, on the contrary, those horrors arose out of the
Coalition, which had for its object to root out not the evil, but the
good of the Revolution in France. (*Life of Napoleon*, Chapter v.)

To Hazlitt the struggle from first to last and in every phase
was simply the struggle of Freedom against Tyranny:

Let all the wrongs public and private produced in France by arbitrary power and exclusive privileges for a thousand years be collected in a volume, and let this volume be read by all who have hearts to feel or capacity to understand, and the strong, stifling sense of oppression and kindling burst of indignation that would follow would be that impulse of public action that led to the French Revolution. Let all the victims that have perished under the mild, paternal sway of the ancient *régime*, in dungeons, and in agony, without a trial, without an accusation, without witnesses, be assembled together, and their chains struck off, and the shout of jubilee and exultation they would make, or that nature would make at the sight, will be the shout that was heard when the Bastille fell! The dead pause that ensued among the gods of the earth, the rankling malice, the panic-fear, when they saw law and justice raised to an equality with their sovereign will, and mankind no longer doomed to be their sport, was that of fiends robbed of their prey: their struggles, their arts, their unyielding perseverance, and their final triumph was that of fiends when it is restored to them. (*Life of Napoleon*, Chap. III.)

That the continental despots, ruling by Right Divine over millions of subjects bound to the soil in a state indistinguishable from slavery, should have viewed with alarm the abatement of royal and noble prerogative in France was entirely explicable; but there was one country that might have been expected to sympathise with the Revolution—the country in which serfdom had long ago disappeared, in which abuse of royal privilege had led to a civil war and the execution of a king, and in which a drastic revolution had driven one ruler from the throne, diverted the succession to a foreign line, and bound all kings to come within the strictest confines of constitutional procedure. That sympathy was not withheld. The brightest spirits in England rejoiced at the downfall of autocracy in France. Some, indeed, were more revolutionary than the Revolutionists themselves. Coleridge and Southey, exalted to the heights of youthful enthusiasm, proposed to emigrate and found a Pantisocracy or Hyper-Utopia on the banks of the Susquehanna.

England and the Revolution

> Bliss was it in that dawn to be alive,
> But to be young was very Heaven!

In all this "pleasant exercise of hope and joy," Hazlitt came to share. Younger than the poets he admired, he believed in them as fervently as in the Revolution. But "universal England" was not with them. One mighty voice had been lifted from the first against the new *régime*. Burke, who had stood for liberty in America and justice in India, now appeared as the champion of tyranny in France. Prematurely aged by a life of struggle and ill-success, he had declined to the state of political pedantry that resists any change if it is made in some other than a prescribed way, and presently comes to resist all change merely

because it is change.   Burke in his latest phase seems to be one
of those described by Hazlitt as

a set of men existing at all times, who never can arrive at a conception
beyond the *still-life* of politics, and in the most critical circumstances
and in the convulsion and agony of states, see only the violation of
forms and etiquette. (*Life of Napoleon*, Chap. v.)

Burke found many willing hearers.   It is a sufficient comment
upon the tendency of his *Reflections* that they were admired
equally in the Court of England and the Court of Russia.   England
had changed.   What France was rejecting, England was accepting.
The French Revolution came in the midst of George III's attempt
to re-erect a royal autocracy upon the ruins of parliamentary
government.   Thirty years of his personal rule had reduced
political life in England to a degraded level of corruption and
incompetence.   An England governed by servile and venal
"King's Friends" could have no sympathy with a Revolution.
A young Englishman, travelling in 1792 with the German forces
gathering to crush France, had formulated a plan for the government of that country.   Its first and chief point was that "the
authority of the king should be perfectly re-established, and that
any liberty the people may afterwards possess should be considered as his indulgence[1]."   It is difficult to understand the
frame of mind that could ever have held in modern times this
view of liberty and government; it is still more incredible that
such a proposal should date from the summer of 1792 when the
immediate result of the Duke of Brunswick's atrocious manifesto
against the French had been the imprisonment of Louis XVI in
the Temple.   It is worth noting that the young English gentleman
who took this enlightened view of national liberty and royal
indulgence was the person who, as Lord Liverpool, held office
here as Prime Minister from 1812 to 1827.

Elated by unexpected success against the German invaders,
France became aggressive, and held that those who
were not with her were against her.   War with
England began in 1793 and lasted with few inter-
missions for twenty-two years.   The continental powers wavered;
sometimes they were leagued against France, sometimes leagued
with her; but England remained steadfastly Anti-Gallican from
1793 to 1815.   Her pretexts for that long animosity changed
from time to time, but her undeclared and unwavering purpose
never changed; and that purpose was the suppression of anything like popular government, and the re-establishment of
unlimited monarchy.   She warred not so much to suppress
revolutionary principles in France as to suppress revolutionary
principles in England.   The events in France had filled the

The Con-
tinental War

---

[1] Lord Granville Leveson Gower, *Private Correspondence*, 1781–1821
Vol. I, p. 49 (1916).

governing classes of England with panic. The excesses of the Revolution there were made the excuse for excesses of repression here. Men of honourable record were transported for advocating the measures of Parliamentary reform that had shortly before been favoured by Pitt himself; and writers of liberal tendencies were shadowed by spies and dragged before the courts upon ridiculous charges of treason. Hazlitt in his impressionable youth had met some of the sufferers. Hatred of Pitt was inhaled with his every breath. Coleridge, whom he revered, had written thus of the detested minister:

> Yon dark Scowler view,
> Who with proud words of dear-loved Freedom came—
> More blasting than the mildew from the South!
> And kissed his country with Iscariot mouth
> Ah! foul apostate from his Father's fame!

Wordsworth's later confession records the horror he felt when England joined in the hunt against France:

> What, then, were my emotions, when in arms
> Britain put forth her freeborn strength in league,
> Oh, pity and shame! with those confederate Powers!
> Not in my single self alone I found,
> But in the minds of all ingenuous youth,
> Change and subversion from that hour. No shock
> Given to my moral nature had I known
> Down to that very moment; neither lapse
> Nor turn of sentiment that might be named
> A revolution, save at this one time;
> All else was progress on the self-same path
> On which, with a diversity of pace,
> I had been travelling: this a stride at once
> Into another region. As a light
> And pliant harebell, swinging in the breeze
> On some grey rock—its birthplace—so had I
> Wantoned, fast rooted on the ancient tower
> Of my belovèd country, wishing not
> A happier fortune than to wither there:
> Now was I from that pleasant station torn
> And tossed about in whirlwind. I rejoiced,
> Yes, afterwards—truth most painful to record!
> Exulted, in the triumph of my soul,
> When Englishmen by thousands were o'erthrown,
> Left without glory on the field, or driven,
> Brave hearts! to shameful flight.   (*Prelude*, Bk x.)

Sentiments even remotely resembling these the Government were determined to suppress. The task was easy, for they were the sentiments of a rapidly dwindling minority. It is always possible to scare the "mutable many" by assuring them that they will lose the privileges they do not possess. That well-tried plan succeeded thoroughly in 1793. The people of England, who had no Parliamentary representation, and, under Pitt's recent statutes, next to no liberties, were assured that the French would rob them of their rights and liberties; and so they fought tremendously.

When the needs of France produced the Man of Destiny the purpose of England was strengthened. That France should make a Revolution was bad enough; that she should make an Emperor was worse. England became the champion of Legitimacy; and just as France, a century earlier, had warred half-heartedly to force the Stewarts back upon England, so England fought with superb and memorable tenacity to force the Bourbons back upon France. That, really, is the story of the war.

Napoleon

Napoleon was our great enemy for many years, yet in such a way that we have now almost forgotten the enmity and remember only the greatness. Seen in contrast to the aims and ideals of the monarchs who combined to crush him, he was a beneficent influence in Europe. There was more real personal and political liberty, more good and sane administration in the France of Napoleon, than in all the rest of Europe put together. An appalling count can be drawn against him; but like Elizabeth or Henry VIII or any other great sinner of history, Napoleon is entitled to be judged by the balance of his career; and no one now disputes that this balance is on the side of good. In the great and ever-changing world of political doctrine, it is presumptuous for anyone to say that this is right or that is wrong; but if we believe that the general course of man for the last hundred years has been wholesomely progressive, we have to admit that, in opposing France, we were opposing the ideals we now call right. Hazlitt had no doubt of it.

The rest of the story is significant. After the triumph of England and the extinction of Napoleon, night settled down upon Europe. It became evident that the liberty which had triumphed at Waterloo was not the liberty of peoples but the liberty of absolute monarchs. For a short time Europe endured the burden of this new-found freedom, and then began to stir uneasily. The three days' revolution of 1830 was the answer of France to the liberty imposed upon it by the infantry of Wellington and the hussars of Blücher. In England the struggles for the Reform Bill acted as a safety-valve of popular discontent; but the states of Central Europe, more used to unenlightened despotism, endured to 1848 before they exploded in revolt. Italy had to wait for half a century before the unity given it by Napoleon was again restored.

> Napoleon! 'twas a high name lifted high;
> It met at last God's thunder sent to clear
> Our compassing and covering atmosphere,
> And open a clear sight, beyond the sky,
> Of supreme empire: this of earth's was done—
> And kings crept out again to feel the sun.

The kings crept out—the peoples sate at home,—
And finding the long invocated peace
A pall embroidered with worn images
Of rights divine, too scant to cover doom
Such as they suffered,—cursed the corn that grew
Rankly, to bitter bread, on Waterloo.

A deep gloom centred in the deep repose—
The nations stood up mute to count their dead—
And *he* who owned the NAME which vibrated
Through silence,—trusting to his noblest foes,
When earth was all too gray for chivalry—
Died of their mercies, 'mid the desert sea.

The words are Mrs Browning's; the sentiments are Hazlitt's.
He grudged France her hero. He thought that
inferior nation did not deserve so great a man.
What he really wanted was an English Napoleon
who should cleanse and purify Britain as the Emperor had
cleansed and purified France. To him Napoleon was not a
tyrant, but a liberator, who had to conquer Europe because
Europe's kings had conspired to conquer France. The Napoleon
whom Hazlitt admired was the Napoleon to whom Beethoven
had first dedicated his Eroica Symphony. He was the symbol
of the French Revolution, the embodiment of a principle that
Hazlitt, as an Englishman and the inheritor of the English
Revolution, held as dear as life, the principle that there is no
Divine Right of reigning inherent in any special family, and that
peoples, therefore, may choose their own form of government.
Thus he writes:

Hazlitt and Napoleon

I have nowhere in anything I may have written declared myself
to be a Republican; nor should I think it worth while to be a martyr
and a confessor to any form or mode of government. But what I
have staked health and wealth, name and fame upon, and am ready
to do so again and to the last gasp, is this, that there is a power in
the people to change its government and its governors. That is,
I am a Revolutionist: for otherwise, I must allow that mankind are
but a herd of slaves, the property of thrones, that no tyranny or insult
can lawfully goad them to a resistance to a particular family. (*Life
of Napoleon*, Chap. XXXIV.)

A fuller confession of his faith appears in another place in the
same work:

Of my object in writing the Life here offered to the public, and of
the general tone that pervades it, it may be proper that I should
render some account (before proceeding farther) in order to prevent
mistakes and false applications. It is true, I admired the man; but
what chiefly attached me to him, was his being, as he had been long
ago designated, "the child and champion of the Revolution." Of this
character he could not divest himself, even though he wished it. He
was nothing, he could be nothing, but what he owed to himself and to
his triumphs over those who claimed mankind as their inheritance

by a divine right; and as long as he was *a thorn in the side of kings* and kept them at bay, his cause rose out of the ruins and defeat of their pride and hopes of revenge. He stood (and he alone stood) between them and their natural prey. He kept off that last indignity and wrong offered to a whole people (and through them to the rest of the world) of being handed over, like a herd of cattle, to a particular family, and chained to the foot of a legitimate throne. This was the chief point at issue—this was the great question, compared with which all others were tame and insignificant—Whether mankind were, from the beginning to the end of time, born slaves or not? As long as he remained, his acts, his very existence, gave a proud and full answer to this question. As long as he interposed a barrier, a gauntlet, and an arm of steel between us and them who alone could set up the plea of old, indefeasible right over us, no increase of power could be too great that tended to shatter this claim to pieces: even his abuse of power and aping the style and title of the imaginary gods of the earth only laughed their pretensions the more to scorn. He did many things wrong and foolish; but they were individual acts, and recoiled upon the head of the doer. They stood upon the ground of their own merits, and could not urge in their vindication "the right divine of kings to govern wrong"; they were not precedents; they were not exempt from public censure or opinion; they were not softened by prescription, nor screened by prejudice, nor sanctioned by super-stition, nor rendered formidable by a principle that imposed them as sacred obligations on all future generations: either they were state-necessities extorted by the circumstances of the time, or violent acts of the will, that carried their own condemnation in their bosom. What-ever fault might be found with them, they did not proceed upon the avowed principle, that "millions are made for one," but one for millions; and as long as this distinction was kept in view, liberty was saved, and the Revolution was untouched; for it was to establish it that the Revolution was commenced, and to overturn it that the enemies of liberty waded through seas of blood and at last succeeded. (*Life of Napoleon*, Chap. XXXI.)

If Hazlitt seems to protest too much, let us recall our incipient Prime Minister of 1792 quoted earlier, and his plan for the govern-ment of France: "the first point is that the authority of the king should be perfectly re-established, and that any liberty the people may afterwards possess should be considered as his indulgence."

All these things are as Hazlitt saw them. We may differ from him as we please, but we must understand his point of view if we are going to read him intelligently. On the whole, however, his beliefs are just the beliefs of the average Briton to-day. Hazlitt was the first of our now many Napoleonists. If he could return to this present world he might exhibit the utmost extreme of his enthusiasm without the least singularity. He would see Englishmen thronging with reverence to the shrine at the Invalides and averting their eyes with shame from the spectacle of St Helena. Hazlitt who set so much store by his "little image" of Napoleon would find the Emperor's portrait a popular picture in the most British of households. He would have to read ravenously to keep abreast of the Napoleonic literature written, translated and published in these islands. Hazlitt was cold to French tragedy but he would unbend to *L'Aiglon* of Edmond Rostand. The enthusiastic lover of Scott might care little for the Wessex novels of Thomas Hardy, but he would certainly rejoice in *The Dynasts*.

These are agreeable speculations. The dull fact is that Hazlitt held his views when they were highly unpopular and savoured of treason. And he held them the more tenaciously the more they were challenged. He began to stand alone. The glorious visions of his youth faded. The Revolution instead of being the beginning of a new life, seemed no more than the end of an old song. His friends, some revered almost to adoration, crept over to the popular and profitable side. The time was gone when

Hazlitt contra Mundum

> Coleridge and Southey, Lloyd and Lamb and Co.
> All tuned their mystic harps to praise Lepaux.

Wordsworth and Coleridge, once apostles, became apostates, and Hazlitt hated them, not only for what they were, but for what they had been. "Into what pit thou seest from what height fall'n." Wordsworth, in his view, had been bought by the Government, and had left the cause for the handful of silver he received as Distributor of Stamps. Southey, the Pantisocrat and eulogist of Wat Tyler, had become the Court Laureate, and, what was even worse, a Quarterly Reviewer. As for Coleridge!— Coleridge, who had preached in the bright dawn of life that memorable sermon against kings, had now become a pensioner of George IV[1], a pillar of Church and State, and dallied with the doctrine of Divine Right. This was the most unkindest cut of all. That Coleridge should turn traitor was the crime of crimes. It was the worse, the second, fall of man. It was sacrilege against those divine and hallowed days of youth when Harmer Hill with all its pines had stooped to listen to a poet as he passed. Upon these false friends the hand of Hazlitt was thereafter heavy. He was impatient even with Lamb, who, thinking much as Hazlitt did, nevertheless thought it more circumspectly. Hazlitt's friends certainly had much to bear. He stalked the world wrathfully, holding his pistol at the heads of all he met, demanding that they should stand and deliver a hymn to the Revolution and a eulogy of the Emperor. Certainly it must have been hard to be patient with a furious essayist who asserted that Trafalgar was a tragedy and Austerlitz a crowning mercy—who, when Napoleon's flotilla was gathered at Boulogne, insisted that all his friends should regard the prospective invader of their country as a universal benefactor. The course of events was not favourable to him. The side he took became more and more a lost cause and was at last swallowed up in total defeat. Hazlitt was not a good loser. If he did not lose his hope, he certainly lost his

[1] Not, however, till 1824.

temper. Indeed, he confesses as much in a little passage of
self-analysis:

I have often been reproached with extravagance for considering
things only in their abstract principles, and with heat or ill-temper,
for getting into a passion about what no ways concerned me. If any
one wishes to see me quite calm, they may cheat me in a bargain,
or tread upon my toes; but a truth repelled, or a sophism repeated,
totally disconcerts me, and I lose all patience. I am not, in the ordinary
acceptation of the term, *a good-natured man*; that is, many things
annoy me besides what interferes with my own ease and interest.
I hate a lie; a piece of injustice wounds me to the quick, though
nothing but the report of it reach me. Therefore I have made many
enemies and few friends; for the public know nothing of well-wishers,
and keep a wary eye on those that would reform them. Coleridge
used to complain of my irascibility in this respect, and not without
reason. Would that he had possessed a little of my tenaciousness
and jealousy of temper; and then, with his eloquence to paint the
wrong, and acuteness to detect it, his country and the cause of liberty
might not have fallen without a struggle! (*Plain Speaker*, "On
Depth and Superficiality.")

It was claimed by Coleridge and others that the first great
revulsion of their feelings towards France dated from the attack
of the Directory on the liberty of Switzerland in 1798. That
invasion, morally indefensible, is difficult to justify even on the
lower ground of military or political necessity. But, even here,
we should know what we are condemning. The Swiss Con-
federacy overthrown by France was in fact nothing like the
later and excellent Swiss Republic. The peasants of Vaud and
the Valais, held in subjection by the petty oligarchs of Berne,
knew little of the "mountain liberty" dear to the poets. When
such a man as Gibbon, the last person in the world to feel
benevolent towards political discontent, permits himself the
criticism to be found in that long youthful letter by him
describing the Swiss constitution[1], the ordinary observer is
tempted to believe that real Swiss liberty began rather than ended
with the Helvetic Republic instituted by France in 1798. But
the great fact remains, that interference with one independent
nation by another is in general utterly wrong, and specially
suspicious when lofty motives are urged in justification. Still,
when we read with admiration that splendid sonnet of Wordsworth, it is well to ask ourselves whether we ought to weep for
the subjugation of the Swiss Republic in 1798 and have no tears
for the attempted subjugation of the French Republic in 1793.

It was this national hypocrisy or inconsistency of ours that
irritated Hazlitt. He held his principles without
thought of compromise, and he had to suffer for
his tenacity. It is difficult for us to understand
the power that was wielded a century ago by the party Reviews,

Hazlitt and
the Reviewers

---

[1] *Works*, 1814, Vol. II, Letter ix.

by such persons as Gifford and Croker in the *Quarterly Review* and John Wilson (called Christopher North) in *Blackwood's Magazine*. The public seem really to have been terrorised by the truculence of these periodicals, and afraid to read or think otherwise than the Reviewers permitted. Ostensibly critical, these magazines had nothing to do with literature. They were purely political organs. If a writer was suspected of any leaning towards liberal views in politics, then the hirelings of Mr Murray in London and of Mr Blackwood in Edinburgh fell upon him with their bludgeons. Thus, Keats was friendly with Leigh Hunt; Leigh Hunt had been imprisoned for criticising the Prince Regent; therefore Keats must be bludgeoned; and bludgeoned he was in articles that are among the ineffaceable shames of our literary history. *The Edinburgh Review*, organ of the Whigs, must not be exempted from general condemnation, though Jeffrey and his contributors at their worst were cleanness itself in comparison with Gifford and Wilson. *The Edinburgh* cannot claim, like *The Quarterly*, to have killed a poet. Its most famous feat is the condemnation of Wordsworth's *Excursion* in an article beginning with the now historic words, "This will never do!"

The Tory reviewers hailed Hazlitt with joy as a fitting victim for their sport. Poor Keats had failed them. He had simply perished without any visible sign of anguish; but Hazlitt, though tough enough to last, was more easily hurt, and (delightful quality) shouted when he was hurt. Let us glance for a moment at the literary methods of that famous time. Perhaps the best of all Hazlitt's books is *Table Talk*. This was reviewed in *Blackwood* for August 1822 by someone who claimed to be a scholar and gentleman, entitled therefore to read the cockney Hazlitt a lesson in good style and manners. Here are a few sentences:

> The whole surface of these volumes is one gaping sore of wounded and festering vanity; and in short...our table-talker "is rather AN ULCER than A MAN." Now, it is one thing to feel sore, and a bad thing it is there is no denying; but to tell all the world the story of one's soreness, to be continually poking at the bandages, and displaying all the ugly things they ought to cover, is quite another, and a far worse affair.

A little of this is quite enough. Hazlitt was maddened by these attacks. He tried to retaliate in various periodicals; but he was attempting the impossible. The rowdy blackguardism that fails may perhaps be corrected, but not the rowdy blackguardism that pays. The combination of vulgarity with success is irresistible. Wilson and Gifford were "in": Hazlitt was "out"; and neither Hazlitt nor anyone else could hurt their very hypothetical feelings.

The actual events of Hazlitt's private life are not important, and only a brief recital need be made of his personal and literary doings. He lived at Winterslow from 1808 to 1812, when he moved to York Street,

Continuation of Authorship

Westminster, the house once occupied by Milton, whose noble spirit, did it haunt this sublunary world, would have consorted rather with the tenant Hazlitt than with the landlord Jeremy Bentham. In 1812 he delivered at the Russell Institution ten lectures on philosophy, some of which survived in manuscript and were printed in the *Literary Remains*. They indicate that Hazlitt's interest in philosophy was after all quite literary. The first wholly characteristic work of his to appear in book form was *The Round Table* (1817) containing matter from his contributions to *The Examiner, The Morning Chronicle* and *The Champion*. Here we have the essential Hazlitt, the Hazlitt of flashing, contentious sentences, full of matter, intimating intense enjoyment in the writer and inciting to intense enjoyment in the reader. The scale of the essays hardly allowed him to wind into his subject as he was to do later, but the imposed brevity gave his aphoristic genius its chance. The same year (1817) saw the publication of his *Characters of Shakespear's Plays*, a book which possibly its own generation found more usefully enlightening than we do. Hazlitt's enjoyment of Shakespeare had (like Lamb's) a singular completeness ensuing from his appreciation of poetry, his sense of drama, and his love for the theatre. He lived in a fortunate hour. He beheld the sunset splendour of Siddons and hailed the meridian brightness of Edmund Kean. The classic dignity of John Kemble and the fervent emotionalism of Miss O'Neill illustrated for him the extremes of Shakespeare's dramatic art. Much that we know of these dead and gone players we learn from Hazlitt. He is, in a special sense, the historian of Kean, whose first impersonations in London he praised in *The Morning Chronicle*. *A View of the English Stage* (1818) reprints a number of dramatic criticisms from *The Chronicle, The Examiner* and *The Champion*. Two years later Hazlitt wrote a fine series of theatrical essays for *The London Magazine*, not fully reprinted until 1903 (*Works*, Vol. VIII).

The years 1819–1820 were in a special sense Hazlitt's "lecture years," for at the Surrey Institution in the Blackfriars Road he delivered those three sets of discourses that form the matter of three excellent and always popular volumes, *Lectures on the English Poets* (1818), *Lectures on the English Comic Writers* (1819) and *Lectures chiefly on the Dramatic Literature of the Reign of Queen Elizabeth* (1820). Talfourd gives an interesting description of Hazlitt as lecturer:

Hazlitt as Lecturer

Mr Hazlitt delivered three courses of lectures at the Surrey Institution ...before audiences with whom he had but "an imperfect sympathy." They consisted chiefly of Dissenters, who agreed with him in his hatred of Lord Castlereagh, but who "loved no plays"; of Quakers, who approved him as the opponent of Slavery and Capital Punishment, but who "heard no music"; of citizens devoted to the main chance, who had a hankering after "the improvement of the mind," but to whom his favourite doctrine of its natural disinterestedness was a riddle; of a few enemies who came to sneer; and a few friends who were eager to learn and admire. The comparative insensibility of the bulk of his audience to his finest passages sometimes provoked him to awaken their attention by points which broke the train of his discourse, after which he could make himself amends by some abrupt paradox which might set their prejudices on edge, and make them fancy they were shocked....He once had an edifying advantage over them. He was enumerating the humanities which endeared Dr Johnson to his mind; and at the close of an agreeable catalogue mentioned, as last and noblest, "his carrying the poor victim of disease and dissipation on his back through Fleet Street," at which a titter rose from some, who were struck by the picture as ludicrous, and a murmur from others, who deemed the allusion unfit for ears polite. He paused for an instant and then added in his sturdiest and most impressive manner, "an act which realises the parable of the Good Samaritan," at which his moral and delicate hearers shrank rebuked into deep silence. He was not eloquent in the true sense of the term; for his thoughts were too weighty to be moved along by the shallow stream of feeling which an evening's excitement can rouse. He wrote all his lectures, and read them as they were written; but his deep voice and earnest manner suited his matter well. He seemed to dig into his subject—and not in vain. (*Literary Remains.*)

But a greater than Talfourd was listening to Hazlitt. Writing to his brother in February 1818, Keats observes:

I hear Hazlitt's lectures regularly, his last was on Gray, Collins, Young, etc., and he gave a very fine piece of discriminating criticism on Swift, Voltaire and Rabelais. I was very disappointed at his treatment of Chatterton.

The poet was then twenty-two and had but another three years of life before him. His first slim volume had already appeared. *Endymion*, dedicated to the memory of that same Chatterton, was being hastily prepared for the printer. A few weeks earlier he had noted "Hazlitt's depth of taste" as being one of three things to rejoice at in the world of his time. The other two were *The Excursion*—and the pictures of Haydon. Upon the last we may remark that much can be forgiven to friendship.

Two other important publications by Hazlitt belong to the year 1819, *A Letter to William Gifford Esq.* and *Political Essays*. The latter work contains many pieces collected from various periodicals (together with some "characters" from his early compilation *The Eloquence of the British Senate*), and exhibits Hazlitt at his best and worst. Some pieces are little more than rancorous journalism with no permanent interest; but others are among his very finest essays. The *Letter to Gifford* was a deliberate attempt to get even with that person. The pamphlet has been highly praised as a piece of tremendous invective, but, really, it is much less vitriolic than some of

Hazlitt and Gifford

Hazlitt's shorter pieces—the character of Gifford, for instance, in *The Spirit of the Age*. It is far too long. Burke's *Letter to a Noble Lord*, which the admiring Hazlitt probably had in mind as a model of scale, is so different in scope as to afford the reader an instructive exercise in the comparison of effective and ineffective polemic. Hazlitt made the tactical mistake of attempting to argue with his adversary. With an insistence that is almost pathetic, Hazlitt tries to convince Gifford (and such of the world as might read the epistle) that he is a metaphysician of parts; and so the Letter concludes with another attempt to restate his views on the Natural Disinterestedness of the Human Mind. As befits a now practised writer, Hazlitt is vastly more lucid than in his efforts of twenty years earlier, but he leaves us without any conviction that his alleged metaphysical discovery is either true or useful.

In 1821 appeared the first volume of his *Table Talk*, the second following a year later. Among several works of high excellence it is hard to choose one and call it best. Still, most lovers of Hazlitt, restricted to one, would probably give their choice to this body of essays, so hard to match for variety of subject, brilliance of style and valid criticism of life and letters. The *Characteristics* of 1823 was an attempt to imitate the *Maxims* of La Rochefoucauld. It cannot be called entirely successful. Hazlitt's best aphorisms are to be found scattered in profusion up and down his longer essays; his deliberate attempts at epigram are more like excised paragraphs than the stamped and coined utterance of genuine aphorism.

Sketches of the Principal Picture Galleries in England (1824) recalls the adventures of the early painting days, and confirms the view that Hazlitt was, on the whole, an excellent critic of pictures. Nowhere does he attempt a purely literary fantasia upon a theme pictorial such as we find, for instance, in Ruskin's description of Tintoretto's "Last Judgment," where much of the critic's ecstasy arises from imagined beauties that are simply not paintable. With Hazlitt a picture is never more than a picture, and so we enjoy his writing as he enjoyed the picture. Sometimes he seems to enjoy certain pictures that later, and presumably better, taste prefers to neglect, but on the whole his judgment is quite remarkably in accord with modern preferences.

In 1825 appeared *The Spirit of the Age or Contemporary Portraits*, a series of character sketches fuller, rounder and less distorted than his earlier efforts in this line. Lamb praises it highly in a letter to Bernard Barton, calling the Horne Tooke "a matchless portrait." It is indeed one of Hazlitt's best works. The essence of a whole period is concentrated in its pungent pages. It was followed in 1826 by *The Plain Speaker*, a collection of essays matching the *Table Talk*, and only slightly less excellent than its companion. To the same year belongs the *Notes of a Journey* mentioned earlier.

During all this busy period Hazlitt had migrated a good deal.

The Life of
Napoleon

He lived at York Street till 1819. We find him in Southampton Buildings during 1820–22, and later in such respectable thoroughfares as Down Street and Half-Moon Street; after which Bouverie Street seems a decline. All these sojournings must be understood as punctuated by frequent flights to Winterslow. His last lodging was in Frith Street, Soho, whither he went in 1830. He was now past his half-century. His health had begun to fail, and his circumstances, depending as they did upon his immediate efforts, naturally grew difficult. Since 1826 he had been labouring at his longest, least read and most unprofitable work, the *Life of Napoleon* Upon this child of his growing age he lavished his tenderest care and his fullest exertions; but it proved a child of sorrow. Three volumes appeared in 1828, and the fourth in 1830, the year of his death. It attracted little notice, and, the publishers failing, Hazlitt got nothing. What interest it still retains centres, of course, in Hazlitt, not in Napoleon. The life of Napoleon could not be written in 1826. It can hardly be written even now. Still, we cannot say that Hazlitt made the best use of the material open to him. He was essentially an essayist, and lost his touch on the large canvas of a great historical picture. Its chief literary fault is a lack of sustained narrative power. Few indeed are the Gibbons, Macaulays and Carlyles, and Hazlitt is not numbered among those who approach the standard of these giants. He cannot compare even with less exalted historians. His account of that epic adventure, the Campaign in Italy, is simply tame; and his story of Brumaire, set by the side of Mr Fisher's, exhibits the difference between forced effort and genuine impulse. Hazlitt's easy and sweeping generalisations about the French and English national character will not do. He could not forgive France for deserting the Emperor so basely, and prostrating herself before the Allied sovereigns so abjectly; and so he rarely loses an opportunity of pouring out contempt. Even his view of the military operations has a political bias. Beside that dazzling line of Marshals the English commanders certainly make very little show; but they were not all fools. Hazlitt's denial of talent to Wellington is as stupid as Tolstoy's denial of genius to Napoleon.

The story of the Emperor's glorious rise and tragic fall was, appropriately, Hazlitt's last work. One other book, however, belongs to 1830, an odd and attractive volume reprinting various magazine articles in which Hazlitt had recorded his conversations with the painter James Northcote. This is not one of the most generally read among his works; yet it contains more keen and sagacious comments on books, pictures and life in general than are dreamt of in the philosophy of many graver authors. How much is Hazlitt and how much is Northcote it is impossible to say; but all of it is delightful.

In August 1830 Hazlitt became seriously ill. For a short
time, during his early days as a Parliamentary
reporter, he had exceeded in the matter of intoxi-
cants, but he soon abandoned an evil habit that
was due more to his surroundings than to his desires. As com-
pensation he took to tea, and for the rest of his life drank that
enchanting liquor not wisely, but too strong. The occasional
references in his work to indigestion are significant. It is even
possible that excess of tea may have shortened his life, for his
fatal illness arose from internal inflammation. Alone, and in
poverty, he gradually sank for several weeks. Material help
came from his old editor Lord Jeffrey and his old friend Charles
Lamb; but he was then beyond the reach of human aid. He
went out with the Bourbons. Some years before, he had said,
"I confess I should like to live to see the downfall of the Bourbons.
That is a vital question with me; and I shall like it the better
the sooner it happens " (*Table Talk*, "On the Fear of Death ").
He had his wish. The last Bourbon king of France fled his
country after the July Revolution of 1830. The news cheered
Hazlitt, but he could scarcely believe that the change was permanent. The other changes he was not to see. He died on the
18th of September 1830 at the age of fifty-two—young for the
child of such long-lived parents. Had he reached the years of
his father he would have seen the best days of Napoleon III;
had he reached the years of his mother he would have seen the
worst.

Sickness and Death (margin note)

Six years after his death appeared two volumes of *Literary
Remains* containing, as preliminaries, a short biography by his son, some *Thoughts on the Genius
of Hazlitt* by Lytton, and a valuable personal sketch by Talfourd.
The bulk of the work was occupied by essays and papers not
republished by Hazlitt in any of his books. Included among
these were such masterpieces as *The Fight* and *My First Acquaintance with Poets*. Some of them were reprinted in a still later
volume called *Winterslow*, embodying pieces written in that loved
retreat. Quite a mass of his work, including sixteen long essays
written for *The Edinburgh Review* between 1814 to 1830, remained
uncollected until the appearance of the complete edition of his
works a few years ago.

Posthuma (margin note)

Hazlitt died, as he had lived, in an attitude of defiance; for
the last recorded utterance of one who had dealt
and suffered many a shrewd blow for the sake of
a lost cause was, "Well, I have had a happy life."
There is no need to doubt it. The man who praised the
English "bruisers" found his joy in combat. Whatever else
Hazlitt is, tame he is never. He enjoyed as strenuously as he
fought. For him a book, a picture, or a walk is an adventure.
Adventures are to the adventurous, Disraeli tells us; and for
Hazlitt the age of adventure was never past. According to

Essays in Adventure (margin note)

Cervantes, adventures should begin at an inn. Hazlitt's usually ended there. Think of such essays as *The Fight* and *On Going a Journey*. Think how many passages in his work can be typified by such a sentence as: "It was on the 10th of April, 1798, that I sat down to a volume of the New Eloise, at the inn at Llangollen, over a bottle of sherry and a cold chicken." Consider the spirit of such a passage as the following:

The greatest pleasure in life is that of reading, while we are young. I have had as much of this pleasure, perhaps, as anyone. As I grow older, it fades; or else the stronger stimulus of writing takes off the edge of it. At present, I have neither time nor inclination for it: yet I should like to devote a year's entire leisure to a course of the English Novelists; and perhaps clap on that old sly knave Sir Walter, to the end of the list. It is astonishing how I used formerly to relish the style of certain authors, at a time when I myself despaired of ever writing a single line. Probably this was the reason. It is not in mental as in natural ascent—intellectual objects seem higher when we survey them from below, than when we look down from any given elevation above the common level. My three favourite writers about the time I speak of were Burke, Junius, and Rousseau. I was never weary of admiring and wondering at the felicities of the style, the turns of expression, the refinements of thought and sentiment: I laid the book down to find out the secret of so much strength and beauty, and took it up again in despair, to read on and admire. So I passed whole days, months, and I may add, years; and have only this to say now, that as my life began, so I could wish it may end. The last time I tasted this luxury in full perfection was one day after a sultry day's walk in summer between Farnham and Alton. I was fairly tired out; I walked into an inn-yard (I think at the latter place); I was shown by the waiter to what looked at first like common out-houses at the other end of it, but they turned out to be a suite of rooms, probably a hundred years old—the one I entered opened into an old-fashioned garden, embellished with beds of larkspur and a leaden Mercury; it was wainscoted, and there was a grave-looking, dark-coloured portrait of Charles II hanging up over the tiled chimney-piece. I had *Love for Love* in my pocket, and began to read; coffee was brought in a silver coffee-pot; the cream, the bread and butter, everything was excellent, and the flavour of Congreve's style prevailed over all. I prolonged the entertainment till a late hour, and relished this divine comedy better even than when I used to see it played by Miss Mellon, as *Miss Prue*; Bob Palmer, as *Tattle*; and Bannister, as honest *Ben*. This circumstance happened just five years ago, and it seems like yesterday. If I count my life so by lustres, it will soon glide away; yet I shall not have to repine, if, while it lasts, it is enriched with a few such recollections! (*Plain Speaker*, "Whether Genius is conscious of its Powers.")

Can we doubt that one in whom the will to adventure was so strong had a happy life? The sense of thrill and discovery in Hazlitt gives to his essays a kinship with the great literature of adventure or wayfaring, the literature that begins for us with *The Odyssey* and includes in later times such different and de-

lightful books as *The Pilgrim's Progress*, *Tom Jones*, the writings
of Borrow and *The Pickwick Papers*. A fondness for Hazlitt is
a fondness for health in literature.

Into any general criticism of his writing this is not the place
Hazlitt's   to enter. One or two points, however, should be
Prose   noticed. Hazlitt's frequent epigrammatic brilliance
is never false glitter. Some later essayists have been tempted to
say brilliant things, not because they are true, but merely because
they are brilliant. Hazlitt is guiltless of this bid for applause.
Whatever virtues he may have lacked, moral and intellectual
honesty he had in unusual fullness. Forcible, and even furious,
he may sometimes be called; but he is no swaggering companion,
he is no Ancient Pistol of prose, merely blusterous and truculent,
like some who have thought to imitate him. Hazlitt wrote from
fierce unshakeable convictions, and his literary rectitude is as
unimpeachable as his political consistency. He is not, like Lamb,
a "quaint" writer. Indeed, he says of himself, "I hate my style
to be known, as I hate all idiosyncracy." Nor is he one of those
whom we may call great architects of prose—like the Burke whose
domed and pinnacled sentences not all the sundering rancour of
the Revolution could prevent Hazlitt from admiring. Much of
his work is what we should call journalism—current criticism,
hastily set down for waiting periodicals; and the wonder is that
its average is so high—so high that Stevenson the fastidious feels
compelled to assure us that, though we are mighty fine fellows
nowadays, we cannot write like William Hazlitt. Now and then
he cheers our imperfection by giving us a bad sentence or a
breathless paragraph, but not often. His most noticeable oddity
is a trick of separating antecedent and relative too far, at times
with unhappy results, as when he writes, "On the contrary, the
celebrated person just alluded to might be said to grind the
sentences between his teeth, which he afterwards committed to
paper" (*Plain Speaker*, "Prose Style of Poets"). But these faults
are lost in the general excellence of his work, which combines
brilliance with unstudied ease of manner in a style altogether his
own. He never strains after "fine writing," but he rises, when
he wishes, to heights of noble and moving eloquence.

Walter Bagehot, who owed something of his own bright style
Hazlitt and   to Hazlitt, and might have learned from him, with
his Con-   advantage, to relax the personal reserve that makes
temporaries   his sparkling utterance just a little frigid, actually
preferred Hazlitt to Lamb, thereby incurring the wrath of his
(and Hazlitt's) old acquaintance Crabb Robinson:

> He nearly quarrelled with me...for urging that Hazlitt was a much
> greater writer than Charles Lamb—a harmless opinion which I still
> hold, but which Mr Robinson met with this outburst: "You, sir,
> YOU prefer the works of that scoundrel, that odious, that malignant
> writer, to the exquisite essays of that angelic creature!" (*Literary
> Studies*, "Henry Crabb Robinson.")

Bagehot is distinguished enough to be entitled to a preference which the normal reader need neither make nor share. The obvious and wholesome thing to do is to avoid invidious distinction between two essayists of very different excellence and to enjoy each for the best he has to give.

Both Lamb and Hazlitt were on the side of the ancients. They are safer guides to us when they write of the poets and dramatists of older and more flavoured times than on the rare occasions when they touch on the newer literature. Hazlitt has occasionally some good references to Byron, but on the whole his attitude is one of suspicion. Neither Lamb nor Hazlitt had a genuine liking for Keats, and their misunderstanding of Shelley was simply abject. On the other hand Hazlitt's admiration for the Waverley novels was as tremendous as Borrow's depreciation of them was ludicrous. Hazlitt's acquaintance with foreign literature (other than a few works by Rousseau) was very very small, and his references to the current music of his day indicate that the higher reaches of that art were quite beyond him.

The portraits of Hazlitt are many, but so various as to leave us with no such clear and instantly recognisable image of the man as we have, say, of Scott, or Burns, or Wordsworth. Talfourd's pen-portrait is admirable:

Hazlitt the Man

In person Mr Hazlitt was of the middle size, with a handsome and eager countenance, worn by sickness and thought, and dark hair, which had curled stiffly over the temples, and was only of late years sprinkled with grey. His gait was slouching and awkward, and his dress neglected; but when he began to talk, he could not be mistaken for a common man. In the company of persons with whom he was not familiar his bashfulness was painful; but when he became entirely at ease, and entered on a favourite topic, no one's conversation was ever more delightful. (*Literary Remains.*)

So much for the outward man. For the rest let us summon another witness. Thus writes Lamb in that *Letter of Elia to Robert Southey* which gave the self-righteous laureate a trouncing he deserved and preserves for us many tributes to Elian friends:

What hath soured him [Hazlitt], and made him to suspect his friends of infidelity towards him, when there was no such matter, I know not. I stood well with him for fifteen years (the proudest of my life), and have ever spoke my full mind of him to some, to whom his panegyric must naturally be least tasteful. I never in thought swerved from him, I never betrayed him, I never slackened in my admiration of him, I was the same to him (neither better nor worse) though he could not see it, as in the days when he thought fit to trust me. At this instant, he may be preparing for me some compliment, above my deserts, as he has sprinkled many such among his admirable books, for which I rest his debtor; or, for anything I know, or can guess to the contrary, he may be about to read a lecture on my weaknesses. He is welcome to them (as he was to my humble hearth), if they can divert a spleen, or ventilate a fit of sullenness. I wish he would not quarrel with the world at the rate he does; but the reconciliation must be effected by himself, and I despair of living to see that day. But, protesting against much that he has written, and some things which he chooses to do; judging him by his conversation which I enjoyed so long, and relished so deeply; or by his books, in those places where no clouding passion intervenes—I should belie my own conscience, if I said less, than that I think W. H. to be, in his natural and healthy state, one of the wisest and finest spirits breathing. So far from being ashamed of that intimacy, which was betwixt us, it is my boast that I was able for so many years to have preserved it entire; and I think I shall go to my grave without finding, or expecting to find, such another companion.

To this it would be an offence to add another word.

MY FIRST ACQUAINTANCE WITH POETS

My father was a Dissenting Minister at W——m in Shropshire; and in the year 1798 (the figures that compose that date are to me like the 'dreaded name of Demogorgon') Mr Coleridge came to Shrewsbury, to succeed Mr Rowe in the spiritual charge of a Unitarian Congregation there. He did not come till late on the Saturday afternoon before he was to preach; and Mr Rowe, who himself went down to the coach in a state of anxiety and expectation, to look for the arrival of his successor, could find no one at all answering the description but a round-faced man in a short black coat (like a shooting jacket) which hardly seemed to have been made for him, but who seemed to be talking at a great rate to his fellow-passengers. Mr Rowe had scarce returned to give an account of his disappointment, when the round-faced man in black entered, and dissipated all doubts on the subject, by beginning to talk. He did not cease while he staid; nor has he since, that I know of. He held the good town of Shrewsbury in delightful suspense for three weeks that he remained there, 'fluttering the *proud Salopians* like an eagle in a dove-cote'; and the Welch mountains that skirt the horizon with their tempestuous confusion, agree to have heard no such mystic sounds since the days of

High-born Hoel's harp or soft Llewellyn's lay!

As we passed along between W——m and Shrewsbury, and I eyed their blue tops seen through the wintry branches, or the red rustling leaves of the sturdy oak-trees by the road-side, a sound was in my ears as of a Siren's song; I was stunned, startled with it, as from deep sleep; but I had no notion then that I should ever be able to express my admiration

to others in motley imagery or quaint allusion, till the light
of his genius shone into my soul, like the sun's rays glittering
in the puddles of the road.   I was at that time dumb, inarticulate, helpless, like a worm by the way-side, crushed, bleeding,
lifeless; but now, bursting from the deadly bands that bound
them,

> With Styx nine times round them,

my ideas float on winged words, and as they expand their
plumes, catch the golden light of other years.   My soul has
indeed remained in its original bondage, dark, obscure, with
longings infinite and unsatisfied; my heart, shut up in the
prison-house of this rude clay, has never found, nor will it
ever find, a heart to speak to; but that my understanding
also did not remain dumb and brutish, or at length found
a language to express itself, I owe to Coleridge.   But this is
not to my purpose.

My father lived ten miles from Shrewsbury, and was in
the habit of exchanging visits with Mr Rowe, and with
Mr Jenkins of Whitchurch (nine miles farther on) according
to the custom of Dissenting Ministers in each other's neighbourhood.   A line of communication is thus established, by which
the flame of civil and religious liberty is kept alive, and
nourishes its smouldering fire unquenchable, like the fires
in the Agamemnon of Æschylus, placed at different stations,
that waited for ten long years to announce with their blazing
pyramids the destruction of Troy.   Coleridge had agreed to
come over to see my father, according to the courtesy of the
country, as Mr Rowe's probable successor; but in the meantime I had gone to hear him preach the Sunday after his
arrival.   A poet and a philosopher getting up into a Unitarian
pulpit to preach the Gospel, was a romance in these degenerate
days, a sort of revival of the primitive spirit of Christianity,
which was not to be resisted.

It was in January, 1798, that I rose one morning before
daylight, to walk ten miles in the mud, and went to hear this
celebrated person preach.   Never, the longest day I have to
live, shall I have such another walk as this cold, raw,
comfortless one, in the winter of the year 1798.   *Il y a des
impressions que ni le tems ni les circonstances peuvent effacer.*

Dusse-je vivre des siècles entiers, le doux tems de ma jeunesse ne peut renaître pour moi, ni s'effacer jamais dans ma mémoire. When I got there, the organ was playing the 100th psalm, and, when it was done, Mr Coleridge rose and gave out his text, 'And he went up into the mountain to pray, HIMSELF, ALONE.' As he gave out this text, his voice 'rose like a steam of rich distilled perfumes,' and when he came to the two last words, which he pronounced loud, deep, and distinct, it seemed to me, who was then young, as if the sounds had echoed from the bottom of the human heart, and as if that prayer might have floated in solemn silence through the universe. The idea of St John came into mind, 'of one crying in the wilderness, who had his loins girt about, and whose food was locusts and wild honey.' The preacher then launched into his subject, like an eagle dallying with the wind. The sermon was upon peace and war; upon church and state—not their alliance, but their separation—on the spirit of the world and the spirit of Christianity, not as the same, but as opposed to one another. He talked of those who had 'inscribed the cross of Christ on banners dripping with human gore.' He made a poetical and pastoral excursion,—and to shew the fatal effects of war, drew a striking contrast between the simple shepherd boy, driving his team afield, or sitting under the hawthorn, piping to his flock, 'as though he should never be old,' and the same poor country-lad, crimped, kidnapped, brought into town, made drunk at an alehouse, turned into a wretched drummer-boy, with his hair sticking on end with powder and pomatum, a long cue at his back, and tricked out in the loathsome finery of the profession of blood.

> Such were the notes our once-lov'd poet sung.

And for myself, I could not have been more delighted if I had heard the music of the spheres. Poetry and Philosophy had met together. Truth and Genius had embraced, under the eye and with the sanction of Religion. This was even beyond my hopes. I returned home well satisfied. The sun that was still labouring pale and wan through the sky, obscured by thick mists, seemed an emblem of the *good cause*; and the cold dank drops of dew that hung half melted on the beard of the thistle, had something genial and refreshing in them;

for there was a spirit of hope and youth in all nature, that turned every thing into good. The face of nature had not then the brand of Jus Divinum on it:

> Like to that sanguine flower inscrib'd with woe.

On the Tuesday following, the half-inspired speaker came. I was called down into the room where he was, and went half-hoping, half-afraid. He received me very graciously, and I listened for a long time without uttering a word. I did not suffer in his opinion by my silence. 'For those two hours,' he afterwards was pleased to say, 'he was conversing with W. H.'s forehead!' His appearance was different from what I had anticipated from seeing him before. At a distance, and in the dim light of the chapel, there was to me a strange wildness in his aspect, a dusky obscurity, and I thought him pitted with the small-pox. His complexion was at that time clear, and even bright—

> As are the children of yon azure sheen.

His forehead was broad and high, light as if built of ivory, with large projecting eyebrows, and his eyes rolling beneath them like a sea with darkened lustre. 'A certain tender bloom his face o'erspread,' a purple tinge as we see it in the pale thoughtful complexions of the Spanish portrait-painters, Murillo and Velasquez. His mouth was gross, voluptuous, open, eloquent; his chin good-humoured and round; but his nose, the rudder of the face, the index of the will, was small, feeble, nothing—like what he has done. It might seem that the genius of his face as from a height surveyed and projected him (with sufficient capacity and huge aspiration) into the world unknown of thought and imagination, with nothing to support or guide his veering purpose, as if Columbus had launched his adventurous course for the New World in a scallop, without oars or compass. So at least I comment on it after the event. Coleridge in his person was rather above the common size, inclining to the corpulent, or like Lord Hamlet, 'somewhat fat and pursy.' His hair (now, alas! grey) was then black and glossy as the raven's, and fell in smooth masses over his forehead. This long pendulous hair is peculiar to enthusiasts, to those whose minds tend heavenward; and is traditionally inseparable (though of a different colour) from the pictures of Christ. It ought to belong, as a character, to all who preach *Christ crucified*, and Coleridge was at that time one of those!

It was curious to observe the contrast between him and my father, who was a veteran in the cause, and then declining into the vale of years. He had been a poor Irish lad, carefully brought up by his parents, and sent to the University of Glasgow (where he studied under Adam Smith) to prepare him for his future destination. It was his mother's proudest wish to see her son a Dissenting Minister. So if we look back to past generations (as far as eye can reach) we see the same hopes, fears, wishes, followed by the same disappointments, throbbing in the human heart; and so we may see them (if we look forward) rising up for ever, and disappearing, like vapourish bubbles, in the human breast! After being tossed about from congregation to congregation in the heats of the Unitarian controversy, and squabbles about the American war, he had been relegated to an obscure village, where he was to spend the last thirty years of his life, far from the only converse that he loved, the talk about disputed texts of Scripture and the cause of civil and religious liberty. Here he passed his days, repining but resigned, in the study of the Bible, and the perusal of the Commentators,—huge folios, not easily got through, one of which would outlast a winter! Why did he pore on these from morn to night (with the exception of a walk in the fields or a turn in the garden to gather broccoli-plants or kidney-beans of his own rearing, with no small degree of pride and pleasure)?—Here were 'no figures nor no fantasies,'—neither poetry nor philosophy— nothing to dazzle, nothing to excite modern curiosity; but to his lack-lustre eyes there appeared, within the pages of the ponderous, unwieldy, neglected tomes, the sacred name of JEHOVAH in Hebrew capitals: pressed down by the weight of the style, worn to the last fading thinness of the understanding, there were glimpses, glimmering notions of the patriarchal wanderings, with palm-trees hovering in the horizon, and processions of camels at the distance of three thousand years; there was Moses with the Burning Bush, the number of the Twelve Tribes, types, shadows, glosses on the law and the prophets; there were discussions (dull enough) on the age of

Methuselah, a mighty speculation! there were outlines, rude guesses at the shape of Noah's Ark and of the riches of Solomon's Temple; questions as to the date of the creation, predictions of the end of all things; the great lapses of time, the strange mutations of the globe were unfolded with the voluminous leaf, as it turned over; and though the soul might slumber with an hieroglyphic veil of inscrutable mysteries drawn over it, yet it was in a slumber ill-exchanged for all the sharpened realities of sense, wit, fancy, or reason. My father's life was comparatively a dream; but it was a dream of infinity and eternity, of death, the resurrection, and a judgment to come!

No two individuals were ever more unlike than were the host and his guest. A poet was to my father a sort of non-descript: yet whatever added grace to the Unitarian cause was to him welcome. He could hardly have been more surprised or pleased, if our visitor had worn wings. Indeed, his thoughts had wings; and as the silken sounds rustled round our little wainscoted parlour, my father threw back his spectacles over his forehead, his white hairs mixing with its sanguine hue; and a smile of delight beamed across his rugged cordial face, to think that Truth had found a new ally in Fancy[1]! Besides, Coleridge seemed to take considerable notice of me, and that of itself was enough. He talked very familiarly, but agreeably, and glanced over a variety of subjects. At dinner-time he grew more animated, and dilated in a very edifying manner on Mary Wolstonecraft and Mackintosh. The last, he said, he considered (on my father's speaking of his *Vindiciæ Gallicæ* as a capital performance) as a clever scholastic man—a master of the topics,—or as the ready warehouseman of letters, who knew exactly where to lay his hand on what he wanted, though the goods were not his own. He thought him no match for Burke, either in style or matter. Burke was a metaphysician, Mackintosh a mere logician. Burke was an orator (almost a poet) who

[1] My father was one of those who mistook his talent after all. He used to be very much dissatisfied that I preferred his Letters to his Sermons. The last were forced and dry; the first came naturally from him. For ease, half-plays on words, and a supine, monkish, indolent pleasantry, I have never seen them equalled.

reasoned in figures, because he had an eye for nature: Mackintosh, on the other hand, was a rhetorician, who had only an eye to common-places. On this I ventured to say that I had always entertained a great opinion of Burke, and that (as far as I could find) the speaking of him with contempt might be made the test of a vulgar democratical mind. This was the first observation I ever made to Coleridge, and he said it was a very just and striking one. I remember the leg of Welsh mutton and the turnips on the table that day had the finest flavour imaginable. Coleridge added that Mackintosh and Tom Wedgwood (of whom, however, he spoke highly) had expressed a very indifferent opinion of his friend Mr Wordsworth, on which he remarked to them—'He strides on so far before you, that he dwindles in the distance!' Godwin had once boasted to him of having carried on an argument with Mackintosh for three hours with dubious success; Coleridge told him—'If there had been a man of genius in the room, he would have settled the question in five minutes.' He asked me if I had ever seen Mary Wolstonecraft, and I said, I had once for a few moments, and that she seemed to me to turn off Godwin's objections to something she advanced with quite a playful, easy air. He replied, that 'this was only one instance of the ascendancy which people of imagination exercised over those of mere intellect.' He did not rate Godwin very high[1] (this was caprice or prejudice, real or affected) but he had a great idea of Mrs Wolstonecraft's powers of conversation, none at all of her talent for bookmaking. We talked a little about Holcroft. He had been asked if he was not much struck *with* him, and he said, he thought himself in more danger of being struck *by* him. I complained that he would not let me get on at all, for he required a definition of every the commonest word, exclaiming, 'What do you mean by a *sensation,* Sir? What do you mean by an *idea*?' This, Coleridge said, was barricadoing the road to truth:—it was setting up a turnpike-gate at every step we took. I forget a great number of things, many more than

[1] He complained in particular of the presumption of attempting to establish the future immortality of man 'without' (as he said) 'knowing what Death was or what Life was'—and the tone in which he pronounced these two words seemed to convey a complete image of both.

I remember; but the day passed off pleasantly, and the next morning Mr Coleridge was to return to Shrewsbury. When I came down to breakfast, I found that he had just received a letter from his friend T. Wedgwood, making him an offer of 150*l.* a-year if he chose to wave his present pursuit, and devote himself entirely to the study of poetry and philosophy. Coleridge seemed to make up his mind to close with this proposal in the act of tying on one of his shoes. It threw an additional damp on his departure. It took the wayward enthusiast quite from us to cast him into Deva's winding vales, or by the shores of old romance. Instead of living at ten miles distance, of being the pastor of a Dissenting congregation at Shrewsbury, he was henceforth to inhabit the Hill of Parnassus, to be a Shepherd on the Delectable Mountains. Alas! I knew not the way thither, and felt very little gratitude for Mr Wedgwood's bounty. I was presently relieved from this dilemma; for Mr Coleridge, asking for a pen and ink, and going to a table to write something on a bit of card, advanced towards me with undulating step, and giving me the precious document, said that that was his address, *Mr Coleridge, Nether-Stowey, Somersetshire*; and that he should be glad to see me there in a few weeks' time, and, if I chose, would come half-way to meet me. I was not less surprised than the shepherd-boy (this simile is to be found in Cassandra) when he sees a thunder-bolt fall close at his feet. I stammered out my acknowledgments and acceptance of this offer (I thought Mr Wedgwood's annuity a trifle to it) as well as I could; and this mighty business being settled, the poet-preacher took leave, and I accompanied him six miles on the road. It was a fine morning in the middle of winter, and he talked the whole way. The scholar in Chaucer is described as going

——Sounding on his way.

So Coleridge went on his. In digressing, in dilating, in passing from subject to subject, he appeared to me to float in air, to slide on ice. He told me in confidence (going along) that he should have preached two sermons before he accepted the situation at Shrewsbury, one on Infant Baptism, the other on the Lord's Supper, shewing that he could not administer either, which would have effectually disqualified him for the object in view. I observed that he continually crossed me on the way by shifting from one side of the foot-path to the other. This struck me as an odd movement; but I did not at that time connect it with any instability of purpose or involuntary change of principle, as I have done since. He seemed unable to keep on in a strait line. He spoke slightingly of Hume (whose Essay on Miracles he said was stolen from an objection started in one of South's sermons—*Credat Judæus Apella!*). I was not very much pleased at this account of Hume, for I had just been reading, with infinite relish, that completest of all metaphysical *choke-pears*, his *Treatise on Human Nature*, to which the *Essays*, in point of scholastic subtlety and close reasoning, are mere elegant trifling, light summer-reading. Coleridge even denied the excellence of Hume's general style, which I think betrayed a want of taste or candour. He however made me amends by the manner in which he spoke of Berkeley. He dwelt particularly on his *Essay on Vision* as a masterpiece of analytical reasoning. So it undoubtedly is. He was exceedingly angry with Dr Johnson for striking the stone with his foot, in allusion to this author's Theory of Matter and Spirit, and saying, 'Thus I confute him, Sir.' Coleridge drew a parallel (I don't know how he brought about the connection) between Bishop Berkeley and Tom Paine. He said the one was an instance of a subtle, the other of an acute mind, than which no two things could be more distinct. The one was a shop-boy's quality, the other the characteristic of a philosopher. He considered Bishop Butler as a true philosopher, a profound and conscientious thinker, a genuine reader of nature and of his own mind. He did not speak of his *Analogy*, but of his *Sermons at the Rolls' Chapel*, of which I had never heard. Coleridge somehow always contrived to prefer the *unknown* to the *known*. In this instance he was right. The *Analogy* is a tissue of sophistry, of wire-drawn, theological special-pleading; the *Sermons* (with the Preface to them) are in a fine vein of deep, matured reflection, a candid appeal to our observation of human nature, without pedantry and without bias. I told Coleridge I had written a few remarks, and was sometimes foolish enough to believe that I had made a discovery on the same subject (the *Natural Disinterestedness of the Human*

Mind)—and I tried to explain my view of it to Coleridge, who listened with great willingness, but I did not succeed in making myself understood. I sat down to the task shortly afterwards for the twentieth time, got new pens and paper, determined to make clear work of it, wrote a few meagre sentences in the skeleton-style of a mathematical demonstration, stopped half-way down the second page; and, after trying in vain to pump up any words, images, notions, apprehensions, facts, or observations, from that gulph of abstraction in which I had plunged myself for four or five years preceding, gave up the attempt as labour in vain, and shed tears of helpless despondency on the blank unfinished paper. I can write fast enough now. Am I better than I was then? Oh no! One truth discovered, one pang of regret at not being able to express it, is better than all the fluency and flippancy in the world. Would that I could go back to what I then was! Why can we not revive past times as we can revisit old places? If I had the quaint Muse of Sir Philip Sidney to assist me, I would write a *Sonnet to the Road between W——m and Shrewsbury*, and immortalise every step of it by some fond enigmatical conceit. I would swear that the very milestones had ears, and that Harmer-hill stooped with all its pines, to listen to a poet, as he passed! I remember but one other topic of discourse in this walk. He mentioned Paley, praised the naturalness and clearness of his style, but condemned his sentiments, thought him a mere time-serving casuist, and said that 'the fact of his work on Moral and Political Philosophy being made a text-book in our Universities was a disgrace to the national character.' We parted at the six-mile stone; and I returned homeward pensive but much pleased. I had met with unexpected notice from a person, whom I believed to have been prejudiced against me. 'Kind and affable to me had been his condescension, and should be honoured ever with suitable regard.' He was the first poet I had known, and he certainly answered to that inspired name. I had heard a great deal of his powers of conversation, and was not disappointed. In fact, I never met with any thing at all like them, either before or since. I could easily credit the accounts which were circulated of his holding forth to a large party of ladies and gentlemen, an evening or two before, on the Berkeleian Theory, when he made the whole material universe look like a transparency of fine words; and another story (which I believe he has somewhere told himself) of his being asked to a party at Birmingham, of his smoking tobacco and going to sleep after dinner on a sofa, where the company found him to their no small surprise, which was increased to wonder when he started up of a sudden, and rubbing his eyes, looked about him, and launched into a three-hours' description of the third heaven, of which he had had a dream, very different from Mr Southey's Vision of Judgment, and also from that other Vision of Judgment, which Mr Murray, the Secretary of the Bridge-street Junto, has taken into his especial keeping!

On my way back, I had a sound in my ears, it was the voice of Fancy: I had a light before me, it was the face of Poetry. The one still lingers there, the other has not quitted my side! Coleridge in truth met me half-way on the ground of philosophy, or I should not have been won over to his imaginative creed. I had an uneasy, pleasurable sensation all the time, till I was to visit him. During those months the chill breath of winter gave me a welcoming; the vernal air was balm and inspiration to me. The golden sunsets, the silver star of evening, lighted me on my way to new hopes and prospects. *I was to visit Coleridge in the spring.* This circumstance was never absent from my thoughts, and mingled with all my feelings. I wrote to him at the time proposed, and received an answer postponing my intended visit for a week or two, but very cordially urging me to complete my promise then. This delay did not damp, but rather increased my ardour. In the meantime, I went to Llangollen Vale, by way of initiating myself in the mysteries of natural scenery; and I must say I was enchanted with it. I had been reading Coleridge's description of England in his fine *Ode on the Departing Year*, and I applied it, *con amore*, to the objects before me. That valley was to me (in a manner) the cradle of a new existence: in the river that winds through it, my spirit was baptised in the waters of Helicon!

I returned home, and soon after set out on my journey with unworn heart and untired feet. My way lay through Worcester and Gloucester, and by Upton, where I thought of Tom Jones and the adventure of the muff. I remember getting completely wet through one day, and stopping at an inn (I think it was at Tewkesbury) where I sat up all night to read Paul and Virginia. Sweet were the showers in early youth that drenched my body, and sweet the drops of pity that fell upon the books I read! I recollect a remark of Coleridge's upon this very book, that nothing could shew the gross indelicacy of French manners and the entire corruption of their imagination more strongly than the behaviour of the heroine in the last fatal scene, who turns away from a person on board the sinking vessel, that offers to save her life, because he has thrown off his clothes to assist him in swimming. Was this a time to think of such a circumstance? I once hinted to Wordsworth, as we were sailing in his boat on Grasmere lake, that I thought he had borrowed the idea of his *Poems on the Naming Of Places* from the local inscriptions of the same kind in Paul and Virginia. He did not own the obligation, and stated some distinction without a difference, in defence of his claim to originality. Any the slightest variation would be sufficient for this purpose in his mind; for whatever *he* added or omitted would inevitably be worth all that any one else had done, and contain the marrow of the sentiment. I was still two days before the time fixed for my arrival, for I had taken care to set out early enough. I stopped these two days at Bridgewater, and when I was tired of sauntering on the banks of its muddy river, returned to the inn, and read Camilla. So have I loitered my life away, reading books, looking at pictures, going to plays, hearing, thinking, writing on what pleased me best. I have wanted only one thing to make me happy; but wanting that, have wanted everything!

I arrived, and was well received. The country about Nether Stowey is beautiful, green and hilly, and near the sea-shore. I saw it but the other day, after an interval of twenty years, from a hill near Taunton. How was the map of my life spread out before me, as the map of the country lay at my feet! In the afternoon, Coleridge took me over to All-Foxden, a romantic old family-mansion of the St Aubins, where Wordsworth lived. It was then in the possession of a friend of the poet's, who gave him the free use of it. Somehow that period (the time just after the French Revolution) was not a time when *nothing was given for nothing*. The mind opened, and a softness might be perceived coming over the heart of individuals, beneath 'the scales that fence' our self-interest. Wordsworth himself was from home, but his sister kept house, and set before us a frugal repast; and we had free access to her brother's poems, the *Lyrical Ballads*, which were still in manuscript, or in the form of *Sybilline Leaves*. I dipped into a few of these with great satisfaction, and with the faith of a novice. I slept that night in an old room with blue hangings, and covered with the round-faced family-portraits of the age of George I and II, and from the wooded declivity of the adjoining park that overlooked my window, at the dawn of day, could

——hear the loud stag speak.

In the outset of life (and particularly at this time I felt it so) our imagination has a body to it. We are in a state between sleeping and waking, and have indistinct but glorious glimpses of strange shapes, and there is always something to come better than what we see. As in our dreams the fulness of the blood gives warmth and reality to the coinage of the brain, so in youth our ideas are clothed, and fed, and pampered with our good spirits; we breathe thick with thoughtless happiness, the weight of future years presses on the strong pulses of the heart, and we repose with undisturbed faith in truth and good. As we advance, we exhaust our fund of enjoyment and of hope. We are no longer wrapped in *lamb's-wool*, lulled in Elysium. As we taste the pleasures of life, their spirit evaporates, the sense palls; and nothing is left but the phantoms, the lifeless shadows of what *has been*!

That morning, as soon as breakfast was over, we strolled out into the park, and seating ourselves on the trunk of an old ash-tree that stretched along the ground, Coleridge read aloud with a sonorous and musical voice, the ballad of *Betty Foy*. I was not critically or sceptically inclined. I saw touches of truth and nature, and took the rest for granted. But in the *Thorn*, the *Mad Mother*, and the *Complaint of a Poor Indian Woman*, I felt that deeper power and pathos which have been since acknowledged,

In spite of pride, in erring reason's spite,

as the characteristics of this author; and the sense of a new style and a new spirit in poetry came over me. It had to me something of the effect that arises from the turning up of the fresh soil, or of the first welcome breath of Spring,

> While yet the trembling year is unconfirmed.

Coleridge and myself walked back to Stowey that evening, and his voice sounded high

> Of Providence, foreknowledge, will, and fate,
> Fix'd fate, free-will, foreknowledge absolute,'

as we passed through echoing grove, by fairy stream or waterfall, gleaming in the summer moonlight! He lamented that Wordsworth was not prone enough to believe in the traditional superstitions of the place, and that there was a something corporeal, a *matter-of-fact-ness*, a clinging to the palpable, or often to the petty, in his poetry, in consequence. His genius was not a spirit that descended to him through the air; it sprung out of the ground like a flower, or unfolded itself from a green spray, on which the gold-finch sang. He said, however (if I remember right) that this objection must be confined to his descriptive pieces, that his philosophic poetry had a grand and comprehensive spirit in it, so that his soul seemed to inhabit the universe like a palace, and to discover truth by intuition, rather than by deduction. The next day Wordsworth arrived from Bristol at Coleridge's cottage. I think I see him now. He answered in some degree to his friend's description of him, but was more gaunt and Don Quixote-like. He was quaintly dressed (according to the *costume* of that unconstrained period) in a brown fustian jacket and striped pantaloons. There was something of a roll, a lounge in his gait, not unlike his own Peter Bell. There was a severe, worn pressure of thought about his temples, a fire in his eye (as if he saw something in objects more than the outward appearance), an intense high narrow forehead, a Roman nose, cheeks furrowed by strong purpose and feeling, and a convulsive inclination to laughter about the mouth, a good deal at variance with the solemn, stately expression of the rest of his face. Chantry's bust wants the marking traits; but he was teazed into making it regular and heavy: Haydon's head of him, introduced into the *Entrance of Christ into Jerusalem*, is the most like his drooping weight of thought and expression. He sat down and talked very naturally and freely, with a mixture of clear gushing accents in his voice, a deep guttural intonation, and a strong tincture of the northern *burr*, like the crust on wine. He instantly began to make havoc of the half of a Cheshire cheese on the table, and said triumphantly that 'his marriage with experience had not been so unproductive as Mr Southey's in teaching him a knowledge of the good things of this life.' He had been to see the *Castle Spectre* by Monk Lewis, while at Bristol, and described it very well. He said 'it fitted the taste of the audience like a glove.' This *ad captandum* merit was however by no means a recommendation of it, according to the severe principles of the new school, which reject rather than court popular effect Wordsworth, looking out of the low, latticed window, said, 'How beautifully the sun sets on that yellow bank!' I thought within myself, 'With what eyes these poets see nature!' and ever after, when I saw the sun-set stream upon the objects facing it, conceived I had made a discovery, or thanked Mr Wordsworth for having made one for me! We went over to All-Foxden again the day following, and Wordsworth read us the story of Peter Bell in the open air; and the comment made upon it by his face and voice was very different from that of some later critics! Whatever might be thought of the poem, 'his face was as a book where men might read strange matters,' and he announced the fate of his hero in prophetic tones. There is a *chaunt* in the recitation both of Coleridge and Wordsworth, which acts as a spell upon the hearer, and disarms the judgment. Perhaps they have deceived themselves by making habitual use of this ambiguous accompaniment. Coleridge's manner is more full, animated, and varied; Wordsworth's more equable, sustained, and internal. The one might be termed more *dramatic*, the other more *lyrical*. Coleridge has told me that he himself liked to compose in walking over uneven ground, or breaking through the straggling branches of a copse-wood; whereas Wordsworth always wrote (if he could) walking up and down a straight gravel-walk, or in some spot where the continuity of his verse met with no collateral interruption. Returning that same evening, I got into a metaphysical argument with Wordsworth, while Coleridge

was explaining the different notes of the nightingale to his
sister, in which we neither of us succeeded in making ourselves
perfectly clear and intelligible. Thus I passed three weeks
at Nether Stowey and in the neighbourhood, generally devoting
the afternoons to a delightful chat in an arbour made of bark
by the poet's friend Tom Poole, sitting under two fine elm-
trees, and listening to the bees humming round us, while
we quaffed our *flip*. It was agreed, among other things,
that we should make a jaunt down the Bristol-Channel, as
far as Linton. We set off together on foot, Coleridge, John
Chester, and I. This Chester was a native of Nether Stowey,
one of those who were attracted to Coleridge's discourse as
flies are to honey, or bees in swarming-time to the sound of a
brass pan. He 'followed in the chase, like a dog who hunts,
not like one that made up the cry.' He had on a brown
cloth coat, boots, and corduroy breeches, was low in stature,
bow-legged, had a drag in his walk like a drover, which he
assisted by a hazel switch, and kept on a sort of trot by the
side of Coleridge, like a running footman by a state coach,
that he might not lose a syllable or sound that fell from
Coleridge's lips. He told me his private opinion, that Coleridge
was a wonderful man. He scarcely opened his lips, much less
offered an opinion the whole way: yet of the three, had I to
chuse during that journey, I would be John Chester. He
afterwards followed Coleridge into Germany, where the
Kantean philosophers were puzzled how to bring him under
any of their categories. When he sat down at table with his
idol, John's felicity was complete; Sir Walter Scott's, or
Mr Blackwood's, when they sat down at the same table with
the King, was not more so. We passed Dunster on our right,
a small town between the brow of a hill and the sea. I remember eying it wistfully as it lay below us: contrasted with
the woody scene around, it looked as clear, as pure, as
embrowned and ideal as any landscape I have seen since, of
Gaspar Poussin's or Domenichino's. We had a long day's
march—(our feet kept time to the echoes of Coleridge's
tongue)—through Minehead and by the Blue Anchor, and on
to Linton, which we did not reach till near midnight, and
where we had some difficulty in making a lodgment. We
however knocked the people of the house up at last, and we

were repaid for our apprehensions and fatigue by some
excellent rashers of fried bacon and eggs. The view in coming
along had been splendid. We walked for miles and miles
on dark brown heaths overlooking the Channel, with the
Welsh hills beyond, and at times descended into little sheltered
valleys close by the seaside, with a smuggler's face scowling
by us, and then had to ascend conical hills with a path winding
up through a coppice to a barren top, like a monk's shaven
crown, from one of which I pointed out to Coleridge's notice
the bare masts of a vessel on the very edge of the horizon
and within the red-orbed disk of the setting sun, like his
own spectre-ship in the *Ancient Mariner*. At Linton the
character of the sea-coast becomes more marked and rugged.
There is a place called the *Valley of Rocks* (I suspect this was
only the poetical name for it) bedded among precipices
overhanging the sea, with rocky caverns beneath, into which
the waves dash, and where the sea-gull for ever wheels its
screaming flight. On the tops of these are huge stones
thrown transverse, as if an earthquake had tossed them
there, and behind these is a fretwork of perpendicular rocks,
something like the *Giant's Causeway*. A thunder-storm came
on while we were at the inn, and Coleridge was running out
bare-headed to enjoy the commotion of the elements in the
Valley of Rocks, but as if in spite, the clouds only muttered
a few angry sounds, and let fall a few refreshing drops.
Coleridge told me that he and Wordsworth were to have
made this place the scene of a prose-tale, which was to have
been in the manner of, but far superior to, the *Death of Abel*,
but they had relinquished the design. In the morning of the
second day, we breakfasted luxuriously in an old-fashioned
parlour, on tea, toast, eggs, and honey, in the very sight of
the bee-hives from which it had been taken, and a garden
full of thyme and wild flowers that had produced it. On this
occasion Coleridge spoke of Virgil's Georgics, but not well.
I do not think he had much feeling for the classical or elegant.
It was in this room that we found a little worn-out copy of
the *Seasons*, lying in a window-seat, on which Coleridge
exclaimed, 'That is true fame!' He said Thomson was a
great poet, rather than a good one; his style was as mere-
tricious as his thoughts were natural. He spoke of Cowper

as the best modern poet. He said the *Lyrical Ballads* were an experiment about to be tried by him and Wordsworth, to see how far the public taste would endure poetry written in a more natural and simple style than had hitherto been attempted; totally discarding the artifices of poetical diction, and making use only of such words as had probably been common in the most ordinary language since the days of Henry II. Some comparison was introduced between Shakespear and Milton. He said 'he hardly knew which to prefer. Shakespear appeared to him a mere stripling in the art; he was as tall and as strong, with infinitely more activity than Milton, but he never appeared to have come to man's estate; or if he had, he would not have been a man, but a monster.' He spoke with contempt of Gray, and with intolerance of Pope. He did not like the versification of the latter. He observed that 'the ears of these couplet-writers might be charged with having short memories, that could not retain the harmony of whole passages.' He thought little of Junius as a writer; he had a dislike of Dr Johnson; and a much higher opinion of Burke as an orator and politician, than of Fox or Pitt. He however thought him very inferior in richness of style and imagery to some of our elder prose-writers, particularly Jeremy Taylor. He liked Richardson, but not Fielding; nor could I get him to enter into the merits of *Caleb Williams*[1]. In short, he was profound and discriminating with respect to those authors whom he liked, and where he gave his judgment fair play; capricious, perverse, and prejudiced in his antipathies and distastes. We loitered on the 'ribbed sea-sands,' in such talk as this, a whole morning, and I recollect met with a curious sea-weed, of which John Chester told us the country name! A fisherman gave Coleridge an account of a boy that had been drowned the day before, and that they had tried to save him at the risk of their own lives. He said

---

[1] He had no idea of pictures, of Claude or Raphael, and at this time I had as little as he. He sometimes gives a striking account at present of the Cartoons at Pisa, by Buffamalco and others; of one in particular, where Death is seen in the air brandishing his scythe, and the great and mighty of the earth shudder at his approach, while the beggars and the wretched kneel to him as their deliverer. He would of course understand so broad and fine a moral as this at any time.

'he did not know how it was that they ventured, but, Sir, we have a *nature* towards one another.' This expression, Coleridge remarked to me, was a fine illustration of that theory of disinterestedness which I (in common with Butler) had adopted. I broached to him an argument of mine to prove that *likeness* was not mere association of ideas. I said that the mark in the sand put one in mind of a man's foot, not because it was part of a former impression of a man's foot (for it was quite new) but because it was like the shape of a man's foot. He assented to the justness of this distinction (which I have explained at length elsewhere, for the benefit of the curious) and John Chester listened; not from any interest in the subject, but because he was astonished that I should be able to suggest any thing to Coleridge that he did not already know. We returned on the third morning, and Coleridge remarked the silent cottage-smoke curling up the valleys where, a few evenings before, we had seen the lights gleaming through the dark.

In a day or two after we arrived at Stowey, we set out, I on my return home, and he for Germany. It was a Sunday morning, and he was to preach that day for Dr Toulmin of Taunton. I asked him if he had prepared anything for the occasion? He said he had not even thought of the text, but should as soon as we parted. I did not go to hear him,— this was a fault,—but we met in the evening at Bridgewater. The next day we had a long day's walk to Bristol, and sat down, I recollect, by a well-side on the road, to cool ourselves and satisfy our thirst, when Coleridge repeated to me some descriptive lines from his tragedy of Remorse; which I must say became his mouth and that occasion better than they, some years after, did Mr Elliston's and the Drury-lane boards,—

> Oh memory! shield me from the world's poor strife,
> And give those scenes thine everlasting life.

I saw no more of him for a year or two, during which period he had been wandering in the Hartz Forest in Germany; and his return was cometary, meteorous, unlike his setting out. It was not till some time after that I knew his friends Lamb and Southey. The last always appears to me (as I first

saw him) with a common-place book under his arm, and the
first with a *bon-mot* in his mouth. It was at Godwin's that
I met him with Holcroft and Coleridge, where they were
disputing fiercely which was the best—*Man as he was, or man
as he is to be*. 'Give me,' says Lamb, 'man as he is *not* to be.'
This saying was the beginning of a friendship between us,
which I believes still continues.—Enough of this for the
present.

> But there is matter for another rhyme,
> And I to this may add a second tale.

An author is bound to write—well or ill, wisely or foolishly: it is his trade. But I do not see that he is bound to talk, any more than he is bound to dance, or ride, or fence better than other people. Reading, study, silence, thought, are a bad introduction to loquacity. It would be sooner learnt of chambermaids and tapsters. He understands the art and mystery of his own profession, which is book-making: what right has any one to expect or require him to do more—to make a bow gracefully on entering or leaving a room, to make love charmingly, or to make a fortune at all? In all things there is a division of labour. A lord is no less amorous for writing ridiculous love-letters, nor a General less successful for wanting wit and honesty. Why then may not a poor author say nothing, and yet pass muster? Set him on the top of a stage-coach, he will make no figure; he is *mum-chance*, while the slang-wit flies about as fast as the dust, with the crack of the whip and the clatter of the horses' heels: put him in a ring of boxers, he is a poor creature—

> And of his port as meek as is a maid.

Introduce him to a tea-party of milliner's girls, and they are ready to split their sides with laughing at him: over his bottle, he is dry: in the drawing-room, rude or awkward: he is too refined for the vulgar, too clownish for the fashion-able:—'he is one that cannot make a good leg, one that cannot eat a mess of broth cleanly, one that cannot ride a horse without spur-galling, one that cannot salute a woman, and look on her directly':—in courts, in camps, in town and country, he is a cypher or a butt: he is good for nothing but a laughing-stock or a scare-crow. You can scarcely get a word out of him for love or money. He knows nothing. He has no notion of pleasure or business, or of what is going on in the world; he does not understand cookery (unless he is a doctor

in divinity) nor surgery, nor chemistry (unless he is a *Quidnunc*)
nor mechanics, nor husbandry and tillage (unless he is as great
an admirer of Tull's Husbandry, and has profited as much
by it as the philosopher of Botley)—no, nor music, painting,
the Drama, nor the Fine Arts in general.

'What the deuce is it then, my good sir, that he does
understand, or know anything about?'

'BOOKS, VENUS, BOOKS!'

'What books?'

'Not receipt-books, Madona, nor account-books, nor books
of pharmacy, or the veterinary art (they belong to their
respective callings and handicrafts) but books of liberal taste
and general knowledge.'

'What do you mean by that general knowledge which
implies not a knowledge of things in general, but an ignorance
(by your own account) of every one in particular: or by that
liberal taste which scorns the pursuits and acquirements of
the rest of the world in succession, and is confined exclusively,
and by way of excellence, to what nobody takes an interest
in but yourself, and a few idlers like yourself? Is this what
the critics mean by the *belles-lettres*, and the study of humanity?'

Book-knowledge, in a word, then, is knowledge *communicable by books*: and it is general and liberal for this reason,
that it is intelligible and interesting on the bare suggestion.
That to which any one feels a romantic attachment, merely
from finding it in a book, must be interesting in itself: that
which he instantly forms a lively and entire conception of,
from seeing a few marks and scratches upon paper, must be
taken from common nature: that which, the first time you
meet with it, seizes upon the attention as a curious speculation,
must exercise the general faculties of the human mind. There
are certain broader aspects of society and views of things
common to every subject, and more or less cognizable to every
mind; and these the scholar treats and founds his claim to
general attention upon them, without being chargeable with
pedantry. The minute descriptions of fishing-tackle, of baits
and flies in Walton's Complete Angler, make that work a great
favourite with sportsmen: the alloy of an amiable humanity,
and the modest but touching descriptions of familiar incidents
and rural objects scattered through it, have made it an equal

favourite with every reader of taste and feeling. Montaigne's Essays, Dilworth's Spelling Book, and Fearn's Treatise on Contingent Remainders, are all equally books, but not equally adapted for all classes of readers. The two last are of no use but to school-masters and lawyers: but the first is a work we may recommend to any one to read who has ever thought at all, or who would learn to think justly on any subject. Persons of different trades and professions—the mechanic, the shop-keeper, the medical practitioner, the artist, &c. may all have great knowledge and ingenuity in their several vocations, the details of which will be very edifying to themselves, and just as incomprehensible to their neighbours: but over and above this professional and technical knowledge, they must be supposed to have a stock of common sense and common feeling to furnish subjects for common conversation, or to give them any pleasure in each other's company. It is to this common stock of ideas, spread over the surface, or striking its roots into the very centre of society, that the popular writer appeals, and not in vain; for he finds readers. It is of this finer essence of wisdom and humanity, 'etherial mould, sky-tinctured,' that books of the better sort are made. They contain the language of thought. It must happen that, in the course of time and the variety of human capacity, some persons will have struck out finer observations, reflections, and sentiments than others. These they have committed to books of memory, have bequeathed as a lasting legacy to posterity; and such persons have become standard authors. We visit at the shrine, drink in some measure of the inspiration, and cannot easily 'breathe in other air less pure, accustomed to immortal fruits.' Are we to be blamed for this, because the vulgar and illiterate do not always understand us? The fault is rather in them, who are 'confined and cabin'd in,' each in their own particular sphere and compartment of ideas, and have not the same refined medium of communication or abstracted topics of discourse. Bring a number of literary, or of illiterate persons together, perfect strangers to each other, and see which party will make the best company. 'Verily, we have our reward.' We have made our election, and have no reason to repent it, if we were wise. But the misfortune is, we wish to have all the advantages on one side.

We grudge, and cannot reconcile it to ourselves, that any one 'should go about to cozen fortune, without the stamp of learning!' We think 'because we are *scholars*, there shall be no more cakes and ale!' We don't know how to account for it, that bar-maids should gossip, or ladies whisper, or bullies roar, or fools laugh, or knaves thrive, without having gone through the same course of select study that we have! This vanity is preposterous, and carries its own punishment with it. Books are a world in themselves, it is true; but they are not the only world. The world itself is a volume larger than all the libraries in it. Learning is a sacred deposit from the experience of ages; but it has not put all future experience on the shelf, or debarred the common herd of mankind from the use of their hands, tongues, eyes, ears, or understandings. Taste is a luxury for the privileged few: but it would be hard upon those who have not the same standard of refinement in their own minds that we suppose ourselves to have, if this should prevent them from having recourse, as usual, to their old frolics, coarse jokes, and horse-play, and getting through the wear and tear of the world, with such homely sayings and shrewd helps as they may. Happy is it, that the mass of mankind eat and drink, and sleep, and perform their several tasks, and do as they like without us—caring nothing for our scribblings, our carpings, and our quibbles; and moving on the same, in spite of our fine-spun distinctions, fantastic theories, and lines of demarcation, which are like the chalk-figures drawn on ball-room floors to be danced out before morning! In the field opposite the window where I write this, there is a country-girl picking stones: in the one next it, there are several poor women weeding the blue and red flowers from the corn: farther on, are two boys, tending a flock of sheep. What do they know or care about what I am writing about them, or ever will—or what would they be the better for it, if they did? Or why need we despise

> The wretched slave,
> Who like a lackey, from the rise to the set,
> Sweats in the eye of Phœbus, and all night
> Sleeps in Elysium; next day, after dawn,
> Doth rise, and help Hyperion to his horse;
> And follows so the ever-running year
> With profitable labour to his grave?

Is not this life as sweet as writing Ephemerides? But we put that which flutters the brain idly for a moment, and then is heard no more, in competition with nature, which exists every where, and lasts always. We not only underrate the force of nature, and make too much of art—but we also over-rate our own accomplishments and advantages derived from art. In the presence of clownish ignorance, or of persons without any great pretensions, real or affected, we are very much inclined to take upon ourselves, as the virtual representa-tives of science, art, and literature. We have a strong itch to show off and do the honours of civilization for all the great men whose works we have ever read, and whose names our auditors have never heard of, as noblemen's lacqueys, in the absence of their masters, give themselves airs of superiority over every one else. But though we have read Congreve, a stage-coachman may be an over-match for us in wit: though we are deep-versed in the excellence of Shakspeare's colloquial style, a village beldam may outscold us: though we have read Machiavel in the original Italian, we may be easily outwitted by a clown: and though we have cried our eyes out over the New Eloise, a poor shepherd-lad, who hardly knows how to spell his own name, may 'tell his tale, under the hawthorn in the dale,' and prove a more thriving wooer. What then is the advantage we possess over the meanest of the mean? Why this, that we have read Congreve, Shakspeare, Machiavel, the New Eloise;—not that we are to have their wit, genius, shrewdness, or melting tenderness.

From speculative pursuits we must be satisfied with speculative benefits. From reading, too, we learn to write. If we have had the pleasure of studying the highest models of perfection in their kind, and can hope to leave any thing ourselves, however slight, to be looked upon as a model, or even a good copy in its way, we may think ourselves pretty well off, without engrossing all the privileges of learning, and all the blessings of ignorance into the bargain.

It has been made a question whether there have not been individuals in common life of greater talents and powers of mind than the most celebrated writers—whether, for instance, such or such a Liverpool merchant, or Manchester manufac-turer, was not a more sensible man than Montaigne, of a longer reach of understanding than the Viscount of St Albans. There is no saying, unless some of these illustrious obscure had communicated their important discoveries to the world. But then they would have been authors!—On the other hand, there is a set of critics who fall into the contrary error; and suppose that unless the proof of capacity is laid before all the world, the capacity itself cannot exist; looking upon all those who have not commenced authors, as literally 'stocks and stones, and worse than senseless things.' I remember trying to convince a person of this class, that a young lady, whom he knew something of, the niece of a celebrated authoress, had just the same sort of fine *tact* and ironical turn in conversation, that her relative had shown in her writings when young. The only answer I could get was an incredulous smile, and the observation that when she wrote any thing as good as ——, or ——, he might think her as clever. I said all I meant was, that she had the same family talents, and asked whether he thought that if Miss —— had not been very clever, as a mere girl, before she wrote her novels, she would ever have written them? It was all in vain. He still stuck to his text, and was convinced that the niece was a little fool compared to her aunt at the same age; and if he had known the aunt formerly, he would have had just the same opinion of *her*. My friend was one of those who have a settled persuasion that it is the book that makes the author, and not the author the book. That's a strange opinion for a great philosopher to hold. But he wilfully shuts his eyes to the germs and indistinct workings of genius, and treats them with supercilious indifference, till they stare him in the face through the press; and then takes cognizance only of the overt acts and published evidence. This is neither a proof of wisdom, nor the way to be wise. It is partly pedantry and prejudice, and partly feebleness of judgment and want of magnanimity. He dare as little commit himself on the character of books, as of individuals, till they are stamped by the public. If you show him any work for his approbation, he asks, 'Whose is the superscription?'—He judges of genius by its shadow, reputation—of the metal by the coin. He is just the reverse of another person whom I know—for, as G—— never allows a particle of merit to any one till it is acknowledged by the whole world, C—— withholds his tribute of applause from every person, in whom any mortal but himself can descry the least glimpse of understanding. He would be thought to look farther into a millstone than any body else. He would have others see with his eyes, and take their opinions from him on trust, in spite of their senses. The more obscure and defective the indications of merit, the greater his sagacity and candour in being the first to point them out. He looks upon what he nicknames *a man of genius*, but as the breath of his nostrils, and the clay in the potter's hands. If any such inert, unconscious mass, under the fostering care of the modern Prometheus, is kindled into life, —begins to see, speak, and move, so as to attract the notice of other people,—our jealous patroniser of latent worth in that case throws aside, scorns, and hates his own handy-work; and deserts his intellectual offspring from the moment they can go alone and shift for themselves.—But to pass on to our more immediate subject.

The conversation of authors is not so good as might be imagined: but, such as it is (and with rare exceptions), it is better than any other. The proof of which is, that, when you are used to it, you cannot put up with any other. That of mixed company becomes utterly intolerable—you cannot sit out a common tea and card party, at least, if they pretend to talk at all. You are obliged in despair to cut all your old acquaintance who are not *au fait* on the prevailing and most smartly contested topics, who are not imbued with the high gusto of criticism and *virtù*. You cannot bear to hear a friend whom you have not seen for many years, tell at how much a yard he sells his laces and tapes when he means to move into his next house, when he heard last from his relations in the country, whether trade is alive or dead, or whether Mr Such-a-one gets to look old. This sort of neighbourly gossip will not go down after the high-raised tone of literary conversation. The last may be very absurd, very unsatisfactory, and full of turbulence and heart-burnings; but it has a zest in it which more ordinary topics of news or family-affairs do not supply. Neither will the conversation of what we understand by *gentlemen* and men of fashion, do after that of men of letters. It is flat, insipid, stale, and unprofitable, in the comparison. They talk about much the same things, pictures, poetry, politics, plays; but they do it worse, and at a sort of vapid secondhand. They, in fact, talk out of newspapers and magazines, what *we write there*. They do not feel the same interest in the subjects they affect to handle with an air of fashionable condescension, nor have they the same knowledge of them, if they were ever so much in earnest in displaying it. If it were not for the wine and the dessert, no author in his senses would accept an invitation to a well-dressed dinner-party, except out of pure good-nature and unwillingness to disoblige by his refusal. Persons in high life talk almost entirely by rote. There are certain established modes of address, and certain answers to them expected as a matter of course, as a point of etiquette. The studied forms of politeness do not give the greatest possible scope to an exuberance of wit or fancy. The fear of giving offence destroys sincerity, and without sincerity there can be no true enjoyment of society, nor unfettered exertion of intellectual activity.—Those who have been accustomed to live with the great are hardly considered as conversible persons in literary society. They are not to be talked with, any more than puppets or echos. They have no opinions but what will please; and you naturally turn away, as a waste of time and words, from attending to a person who just before assented to what you said, and whom you find, the moment after, from something that unexpectedly or perhaps by design drops from him, to be of a totally different way of thinking. This *bush-fighting* is not regarded as fair play among scientific men. As fashionable conversation is a sacrifice to politeness, so the conversation of low life is nothing but rudeness. They contradict you without giving a reason, or if they do, it is a very bad one—swear, talk loud, repeat the same thing fifty times over, get to calling names, and from words proceed to blows. You cannot make companions of servants, or persons in an inferior station in life. You may talk to them on matters of business, and what they have to do for you (as lords talk to bruisers on subjects of *fancy*, or country-squires to their grooms on horse-racing), but out of that narrow sphere, to any general topic, you cannot lead them; the conversation soon flags, and you go back to the old question, or are obliged to break up the sitting for want of ideas in common. The conversation of authors is better than that of most professions. It is better than that of lawyers, who talk nothing but *double entendre*—than that of physicians, who talk of the approaching deaths of the College, or the marriage of some new practitioner with some rich widow—than that of divines, who talk of the last place they dined at—than that of University-men, who make stale puns, repeat the refuse of the London newspapers, and affect an ignorance of Greek and mathematics—it is better than that of players, who talk of nothing but the green-room, and rehearse the scholar, the wit, or the fine gentleman, like a part on the stage—or than that of ladies, who, whatever you talk of, think of nothing, and expect you to think of nothing, but themselves. It is not easy to keep up a conversation with women in company. It is thought a piece of rudeness to differ from them: it is not quite fair to ask them a reason for what they say. You are afraid of pressing too hard upon them: but where you cannot differ openly and unreservedly, you cannot heartily agree. It is not so in France. There the women talk of things in general, and reason better than the men in this country. They are mistresses of the intellectual foils. They are adepts in all the topics. They know what is to be said for and against all sorts of questions, and are lively and full of mischief into the bargain. They are very subtle. They put you to your trumps immediately. Your logic is more in requisition even than your gallantry. You must argue as well as bow yourself into the good graces of these modern Amazons. What a situation for an Englishman to be placed in[1]!

The fault of literary conversation in general is its too great tenaciousness. It fastens upon a subject, and will not let it go. It resembles a battle rather than a skirmish, and makes a toil of a pleasure. Perhaps it does this from necessity, from a consciousness of wanting the more familiar graces, the power to sport and trifle, to touch lightly and adorn agreeably, every view or turn of a question *en passant*, as it

---

[1] The topics of metaphysical argument having got into female society in France, is a proof how much they must have been discussed there generally, and how unfounded the charge is which we bring against them of excessive thoughtlessness and frivolity. The French (taken all together) are a more sensible, reflecting, and better informed people than the English.

arises.   Those who have a reputation to lose are too ambitious of shining, to please. 'To excel in conversation,' said an ingenious man, 'one must not be always striving to say good things: to say one good thing, one must say many bad, and more indifferent ones.' This desire to shine without the means at hand, often makes men silent:—

> The fear of being silent strikes us dumb.

A writer who has been accustomed to take a connected view of a difficult question, and to work it out gradually in all its bearings, may be very deficient in that quickness and ease, which men of the world, who are in the habit of hearing a variety of opinions, who pick up an observation on one subject, and another on another, and who care about none any farther than the passing away of an idle hour, usually acquire. An author has studied a particular point—he has read, he has inquired, he has thought a great deal upon it: he is not contented to take it up casually in common with others, to throw out a hint, to propose an objection: he will either remain silent, uneasy, and dissatisfied, or he will begin at the beginning and go through with it to the end. He is for taking the whole responsibility upon himself. He would be thought to understand the subject better than others, or indeed would show that nobody else knows any thing about it. There are always three or four points on which the literary novice at his first outset in life fancies he can enlighten every company, and bear down all opposition: but he is cured of this Quixotic and pugnacious spirit, as he goes more into the world, where he finds that there are other opinions and other pretensions to be adjusted besides his own. When this asperity wears off, and a certain scholastic precocity is mellowed down, the conversation of men of letters becomes both interesting and instructive. Men of the world have no fixed principles, no ground-work of thought: mere scholars have too much an object, a theory always in view, to which they wrest every thing, and not unfrequently, common sense itself. By mixing with society, they rub off their hardness of manner, and impracticable, offensive singularity, while they retain a greater depth and coherence of understanding. There is more to be learnt from them than from their books. This was a remark

of Rousseau's, and it is a very true one. In the confidence
and unreserve of private intercourse, they are more at liberty
to say what they think, to put the subject in different and
opposite points of view, to illustrate it more briefly and pithily
by familiar expressions, by an appeal to individual character
and personal knowledge—to bring in the limitation, to obviate
misconception, to state difficulties on their own side of the
argument, and answer them as well as they can. This would
hardly agree with the prudery, and somewhat ostentatious
claims of authorship. Dr Johnson's conversation in Boswell's
Life is much better than his published works: and the fragments
of the opinions of celebrated men, preserved in their letters
or in anecdotes of them, are justly sought after as invaluable
for the same reason. For instance, what a fund of sense
there is in Grimm's Memoirs! We thus get at the essence
of what is contained in their more laboured productions,
without the affectation or formality.—Argument, again, is
the death of conversation, if carried on in a spirit of hostility:
but discussion is a pleasant and profitable thing, where you
advance and defend your opinions as far as you can, and
admit the truth of what is objected against them with equal
impartiality; in short, where you do not pretend to set up
for an oracle, but freely declare what you really know about
any question, or suggest what has struck you as throwing a
new light upon it, and let it pass for what it is worth. This
tone of conversation was well described by Dr Johnson, when
he said of some party at which he had been present the night
before—'We had good talk, sir!' As a general rule, there
is no conversation worth any thing but between friends, or
those who agree in the same leading views of a subject. Nothing
was ever learnt by either side in a dispute. You contradict
one another, will not allow a grain of sense in what your
adversary advances, are blind to whatever makes against
yourself, dare not look the question fairly in the face, so that
you cannot avail yourself even of your real advantages, insist
most on what you feel to be the weakest points of your argument, and get more and more absurd, dogmatical, and violent
every moment. Disputes for victory generally end to the
dissatisfaction of all parties; and the one recorded in Gil Blas
breaks up just as it ought. I once knew a very ingenious

man, than whom, to take him in the way of common chit-chat
or fireside gossip, no one could be more entertaining or rational.
He would make an apt classical quotation, propose an explanation of a curious passage in Shakspeare's Venus and
Adonis, detect a metaphysical error in Locke, would infer the
volatility of the French character from the chapter in Sterne
where the Count mistakes the feigned name of Yorick for
a proof of his being the identical imaginary character in
Hamlet (*Et vous êtes Yorick!*)—thus confounding words with
things twice over—but let a difference of opinion be once
hitched in, and it was all over with him.   His only object
from that time was to shut out common sense, and to be proof
against conviction.   He would argue the most ridiculous point
(such as that there were two original languages) for hours
together, nay, through the horologe.   You would not suppose
it was the same person.   He was like an obstinate run-away
horse, that takes the bit in his mouth, and becomes mischievous
and unmanageable.   He had made up his mind to one thing,
not to admit a single particle of what any one else said for or
against him.   It was all the difference between a man drunk
or sober, sane or mad.   It is the same when he once gets the
pen in his hand.   He has been trying to prove a contradiction
in terms for the ten last years of his life, *viz.* that the Bourbons
have the same right to the throne of France that the Brunswick
family have to the throne of England.   Many people think
there is a want of honesty or a want of understanding in this.
There is neither.   But he will persist in an argument to the
last pinch; he will yield, in absurdity, to no man!

This litigious humour is bad enough: but there is one
character still worse, that of a person who goes into company,
not to contradict, but to *talk at* you.   This is the greatest
nuisance in civilised society.   Such a person does not come
armed to defend himself at all points, but to unsettle, if he
can, and throw a slur on all your favourite opinions.   If he
has a notion that any one in the room is fond of poetry, he
immediately volunteers a contemptuous tirade against the
idle jingle of verse.   If he suspects you have a delight in
pictures, he endeavours, not by fair argument, but by a
side-wind, to put you out of conceit with so frivolous an art.
If you have a taste for music, he does not think much good

is to be done by this tickling of the ears. If you speak in praise of a comedy, he does not see the use of wit: if you say you have been to a tragedy, he shakes his head at this mockery of human misery, and thinks it ought to be prohibited. He tries to find out beforehand whatever it is that you take a particular pride or pleasure in, that he may annoy your self-love in the tenderest point (as if he were probing a wound) and make you dissatisfied with yourself and your pursuits for several days afterwards. A person might as well make a practice of throwing out scandalous aspersions against your dearest friends or nearest relations, by way of ingratiating himself into your favour. Such ill-timed impertinence is 'villainous, and shews a pitiful ambition in the fool that uses it.'

The soul of conversation is sympathy.—Authors should converse chiefly with authors, and their talk should be of books. 'When Greek meets Greek, then comes the tug of war.' There is nothing so pedantic as pretending not to be pedantic. No man can get above his pursuit in life: it is getting above himself, which is impossible. There is a Free-masonry in all things. You can only speak to be understood, but this you cannot be, except by those who are in the secret. Hence an argument has been drawn to supersede the necessity of conversation altogether; for it has been said, that there is no use in talking to people of sense, who know all that you can tell them, nor to fools, who will not be instructed. There is, however, the smallest encouragement to proceed, when you are conscious that the more you really enter into a subject, the farther you will be from the comprehension of your hearers—and that the more proofs you give of any position, the more odd and out-of-the-way they will think your notions. C—— is the only person who can talk to all sorts of people, on all sorts of subjects, without caring a farthing for their understanding one word he says—and *he* talks only for admiration and to be listened to, and accordingly the least interruption puts him out. I firmly believe he would make just the same impression on half his audiences, if he purposely repeated absolute nonsense with the same voice and manner and inexhaustible flow of undulating speech! In general, wit shines only by reflection. You must take your

cue from your company—must rise as they rise, and sink as
they fall. You must see that your good things, your knowing
allusions, are not flung away, like the pearls in the adage.
What a check it is to be asked a foolish question; to find that
the first principles are not understood! You are thrown on
your back immediately, the conversation is stopped like a
country-dance by those who do not know the figure. But
when a set of adepts, of *illuminati*, get about a question, it is
worth while to hear them talk. They may snarl and quarrel
over it, like dogs; but they pick it bare to the bone, they
masticate it thoroughly.

This was the case formerly at L——'s—where we used to have many lively skirmishes at their Thursday evening parties. I doubt whether the Small-coal man's musical parties could exceed them. Oh! for the pen of John Buncle to consecrate a *petit souvenir* to their memory!—There was L—— himself, the most delightful, the most provoking, the most witty and sensible of men. He always made the best pun, and the best remark in the course of the evening. His serious conversation, like his serious writing, is his best. No one ever stammered out such fine, piquant, deep, eloquent things in half a dozen half sentences as he does. His jests scald like tears: and he probes a question with a play upon words. What a keen, laughing, hair-brained vein of home-felt truth! What choice venom! How often did we cut into the haunch of letters, while we discussed the haunch of mutton on the table! How we skimmed the cream of criticism! How we got into the heart of controversy! How we picked out the marrow of authors! 'And, in our flowing cups, many a good name and true was freshly remembered.' Recollect (most sage and critical reader) that in all this I was but a guest! Need I go over the names? They were but the old everlasting set—Milton and Shakspeare, Pope and Dryden, Steele and Addison, Swift and Gay, Fielding, Smollet, Sterne, Richardson, Hogarth's prints, Claude's land-scapes, the Cartoons at Hampton-court, and all those things, that, having once been, must ever be. The Scotch Novels had not then been heard of: so we said nothing about them. In general, we were hard upon the moderns. The author of the Rambler was only tolerated in Boswell's Life of him; and it was as much as any one could do to edge in a word for Junius. L—— could not bear Gil Blas. This was a fault. I remember the greatest triumph I ever had was in persuading him, after some years' difficulty, that Fielding was better than Smollet. On one occasion, he was for making out a list of persons famous in history that one would wish to see again —at the head of whom were Pontius Pilate, Sir Thomas Browne, and Dr Faustus—but we black-balled most of his list! But with what a gusto would he describe his favourite authors, Donne, or Sir Philip Sidney, and call their most crabbed passages *delicious*! He tried them on his palate as epicures taste olives, and his observations had a smack in them, like a roughness on the tongue. With what discrimination he hinted a defect in what he admired most—as in saying that the display of the sumptuous banquet in Paradise Regained was not in true keeping, as the simplest fare was all that was necessary to tempt the extremity of hunger—and stating that Adam and Eve in Paradise Lost were too much like married people. He has furnished many a text for C—— to preach upon. There was no fuss or cant about him: nor were his sweets or his sours ever diluted with one particle of affectation. I cannot say that the party at L——'s were all of one description. There were honorary members, lay-brothers. Wit and good fellowship was the motto inscribed over the door. When a stranger came in, it was not asked, 'Has he written any thing?'—we were above that pedantry; but we waited to see what he could do. If he could take a hand at piquet, he was welcome to sit down. If a person liked any thing, if he took snuff heartily, it was sufficient. He would understand, by analogy, the pungency of other things, besides Irish blackguard, or Scotch rappee. A character was good any where, in a room or on paper. But we abhorred insipidity, affectation, and fine gentlemen. There was one of our party who never failed to mark 'two for his Nob' at cribbage, and he was thought no mean person. This was Ned P——, and a better fellow in his way breathes not. There was ——, who asserted some incredible matter of fact as a likely paradox, and settled all controversies by an *ipse dixit*, a *fiat* of his will, hammering out many a hard theory on the anvil of his brain— the Baron Munchausen of politics and practical philosophy:— there was Captain ——, who had you at an advantage by never understanding you:—there was Jem White, the author of Falstaff's Letters, who the other day left this dull world to go in search of more kindred spirits, 'turning like the latter end of a lover's lute':—there was A——, who sometimes dropped in, the Will Honeycomb of our set—and Mrs R——, who being of a quiet turn, loved to hear a noisy debate. An utterly uninformed person might have supposed this a scene of vulgar confusion and uproar. While the most critical question was pending, while the most difficult problem in philosophy was solving, P—— cried out, 'That's game,' and M. B. muttered a quotation over the last remains of a veal-pie at a side-table. Once, and once only, the literary interest overcame the general. For C—— was riding the high German horse, and demonstrating the Categories of the Transcendental philosophy to the author of the Road to Ruin; who insisted on his knowledge of German, and German metaphysics, having read the *Critique of Pure Reason* in the original. 'My dear Mr Holcroft,' said C——, in a tone of infinitely provoking conciliation, 'you really put me in mind of a sweet pretty German girl, about fifteen, that I met with in the Hartz forest in Germany—and who one day, as I was reading the Limits of the Knowable and the Unknowable, the profoundest of all his works, with great attention, came behind my chair, and leaning over, said, What, *you* read Kant? Why, *I* that am German born, don't understand him!' This was too much to bear, and Holcroft, starting up, called out in no measured tone, 'Mr C——, you are the most eloquent man I ever met with, and the most troublesome with your eloquence!' P—— held the cribbage-peg that was to mark him game, suspended in his hand; and the whist table was silent for a moment. I saw Holcroft down stairs, and, on coming to the landing-place in Mitre-court, he stopped me to observe, that 'he thought Mr C—— a very clever man, with a great command of language, but that he feared he did not always affix very precise ideas to the words he used.' After he was gone, we had our laugh out, and went on with the argument on the nature of Reason, the Imagination, and the Will. I wish I could find a publisher for it: it would make a supplement to the *Biographia Literaria* in a volume and a half octavo.

Those days are over! An event, the name of which I wish never to mention, broke up our party, like a bomb-shell thrown into the room: and now we seldom meet—

Like angels' visits, short and far between.

There is no longer the same set of persons, nor of associations. L—— does not live where he did. By shifting his abode, his notions seem less fixed. He does not wear his old snuff-coloured coat and breeches. It looks like an alteration in his style. An author and a wit should have a separate costume, a particular cloth: he should present something positive and singular to the mind, like Mr Douce of the Museum. Our faith in the religion of letters will not bear to be taken to pieces, and put together again by caprice or accident. L. H—— goes there sometimes. He has a fine vinous spirit about him, and tropical blood in his veins: but he is better at his own table. He has a great flow of pleasantry and delightful animal spirits: but his hits do not tell like L——'s; you cannot repeat them the next day. He requires not only to be appreciated, but to have a select circle of admirers and devotees, to feel himself quite at home. He sits at the head of a party with great gaiety and grace; has an elegant manner and turn of features; is never at a loss—*aliquando sufflaminandus erat*—has continual sportive sallies of wit or fancy; tells a story capitally; mimics an actor, or an acquaintance, to admiration; laughs with great glee and good humour at his own or other people's jokes; understands the point of an equivoque, or an observation immediately; has a taste and knowledge of books, of music, of medals; manages an argument adroitly; is genteel and gallant, and has a set of bye-phrases and quaint allusions always at hand to produce a laugh:—if he has a fault, it is that he does not listen so well as he speaks, is impatient of interruption, and is fond of being looked up to, without considering by whom. I believe, however, he has pretty well seen the folly of this. Neither is his ready display of personal accomplishment and variety of resources an advantage to his writings. They sometimes present a desultory and slip-shod appearance, owing to this very circumstance. The same things that tell, perhaps, best, to a private circle round the fireside, are not always intelligible to the public, nor does he take pains to make them so. He is too confident and secure of his audience. That which may be entertaining enough with the assistance of a certain liveliness of manner, may read very flat on paper, because it is abstracted from all the circumstances that had

set it off to advantage.   A writer should recollect that he has
only to trust to the immediate impression of words, like a
musician who sings without the accompaniment of an instrument.   There is nothing to help out, or slubber over, the defects
of the voice in the one case, nor of the style in the other.   The
reader may, if he pleases, get a very good idea of L. H——'s
conversation from a very agreeable paper he has lately
published, called the *Indicator*, than which nothing can be
more happily conceived or executed.

The art of conversation is the art of hearing as well as of
being heard.   Authors in general are not good listeners.
Some of the best talkers are, on this account, the worst
company; and some who are very indifferent, but very great
talkers, are as bad.   It is sometimes wonderful to see how
a person, who has been entertaining or tiring a company by
the hour together, drops his countenance as if he had been
shot, or had been seized with a sudden lock-jaw, the moment
any one interposes a single observation.   The best converser
I know is, however, the best listener.   I mean Mr Northcote,
the painter.   Painters by their profession are not bound to
shine in conversation, and they shine the more.   He lends
his ear to an observation, as if you had brought him a piece
of news, and enters into it with as much avidity and earnest-
ness, as if it interested himself personally.   If he repeats an
old remark or story, it is with the same freshness and point
as for the first time.   It always arises out of the occasion,
and has the stamp of originality.   There is no parroting of
himself.   His look is a continual, ever-varying history-piece
of what passes in his mind.   His face is as a book.   There
need no marks of interjection or interrogation to what he says.
His manner is quite picturesque.   There is an excess of
character and *naiveté* that never tires.   His thoughts bubble
up and sparkle, like beads on old wine.   The fund of anecdote,
the collection of curious particulars, is enough to set up any
common retailer of jests, that dines out every day; but these
are not strung together like a row of galley-slaves, but are
always introduced to illustrate some argument or bring out
some fine distinction of character.   The mixture of spleen
adds to the sharpness of the point, like poisoned arrows.
Mr Northcote enlarges with enthusiasm on the old painters,

and tells good things of the new. The only thing he ever vexed me in was his liking the *Catalogue Raisonné*. I had almost as soon hear him talk of Titian's pictures (which he does with tears in his eyes, and looking just like them) as see the originals, and I had rather hear him talk of Sir Joshua's than see them. He is the last of that school who knew Goldsmith and Johnson. How finely he describes Pope! His elegance of mind, his figure, his character were not unlike his own. He does not resemble a modern Englishman, but puts one in mind of a Roman Cardinal or Spanish Inquisitor. I never ate or drank with Mr Northcote; but I have lived on his conversation with undiminished relish ever since I can remember,—and when I leave it, I come out into the street with feelings lighter and more etherial than I have at any other time.—One of his *tête-à-têtes* would at any time make an Essay; but he cannot write himself, because he loses himself in the connecting passages, is fearful of the effect, and wants the habit of bringing his ideas into one focus or point of view. A *lens* is necessary to collect the diverging rays, the refracted and broken angular lights of conversation on paper. Contradiction is half the battle in talking—the being startled by what others say, and having to answer on the spot. You have to defend yourself, paragraph by paragraph, parenthesis within parenthesis. Perhaps it might be supposed that a person who excels in conversation and cannot write, would succeed better in dialogue. But the stimulus, the immediate irritation, would be wanting; and the work would read flatter than ever, from not having the very thing it pretended to have.

Lively sallies and connected discourse are very different things. There are many persons of that impatient and restless turn of mind, that they cannot wait a moment for a conclusion, or follow up the thread of any argument. In the hurry of conversation their ideas are somehow huddled into sense; but in the intervals of thought, leave a great gap between. Montesquieu said, he often lost an idea before he could find words for it: yet he dictated, by way of saving time, to an amanuensis. This last is, in my opinion, a vile method, and a solecism in authorship. Horne Tooke, among other paradoxes, used to maintain, that no one could write a good style who was not in the habit of talking and hearing the sound of his own voice. He might as well have said that no one could relish a good style without reading it aloud, as we find common people do to assist their apprehension. But there is a method of trying periods on the ear, or weighing them with the scales of the breath, without any articulate sound. Authors, as they write, may be said to 'hear a sound so fine, there's nothing lives 'twixt it and silence.' Even musicians generally compose in their heads. I agree that no style is good, that is not fit to be spoken or read aloud with effect. This holds true not only of emphasis and cadence, but also with regard to natural idiom and colloquial freedom. Sterne's was in this respect the best style that ever was written. You fancy that you hear the people talking. For a contrary reason, no college-man writes a good style, or understands it when written. Fine writing is with him all verbiage and monotony—a translation into classical centos or hexameter lines.

That which I have just mentioned is among many instances I could give of ingenious absurdities advanced by Mr Tooke in the heat and pride of controversy. A person who knew him well, and greatly admired his talents, said of him that he never (to his recollection) heard him defend an opinion which he thought right, or in which he believed him to be himself sincere. He indeed provoked his antagonists into the toils by the very extravagance of his assertions, and the teasing sophistry by which he rendered them plausible. His temper was prompter to his skill. He had the manners of a man of the world, with great scholastic resources. He flung every one else off his guard, and was himself immoveable. I never knew any one who did not admit his superiority in this kind of warfare. He put a full stop to one of C——'s long-winded prefatory apologies for his youth and inexperience, by saying abruptly, 'Speak up, young man!' and, at another time, silenced a learned professor, by desiring an explanation of a word which the other frequently used, and which, he said, he had been many years trying to get at the meaning of,—the copulative Is! He was the best intellectual fencer of his day. He made strange havoc of Fuseli's fantastic hieroglyphics, violent humours, and oddity of dialect.—Curran, who was sometimes of the same party, was lively and animated in convivial conversation, but dull in argument; nay, averse to any thing like reasoning or serious observation, and had the worst taste I ever knew. His favourite critical topics were to abuse Milton's Paradise Lost, and Romeo and Juliet. Indeed, he confessed a want of sufficient acquaintance with books when he found himself in literary society in London. He and Sheridan once dined at John Kemble's with Mrs Inchbald and Mary Woolstonecroft, when the discourse almost wholly turned on Love, 'from noon to dewy eve, a summer's day!' What a subject! What speakers, and what hearers! What would I not give to have been there, had I not learned it all from the bright eyes of Amaryllis, and may one day make a *Table-talk* of it!—Peter Pindar was rich in anecdote and grotesque humour, and profound in technical knowledge both of music, poetry, and painting, but he was gross and over-bearing. Wordsworth sometimes talks like a man inspired on subjects of poetry (his own out of the question)—Coleridge well on every subject, and G—dwin on none. To finish this subject—Mrs M——'s conversation is as fine-cut as her features, and I like to sit in the room with that sort of coronet face. What she says leaves a flavour, like fine green tea. H—t's is like champaigne, and N——'s like anchovy sandwiches. H—yd—n's is like a game at trap-ball: L—'s like snap-dragon: and my own (if I do not mistake the matter) is not very much unlike a game at nine-pins!...One source of the conversation of authors, is the character of other authors, and on that they are rich indeed. What things they say! What stories they tell of one another, more par-ticularly of their friends! If I durst only give some of these confidential communications!...The reader may perhaps think the foregoing a specimen of them:—but indeed he is mistaken.

I do not know of any greater impertinence, than for an obscure individual to set about pumping a character of celebrity. 'Bring him to me,' said a Doctor Tronchin, speaking of Rousseau, 'that I may see whether he has any thing in him.' Before you can take measure of the capacity of others, you ought to be sure that they have not taken measure of yours. They may think you a spy on them, and may not like their company. If you really want to know whether another person can talk well, begin by saying a good thing yourself, and you will have a right to look for a rejoinder. 'The best tennis-players,' says Sir Fopling Flutter, 'make the best matches.'

> ————————For wit is like a rest
> Held up at tennis, which men do the best
> With the best players.

We hear it often said of a great author, or a great actress, that they are very stupid people in private. But he was a fool that said so. *Tell me your company, and I'll tell you your manners.* In conversation, as in other things, the action and reaction should bear a certain proportion to each other.— Authors may, in some sense, be looked upon as foreigners, who are not naturalized even in their native soil. L—— once came down into the country to see us. He was 'like the most capricious poet Ovid among the Goths.' The country people thought him an oddity, and did not understand his jokes. It would be strange if they had; for he did not make any, while he staid. But when we crossed the country to Oxford, then he spoke a little. He and the old colleges were hail-fellow well met; and in the quadrangles, he 'walked gowned.'

There is a character of a gentleman; so there is a character of a scholar, which is no less easily recognised. The one has an air of books about him, as the other has of good-breeding. The one wears his thoughts as the other does his clothes, gracefully; and even if they are a little old-fashioned, they are not ridiculous: they have had their day. The gentleman shows, by his manner, that he has been used to respect from others: the scholar that he lays claim to self-respect and to a certain independence of opinion. The one has been accustomed to the best company; the other has passed his time in cultivating an intimacy with the best authors. There is nothing forward or vulgar in the behaviour of the one; nothing shrewd or petulant in the observations of the other, as if he should astonish the bye-standers, or was astonished himself at his own discoveries. Good taste and good sense, like common politeness, are, or are supposed to be, matters of course. One is distinguished by an appearance of marked attention to every one present; the other manifests an habitual air of abstraction and absence of mind. The one is not an upstart with all the self-important airs of the founder of his own fortune; nor the other a self-taught man, with the repulsive self-sufficiency which arises from an ignorance of what hundreds have known before him. We must excuse perhaps a little conscious family-pride in the one, and a little harmless pedantry in the other.—As there is a class of the first character which sinks into the mere gentleman, that is, which has nothing but this sense of respectability and propriety to support it—so the character of a scholar not unfrequently dwindles down into the shadow of a shade, till nothing is left of it but the mere book-worm. There is often something amiable as well as enviable in this last character. I know one such instance, at least. The person I mean has an admiration for learning, if he is only dazzled by its light. He lives among old authors, if he does not enter much into their spirit. He handles the covers, and turns over the page, and is familiar with the names and dates. He is busy and self-involved. He hangs like a film and cobweb upon letters, or is like the dust upon the outside of knowledge, which should not be rudely brushed aside. He follows learning as its shadow; but as such, he is respectable. He browzes on the husk and leaves of books, as the young fawn browzes on the bark and leaves of trees. Such a one lives all his life in a dream of learning, and has never once had his sleep broken by a real sense of things. He believes implicitly in genius, truth, virtue, liberty, because he finds the names of these things in books. He thinks that love and friendship are the finest things imaginable, both in practice and theory. The legend of good women is to him no fiction. When he steals from the twilight of his cell, the scene breaks upon him like an illuminated missal, and all the people he sees are but so many figures in a *camera obscura*. He reads the world, like a favourite volume, only to find beauties in it, or like an edition of some old work which he is preparing for the press, only to make emendations in it, and correct the errors that have inadvertently slipt in. He and his dog Tray are much the same honest, simple-hearted, faithful, affectionate creatures—if Tray could but read! His

mind cannot take the impression of vice: but the gentleness
of his nature turns gall to milk. He would not hurt a fly.
He draws the picture of mankind from the guileless simplicity
of his own heart: and when he dies, his spirit will take its
smiling leave, without having ever had an ill thought of
others, or the consciousness of one in itself!

OF PERSONS ONE WOULD WISH TO HAVE SEEN

Come like shadows—so depart.

B—— it was, I think, who suggested this subject, as well as the defence of Guy Faux, which I urged him to execute. As, however, he would undertake neither, I suppose I must do both—a task for which he would have been much fitter, no less from the temerity than the felicity of his pen—

Never so sure our rapture to create
As when it touch'd the brink of all we hate.

Compared with him I shall, I fear, make but a common-place piece of business of it; but I should be loth the idea was entirely lost, and besides I may avail myself of some hints of his in the progress of it. I am sometimes, I suspect, a better reporter of the ideas of other people than expounder of my own. I pursue the one too far into paradox or mysticism; the others I am not bound to follow farther than I like, or than seems fair and reasonable.

On the question being started, A—— said, 'I suppose the two first persons you would choose to see would be the two greatest names in English literature, Sir Isaac Newton and Mr Locke?' In this A——, as usual, reckoned without his host. Every one burst out a laughing at the expression of B——'s face, in which impatience was restrained by courtesy. 'Yes, the greatest names,' he stammered out hastily, 'but they were not persons—not persons.'—'Not persons?' said A——, looking wise and foolish at the same time, afraid his triumph might be premature. 'That is,' rejoined B——, 'not characters, you know. By Mr Locke and Sir Isaac Newton, you mean the Essay on the Human Understanding, and the *Principia*, which we have to this day. Beyond their contents there is nothing personally interesting in the men. But what we want to see any one *bodily* for, is when there is something peculiar, striking in the individuals, more than we can learn from their writings, and yet are curious to know.

I dare say Locke and Newton were very like Kneller's portraits
of them.   But who could paint Shakspeare?'—'Ay,' retorted
A——, 'there it is; then I suppose you would prefer seeing him
and Milton instead?'—'No,' said B——, 'neither.   I have
seen so much of Shakspeare on the stage and on book-stalls,
in frontispieces and on mantle-pieces, that I am quite tired
of the everlasting repetition: and as to Milton's face, the
impressions that have come down to us of it I do not like;
it is too starched and puritanical; and I should be afraid
of losing some of the manna of his poetry in the leaven of
his countenance and the precisian's band and gown.'—'I shall
guess no more,' said A——.   'Who is it, then, you would like
to see "in his habit as he lived," if you had your choice of the
whole range of English literature?'   B—— then named
Sir Thomas Brown and Fulke Greville, the friend of Sir Philip
Sidney, as the two worthies whom he should feel the greatest
pleasure to encounter on the floor of his apartment in their
night-gown and slippers, and to exchange friendly greeting
with them.   At this A—— laughed outright, and conceived
B—— was jesting with him; but as no one followed his
example, he thought there might be something in it, and
waited for an explanation in a state of whimsical suspense.
B—— then (as well as I can remember a conversation that
passed twenty years ago—how time slips!) went on as follows.
'The reason why I pitch upon these two authors is, that their
writings are riddles, and they themselves the most mysterious
of personages.   They resemble the soothsayers of old, who
dealt in dark hints and doubtful oracles; and I should like
to ask them the meaning of what no mortal but themselves,
I should suppose, can fathom.   There is Dr Johnson, I have
no curiosity, no strange uncertainty about him: he and Boswell
together have pretty well let me into the secret of what passed
through his mind.   He and other writers like him are sufficiently explicit: my friends, whose repose I should be tempted
to disturb, (were it in my power) are implicit, inextricable,
inscrutable.

> And call up him who left half-told
> The story of Cambuscan bold.

'When I look at that obscure but gorgeous prose-composi-
tion (the *Urn-burial*) I seem to myself to look into a deep abyss,

at the bottom of which are hid pearls and rich treasure; or it is like a stately labyrinth of doubt and withering speculation, and I would invoke the spirit of the author to lead me through it. Besides, who would not be curious to see the lineaments of a man who, having himself been twice married, wished that mankind were propagated like trees! As to Fulke Greville, he is like nothing but one of his own "Prologues spoken by the ghost of an old king of Ormus," a truly formidable and inviting personage: his style is apocalyptical, cabalistical, a knot worthy of such an apparition to untie; and for the unravelling a passage or two, I would stand the brunt of an encounter with so portentous a commentator!'— 'I am afraid in that case,' said A——, 'that if the mystery were once cleared up, the merit might be lost';—and turning to me, whispered a friendly apprehension, that while B—— continued to admire these old crabbed authors, he would never become a popular writer. Dr Donne was mentioned as a writer of the same period, with a very interesting countenance, whose history was singular, and whose meaning was often quite as *uncomeatable*, without a personal citation from the dead, as that of any of his contemporaries. The volume was produced; and while some one was expatiating on the exquisite simplicity and beauty of the portrait prefixed to the old edition, A—— got hold of the poetry, and exclaiming 'What have we here?' read the following:—

> Here lies a She-Sun and a He-Moon here,
> She gives the best light to his sphere,
> Or each is both and all, and so
> They unto one another nothing owe.

There was no resisting this, till B——, seizing the volume, turned to the beautiful 'Lines to his Mistress,' dissuading her from accompanying him abroad, and read them with suffused features and a faltering tongue.

> By our first strange and fatal interview,
> By all desires which thereof did ensue,
> By our long starving hopes, by that remorse
> Which my words' masculine persuasive force
> Begot in thee, and by the memory
> Of hurts, which spies and rivals threaten'd me,
> I calmly beg. But by thy father's wrath,
> By all pains which want and divorcement hath,

I conjure thee; and all the oaths which I
And thou have sworn to seal joint constancy
Here I unswear, and overswear them thus,
Thou shalt not love by ways so dangerous.
Temper, oh fair Love! love's impetuous rage,
Be my true mistress still, not my feign'd Page;
I'll go, and, by thy kind leave, leave behind
Thee, only worthy to nurse in my mind.
Thirst to come back; oh, if thou die before,
My soul from other lands to thee shall soar.
Thy (else Almighty) beauty cannot move
Rage from the seas, nor thy love teach them love,
Nor tame wild Boreas' harshness; thou hast read
How roughly he in pieces shivered
Fair Orithea, whom he swore he lov'd.
Fall ill or good, 'tis madness to have prov'd
Dangers unurg'd: Feed on this flattery,
That absent lovers one in th' other be.
Dissemble nothing, not a boy, nor change
Thy body's habit, nor mind; be not strange
To thyself only. All will spy in thy face
A blushing, womanly, discovering grace.
Richly cloth'd apes are called apes, and as soon
Eclips'd as bright we call the moon the moon.
Men of France, changeable cameleons,
Spittles of diseases, shops of fashions,
Love's fuellers, and the rightest company
Of players, which upon the world's stage be,
Will quickly know thee....O stay here! for, for thee
England is only a worthy gallery,
To walk in expectation; till from thence
Our greatest King call thee to his presence.
When I am gone, dream me some happiness,
Nor let thy looks our long hid love confess,
Nor praise, nor dispraise me; nor bless, nor curse
Openly love's force, nor in bed fright thy nurse
With midnight startings, crying out, Oh, oh,
Nurse, oh, my love is slain, I saw him go
O'er the white Alps alone; I saw him, I,
Assail'd, fight, taken, stabb'd, bleed, fall, and die.
Augur me better chance, except dread Jove
Think it enough for me to have had thy love.

Some one then inquired of B—— if we could not see from
the window the Temple-walk in which Chaucer used to take
his exercise; and on his name being put to the vote, I was
pleased to find that there was a general sensation in his favour
in all but A——, who said something about the ruggedness

of the metre, and even objected to the quaintness of the
orthography. I was vexed at this superficial gloss, per-
tinaciously reducing every thing to its own trite level, and
asked 'if he did not think it would be worth while to scan the
eye that had first greeted the Muse in that dim twilight and
early dawn of English literature; to see the head, round
which the visions of fancy must have played like gleams of
inspiration or a sudden glory; to watch those lips that
"lisped in numbers, for the numbers came"—as by a miracle,
or as if the dumb should speak? Nor was it alone that he
had been the first to tune his native tongue (however imper-
fectly to modern ears); but he was himself a noble, manly
character, standing before his age and striving to advance it;
a pleasant humourist withal, who has not only handed down
to us the living manners of his time, but had, no doubt, store
of curious and quaint devices, and would make as hearty
a companion as Mine Host of Tabard. His interview with
Petrarch is fraught with interest. Yet I would rather have
seen Chaucer in company with the author of the Decameron,
and have heard them exchange their best stories together,
the Squire's Tale against the Story of the Falcon, the Wife of
Bath's Prologue against the Adventures of Friar Albert. How
fine to see the high mysterious brow which learning then
wore, relieved by the gay, familiar tone of men of the world,
and by the courtesies of genius. Surely, the thoughts and
feelings which passed through the minds of these great revivers
of learning, these Cadmuses who sowed the teeth of letters,
must have stamped an expression on their features, as different
from the moderns as their books, and well worth the perusal.
Dante,' I continued, 'is as interesting a person as his own
Ugolino, one whose lineaments curiosity would as eagerly
devour in order to penetrate his spirit, and the only one of
the Italian poets I should care much to see. There is a fine
portrait of Ariosto by no less a hand than Titian's; light,
Moorish, spirited, but not answering our idea. The same
artist's large colossal profile of Peter Aretine is the only
likeness of the kind that has the effect of conversing with
"the mighty dead," and this is truly spectral, ghastly,
necromantic.' B—— put it to me if I should like to see
Spenser as well as Chaucer; and I answered without hesitation,

'No; for that his beauties were ideal, visionary, not palpable or personal, and therefore connected with less curiosity about the man. His poetry was the essence of romance, a very halo round the bright orb of fancy; and the bringing in the individual might dissolve the charm. No tones of voice could come up to the mellifluous cadence of his verse; no form but of a winged angel could vie with the airy shapes he has described. He was (to our apprehensions) rather "a creature of the element, that lived in the rainbow and played in the plighted clouds," than an ordinary mortal. Or if he did appear, I should wish it to be as a mere vision, like one of his own pageants, and that he should pass by unquestioned like a dream or sound—

> ——That was Arion crown'd:
> So went he playing on the wat'ry plain!

Captain C. muttered something about Columbus, and M. C. hinted at the Wandering Jew; but the last was set aside as spurious, and the first made over to the New World.

'I should like,' said Miss D——, 'to have seen Pope talking with Patty Blount; and I *have* seen Goldsmith.' Every one turned round to look at Miss D——, as if by so doing they too could get a sight of Goldsmith.

'Where,' asked a harsh croaking voice, 'was Dr Johnson in the years 1745–6? He did not write any thing that we know of, nor is there any account of him in Boswell during those two years. Was he in Scotland with the Pretender? He seems to have passed through the scenes in the Highlands in company with Boswell many years after "with lack-lustre eye," yet as if they were familiar to him, or associated in his mind with interests that he durst not explain. If so, it would be an additional reason for my liking him; and I would give something to have seen him seated in the tent with the youthful Majesty of Britain, and penning the Proclamation to all true subjects and adherents of the legitimate Government.'

'I thought,' said A——, turning short round upon B——, 'that you of the Lake School did not like Pope?'—'Not like Pope! My dear sir, you must be under a mistake—I can read him over and over for ever!'—'Why certainly, the

"Essay on Man" must be allowed to be a master-piece.'—'It may be so, but I seldom look into it.'—'Oh! then it's his Satires you admire?'—'No, not his Satires, but his friendly Epistles and his compliments.'—'Compliments! I did not know he ever made any.'—'The finest,' said B——, 'that were ever paid by the wit of man. Each of them is worth an estate for life—nay, is an immortality. There is that superb one to Lord Cornbury:

> Despise low joys, low gains;
> Disdain whatever Cornbury disdains;
> Be virtuous, and be happy for your pains.

'Was there ever more artful insinuation of idolatrous praise? And then that noble apotheosis of his friend Lord Mansfield (however little deserved), when, speaking of the House of Lords, he adds—

> Conspicuous scene! another yet is nigh,
> (More silent far) where kings and poets lie;
> Where Murray (long enough his country's pride)
> Shall be no more than Tully or than Hyde!

'And with what a fine turn of indignant flattery he addresses Lord Bolingbroke—

> Why rail they then, if but one wreath of mine,
> Oh! all accomplish'd St John, deck thy shrine?

'Or turn,' continued B——, with a slight hectic on his cheek and his eye glistening, 'to his list of early friends:

> But why then publish? Granville the polite,
> And knowing Walsh, would tell me I could write;
> Well-natured Garth inflamed with early praise,
> And Congreve loved and Swift endured my lays:
> The courtly Talbot, Somers, Sheffield read,
> Ev'n mitred Rochester would nod the head;
> And St John's self (great Dryden's friend before)
> Received with open arms one poet more.
> Happy my studies, if by these approved!
> Happier their author, if by these beloved!
> From these the world will judge of men and books,
> Not from the Burnets, Oldmixons, and Cooks.

Here his voice totally failed him, and throwing down the book, he said, 'Do you think I would not wish to have been friends with such a man as this?'

'What say you to Dryden?'—'He rather made a show of himself, and courted popularity in that lowest temple of Fame, a coffee-house, so as in some measure to vulgarize one's idea of him. Pope, on the contrary, reached the very *beau ideal* of what a poet's life should be; and his fame while living seemed to be an emanation from that which was to circle his name after death. He was so far enviable (and one would feel proud to have witnessed the rare spectacle in him) that he was almost the only poet and man of genius who met with his reward on this side of the tomb, who realized in friends, fortune, the esteem of the world, the most sanguine hopes of a youthful ambition, and who found that sort of patronage from the great during his lifetime which they would be thought anxious to bestow upon him after his death. Read Gay's verses to him on his supposed return from Greece, after his translation of Homer was finished, and say if you would not gladly join the bright procession that welcomed him home, or see it once more land at Whitehall-stairs.'— 'Still,' said Miss D——, 'I would rather have seen him talking with Patty Blount, or riding by in a coronet-coach with Lady Mary Wortley Montagu!'

E——, who was deep in a game of piquet at the other end of the room, whispered to M. C. to ask if Junius would not be a fit person to invoke from the dead. 'Yes,' said B——, 'provided he would agree to lay aside his mask.'

We were now at a stand for a short time, when Fielding was mentioned as a candidate: only one, however, seconded the proposition. 'Richardson?'—'By all means, but only to look at him through the glass-door of his back-shop, hard at work upon one of his novels (the most extraordinary contrast that ever was presented between an author and his works), but not to let him come behind his counter lest he should want you to turn customer, nor to go upstairs with him, lest he should offer to read the first manuscript of Sir Charles Grandison, which was originally written in eight and twenty volumes octavo, or get out the letters of his female correspondents, to prove that Joseph Andrews was low.'

There was but one statesman in the whole of English history that any one expressed the least desire to see—Oliver Cromwell, with his fine, frank, rough, pimply face, and wily policy;—and one enthusiast, John Bunyan, the immortal author of the Pilgrim's Progress. It seemed that if he came into the room, dreams would follow him, and that each person would nod under his golden cloud, 'nigh-sphered in Heaven,' a canopy as strange and stately as any in Homer.

Of all persons near our own time, Garrick's name was received with the greatest enthusiasm, who was proposed by J. F——. He presently superseded both Hogarth and Handel, who had been talked of, but then it was on condition that he should act in tragedy and comedy, in the play and the farce, Lear and Wildair and Abel Drugger. What a *sight for sore eyes* that would be! Who would not part with a year's income at least, almost with a year of his natural life, to be present at it? Besides, as he could not act alone, and recitations are unsatisfactory things, what a troop he must bring with him—the silver-tongued Barry, and Quin, and Shuter and Weston, and Mrs Clive and Mrs Pritchard, of whom I have heard my father speak as so great a favourite when he was young! This would indeed be a revival of the dead, the restoring of art; and so much the more desirable, as such is the lurking scepticism mingled with our overstrained admiration of past excellence, that though we have the speeches of Burke, the portraits of Reynolds, the writings of Goldsmith, and the conversation of Johnson, to show what people could do at that period, and to confirm the universal testimony to the merits of Garrick; yet, as it was before our time, we have our misgivings, as if he was probably after all little better than a Bartlemy-fair actor, dressed out to play Macbeth in a scarlet coat and laced cocked-hat. For one, I should like to have seen and heard with my own eyes and ears. Certainly, by all accounts, if any one was ever moved by the true histrionic *æstus*, it was Garrick. When he followed the Ghost in Hamlet, he did not drop the sword, as most actors do behind the scenes, but kept the point raised the whole way round, so fully was he possessed with the idea, or so anxious not to lose sight of his part for a moment. Once at a splendid dinner-party at Lord ——'s, they suddenly missed Garrick, and could not imagine what was become of him, till they were drawn to the window by the convulsive screams and peals of laughter of a young negro boy, who was rolling on the ground in an ecstacy of delight to see Garrick mimicing a turkey-cock in the court-yard, with his coat-tail stuck out behind, and in a seeming flutter of feathered rage and pride. Of our party only two persons present had seen the British Roscius; and they seemed as willing as the rest to renew their acquaintance with their old favourite.

We were interrupted in the hey-day and mid-career of this fanciful speculation, by a grumbler in a corner, who declared it was a shame to make all this rout about a mere player and farce-writer, to the neglect and exclusion of the fine old dramatists, the contemporaries and rivals of Shakespeare. B—— said he had anticipated this objection when he had named the author of Mustapha and Alaham; and out of caprice insisted upon keeping him to represent the set, in preference to the wild hair-brained enthusiast Kit Marlowe; to the sexton of St Ann's, Webster, with his melancholy yew-trees and death's-heads; to Deckar, who was but a garrulous proser; to the voluminous Heywood; and even to Beaumont and Fletcher, whom we might offend by complimenting the wrong author on their joint productions. Lord Brook, on the contrary, stood quite by himself, or in Cowley's words, was 'a vast species alone.' Some one hinted at the circumstance of his being a lord, which rather startled B——, but he said a *ghost* would perhaps dispense with strict etiquette, on being regularly addressed by his title. Ben Jonson divided our suffrages pretty equally. Some were afraid he would begin to traduce Shakspeare, who was not present to defend himself. 'If he grows disagreeable,' it was whispered aloud, 'there is G—— can match him.' At length, his romantic visit to Drummond of Hawthornden was mentioned, and turned the scale in his favour.

B—— inquired if there was any one that was hanged that I would choose to mention? And I answered, Eugene Aram[1]. The name of the 'Admirable Crichton' was suddenly started as a splendid example of *waste* talents, so different from the generality of his countrymen. This choice was mightily approved by a North-Briton present, who declared himself descended from that prodigy of learning and accomplishment, and said he had family-plate in his possession as

[1] See Newgate Calendar for 1758.

vouchers for the fact, with the initials A. C.—*Admirable Crichton!* H—— laughed or rather roared as heartily at this as I should think he has done for many years.

The last-named Mitre-courtier[1] then wished to know whether there were any metaphysicians to whom one might be tempted to apply the wizard spell? I replied, there were only six in modern times deserving the name—Hobbes, Berkeley, Butler, Hartley, Hume, Leibnitz; and perhaps Jonathan Edwards, a Massachusets man[2]. As to the French, who talked fluently of having *created* this science, there was not a title in any of their writings, that was not to be found literally in the authors I had mentioned. [Horne Tooke, who might have a claim to come in under the head of Grammar, was still living.] None of these names seemed to excite much interest, and I did not plead for the re-appearance of those who might be thought best fitted by the abstracted nature of their studies for their present spiritual and disembodied state, and who, even while on this living stage, were nearly divested of common flesh and blood. As A—— with an uneasy fidgetty face was about to put some question about Mr Locke and Dugald Stewart, he was prevented by M. C. who observed, 'If J—— was here, he would undoubtedly be for having up those profound and redoubted scholiasts, Thomas Aquinas and Duns Scotus.' I said this might be fair enough in him who had read or fancied he had read the original works, but I did not see how we could have any right to call up these authors to give an account of themselves in person, till we had looked into their writings.

By this time it should seem that some rumour of our whimsical deliberation had got wind, and had disturbed the *irritabile genus* in their shadowy abodes, for we received

---

[1] B—— at this time occupied chambers in Mitre Court, Fleet Street.

[2] Lord Bacon is not included in this list, nor do I know where he should come in. It is not easy to make room for him and his reputation together. This great and celebrated man in some of his works recommends it to pour a bottle of claret into the ground of a morning, and to stand over it, inhaling the perfumes. So he sometimes enriched the dry and barren soil of speculation with the fine aromatic spirit of his genius. His 'Essays' and his 'Advancement of Learning' are works of vast depth and scope of observation. The last, though it contains no positive discoveries, is a noble chart of the human intellect, and a guide to all future inquirers.

messages from several candidates that we had just been
thinking of. Gray declined our invitation, though he had not
yet been asked: Gay offered to come and bring in his hand
the Duchess of Bolton, the original Polly: Steele and Addison
left their cards as Captain Sentry and Sir Roger de Coverley:
Swift came in and sat down without speaking a word, and
quitted the room as abruptly: Otway and Chatterton were
seen lingering on the opposite side of the Styx, but could
not muster enough between them to pay Charon his fare:
Thomson fell asleep in the boat, and was rowed back again—
and Burns sent a low fellow, one John Barleycorn, an old
companion of his who had conducted him to the other world,
to say that he had during his lifetime been drawn out of his
retirement as a show, only to be made an exciseman of, and
that he would rather remain where he was. He desired,
however, to shake hands by his representative—the hand,
thus held out, was in a burning fever, and shook prodigiously.

The room was hung round with several portraits of eminent
painters. While we were debating whether we should demand
speech with these masters of mute eloquence, whose features
were so familiar to us, it seemed that all at once they glided
from their frames, and seated themselves at some little distance
from us. There was Leonardo with his majestic beard and
watchful eye, having a bust of Archimedes before him; next
him was Raphael's graceful head turned round to the Fornarina; and on his other side was Lucretia Borgia, with calm,
golden locks; Michael Angelo had placed the model of St
Peter's on the table before him; Corregio had an angel at his
side; Titian was seated with his Mistress between himself and
Giorgioni; Guido was accompanied by his own Aurora, who
took a dice-box from him; Claude held a mirror in his hand;
Rubens patted a beautiful panther (led in by a satyr) on the
head; Vandyke appeared as his own Paris, and Rembrandt
was hid under furs, gold chains and jewels, which Sir Joshua
eyed closely, holding his hand so as to shade his forehead.
Not a word was spoken; and as we rose to do them homage,
they still presented the same surface to the view. Not being
bonâ-fide representations of living people, we got rid of the
splendid apparitions by signs and dumb show. As soon as
they had melted into thin air, there was a loud noise at the

outer door, and we found it was Giotto, Cimabue, and Ghirlandaio, who had been raised from the dead by their earnest desire to see their illustrious successors—

Whose names on earth
In Fame's eternal records live for aye!

Finding them gone, they had no ambition to be seen after them, and mournfully withdrew. 'Egad!' said B——, 'those are the very fellows I should like to have had some talk with, to know how they could see to paint when all was dark around them?'

'But shall we have nothing to say,' interrogated G. J——, 'to the Legend of Good Women?'—'Name, name, Mr J——,' cried H—— in a boisterous tone of friendly exultation, 'name as many as you please, without reserve or fear of molestation!' J—— was perplexed between so many amiable recollections, that the name of the lady of his choice expired in a pensive whiff of his pipe; and B—— impatiently declared for the Duchess of Newcastle. Mrs Hutchinson was no sooner mentioned, than she carried the day from the Duchess. We were the less solicitous on this subject of filling up the post-humous lists of Good Women, as there was already one in the room as good, as sensible, and in all respects as exemplary, as the best of them could be for their lives! 'I should like vastly to have seen Ninon de l'Enclos,' said that incomparable person; and this immediately put us in mind that we had neglected to pay honour due to our friends on the other side of the Channel: Voltaire, the patriarch of levity, and Rousseau, the father of sentiment, Montaigne and Rabelais (great in wisdom and in wit), Molière and that illustrious group that are collected round him (in the print of that subject) to hear him read his comedy of the Tartuffe at the house of Ninon; Racine, La Fontaine, Rochefoucault, St Evremont, &c.

'There is one person,' said a shrill, querulous voice, 'I would rather see than all these—Don Quixote!'

'Come, come!' said H——; 'I thought we should have no heroes, real or fabulous. What say you, Mr B——? Are you for eking out your shadowy list with such names as Alexander, Julius Cæsar, Tamerlane, or Ghengis Khan?' —'Excuse me,' said B——, 'on the subject of characters in active life, plotters and disturbers of the world, I have a crotchet of my own, which I beg leave to reserve.'—'No, no! come, out with your worthies!'—'What do you think of Guy Faux and Judas Iscariot?' H—— turned an eye upon him like a wild Indian, but cordial and full of smothered glee. 'Your most exquisite reason!' was echoed on all sides; and A—— thought that B—— had now fairly entangled himself. 'Why, I cannot but think,' retorted he of the wistful countenance, 'that Guy Faux, that poor fluttering annual scare-crow of straw and rags, is an ill-used gentleman. I would give something to see him sitting pale and emaciated, surrounded by his matches and his barrels of gunpowder, and expecting the moment that was to transport him to Paradise for his heroic self-devotion; but if I say any more, there is that fellow G—— will make something of it. And as to Judas Iscariot, my reason is different. I would fain see the face of him, who, having dipped his hand in the same dish with the Son of Man, could afterwards betray him. I have no conception of such a thing; nor have I ever seen any picture (not even Leonardo's very fine one) that gave me the least idea of it.'— 'You have said enough, Mr B——, to justify your choice.'

'Oh! ever right, Menenius,—ever right!'

'There is only one other person I can ever think of after this,' continued H——; but without mentioning a name that once put on a semblance of mortality. 'If Shakspeare was to come into the room, we should all rise up to meet him; but if that person was to come into it, we should all fall down and try to kiss the hem of his garment!'

As a lady present seemed now to get uneasy at the turn the conversation had taken, we rose up to go. The morning broke with that dim, dubious light by which Giotto, Cimabue, and Ghirlandaio must have seen to paint their earliest works; and we parted to meet again and renew similar topics at night, the next night, and the night after that, till that night over-spread Europe which saw no dawn. The same event, in truth, broke up our little Congress that broke up the great one. But that was to meet again: our deliberations have never been resumed.

ON READING OLD BOOKS

I hate to read new books. There are twenty or thirty volumes that I have read over and over again, and these are the only ones that I have any desire ever to read at all. It was a long time before I could bring myself to sit down to the Tales of My Landlord, but now that author's works have made a considerable addition to my scanty library. I am told that some of Lady Morgan's are good, and have been recommended to look into Anastasius; but I have not yet ventured upon that task. A lady, the other day, could not refrain from expressing her surprise to a friend, who said he had been reading Delphine:—she asked,—If it had not been published some time back? Women judge of books as they do of fashions or complexions, which are admired only 'in their newest gloss.' That is not my way. I am not one of those who trouble the circulating libraries much, or pester the booksellers for mail-coach copies of standard periodical publications. I cannot say that I am greatly addicted to black-letter, but I profess myself well versed in the marble bindings of Andrew Millar, in the middle of the last century; nor does my taste revolt at Thurloe's State Papers, in Russia leather; or an ample impression of Sir William Temple's Essays, with a portrait after Sir Godfrey Kneller in front. I do not think altogether the worse of a book for having survived the author a generation or two. I have more confidence in the dead than the living. Contemporary writers may generally be divided into two classes—one's friends or one's foes. Of the first we are compelled to think too well, and of the last we are disposed to think too ill, to receive much genuine pleasure from the perusal, or to judge fairly of the merits of either. One candidate for literary fame, who happens to be of our acquaintance, writes finely, and like a man of genius; but unfortunately has a foolish face, which spoils a delicate passage:—another inspires us with the highest respect for his personal talents and character, but does not quite come up to our expectations in print. All these contradictions and petty details interrupt the calm current of our reflections. If you want to know what any of the authors were who lived before our time, and are still objects of anxious inquiry, you have only to look into their works. But the dust and smoke and noise of modern literature have nothing in common with the pure, silent air of immortality.

When I take up a work that I have read before (the oftener the better) I know what I have to expect. The satisfaction is not lessened by being anticipated. When the entertainment is altogether new, I sit down to it as I should to a strange dish, —turn and pick out a bit here and there, and am in doubt what to think of the composition. There is a want of confidence and security to second appetite. New-fangled books are also like made-dishes in this respect, that they are generally little else than hashes and *rifacimentos* of what has been served up entire and in a more natural state at other times. Besides, in thus turning to a well-known author, there is not only an assurance that my time will not be thrown away, or my palate nauseated with the most insipid or vilest trash,— but I shake hands with, and look an old, tried, and valued friend in the face,—compare notes, and chat the hours away. It is true, we form dear friendships with such ideal guests— dearer, alas! and more lasting, than those with our most intimate acquaintance. In reading a book which is an old favourite with me (say the first novel I ever read) I not only have the pleasure of imagination and of a critical relish of the work, but the pleasures of memory added to it. It recals the same feelings and associations which I had in first reading it, and which I can never have again in any other way. Standard productions of this kind are links in the chain of our conscious being. They bind together the different scattered divisions of our personal identity. They are landmarks and guides in our journey through life. They are pegs and loops on which we can hang up, or from which we can take down, at pleasure, the wardrobe of a moral imagination, the relics of our best affections, the tokens and records of our happiest hours. They are 'for thoughts and for remembrance!' They are like Fortunatus's Wishing-Cap —they give us the best riches—those of Fancy; and transport us, not over half the globe, but (which is better) over half our lives, at a word's notice!

My father Shandy solaced himself with Bruscambille. Give me for this purpose a volume of Peregrine Pickle or Tom Jones. Open either of them any where—at the Memoirs of Lady Vane, or the adventures at the masquerade with Lady Bellaston, or the disputes between Thwackum and Square, or the escape of Molly Seagrim, or the incident of Sophia and her muff, or the edifying prolixity of her aunt's lecture—and there I find the same delightful, busy, bustling scene as ever, and feel myself the same as when I was first introduced into the midst of it. Nay, sometimes the sight of an odd volume of these good old English authors on a stall, or the name lettered on the back among others on the shelves of a library, answers the purpose, revives the whole train of ideas, and sets 'the puppets dallying.' Twenty years are struck off the list, and I am a child again. A sage philosopher, who was not a very wise man, said, that he should like very well to be young again, if he could take his experience along with him. This ingenious person did not seem to be aware, by the gravity of his remark, that the great advantage of being young is to be without this weight of experience, which he would fain place upon the shoulders of youth, and which never comes too late with years. Oh! what a privilege to be able to let this hump, like Christian's burthen, drop from off one's back, and transport one's self, by the help of a little musty duodecimo, to the time when 'ignorance was bliss,' and when we first got a peep at the rarée-show of the world, through the glass of fiction—gazing at mankind, as we do at wild beasts in a menagerie, through the bars of their cages,— or at curiosities in a museum, that we must not touch! For myself, not only are the old ideas of the contents of the work brought back to my mind in all their vividness, but the old associations of the faces and persons of those I then knew, as they were in their life-time—the place where I sat to read the volume, the day when I got it, the feeling of the air, the fields, the sky—return, and all my early impressions with them. This is better to me—those places, those times, those persons,

and those feelings that come across me as I retrace the story
and devour the page, are to me better far than the wet sheets
of the last new novel from the Ballantyne press, to say nothing
of the Minerva press in Leadenhall-street. It is like visiting
the scenes of early youth. I think of the time 'when I was
in my father's house, and my path ran down with butter and
honey,'—when I was a little, thoughtless child, and had no
other wish or care but to con my daily task, and be happy!—
Tom Jones, I remember, was the first work that broke the
spell. It came down in numbers once a fortnight, in Cooke's
pocket-edition, embellished with cuts. I had hitherto read
only in school-books, and a tiresome ecclesiastical history
(with the exception of Mrs Radcliffe's Romance of the Forest):
but this had a different relish with it,—'sweet in the mouth,'
though not 'bitter in the belly.' It smacked of the world
I lived in, and in which I was to live—and shewed me groups,
'gay creatures' not 'of the element,' but of the earth; not
'living in the clouds,' but travelling the same road that I
did;—some that had passed on before me, and others that
might soon overtake me. My heart had palpitated at the
thoughts of a boarding-school ball, or gala-day at Midsummer
or Christmas: but the world I had found out in Cooke's
edition of the British Novelists was to me a dance through
life, a perpetual gala-day. The sixpenny numbers of this
work regularly contrived to leave off just in the middle of
a sentence, and in the nick of a story, where Tom Jones
discovers Square behind the blanket; or where Parson Adams,
in the inextricable confusion of events, very undesignedly gets
to bed to Mrs Slip-slop. Let me caution the reader against
this impression of Joseph Andrews; for there is a picture
of Fanny in it which he should not set his heart on, lest he
should never meet with any thing like it; or if he should,
it would, perhaps, be better for him that he had not. It was
just like —— ——! With what eagerness I used to look
forward to the next number, and open the prints! Ah!
never again shall I feel the enthusiastic delight with which
I gazed at the figures, and anticipated the story and adventures
of Major Bath and Commodore Trunnion, of Trim and my Uncle
Toby, of Don Quixote and Sancho and Dapple, of Gil Blas
and Dame Lorenza Sephora, of Laura and the fair Lucretia,

whose lips open and shut like buds of roses. To what nameless
ideas did they give rise,—with what airy delights I filled up
the outlines, as I hung in silence over the page!—Let me still
recal them, that they may breathe fresh life into me, and
that I may live that birthday of thought and romantic pleasure
over again! Talk of the *ideal*! This is the only true ideal—
the heavenly tints of Fancy reflected in the bubbles that
float upon the spring-tide of human life.

> Oh! Memory! shield me from the world's poor strife,
> And give those scenes thine everlasting life!

The paradox with which I set out is, I hope, less startling
than it was; the reader will, by this time, have been let into
my secret. Much about the same time, or I believe rather
earlier, I took a particular satisfaction in reading Chubb's
Tracts, and I often think I will get them again to wade through.
There is a high gusto of polemical divinity in them; and you
fancy that you hear a club of shoemakers at Salisbury, debating
a disputable text from one of St Paul's Epistles in a workman-
like style, with equal shrewdness and pertinacity. I cannot
say much for my metaphysical studies, into which I launched
shortly after with great ardour, so as to make a toil of a
pleasure. I was presently entangled in the briars and thorns
of subtle distinctions,—of 'fate, free-will, fore-knowledge
absolute,' though I cannot add that 'in their wandering mazes
I found no end'; for I did arrive at some very satisfactory
and potent conclusions; nor will I go so far, however ungrateful
the subject might seem, as to exclaim with Marlowe's Faustus
—'Would I had never seen Wittenberg, never read book'—
that is, never studied such authors as Hartley, Hume,
Berkeley, &c. Locke's Essay on the Human Understanding
is, however, a work from which I never derived either pleasure
or profit; and Hobbes, dry and powerful as he is, I did not
read till long afterwards. I read a few poets, which did not
much hit my taste,—for I would have the reader understand,
I am deficient in the faculty of imagination; but I fell early
upon French romances and philosophy, and devoured them
tooth-and-nail. Many a dainty repast have I made of the
New Eloise;—the description of the kiss; the excursion on
the water; the letter of St Preux, recalling the time of their

first loves; and the account of Julia's death; these I read
over and over again with unspeakable delight and wonder.
Some years after, when I met with this work again, I found
I had lost nearly my whole relish for it (except some few
parts) and was, I remember, very much mortified with the
change in my taste, which I sought to attribute to the smallness
and gilt edges of the edition I had bought, and its being
perfumed with rose-leaves. Nothing could exceed the gravity,
the solemnity with which I carried home and read the
Dedication to the Social Contract, with some other pieces of
the same author, which I had picked up at a stall in a coarse
leathern cover. Of the Confessions I have spoken elsewhere,
and may repeat what I have said—'Sweet is the dew of their
memory, and pleasant the balm of their recollection!' Their
beauties are not 'scattered like stray-gifts o'er the earth,'
but sown thick on the page, rich and rare. I wish I had never
read the Emilius, or read it with less implicit faith. I had
no occasion to pamper my natural aversion to affectation or
pretence, by romantic and artificial means. I had better
have formed myself on the model of Sir Fopling Flutter.
There is a class of persons whose virtues and most shining
qualities sink in, and are concealed by, an absorbent ground
of modesty and reserve; and such a one I do, without vanity,
profess myself[1]. Now these are the very persons who are
likely to attach themselves to the character of Emilius, and
of whom it is sure to be the bane. This dull, phlegmatic,
retiring humour is not in a fair way to be corrected, but
confirmed and rendered desperate, by being in that work
held up as an object of imitation, as an example of simplicity
and magnanimity—by coming upon us with all the recommen-
dations of novelty, surprise, and superiority to the prejudices
of the world—by being stuck upon a pedestal, made amiable,
dazzling, a *leurre de dupe*! The reliance on solid worth which
it inculcates, the preference of sober truth to gaudy tinsel,
hangs like a mill-stone round the neck of the imagination—

---

[1] Nearly the same sentiment was wittily and happily expressed by a
friend, who had some lottery puffs, which he had been employed to write,
returned on his hands for their too great severity of thought and classical
terseness of style, and who observed on that occasion, that 'Modest merit
never can succeed!'

'a load to sink a navy'—impedes our progress, and blocks up every prospect in life. A man, to get on, to be successful, conspicuous, applauded, should not retire upon the centre of his conscious resources, but be always at the circumference of appearances. He must envelop himself in a halo of mystery —he must ride in an equipage of opinion—he must walk with a train of self-conceit following him—he must not strip himself to a buff-jerkin, to the doublet and hose of his real merits, but must surround himself with a *cortège* of prejudices, like the signs of the Zodiac—he must seem any thing but what he is, and then he may pass for any thing he pleases. The world love to be amused by hollow professions, to be deceived by flattering appearances, to live in a state of hallucination; and can forgive every thing but the plain, downright, simple honest truth—such as we see it chalked out in the character of Emilius.—To return from this digression, which is a little out of place here.

Books have in a great measure lost their power over me; nor can I revive the same interest in them as formerly. I perceive when a thing is good, rather than feel it. It is true,

Marcian Colonna is a dainty book;

and the reading of Mr Keats's Eve of Saint Agnes lately made me regret that I was not young again. The beautiful and tender images there conjured up, 'come like shadows—so depart.' The 'tiger-moth's wings,' which he has spread over his rich poetic blazonry, just flit across my fancy; the gorgeous twilight window which he has painted over again in his verse, to me 'blushes' almost in vain 'with blood of queens and kings.' I know how I should have felt at one time in reading such passages; and that is all. The sharp luscious flavour, the fine *aroma* is fled, and nothing but the stalk, the bran, the husk of literature is left. If any one were to ask me what I read now, I might answer with my Lord Hamlet in the play—'Words, words, words.'—'What is the matter?' —*Nothing!*'—They have scarce a meaning. But it was not always so. There was a time when to my thinking, every word was a flower or a pearl, like those which dropped from the mouth of the little peasant-girl in the Fairy tale, or like those that fall from the great preacher in the Caledonian

Chapel! I drank of the stream of knowledge that tempted, but did not mock my lips, as of the river of life, freely. How eagerly I slaked my thirst of German sentiment, 'as the hart that panteth for the water-springs'; how I bathed and revelled, and added my floods of tears to Goethe's Sorrows of Werter, and to Schiller's Robbers—

> Giving my stock of more to that which had too much!

I read, and assented with all my soul to Coleridge's fine Sonnet, beginning—

> Schiller! that hour I would have wish'd to die,
> If through the shuddering midnight I had sent,
> From the dark dungeon of the tow'r time-rent,
> That fearful voice, a famish'd father's cry!

I believe I may date my insight into the mysteries of poetry from the commencement of my acquaintance with the authors of the Lyrical Ballads; at least, my discrimination of the higher sorts—not my predilection for such writers as Goldsmith or Pope: nor do I imagine they will say I got my liking for the Novelists, or the comic writers,—for the characters of Valentine, Tattle, or Miss Prue, from them. If so, I must have got from them what they never had themselves. In points where poetic diction and conception are concerned, I may be at a loss, and liable to be imposed upon: but in forming an estimate of passages relating to common life and manners, I cannot think I am a plagiarist from any man. I there 'know my cue without a prompter.' I may say of such studies—*Intus et in cute*. I am just able to admire those literal touches of observation and description, which persons of loftier pretensions over-look and despise. I think I comprehend something of the characteristic part of Shakspeare; and in him indeed, all is characteristic, even the nonsense and poetry. I believe it was the celebrated Sir Humphrey Davy who used to say, that Shakspeare was rather a metaphysician than a poet. At any rate, it was not ill said. I wish that I had sooner known the dramatic writers contemporary with Shakspeare; for in looking them over about a year ago, I almost revived my old passion for reading, and my old delight in books, though they were very nearly new to me. The Periodical Essayists I read long ago. The

5—2

Spectator I liked extremely: but the Tatler took my fancy most. I read the others soon after, the Rambler, the Adventurer, the World, the Connoisseur: I was not sorry to get to the end of them, and have no desire to go regularly through them again. I consider myself a thorough adept in Richardson. I like the longest of his novels best, and think no part of them tedious; nor should I ask to have any thing better to do than to read them from beginning to end, to take them up when I chose, and lay them down when I was tired, in some old family mansion in the country, till every word and syllable relating to the bright Clarissa, the divine Clementina, the beautiful Pamela, 'with every trick and line of their sweet favour,' were once more 'graven in my heart's table[1].' I have a sneaking kindness for Mackenzie's Julia de Roubigné—for the deserted mansion, and straggling gilli-flowers on the mouldering garden-wall; and still more for his Man of Feeling; not that it is better, nor so good; but at the time I read it, I sometimes thought of the heroine, Miss Walton, and of Miss —— together, and 'that ligament, fine as it was, was never broken!'—One of the poets that I have always read with most pleasure, and can wander about in for ever with a sort of voluptuous indolence, is Spenser; and I like Chaucer even better. The only writer among the Italians I can pretend to any knowledge of, is Boccacio, and of him I cannot express half my admiration. His story of the Hawk I could read and think of from day to day, just as I would look at a picture of Titian's!—

I remember, as long ago as the year 1798, going to a neighbouring town (Shrewsbury, where Farquhar has laid the plot of his Recruiting Officer) and bringing home with me, 'at one proud swoop,' a copy of Milton's Paradise Lost, and another of Burke's Reflections on the French Revolution—both

---

[1] During the peace of Amiens, a young English officer, of the name of Lovelace, was presented at Buonaparte's levee. Instead of the usual question, 'Where have you served, Sir?' the First Consul immediately addressed him, 'I perceive your name, Sir, is the same as that of the hero of Richardson's Romance!' Here was a Consul. The young man's uncle, who was called Lovelace, told me this anecdote while we were stopping together at Calais. I had also been thinking that his was the same name as that of the hero of Richardson's Romance. This is one of my reasons for liking Buonaparte.

which I have still; and I still recollect, when I see the covers, the pleasure with which I dipped into them as I returned with my double prize. I was set up for one while. That time is past 'with all its giddy raptures': but I am still anxious to preserve its memory, 'embalmed with odours.'— With respect to the first of these works, I would be permitted to remark here in passing, that it is a sufficient answer to the German criticism which has since been started against the character of Satan (*viz.* that it is not one of disgusting deformity, or pure, defecated malice) to say that Milton has there drawn, not the abstract principle of evil, not a devil incarnate, but a fallen angel. This is the scriptural account, and the poet has followed it. We may safely retain such passages as that well-known one—

> ——His form had not yet lost
> All her original brightness; nor appear'd
> Less than archangel ruin'd; and the excess
> Of glory obscur'd——

for the theory, which is opposed to them, 'falls flat upon the grunsel edge, and shames its worshippers.' Let us hear no more then of this monkish cant, and bigotted outcry for the restoration of the horns and tail of the devil!—Again, as to the other work, Burke's Reflections, I took a particular pride and pleasure in it, and read it to myself and others for months afterwards. I had reason for my prejudice in favour of this author. To understand an adversary is some praise: to admire him is more. I thought I did both: I knew I did one. From the first time I ever cast my eyes on any thing of Burke's (which was an extract from his Letter to a Noble Lord in a three-times a week paper, The St James's Chronicle, in 1796), I said to myself, 'This is true eloquence: this is a man pouring out his mind on paper.' All other style seemed to me pedantic and impertinent. Dr Johnson's was walking on stilts; and even Junius's (who was at that time a favourite with me) with all his terseness, shrunk up into little antithetic points and well-trimmed sentences. But Burke's style was forked and playful as the lightning, crested like the serpent. He delivered plain things on a plain ground; but when he rose, there was no end of his flights and circumgyrations— and in this very Letter, 'he, like an eagle in a dove-cot,

fluttered *his* Volscians' (the Duke of Bedford and the Earl
of Lauderdale)[1] 'in Corioli.'   I did not care for his doctrines.
I was then, and am still, proof against their contagion; but
I admired the author, and was considered as not a very staunch
partisan of the opposite side, though I thought myself that
an abstract proposition was one thing—a masterly transition,
a brilliant metaphor, another.   I conceived too that he might
be wrong in his main argument, and yet deliver fifty truths in
arriving at a false conclusion.   I remember Coleridge assuring
me, as a poetical and political set-off to my sceptical admiration,
that Wordsworth had written an Essay on Marriage, which,
for manly thought and nervous expression, he deemed in-
comparably superior.   As I had not, at that time, seen any
specimens of Mr Wordsworth's prose style, I could not express
my doubts on the subject.   If there are greater prose-writers
than Burke, they either lie out of my course of study, or are
beyond my sphere of comprehension.   I am too old to be
a convert to a new mythology of genius.   The niches are
occupied, the tables are full.   If such is still my admiration
of this man's misapplied powers, what must it have been at
a time when I myself was in vain trying, year after year,
to write a single Essay, nay, a single page or sentence; when
I regarded the wonders of his pen with the longing eyes of
one who was dumb and a changeling; and when, to be able
to convey the slightest conception of my meaning to others
in words, was the height of an almost hopeless ambition!
But I never measured others' excellences by my own defects:
though a sense of my own incapacity, and of the steep,
impassable ascent from me to them, made me regard them
with greater awe and fondness.   I have thus run through
most of my early studies and favourite authors, some of whom
I have since criticised more at large.   Whether those observations will survive me, I neither know nor do I much care:
but to the works themselves, 'worthy of all acceptation,'
and to the feelings they have always excited in me since I
could distinguish a meaning in language, nothing shall ever
prevent me from looking back with gratitude and triumph.
To have lived in the cultivation of an intimacy with such

---

[1] He is there called 'Citizen Lauderdale.'   Is this the present Earl?

works, and to have familiarly relished such names, is not to have lived quite in vain.

There are other authors whom I have never read, and yet whom I have frequently had a great desire to read, from some circumstance relating to them. Among these is Lord Clarendon's History of the Grand Rebellion, after which I have a hankering, from hearing it spoken of by good judges—from my interest in the events, and knowledge of the characters from other sources, and from having seen fine portraits of most of them. I like to read a well-penned character, and Clarendon is said to have been a master in this way. I should like to read Froissart's Chronicles, Hollingshed and Stowe, and Fuller's Worthies. I intend, whenever I can, to read Beaumont and Fletcher all through. There are fifty-two of their plays, and I have only read a dozen or fourteen of them. A Wife for a Month, and Thierry and Theodoret, are, I am told, delicious, and I can believe it. I should like to read the speeches in Thucydides, and Guicciardini's History of Florence, and Don Quixote in the original. I have often thought of reading the Loves of Persiles and Sigismunda, and the Galatea of the same author. But I somehow reserve them like 'another Yarrow.' I should also like to read the last new novel (if I could be sure it was so) of the author of Waverley:—no one would be more glad than I to find it the best!—

Players are 'the abstracts and brief chronicles of the time'; the motley representatives of human nature. They are the only honest hypocrites. Their life is a voluntary dream; a studied madness. The height of their ambition is to be *beside themselves*. To-day kings, to-morrow beggars, it is only when they are themselves, that they are nothing. Made up of mimic laughter and tears, passing from the extremes of joy or woe at the prompter's call, they wear the livery of other men's fortunes; their very thoughts are not their own. They are, as it were, train-bearers in the pageant of life, and hold a glass up to humanity, frailer than itself. We see ourselves at second-hand in them: they shew us all that we are, all that we wish to be, and all that we dread to be. The stage is an epitome, a bettered likeness of the world, with the dull part left out: and, indeed, with this omission, it is nearly big enough to hold all the rest. What brings the resemblance nearer is, that, as *they* imitate us, we, in our turn, imitate them. How many fine gentlemen do we owe to the stage? How many romantic lovers are mere Romeos in masquerade? How many soft bosoms have heaved with Juliet's sighs? They teach us when to laugh and when to weep, when to love and when to hate, upon principle and with a good grace! Wherever there is a play-house, the world will go on not amiss. The stage not only refines the manners, but it is the best teacher of morals, for it is the truest and most intelligible picture of life. It stamps the image of virtue on the mind by first softening the rude materials of which it is composed, by a sense of pleasure. It regulates the passions by giving a loose to the imagination. It points out the selfish and depraved to our detestation, the amiable and generous to our admiration; and if it clothes the more seductive vices with the borrowed graces of wit and fancy, even those graces operate as a diversion to the coarser poison of experience and bad example, and often prevent or carry off the infection by inoculating the mind with a certain taste and elegance. To shew how little we agree with the common declamations against the immoral tendency of the stage on this score, we will hazard a conjecture, that the acting of the Beggar's Opera a certain number of nights every year since it was first brought out, has done more towards putting down the practice of highway robbery, than all the gibbets that ever were erected. A person, after seeing this piece, is too deeply imbued with a sense of humanity, is in too good humour with himself and the rest of the world, to set about cutting throats or rifling pockets. Whatever makes a jest of vice, leaves it too much a matter of indifference for any one in his senses to rush desperately on his ruin for its sake. We suspect that just the contrary effect must be produced by the representation of George Barnwell, which is too much in the style of the Ordinary's sermon to meet with any better success. The mind, in such cases, instead of being deterred by the alarming consequences held out to it, revolts against the denunciation of them as an insult offered to its free-will, and, in a spirit of defiance, returns a practical answer to them, by daring the worst that can happen. The most striking lesson ever read to levity and licentiousness, is in the last act of the Inconstant, where young Mirabel is preserved by the fidelity of his mistress, Orinda, in the disguise of a page, from the hands of assassins, into whose power he has been allured by the temptations of vice and beauty. There never was a rake who did not become in imagination a reformed man, during the representation of the last trying scenes of this admirable comedy.

If the stage is useful as a school of instruction, it is no less so as a source of amusement. It is the source of the greatest enjoyment at the time, and a never-failing fund of agreeable reflection afterwards. The merits of a new play, or of a new actor, are always among the first topics of polite conversation. One way in which public exhibitions contribute to refine and humanise mankind, is by supplying them with ideas and subjects of conversation and interest in common. The progress of civilisation is in proportion to the number of commonplaces current in society. For instance, if we meet with a stranger at an inn or in a stage-coach, who knows nothing but his own affairs, his shop, his customers, his farm, his pigs, his poultry, we can carry on no conversation with him on these local and personal matters: the only way is to let him have all the talk to himself. But if he has fortunately ever seen Mr Liston act, this is an immediate topic of mutual conversation, and we agree together the rest of the evening in discussing the merits of that inimitable actor, with the same satisfaction as in talking over the affairs of the most intimate friend.

If the stage thus introduces us familiarly to our contemporaries, it also brings us acquainted with former times. It is an interesting revival of past ages, manners, opinions, dresses, persons, and actions,—whether it carries us back to the wars of York and Lancaster, or half way back to the heroic times of Greece and Rome, in some translation from the French, or quite back to the age of Charles II in the scenes of Congreve and of Etherege, (the gay Sir George!)—happy age, when kings and nobles led purely ornamental lives; when the utmost stretch of a morning's study went no further than the choice of a sword-knot, or the adjustment of a side-curl; when the soul spoke out in all the pleasing eloquence of dress; and beaux and belles, enamoured of themselves in one another's follies, fluttered like gilded butterflies in giddy mazes through the walks of St James's Park!

A good company of comedians, a Theatre-Royal judiciously managed, is your true Herald's College; the only Antiquarian Society, that is worth a rush. It is for this reason that there is such an air of romance about players, and that it is pleasanter to see them, even in their own persons, than any of the three learned professions. We feel more respect for John Kemble in a plain coat, than for the Lord Chancellor on the woolsack. He is surrounded, to our eyes, with a greater number of imposing recollections: he is a more reverend piece of formality; a more complicated tissue of costume. We do not know whether to look upon this accomplished actor as Pierre or King John or Coriolanus or Cato or Leontes or the Stranger. But we see in him a stately hieroglyphic of humanity; a living monument of departed greatness, a sombre comment on the rise and fall of kings. We look after him till he is out of sight, as we listen to a story of one of Ossian's heroes, to 'a tale of other times!'

One of the most affecting things we know is to see a favourite actor take leave of the stage. We were present not long ago when Mr Bannister quitted it. We do not wonder that his feelings were overpowered on the occasion: ours were nearly so too. We remembered him, in the first heydey of our youthful spirits, in the *Prize*, in which he played so delightfully with that fine old croaker Suett, and Madame Storace,—in the farce of *My Grandmother*, in the *Son-in-Law*, in *Autolycus*, and in *Scrub*, in which our satisfaction was at its height. At that time, King and Parsons, and Dodd, and Quick, and Edwin were in the full vigour of their reputation, who are now all gone. We still feel the vivid delight with which we used to see their names in the play-bills, as we went along to the Theatre. Bannister was one of the last of these that remained; and we parted with him as we should with one of our oldest and best friends. The most pleasant feature in the profession of a player, and which, indeed, is peculiar to it, is that we not only admire the talents of those who adorn it, but we contract a personal intimacy with them. There is no class of society whom so many persons regard with affection as actors. We greet them on the stage; we like to meet them in the streets; they almost always recall to us pleasant associations; and we feel our gratitude excited, without the uneasiness of a sense of obligation. The very gaiety and popularity, however, which surround the life of a favourite performer, make the retiring from it a very serious business. It glances a mortifying reflection on the shortness of human life, and the vanity of human pleasures. Something reminds us, that 'all the world's a stage, and all the men and women merely players.'

It has been considered as the misfortune of first-rate talents for the stage, that they leave no record behind them except that of vague rumour, and that the genius of a great actor perishes with him, 'leaving the world no copy.' This is a misfortune, or at least an unpleasant circumstance, to actors; but it is, perhaps, an advantage to the stage. It leaves an opening to originality. The stage is always beginning anew; the candidates for theatrical reputation are always setting out afresh, unencumbered by the affectation of the faults or excellences of their predecessors. In this respect, we should imagine that the average quantity of dramatic talent remains more nearly the same than that in any other walk of art. In no other instance do the complaints of the degeneracy of the moderns seem so unfounded as in this; and Colley Cibber's account of the regular decline of the stage, from the time of Shakspeare to that of Charles II, and from the time of Charles II to the beginning of George II, appears quite ridiculous. The stage is a place where genius is sure to come upon its legs, in a generation or two at farthest. In the other arts, (as painting and poetry), it has been contended that what has been well done already, by giving rise to endless vapid imitations, is an obstacle to what might be done well hereafter: that the models or *chef-d'œuvres* of art, where they are accumulated, choke up the path to excellence; and that the works of genius, where they can be rendered permanent and handed down from age to age, not only prevent, but render superfluous, future productions of the same kind. We have not, neither do we want, two Shakspeares, two Miltons, two Raphaels, any more than we require two suns in the same sphere. Even Miss O'Neill stands a little in the way of our recollections of Mrs Siddons. But Mr Kean is an excellent substitute for the memory of Garrick, whom we never saw. When an author dies, it is no matter, for his works remain. When a great actor dies, there is a void produced in society, a gap which requires to be filled up. Who does not go to see Kean? Who, if Garrick were alive, would go to see him? At least one or the other must have quitted the stage. We have seen what a ferment has been excited among our living artists by the exhibition of the works of the old Masters at the British Gallery. What would the actors say to it, if, by any spell or power of necromancy, all the celebrated actors, for the last hundred years, could be made to appear again on the boards of Covent Garden and Drury-Lane, for the last time, in all their most brilliant parts? What a rich treat to the town, what a feast for the critics, to go and see Betterton, and Booth, and Wilks, and Sandford, and Nokes, and Leigh, and Penkethman, and Bullock, and Estcourt, and Dogget, and Mrs Barry, and Mrs Montfort, and Mrs Oldfield, and Mrs Bracegirdle, and Mrs Cibber, and Cibber himself, the prince of coxcombs, and Macklin, and Quin, and Rich, and Mrs Clive, and Mrs Pritchard, and Mrs Abington, and Weston, and Shuter, and Garrick, and all the rest of those who 'gladdened life, and whose deaths eclipsed the gaiety of nations'! We should certainly be there. We should buy a ticket for the season. We should enjoy *our hundred days* again. We should not lose a single night. We would not, for a great deal, be absent from Betterton's Hamlet or his Brutus, or from Booth's Cato, as it was first acted to the contending applause of Whigs and Tories. We should be in the first row when Mrs Barry (who was kept by Lord Rochester, and with whom Otway was in love) played Monimia or Belvidera; and we suppose we should go to see Mrs Bracegirdle (with whom all the world was in love) in all her parts. We should then know exactly whether Penkethman's manner of picking a chicken, and Bullock's mode of devouring asparagus, answered to the ingenious account of them in the Tatler; and whether Dogget was equal to Dowton—whether Mrs Montfort[1] or Mrs Abington

---

[1] The following lively description of this actress is given by Cibber in his Apology:—

'What found most employment for her whole various excellence at once, was the part of Melantha, in Marriage-à-la-mode. Melantha is as finished an impertinent as ever fluttered in a drawing-room, and seems to contain the most complete system of female foppery that could possibly be crowded

was the finest lady—whether Wilks or Cibber was the best
Sir Harry Wildair—whether Macklin was really 'the Jew
that Shakspeare drew,' and whether Garrick was, upon the
whole, so great an actor as the world have made him out!
Many people have a strong desire to pry into the secrets of
futurity: for our own parts, we should be satisfied if we had
the power to recall the dead, and live the past over again
as often as we pleased! Players, after all, have little reason
to complain of their hard-earned, short-lived popularity.
One thunder of applause from pit, boxes, and gallery, is equal
to a whole immortality of posthumous fame: and when we
hear an actor, whose modesty is equal to his merit, declare,
that he would like to see a dog wag his tail in approbation,
what must he feel when he sees the whole house in a roar!
Besides, Fame, as if their reputation had been entrusted to
her alone, has been particularly careful of the renown of her
theatrical favourites: she forgets one by one, and year by

into the tortured form of a fine lady. Her language, dress, motion, manners,
soul, and body, are in a continual hurry to be something more than is
necessary or commendable. And though I doubt it will be a vain labour
to offer you a just likeness of Mrs Montfort's action, yet the fantastic
impression is still so strong in my memory, that I cannot help saying
something, though fantastically, about it. The first ridiculous airs that
break from her are upon a gallant never seen before, who delivers her a letter
from her father, recommending him to her good graces as an honourable
lover. Here now, one would think she might naturally shew a little of the
sex's decent reserve, though never so slightly covered! No, sir; not
a tittle of it; modesty is the virtue of a poor-soul'd country gentlewoman:
she is too much a court-lady, to be under so vulgar a confusion: she reads
the letter, therefore, with a careless, dropping lip, and an erected brow,
humming it hastily over, as if she were impatient to outgo her father's
commands, by making a complete conquest of him at once: and that the
letter might not embarrass her attack, crack! she crumbles it at once into
her palm, and pours upon him her whole artillery of airs, eyes, and motion;
down goes her dainty, diving body to the ground, as if she were sinking
under the conscious load of her own attractions; then launches into a flood
of fine language and compliment, still playing her chest forward in fifty
falls and risings, like a swan upon waving water; and, to complete her
impertinence, she is so rapidly fond of her own wit, that she will not give
her lover leave to praise it: Silent assenting bows, and vain endeavours to
speak, are all the share of the conversation he is admitted to, which at last
he is relieved from, by her engagement to half a score visits, which she
swims from him to make, with a promise to return in a twinkling.'—*The
Life of Colley Cibber*, p. 138.

year, those who have been great lawyers, great statesmen, and great warriors in their day; but the name of Garrick still survives with the works of Reynolds and of Johnson.

Actors have been accused, as a profession, of being extravagant and dissipated. While they are said to be so as a piece of common cant, they are likely to continue so. But there is a sentence in Shakspeare which should be stuck as a label in the mouths of our beadles and whippers-in of morality: 'The web of our life is of a mingled yarn, good and ill together: our virtues would be proud if our faults whipped them not: and our vices would despair if they were not cherished by our virtues.' With respect to the extravagance of actors, as a traditional character, it is not to be wondered at. They live from hand to mouth: they plunge from want into luxury; they have no means of making money *breed*, and all professions that do not live by turning money into money, or have not a certainty of accumulating it in the end by parsimony, spend it. Uncertain of the future, they make sure of the present moment. This is not unwise. Chilled with poverty, steeped in contempt, they sometimes pass into the sunshine of fortune, and are lifted to the very pinnacle of public favour; yet even there cannot calculate on the continuance of success, but are, 'like the giddy sailor on the mast, ready with every blast to topple down into the fatal bowels of the deep!' Besides, if the young enthusiast, who is smitten with the stage, and with the public as a mistress, were naturally a close *hunks*, he would become or remain a city clerk, instead of turning player. Again, with respect to the habit of convivial indulgence, an actor, to be a good one, must have a great spirit of enjoyment in himself, strong impulses, strong passions, and a strong sense of pleasure: for it is his business to imitate the passions, and to communicate pleasure to others. A man of genius is not a machine. The neglected actor may be excused if he drinks oblivion of his disappointments; the successful one, if he quaffs the applause of the world, and enjoys the friendship of those who are the friends of the favourites of fortune, in draughts of nectar. There is no path so steep as that of fame: no labour so hard as the pursuit of excellence. The intellectual excitement, inseparable from those professions which call forth all our sensibility to pleasure and pain,

requires some corresponding physical excitement to support
our failure, and not a little to allay the ferment of the spirits
attendant on success.   If there is any tendency to dissipation
beyond this in the profession of a player, it is owing to the
prejudices entertained against them, to that spirit of bigotry
which in a neighbouring country would deny actors Christian
burial after their death, and to that cant of criticism, which,
in our own, slurs over their characters, while living, with
a half-witted jest.

A London engagement is generally considered by actors
as the *ne plus ultra* of their ambition, as 'a consummation
devoutly to be wished,' as the great prize in the lottery of
their professional life.   But this appears to us, who are not
in the secret, to be rather the prose termination of their
adventurous career: it is the provincial commencement that
is the poetical and truly enviable part of it.   After that, they
have comparatively little to hope or fear. 'The wine of
life is drunk, and but the lees remain.'   In London, they
become gentlemen, and the King's servants: but it is the
romantic mixture of the hero and the vagabond that constitutes
the essence of the player's life.   It is the transition from
their real to their assumed characters, from the contempt
of the world to the applause of the multitude, that gives
its zest to the latter, and raises them as much above common
humanity at night, as in the daytime they are depressed
below it. 'Hurried from fierce extremes, by contrast made
more fierce,'—it is rags and a flock-bed which give their
splendour to a plume of feathers and a throne. We should
suppose, that if the most admired actor on the London stage
were brought to confession on this point, he would acknowledge
that all the applause he had received from 'brilliant and
overflowing audiences,' was nothing to the light-headed
intoxication of unlooked-for success in a barn.   In town,
actors are criticised: in country-places, they are wondered
at, or hooted at: it is of little consequence which, so that
the interval is not too long between.   For ourselves, we own
that the description of the strolling player in Gil Blas, soaking
his dry crusts in the well by the roadside, presents to us a
perfect picture of human felicity.

ON A LANDSCAPE OF NICOLAS POUSSIN

And blind Orion hungry for the morn.

Orion, the subject of this landscape, was the classical
Nimrod; and is called by Homer, 'a hunter of shadows,
himself a shade.' He was the son of Neptune; and having
lost an eye in some affray between the Gods and men, was
told that if he would go to meet the rising sun, he would
recover his sight. He is represented setting out on his journey,
with men on his shoulders to guide him, a bow in his hand,
and Diana in the clouds greeting him. He stalks along, a
giant upon earth, and reels and falters in his gait, as if just
awaked out of sleep, or uncertain of his way;—you see his
blindness, though his back is turned. Mists rise around him,
and veil the sides of the green forests; earth is dank and
fresh with dews, the 'grey dawn and the Pleiades before him
dance,' and in the distance are seen the blue hills and sullen
ocean. Nothing was ever more finely conceived or done.
It breathes the spirit of the morning; its moisture, its repose,
its obscurity, waiting the miracle of light to kindle it into
smiles: the whole is, like the principal figure in it, 'a fore-
runner of the dawn.' The same atmosphere tinges and imbues
every object, the same dull light 'shadowy sets off' the face
of nature: one feeling of vastness, of strangeness, and of
primeval forms pervades the painter's canvas, and we are
thrown back upon the first integrity of things. This great
and learned man might be said to see nature through the
glass of time: he alone has a right to be considered as the
painter of classical antiquity. Sir Joshua has done him justice
in this respect. He could give to the scenery of his heroic
fables that unimpaired look of original nature, full, solid,
large, luxuriant, teeming with life and power; or deck it with
all the pomp of art, with temples and towers, and mythologic

groves. His pictures 'denote a foregone conclusion.' He applies nature to his purposes, works out her images according to the standard of his thoughts, embodies high fictions; and the first conception being given, all the rest seems to grow out of, and be assimilated to it, by the unfailing process of a studious imagination. Like his own Orion, he overlooks the surrounding scene, appears to 'take up the isles as a very little thing, and to lay the earth in a balance.' With a laborious and mighty grasp, he put nature into the mould of the ideal and antique; and was among painters (more than any one else) what Milton was among poets. There is in both something of the same pedantry, the same stiffness, the same elevation, the same grandeur, the same mixture of art and nature, the same richness of borrowed materials, the same unity of character. Neither the poet nor the painter lowered the subjects they treated, but filled up the outline in the fancy, and added strength and reality to it; and thus not only satisfied, but surpassed the expectations of the spectator and the reader. This is held for the triumph and the perfection of works of art. To give us nature, such as we see it, is well and deserving of praise; to give us nature, such as we have never seen, but have often wished to see it, is better, and deserving of higher praise. He who can show the world in its first naked glory, with the hues of fancy spread over it, or in its high and palmy state, with the gravity of history stamped on the proud monuments of vanished empire,—who, by his 'so potent art,' can recal time past, transport us to distant places, and join the regions of imagination (a new conquest) to those of reality,—who shows us not only what nature is, but what she has been, and is capable of,—he who does this, and does it with simplicity, with truth, and grandeur, is lord of nature and her powers; and his mind is universal, and his art the master-art!

There is nothing in this 'more than natural,' if criticism could be persuaded to think so. The historic painter does not neglect or contravene nature, but follows her more closely up into her fantastic heights, or hidden recesses. He demonstrates what she would be in conceivable circumstances, and under implied conditions. He 'gives to airy nothing a local habitation,' not 'a name.' At his touch, words start up into

images, thoughts become things. He clothes a dream, a
phantom with form and colour and the wholesome attributes
of reality. *His* art is a second nature; not a different one.
There are those, indeed, who think that not to copy nature,
is the rule for attaining perfection. Because they cannot
paint the objects which they have seen, they fancy themselves
qualified to paint the ideas which they have not seen. But
it is possible to fail in this latter and more difficult style
of imitation, as well as in the former humbler one. The
detection, it is true, is not so easy, because the objects are not
so nigh at hand to compare, and therefore there is more room
both for false pretension and for self-deceit. They take an
epic motto or subject, and conclude that the spirit is implied
as a thing of course. They paint inferior portraits, maudlin
lifeless faces, without ordinary expression, or one look, feature,
or particle of nature in them, and think that this is to rise to
the truth of history. They vulgarise and degrade whatever
is interesting or sacred to the mind, and suppose that they
thus add to the dignity of their profession. They represent
a face that seems as if no thought or feeling of any kind had
ever passed through it, and would have you believe that this
is the very sublime of expression, such as it would appear
in heroes, or demi-gods of old, when rapture or agony was
raised to its height. They show you a landscape that looks
as if the sun never shone upon it, and tell you that it is not
modern—that so earth looked when Titan first kissed it with
his rays. This is not the true *ideal*. It is not to fill the moulds
of the imagination, but to deface and injure them: it is not
to come up to, but to fall short of the poorest conception in
the public mind. Such pictures should not be hung in the
same room with that of Orion[1].

[1] Every thing tends to show the manner in which a great artist is formed.
If any person could claim an exemption from the careful imitation of individual objects, it was Nicolas Poussin. He studied the antique, but he also
studied nature. 'I have often admired,' says Vignuel de Marville, who
knew him at a late period of his life, 'the love he had for his art. Old as
he was, I frequently saw him among the ruins of ancient Rome, out in the
Campagna, or along the banks of the Tyber, sketching a scene that had
pleased him; and I often met him with his handkerchief full of stones,
moss, or flowers, which he carried home, that he might copy them exactly
from nature. One day I asked him how he had attained to such a degree

Poussin was, of all painters, the most poetical. He was the painter of ideas. No one ever told a story half so well, nor so well knew what was capable of being told by the pencil. He seized on, and struck off with grace and precision, just that point of view which would be likely to catch the reader's fancy. There is a significance, a consciousness in whatever he does (sometimes a vice, but oftener a virtue) beyond any other painter. His Giants sitting on the tops of craggy mountains, as huge themselves, and playing idly on their Pan's-pipes, seem to have been seated there these three thousand years, and to know the beginning and the end of their own story. An infant Bacchus or Jupiter is big with his future destiny. Even inanimate and dumb things speak a language of their own. His snakes, the messengers of fate, are inspired with human intellect. His trees grow and expand their leaves in the air, glad of the rain, proud of the sun, awake to the winds of heaven. In his Plague of Athens, the very buildings seem stiff with horror. His picture of the Deluge is, perhaps, the finest historical landscape in the world. You see a waste of waters, wide, interminable: the sun is labouring, wan and weary, up the sky; the clouds, dull and leaden, lie like a load upon the eye, and heaven and earth seem commingling into one confused mass! His human figures are sometimes 'o'er-informed' with this kind of feeling. Their actions have too much gesticulation, and the set expression of the features borders too much on the mechanical and caricatured style. In this respect, they form a contrast to Raphael's, whose figures never appear to be sitting for their pictures, or to be conscious of a spectator, or to have come from the painter's

of perfection, as to have gained so high a rank among the great painters of Italy? He answered, I HAVE NEGLECTED NOTHING.'—*See his Life lately published.* It appears from this account that he had not fallen into a recent error, that Nature puts the man of genius out. As a contrast to the foregoing description, I might mention, that I remember an old gentleman once asking Mr West in the British Gallery, if he had ever been at Athens? To which the President made answer, No; nor did he feel any great desire to go; for that he thought he had as good an idea of the place from the Catalogue, as he could get by living there for any number of years. What would he have said, if any one had told him, he could get as good an idea of the subject of one of his great works from reading the Catalogue of it, as from seeing the picture itself! Yet the answer was characteristic of the genius of the painter.

hand. In Nicolas Poussin, on the contrary, every thing seems to have a distinct understanding with the artist: 'the very stones prate of their whereabout': each object has its part and place assigned, and is in a sort of compact with the rest of the picture. It is this conscious keeping, and, as it were, *internal* design, that gives their peculiar character to the works of this artist. There was a picture of Aurora in the British Gallery a year or two ago. It was a suffusion of golden light. The Goddess wore her saffron-coloured robes, and appeared just risen from the gloomy bed of old Tithonus. Her very steeds, milk-white, were tinged with the yellow dawn. It was a personification of the morning.—Poussin succeeded better in classic than in sacred subjects. The latter are comparatively heavy, forced, full of violent contrasts of colour, of red, blue, and black, and without the true prophetic inspiration of the characters. But in his Pagan allegories and fables he was quite at home. The native gravity and native levity of the Frenchman were combined with Italian scenery and an antique gusto, and gave even to his colouring an air of learned indifference. He wants, in one respect, grace, form, expression; but he has every where sense and meaning, perfect costume and propriety. His personages always belong to the class and time represented, and are strictly versed in the business in hand. His grotesque compositions in particular, his Nymphs and Fauns, are superior (at least, as far as style is concerned) even to those of Rubens. They are taken more immediately out of fabulous history. Rubens's Satyrs and Bacchantes have a more jovial and voluptuous aspect, are more drunk with pleasure, more full of animal spirits and riotous impulses; they laugh and bound along—

> Leaping like wanton kids in pleasant spring:

but those of Poussin have more of the intellectual part of the character, and seem vicious on reflection, and of set purpose. Rubens's are noble specimens of a class; Poussin's are allegorical abstractions of the same class, with bodies less pampered, but with minds more secretly depraved. The Bacchanalian groups of the Flemish painter were, however, his masterpieces in composition. Witness those prodigies of colour, character, and expression, at Blenheim. In the more chaste and refined delineation of classic fable, Poussin was without a rival. Rubens, who was a match for him in the wild and picturesque, could not pretend to vie with the elegance and purity of thought in his picture of Apollo giving a poet a cup of water to drink, nor with the gracefulness of design in the figure of a nymph squeezing the juice of a bunch of grapes from her fingers (a rosy wine-press) which falls into the mouth of a chubby infant below. But, above all, who shall celebrate, in terms of fit praise, his picture of the shepherds in the Vale of Tempe going out in a fine morning of the spring, and coming to a tomb with this inscription:—ET EGO IN ARCADIA VIXI! The eager curiosity of some, the expression of others who start back with fear and surprise, the clear breeze playing with the branches of the shadowing trees, 'the valleys low, where the mild zephyrs use,' the distant, uninterrupted, sunny prospect speak (and for ever will speak on) of ages past to ages yet to come[1]!

Pictures are a set of chosen images, a stream of pleasant thoughts passing through the mind. It is a luxury to have the walls of our rooms hung round with them, and no less so to have such a gallery in the mind, to con over the relics of ancient art bound up 'within the book and volume of the brain, unmixed (if it were possible) with baser matter!' A life passed among pictures, in the study and the love of art, is a happy noiseless dream: or rather, it is to dream and to be awake at the same time; for it has all 'the sober certainty of waking bliss,' with the romantic voluptuousness of a visionary and abstracted being. They are the bright consummate essences of things, and 'he who knows of these delights to taste and interpose them oft, is not unwise!'—The Orion, which I have here taken occasion to descant upon, is one of a collection of excellent pictures, as this collection is itself one of a series from the old masters, which have for some years back embrowned the walls of the British Gallery, and

---

[1] Poussin has repeated this subject more than once, and appears to have revelled in its witcheries. I have before alluded to it, and may again. It is hard that we should not be allowed to dwell as often as we please on what delights us, when things that are disagreeable recur so often against our will.

enriched the public eye.   What hues (those of nature mellowed
by time) breathe around, as we enter!   What forms are there,
woven into the memory!   What looks, which only the answering looks of the spectator can express!   What intellectual
stores have been yearly poured forth from the shrine of
ancient art!   The works are various, but the names the same
—heaps of Rembrandts frowning from the darkened walls,
Rubens's glad gorgeous groups, Titians more rich and rare,
Claudes always exquisite, sometimes beyond compare, Guido's
endless cloying sweetness, the learning of Poussin and the
Caracci, and Raphael's princely magnificence, crowning all.
We read certain letters and syllables in the catalogue, and at
the well-known magic sound, a miracle of skill and beauty
starts to view.   One might think that one year's prodigal
display of such perfection would exhaust the labours of one
man's life; but the next year, and the next to that, we find
another harvest reaped and gathered in to the great garner
of art, by the same immortal hands—

> Old GENIUS the porter of them was;
> He letteth in, he letteth out to wend.—

Their works seem endless as their reputation—to be many as
they are complete—to multiply with the desire of the mind
to see more and more of them; as if there were a living power
in the breath of Fame, and in the very names of the great
heirs of glory 'there were propagation too!'   It is something
to have a collection of this sort to count upon once a year;
to have one last, lingering look yet to come.   Pictures are
scattered like stray gifts through the world; and while they
remain, earth has yet a little gilding left, not quite rubbed
off, dishonoured, and defaced.   There are plenty of standard
works still to be found in this country, in the collections at
Blenheim, at Burleigh, and in those belonging to Mr Angerstein,
Lord Grosvenor, the Marquis of Stafford, and others, to keep
up this treat to the lovers of art for many years: and it is
the more desirable to reserve a privileged sanctuary of this
sort, where the eye may dote, and the heart take its fill of
such pictures as Poussin's Orion, since the Louvre is stripped
of its triumphant spoils, and since he, who collected it, and
wore it as a rich jewel in his Iron Crown, the hunter of greatness
and of glory, is himself a shade!—

'There is a pleasure in painting which none but painters know.' In writing, you have to contend with the world; in painting, you have only to carry on a friendly strife with Nature. You sit down to your task, and are happy. From the moment that you take up the pencil, and look Nature in the face, you are at peace with your own heart. No angry passions rise to disturb the silent progress of the work, to shake the hand, or dim the brow: no irritable humours are set afloat: you have no absurd opinions to combat, no point to strain, no adversary to crush, no fool to annoy—you are actuated by fear or favour to no man. There is 'no juggling here,' no sophistry, no intrigue, no tampering with the evidence, no attempt to make black white, or white black: but you resign yourself into the hands of a greater power, that of Nature, with the simplicity of a child, and the devotion of an enthusiast—'study with joy her manner, and with rapture taste her style.' The mind is calm, and full at the same time. The hand and eye are equally employed. In tracing the commonest object, a plant or the stump of a tree, you learn something every moment. You perceive unexpected differences, and discover likenesses where you looked for no such thing. You try to set down what you see—find out your error, and correct it. You need not play tricks, or purposely mistake: with all your pains, you are still far short of the mark. Patience grows out of the endless pursuit, and turns it into a luxury. A streak in a flower, a wrinkle in a leaf, a tinge in a cloud, a stain in an old wall or ruin grey, are seized with avidity as the *spolia opima* of this sort of mental warfare, and furnish out labour for another half day. The hours pass away untold, without chagrin, and without weariness; nor would you ever wish to pass them otherwise.

Innocence is joined with industry, pleasure with business; and the mind is satisfied, though it is not engaged in thinking or in doing any mischief[1].

I have not much pleasure in writing these Essays, or in reading them afterwards; though I own I now and then meet with a phrase that I like, or a thought that strikes me as a true one. But after I begin them, I am only anxious to get to the end of them, which I am not sure I shall do, for I seldom see my way a page or even a sentence beforehand; and when I have as by a miracle escaped, I trouble myself little more about them. I sometimes have to write them twice over: then it is necessary to read the *proof*, to prevent mistakes by the printer; so that by the time they appear in a tangible shape, and one can con them over with a conscious, sidelong glance to the public approbation, they have lost their gloss and relish, and become 'more tedious than a twice-told tale.' For a person to read his own works over with any great delight, he ought first to forget that he ever wrote them. Familiarity naturally breeds contempt. It is, in fact, like

---

[1] There is a passage in Werter which contains a very pleasing illustration of this doctrine, and is as follows.

'About a league from the town is a place called Walheim. It is very agreeably situated on the side of a hill: from one of the paths which leads out of the village, you have a view of the whole country; and there is a good old woman who sells wine, coffee, and tea there: but better than all this are two lime-trees before the church, which spread their branches over a little green, surrounded by barns and cottages. I have seen few places more retired and peaceful. I send for a chair and table from the old woman's, and there I drink my coffee and read Homer. It was by accident that I discovered this place one fine afternoon: all was perfect stillness; every body was in the fields, except a little boy about four years old, who was sitting on the ground, and holding between his knees a child of about six months; he pressed it to his bosom with his little arms, which made a sort of great chair for it, and notwithstanding the vivacity which sparkled in his eyes, he sat perfectly still. Quite delighted with the scene, I sat down on a plough opposite, and had great pleasure in drawing this little picture of brotherly tenderness. I added a bit of the hedge, the barn-door, and some broken cart-wheels, without any order, just as they happened to lie; and in about an hour I found I had made a drawing of great expression and very correct design, without having put in any thing of my own. This confirmed me in the resolution I had made before, only to copy nature for the future. Nature is inexhaustible, and alone forms the greatest masters. Say what you will of rules, they alter the true features, and the natural expression.' Page 15.

poring fondly over a piece of blank paper: from repetition, the words convey no distinct meaning to the mind, are mere idle sounds, except that our vanity claims an interest and property in them.   I have more satisfaction in my own thoughts than in dictating them to others: words are necessary to explain the impression of certain things upon me to the reader, but they rather weaken and draw a veil over than strengthen it to myself.   However I might say with the poet, 'My mind to me a kingdom is,' yet I have little ambition 'to set a throne or chair of state in the understandings of other men.'   The ideas we cherish most, exist best in a kind of shadowy abstraction,

> Pure in the last recesses of the mind;

and derive neither force nor interest from being exposed to public view.   They are old familiar acquaintance, and any change in them, arising from the adventitious ornaments of style or dress, is little to their advantage.   After I have once written on a subject, it goes out of my mind: my feelings about it have been melted down into words, and *them* I forget. I have, as it were, discharged my memory of its old habitual reckoning, and rubbed out the score of real sentiment.   For the future, it exists only for the sake of others.—But I cannot say, from my own experience, that the same process takes place in transferring our ideas to canvas; they gain more than they lose in the mechanical transformation.   One is never tired of painting, because you have to set down not what you knew already, but what you have just discovered. In the former case, you translate feelings into words; in the latter, names into things.   There is a continual creation out of nothing going on.   With every stroke of the brush, a new field of inquiry is laid open; new difficulties arise, and new triumphs are prepared over them.   By comparing the imitation with the original, you see what you have done, and how much you have still to do.   The test of the senses is severer than that of fancy, and an over-match even for the delusions of our self-love.   One part of a picture shames another, and you determine to paint up to yourself, if you cannot come up to nature.   Every object becomes lustrous from the light thrown back upon it by the mirror of art: and by the aid of the pencil

we may be said to touch and handle the objects of sight.
The air-drawn visions that hover on the verge of existence
have a bodily presence given them on the canvas: the form
of beauty is changed into a substance: the dream and the
glory of the universe is made 'palpable to feeling as to sight.'
—And see! a rainbow starts from the canvas, with all its
humid train of glory, as if it were drawn from its cloudy arch
in heaven. The spangled landscape glitters with drops of
dew after the shower. The 'fleecy fools' show their coats
in the gleams of the setting sun. The shepherds pipe their
farewell notes in the fresh evening air. And is this bright
vision made from a dead dull blank, like a bubble reflecting
the mighty fabric of the universe? Who would think this
miracle of Rubens' pencil possible to be performed? Who,
having seen it, would not spend his life to do the like? See
how the rich fallows, the bare stubble-field, the scanty harvest-
home, drag in Rembrandt's landscapes! How often have
I looked at them and nature, and tried to do the same, till
the very 'light thickened,' and there was an earthiness in
the feeling of the air! There is no end of the refinements of
art and nature in this respect. One may look at the misty
glimmering horizon till the eye dazzles and the imagination
is lost, in hopes to transfer the whole interminable expanse
at one blow upon canvas. Wilson said, he used to try to paint
the effect of the motes dancing in the setting sun. At another
time, a friend coming into his painting-room when he was
sitting on the ground in a melancholy posture, observed that
his picture looked like a landscape after a shower: he started
up with the greatest delight, and said, 'That is the effect
I intended to produce, but thought I had failed.' Wilson
was neglected; and, by degrees, neglected his art to apply
himself to brandy. His hand became unsteady, so that it
was only by repeated attempts that he could reach the place,
or produce the effect he aimed at; and when he had done
a little to a picture, he would say to any acquaintance who
chanced to drop in, 'I have painted enough for one day:
come, let us go somewhere.' It was not so Claude left his
pictures, or his studies on the banks of the Tiber, to go in
search of other enjoyments, or ceased to gaze upon the glittering
sunny vales and distant hills; and while his eye drank in

the clear sparkling hues and lovely forms of nature, his hand stamped them on the lucid canvas to last there for ever!—One of the most delightful parts of my life was one fine summer, when I used to walk out of an evening to catch the last light of the sun, gemming the green slopes or russet lawns, and gilding tower or tree, while the blue sky gradually turning to purple and gold, or skirted with dusky grey, hung its broad marble pavement over all, as we see it in the great master of Italian landscape. But to come to a more particular explanation of the subject.

The first head I ever tried to paint was an old woman with the upper part of the face shaded by her bonnet, and I certainly laboured it with great perseverance. It took me numberless sittings to do it. I have it by me still, and sometimes look at it with surprise, to think how much pains were thrown away to little purpose,—yet not altogether in vain if it taught me to see good in every thing, and to know that there is nothing vulgar in nature seen with the eye of science or of true art. Refinement creates beauty everywhere: it is the grossness of the spectator that discovers nothing but grossness in the object. Be this as it may, I spared no pains to do my best. If art was long, I thought that life was so too at that moment. I got in the general effect the first day; and pleased and surprised enough I was at my success. The rest was a work of time—of weeks and months (if need were) of patient toil and careful finishing. I had seen an old head by Rembrandt at Burleigh-House, and if I could produce a head at all like Rembrandt in a year, in my life-time, it would be glory and felicity, and wealth and fame enough for me! The head I had seen at Burleigh was an exact and wonderful fac-simile of nature, and I resolved to make mine (as nearly as I could) an exact fac-simile of nature. I did not then, nor do I now believe, with Sir Joshua, that the perfection of art consists in giving general appearances without individual details, but in giving general appearances with individual details. Otherwise, I had done my work the first day. But I saw something more in nature than general effect, and I thought it worth my while to give it in the picture. There was a gorgeous effect of light and shade: but there was a delicacy as well as depth in the *chiaro scuro*, which I was bound to follow into

all its dim and scarce perceptible variety of tone and shadow.
Then I had to make the transition from a strong light to as
dark a shade, preserving the masses, but gradually softening
off the intermediate parts.   It was so in nature: the difficulty
was to make it so in the copy.   I tried, and failed again and
again; I strove harder, and succeeded as I thought.   The
wrinkles in Rembrandt were not hard lines; but broken and
irregular.   I saw the same appearance in nature, and strained
every nerve to give it.   If I could hit off this edgy appearance,
and insert the reflected light in the furrows of old age in half
a morning, I did not think I had lost a day.   Beneath the
shrivelled yellow parchment look of the skin, there was here
and there a streak of the blood colour tinging the face; this
I made a point of conveying, and did not cease to compare
what I saw with what I did (with jealous lynx-eyed watchful-
ness) till I succeeded to the best of my ability and judgment.
How many revisions were there!   How many attempts to
catch an expression which I had seen the day before!   How
often did we try to get the old position, and wait for the return
of the same light!   There was a puckering up of the lips,
a cautious introversion of the eye under the shadow of the
bonnet, indicative of the feebleness and suspicion of old age,
which at last we managed, after many trials and some quarrels,
to a tolerable nicety.   The picture was never finished, and
I might have gone on with it to the present hour[1].   I used to
set it on the ground when my day's work was done, and saw
revealed to me with swimming eyes the birth of new hopes,
and of a new world of objects.   The painter thus learns to
look at nature with different eyes.   He before saw her 'as in
a glass darkly, but now face to face.'   He understands the
texture and meaning of the visible universe, and 'sees into
the life of things,' not by the help of mechanical instruments,
but of the improved exercise of his faculties, and an intimate
sympathy with nature.   The meanest thing is not lost upon
him, for he looks at it with an eye to itself, not merely to his
own vanity or interest, or the opinion of the world.   Even
where there is neither beauty nor use—if that ever were—

---

[1] It is at present covered with a thick slough of oil and varnish (the
perishable vehicle of the English school) like an envelope of gold-beaters'
skin, so as to be hardly visible.

still there is truth, and a sufficient source of gratification in the indulgence of curiosity and activity of mind. The humblest painter is a true scholar; and the best of scholars— the scholar of nature. For myself, and for the real comfort and satisfaction of the thing, I had rather have been Jan Steen, or Gerard Dow, than the greatest casuist or philologer that ever lived. The painter does not view things in clouds or 'mist, the common gloss of theologians,' but applies the same standard of truth and disinterested spirit of inquiry, that influence his daily practice, to other subjects. He perceives form, he distinguishes character. He reads men and books with an intuitive eye. He is a critic as well as a connoisseur. The conclusions he draws are clear and convincing, because they are taken from the things themselves. He is not a fanatic, a dupe, or a slave: for the habit of seeing for himself also disposes him to judge for himself. The most sensible men I know (taken as a class) are painters; that is, they are the most lively observers of what passes in the world about them, and the closest observers of what passes in their own minds. From their profession they in general mix more with the world than authors; and if they have not the same fund of acquired knowledge, are obliged to rely more on individual sagacity. I might mention the names of Opie, Fuseli, Northcote, as persons distinguished for striking description and acquaintance with the subtle traits of character[1]. Painters in ordinary society, or in obscure situations where their value is not known, and they are treated with neglect and indifference, have sometimes a forward self-sufficiency of manner: but this is not so much their fault as that of others. Perhaps their want of regular education may also be in fault in such cases. Richardson, who is very tenacious of the respect in which the profession ought to be held, tells a story of Michael Angelo, that after a quarrel between him and Pope Julius II 'upon account of a slight the artist conceived the

[1] Men in business, who are answerable with their fortunes for the consequences of their opinions, and are therefore accustomed to ascertain pretty accurately the grounds on which they act, before they commit themselves on the event, are often men of remarkably quick and sound judgments. Artists in like manner must know tolerably well what they are about, before they can bring the result of their observations to the test of ocular demonstration.

pontiff had put upon him, Michael Angelo was introduced by
a bishop, who, thinking to serve the artist by it, made it an
argument that the Pope should be reconciled to him, because
men of his profession were commonly ignorant, and of no
consequence otherwise : his holiness, enraged at the bishop,
struck him with his staff, and told him, it was he that was the
blockhead, and affronted the man himself would not offend;
the prelate was driven out of the chamber, and Michael
Angelo had the Pope's benediction accompanied with presents.
This bishop had fallen into the vulgar error, and was rebuked
accordingly.'

Besides the exercise of the mind, painting exercises the
body. It is a mechanical as well as a liberal art. To do
any thing, to dig a hole in the ground, to plant a cabbage,
to hit a mark, to move a shuttle, to work a pattern,—in a
word, to attempt to produce any effect, and to *succeed*, has
something in it that gratifies the love of power, and carries
off the restless activity of the mind of man. Indolence is
a delightful but distressing state : we must be doing something
to be happy. Action is no less necessary than thought to
the instinctive tendencies of the human frame; and painting
combines them both incessantly[1]. The hand furnishes a
practical test of the correctness of the eye; and the eye thus
admonished, imposes fresh tasks of skill and industry upon
the hand. Every stroke tells, as the verifying of a new
truth; and every new observation, the instant it is made,
passes into an act and emanation of the will. Every step is
nearer what we wish, and yet there is always more to do.
In spite of the facility, the fluttering grace, the evanescent
hues, that play round the pencil of Rubens and Vandyke,
however I may admire, I do not envy them this power so
much as I do the slow, patient, laborious execution of
Correggio, Leonardo da Vinci, and Andrea del Sarto, where
every touch appears conscious of its charge, emulous of truth,
and where the painful artist has so distinctly wrought,

That you might almost say his picture thought!

In the one case, the colours seem breathed on the canvas
as by magic, the work and the wonder of a moment : in the

[1] The famous Schiller used to say, that he found the great happiness
of life, after all, to consist in the discharge of some mechanical duty.

other, they seem inlaid in the body of the work, and as if it took the artist years of unremitting labour, and of delightful never-ending progress to perfection[1]. Who would wish ever to come to the close of such works,—not to dwell on them, to return to them, to be wedded to them to the last? Rubens, with his florid, rapid style, complained that when he had just learned his art, he should be forced to die. Leonardo, in the slow advances of his, had lived long enough!

Painting is not, like writing, what is properly understood by a sedentary employment. It requires not indeed a strong, but a continued and steady exertion of muscular power. The precision and delicacy of the manual operation makes up for the want of vehemence,—as to balance himself for any time in the same position the rope-dancer must strain every nerve. Painting for a whole morning gives one as excellent an appetite for one's dinner, as old Abraham Tucker acquired for his by riding over Banstead Downs. It is related of Sir Joshua Reynolds, that 'he took no other exercise than what he used in his painting-room,'—the writer means, in walking backwards and forwards to look at his picture; but the act of painting itself, of laying on the colours in the proper place, and proper quantity, was a much harder exercise than this alternate receding from and returning to the picture. This last would be rather a relaxation and relief than an effort. It is not to be wondered at, that an artist like Sir Joshua, who delighted so much in the sensual and practical part of his art, should have found himself at a considerable loss when the decay of his sight precluded him, for the last year or two of his life, from the following up of his profession,—'the source,' according to his own remark, 'of thirty years uninterrupted enjoyment and prosperity to him.' It is only those who never think at all, or else who have accustomed themselves to brood incessantly on abstract ideas, that never feel *ennui*.

To give one instance more, and then I will have done with this rambling discourse. One of my first attempts was a picture of my father, who was then in a green old age, with strong-marked features, and scarred with the small-pox.

---

[1] The rich *impasting* of Titian and Giorgione combines something of the advantages of both these styles, the felicity of the one with the carefulness of the other, and is perhaps to be preferred to either.

I drew it with a broad light crossing the face, looking down, with
spectacles on, reading.   The book was Shaftesbury's Characteristics, in a fine old binding, with Gribelin's etchings.   My
father would as lieve it had been any other book; but for him
to read was to be content, was 'riches fineless.'   The sketch
promised well; and I set to work to finish it, determined to
spare no time nor pains.   My father was willing to sit as long
as I pleased; for there is a natural desire in the mind of man
to sit for one's picture, to be the object of continued attention,
to have one's likeness multiplied; and besides his satisfaction
in the picture, he had some pride in the artist, though he would
rather I should have written a sermon than painted like
Rembrandt or like Raphael.   Those winter days, with the
gleams of sunshine coming through the chapel-windows, and
cheered by the notes of the robin-redbreast in our garden
(that 'ever in the haunch of winter sings')—as my afternoon's
work drew to a close,—were among the happiest of my life.
When I gave the effect I intended to any part of the picture
for which I had prepared my colours, when I imitated the
roughness of the skin by a lucky stroke of the pencil, when
I hit the clear pearly tone of a vein, when I gave the ruddy
complexion of health, the blood circulating under the broad
shadows of one side of the face, I thought my fortune made;
or rather it was already more than made, in my fancying
that I might one day be able to say with Correggio, '*I also
am a painter!*'   It was an idle thought, a boy's conceit; but
it did not make me less happy at the time.   I used regularly
to set my work in the chair to look at it through the long
evenings; and many a time did I return to take leave of it
before I could go to bed at night.   I remember sending it
with a throbbing heart to the Exhibition, and seeing it hung
up there by the side of one of the Honourable Mr Skeffington
(now Sir George).   There was nothing in common between
them, but that they were the portraits of two very good-
natured men.   I think, but am not sure, that I finished
this portrait (or another afterwards) on the same day that
the news of the battle of Austerlitz came; I walked out in
the afternoon, and, as I returned, saw the evening star set
over a poor man's cottage with other thoughts and feelings
than I shall ever have again.   Oh for the revolution of the

great Platonic year, that those times might come over again!
I could sleep out the three hundred and sixty-five thousand
intervening years very contentedly!—The picture is left:
the table, the chair, the window where I learned to construe
Livy, the chapel where my father preached, remain where
they were; but he himself is gone to rest, full of years, of faith,
of hope, and charity!

ON THE PLEASURE OF PAINTING II

The painter not only takes a delight in nature, he has a new and exquisite source of pleasure opened to him in the study and contemplation of works of art—

> Whate'er Lorraine light touch'd with soft'ning hue,
> Or savage Rosa dash'd, or learned Poussin drew.

He turns aside to view a country-gentleman's seat with eager looks, thinking it may contain some of the rich products of art. There is an air round Lord Radnor's park, for there hang the two Claudes, the Morning and Evening of the Roman Empire—round Wilton-house, for there is Vandyke's picture of the Pembroke family—round Blenheim, for there is his picture of the Duke of Buckingham's children, and the most magnificent collection of Rubenses in the world—at Knowsley, for there is Rembrandt's Hand-writing on the Wall—and at Burleigh, for there are some of Guido's angelic heads. The young artist makes a pilgrimage to each of these places, eyes them wistfully at a distance, 'bosomed high in tufted trees,' and feels an interest in them of which the owner is scarce conscious: he enters the well-swept walks and echoing archways, passes the threshold, is led through wainscoted rooms, is shown the furniture, the rich hangings, the tapestry, the massy services of plate—and, at last, is ushered into the room where his treasure is, the idol of his vows—some speaking face or bright landscape! It is stamped on his brain, and lives there thenceforward, a tally for nature, and a test of art. He furnishes out the chambers of the mind from the spoils of time, picks and chooses which shall have the best places—nearest his heart. He goes away richer than he came, richer than the possessor; and thinks that he may one day return, when he perhaps shall have done something like them, or even from failure shall have learned to admire truth and genius more.

My first initiation in the mysteries of the art was at the
Orleans Gallery: it was there I formed my taste, such as
it is; so that I am irreclaimably of the old school in painting.
I was staggered when I saw the works there collected, and
looked at them with wondering and with longing eyes. A mist
passed away from my sight: the scales fell off. A new sense
came upon me, a new heaven and a new earth stood before
me. I saw the soul speaking in the face—'hands that the
rod of empire had swayed' in mighty ages past—'a forked
mountain or blue promontory,'

——with trees upon't
That nod unto the world, and mock our eyes with air.

Old Time had unlocked his treasures, and Fame stood portress
at the door. We had all heard of the names of Titian, Raphael,
Guido, Domenichino, the Caracci—but to see them face to
face, to be in the same room with their deathless productions,
was like breaking some mighty spell—was almost an effect of
necromancy! From that time I lived in a world of pictures.
Battles, sieges, speeches in parliament seemed mere idle noise
and fury, 'signifying nothing,' compared with those mighty
works and dreaded names that spoke to me in the eternal
silence of thought. This was the more remarkable, as it was
but a short time before that I was not only totally ignorant
of, but insensible to the beauties of art. As an instance,
I remember that one afternoon I was reading the Provoked
Husband with the highest relish, with a green woody landscape
of Ruysdael or Hobbima just before me, at which I looked
off the book now and then, and wondered what there could
be in that sort of work to satisfy or delight the mind—at the
same time asking myself, as a speculative question, whether
I should ever feel an interest in it like what I took in reading
Vanbrugh and Cibber?

I had made some progress in painting when I went to
the Louvre to study, and I never did any thing afterwards.
I never shall forget conning over the Catalogue which a friend
lent me just before I set out. The pictures, the names of the
painters, seemed to relish in the mouth. There was one of
Titian's Mistress at her toilette. Even the colours with which
the painter had adorned her hair were not more golden, more

amiable to sight, than those which played round and tantalised my fancy ere I saw the picture. There were two portraits by the same hand—'A young Nobleman with a glove'—Another, 'a companion to it'—I read the description over and over with fond expectancy, and filled up the imaginary outline with whatever I could conceive of grace, and dignity, and an antique *gusto*—all but equal to the original. There was the Transfiguration too. With what awe I saw it in my mind's eye, and was overshadowed with the spirit of the artist! Not to have been disappointed with these works afterwards, was the highest compliment I can pay to their transcendant merits. Indeed, it was from seeing other works of the same great masters that I had formed a vague, but no disparaging idea of these.—The first day I got there, I was kept for some time in the French Exhibition-room, and thought I should not be able to get a sight of the old masters. I just caught a peep at them through the door (vile hindrance!) like looking out of purgatory into paradise—from Poussin's noble mellow-looking landscapes to where Rubens hung out his gaudy banner, and down the glimmering vista to the rich jewels of Titian and the Italian school. At last, by much importunity, I was admitted, and lost not an instant in making use of my new privilege.—It was *un beau jour* to me. I marched delighted through a quarter of a mile of the proudest efforts of the mind of man, a whole creation of genius, a universe of art! I ran the gauntlet of all the schools from the bottom to the top; and in the end got admitted into the inner room, where they had been repairing some of their greatest works. Here the Transfiguration, the St Peter Martyr, and the St Jerome of Domenichino stood on the floor, as if they had bent their knees, like camels stooping, to unlade their riches to the spectator. On one side, on an easel, stood Hippolito de Medici (a portrait by Titian) with a boar-spear in his hand, looking through those he saw, till you turned away from the keen glance: and thrown together in heaps were landscapes of the same hand, green pastoral hills and vales, and shepherds piping to their mild mistresses underneath the flowering shade. Reader, 'if thou hast not seen the Louvre, thou art damned!'—for thou hast not seen the choicest remains of the works of art; or thou hast not seen all these together, with their mutually reflected glories. I say nothing of the statues; for I know but little of sculpture, and never liked any till I saw the Elgin marbles....Here, for four months together, I strolled and studied, and daily heard the warning sound—'*Quatre heures passées, il faut fermer, Citoyens*,' (ah! why did they ever change their style?) muttered in coarse provincial French; and brought away with me some loose draughts and fragments, which I have been forced to part with, like drops of life-blood, for 'hard money.' How often, thou tenantless mansion of godlike magnificence—how often has my heart since gone a pilgrimage to thee!

It has been made a question, whether the artist, or the mere man of taste and natural sensibility, receives most pleasure from the contemplation of works of art? and I think this question might be answered by another as a sort of *experimentum crucis*, namely, whether any one out of that 'number numberless' of mere gentlemen and amateurs, who visited Paris at the period here spoken of, felt as much interest, as much pride or pleasure in this display of the most striking monuments of art as the humblest student would? The first entrance into the Louvre would be only one of the events of his journey, not an event in his life, remembered ever after with thankfulness and regret. He would explore it with the same unmeaning curiosity and idle wonder as he would the Regalia in the Tower, or the Botanic Garden in the Thuilleries, but not with the fond enthusiasm of an artist. How should he? His is 'casual fruition, joyless, unendeared.' But the painter is wedded to his art, the mistress, queen, and idol of his soul. He has embarked his all in it, fame, time, fortune, peace of mind, his hopes in youth, his consolation in age: and shall he not feel a more intense interest in whatever relates to it than the mere indolent trifler? Natural sensibility alone, without the entire application of the mind to that one object, will not enable the possessor to sympathise with all the degrees of beauty and power in the conception of a Titian or a Correggio; but it is he only who does this, who follows them into all their force and matchless grace, that does or can feel their full value. Knowledge is pleasure as well as power. No one but the artist who has studied nature and contended with the difficulties of art, can be aware of the beauties, or intoxicated with a passion for painting. No one who has not devoted his life and soul to the pursuit of art, can feel the same exultation in its brightest ornaments and loftiest triumphs which an artist does. Where the treasure is, there the heart is also. It is now seventeen years since I was studying in the Louvre (and I have long since given up all thoughts of the art as a profession), but long after I returned, and even still, I sometimes dream of being there again—of asking for the old pictures—and not finding them, or finding them changed or faded from what they were, I cry myself awake! What gentleman-amateur ever does this at such a distance of time,—that is, ever received pleasure or took interest enough in them to produce so lasting an impression?

But it is said that if a person had the same natural taste, and the same acquired knowledge as an artist, without the petty interests and technical notions, he would derive a purer pleasure from seeing a fine portrait, a fine landscape, and so on. This however is not so much begging the question as asking an impossibility: he cannot have the same insight into the end without having studied the means; nor the same love of art without the same habitual and exclusive attachment to it. Painters are, no doubt, often actuated by jealousy, partiality, and a sordid attention to that only which they find useful to themselves in painting. W—— has been seen poring over the texture of a Dutch cabinet-picture, so that he could not see the picture itself. But this is the perversion and pedantry of the profession, not its true or genuine spirit. If W—— had never looked at any thing but megilps and handling, he never would have put the soul of life and manners into his pictures, as he has done. Another objection is, that the instrumental parts of the art, the means, the first rudiments, paints, oils, and brushes, are painful and disgusting; and that the consciousness of the difficulty and anxiety with which perfection has been attained, must take away from the pleasure of the finest performance. This, however, is only an additional proof of the greater pleasure derived by the artist from his profession; for these things which are said to interfere with and destroy the common interest in works of art, do not disturb him; he never once thinks of them, he is absorbed in the pursuit of a higher object; he is intent, not on the means but the end; he is taken up, not with the difficulties, but with the triumph over them. As in the case of the anatomist, who overlooks many things in the eagerness of his search after abstract truth; or the alchemist who, while he is raking into his soot and furnaces, lives in a golden dream; a lesser gives way to a greater object. But it is pretended that the painter may be supposed to submit to the unpleasant part of the process only for the sake of the fame or profit in view. So far is this from being a true state of the case, that I will venture to say, in the instance of a friend of mine who has lately succeeded in an important undertaking in his art, that not all the fame he has acquired, not all the money he has received from thousands of admiring spectators, not all the newspaper puffs,—nor even the praise of the Edinburgh Review,—not all these, put together, ever gave him at any time the same genuine, undoubted satisfaction as any one half-hour employed in the ardent and propitious pursuit of his art—in finishing to his heart's content a foot, a hand, or even a piece of drapery. What is the state of mind of an artist while he is at work? He is then in the act of realising the highest idea he can form of beauty or grandeur: he conceives, he embodies that which he understands and loves best: that is, he is in full and perfect possession of that which is to him the source of the highest happiness and intellectual excitement which he can enjoy.

In short, as a conclusion to this argument, I will mention a circumstance which fell under my knowledge the other day. A friend had bought a print of Titian's Mistress, the same to which I have alluded above. He was anxious to shew it me on this account. I told him it was a spirited engraving, but it had not the look of the original. I believe he thought this fastidious, till I offered to shew him a rough sketch of it, which I had by me. Having seen this, he said he perceived exactly what I meant, and could not bear to look at the print afterwards. He had good sense enough to see the difference in the individual instance; but a person better acquainted with Titian's manner and with art in general, that is, of a more cultivated and refined taste, would know that it was a bad print, without having any immediate model to compare it with. He would perceive with a glance of the eye, with a sort of instinctive feeling, that it was hard, and without that bland, expansive, and nameless expression which always distinguished Titian's most famous works. Any one who is accustomed to a head in a picture can never reconcile himself to a print from it: but to the ignorant they are both the same. To a vulgar eye there is no difference between a Guido and a daub, between a penny-print or the vilest scrawl, and the most finished performance. In other words, all that excellence which lies between these two extremes,—all, at least, that marks the excess above mediocrity,—all that constitutes true beauty, harmony, refinement, grandeur, is lost upon the common observer. But it is from this point that the delight, the glowing raptures of the true adept commence. An uninformed spectator may like an ordinary drawing better than the ablest connoisseur; but for that very reason he cannot like the highest specimens of art so well. The refinements not only of execution but of truth and nature are inaccessible to unpractised eyes. The exquisite gradations in a sky of Claude's are not perceived by such persons, and consequently the harmony cannot be felt. Where there is no conscious apprehension, there can be no conscious pleasure. Wonder at the first sight of works of art may be the effect of ignorance and novelty; but real admiration and permanent delight in them are the growth of taste and knowledge. 'I would not wish to have your eyes,' said a good-natured man to a critic, who was finding fault with a picture, in which the other saw no blemish. Why so? The idea which prevented him from admiring this inferior production was a higher idea of truth and beauty which was ever present with him, and a continual source of pleasing and lofty contemplations. It may be different in a taste for outward luxuries and the privations of mere sense; but the idea of perfection, which acts as an intellectual foil, is always an addition, a support, and a proud consolation!

Richardson, in his Essays, which ought to be better known, has left some striking examples of the felicity and infelicity of artists, both as it relates to their external fortune, and to the practice of their art. In speaking of *the knowledge of hands*, he exclaims—'When one is considering a picture or a drawing, one at the same time thinks this was done by him[1] who had many extraordinary endowments of body and mind, but was withal very capricious; who was honoured in life and death, expiring in the arms of one of the greatest princes of that age, Francis I King of France, who loved him as a friend. Another is of him[2] who lived a long and happy life, beloved of Charles V emperour; and many others of the first princes of Europe. When one has another in hand, we think this was done by one[3] who so excelled in three arts, as that any of them in that degree had rendered him worthy of immortality; and one moreover that durst contend with his sovereign (one of the haughtiest popes that ever was) upon a slight offered to him, and extricated himself with honour. Another is the work of him[4] who, without any one exterior advantage but mere strength of genius, had the most sublime imaginations, and executed them accordingly, yet lived and died obscurely. Another we shall consider as the work of him[5] who restored Painting when it had almost sunk; of him whom art made honourable, but who, neglecting and despising greatness with a sort of cynical pride, was treated suitably to the figure he gave himself, not his intrinsic worth; which, not having philosophy enough to bear it, broke his heart. Another is done by one[6] who (on the contrary) was a fine gentleman, and lived in great magnificence, and was much honoured by his own and foreign princes; who was a courtier, a statesman, and a painter; and so much all these, that when he acted in either character, *that* seemed to be his business, and the others his diversion. I say when one thus reflects, besides the pleasure arising from the beauties and excellences of the work, the fine ideas it gives us of natural things, the noble way of thinking it may suggest to us, an additional pleasure results from the above considerations. But, oh! the pleasure, when a connoisseur and lover of art has before him a picture or drawing, of which he can say this is the hand, these are the thoughts of him[7] who was one of the politest, best-natured gentlemen that ever was; and beloved and assisted by the

---

[1] Leonardo da Vinci.   [2] Titian.
[3] Michael Angelo.   [4] Correggio.
[5] Annibal Caracci.   [6] Rubens.
[7] Rafaelle.

greatest wits and the greatest men then in Rome: of him who lived in great fame, honour, and magnificence, and died extremely lamented; and missed a Cardinal's hat only by dying a few months too soon; but was particularly esteemed and favoured by two Popes, the only ones who filled the chair of St Peter in his time, and as great men as ever sat there since that apostle, if at least he ever did: one, in short, who could have been a Leonardo, a Michael Angelo, a Titian, a Correggio, a Parmegiano, an Annibal, a Rubens, or any other whom he pleased, but none of them could ever have been a Rafaelle.'   Page 251.

The same writer speaks feelingly of the change in the style of different artists from their change of fortune, and as the circumstances are little known, I will quote the passage relating to two of them.

'Guido Reni from a prince-like affluence of fortune (the just reward of his angelic works) fell to a condition like that of a hired servant to one who supplied him with money for what he did at a fixed rate; and that by his being bewitched with a passion for gaming, whereby he lost vast sums of money; and even what he got in this his state of servitude by day, he commonly lost at night: nor could he ever be cured of this cursed madness. Those of his works, therefore, which he did in this unhappy part of his life, may easily be conceived to be in a different style to what he did before, which in some things, that is, in the airs of his heads (in the gracious kind), had a delicacy in them peculiar to himself, and almost more than human. But I must not multiply instances. Parmegiano is one that alone takes in all the several kinds of variation, and all the degrees of goodness, from the lowest of the indifferent up to the sublime. I can produce evident proofs of this in so easy a gradation, that one cannot deny but that he that did this, might do that, and very probably did so; and thus one may ascend and descend, like the angels on Jacob's ladder, whose foot was upon the earth, but its top reached to Heaven.

'And this great man had his unlucky circumstance: he became mad after the philosopher's stone, and did but very little in painting or drawing afterwards. Judge what that was, and whether there was not an alteration of style from what he had done, before this devil possessed him. His creditors

endeavoured to exorcise him, and did him some good, for he
set himself to work again in his own way: but if a drawing
I have of a Lucretia be that he made for his last picture, as
it probably is (Vasari says that was the subject of it), it is
an evident proof of his decay: it is good indeed, but it wants
much of the delicacy which is commonly seen in his works;
and so I always thought before I knew or imagined it to be
done in this his ebb of genius.' Page 153.

We have had two artists of our own country, whose fate
has been as singular as it was hard. Gandy was a portrait-
painter in the beginning of the last century, whose heads were
said to have come near to Rembrandt's, and he was the undoubted prototype of Sir Joshua Reynolds's style. Yet his
name has scarcely been heard of; and his reputation, like his
works, never extended beyond his own county. What did
he think of himself and of a fame so bounded! Did he ever
dream he was indeed an artist? Or how did this feeling in
him differ from the vulgar conceit of the lowest pretender?
The best known of his works is a portrait of an alderman of
Exeter, in some public building in that city.

Poor Dan. Stringer! Forty years ago he had the finest
hand and the clearest eye of any artist of his time, and produced
heads and drawings that would not have disgraced a brighter
period in the art. But he fell a martyr (like Burns) to the
society of country-gentlemen, and then of those whom they
would consider as more his equals. I saw him many years
ago, when he treated the masterly sketches he had by him
(one in particular of the group of citizens in Shakespear
'swallowing the tailor's news') as 'bastards of his genius,
not his children'; and seemed to have given up all thoughts
of his art. Whether he is since dead, I cannot say: the world
do not so much as know that he ever lived!

THE FIGHT

——The *fight*, the *fight*'s the thing,
Wherein I'll catch the conscience of the king.

Where there's a will, there's a way.—I said so to myself,
as I walked down Chancery-lane, about half-past six o'clock
on Monday the 10th of December, to inquire at Jack Randall's
where the fight the next day was to be; I found 'the proverb'
nothing 'musty' in the present instance. I was determined
to see this fight, come what would, and see it I did, in great
style. It was my *first fight*, yet it more than answered my
expectations. Ladies! it is to you I dedicate this description;
nor let it seem out of character for the fair to notice the exploits
of the brave. Courage and modesty are the old English virtues;
and may they never look cold and askance on one another!
Think, ye fairest of the fair, loveliest of the lovely kind, ye
practisers of soft enchantment, how many more ye kill with
poisoned baits than ever fell in the ring; and listen with
subdued air and without shuddering, to a tale tragic only in
appearance, and sacred to the FANCY!

I was going down Chancery-lane, thinking to ask at Jack
Randall's where the fight was to be, when looking through the
glass-door of the *Hole in the Wall*, I heard a gentleman asking
the same question *at* Mrs Randall, as the author of Waverley
would express it. Now Mrs Randall stood answering the
gentleman's question, with the authenticity of the lady of
the Champion of the Light Weights. Thinks I, I'll wait till
this person comes out, and learn from him how it is. For to
say a truth, I was not fond of going into this house of call for
heroes and philosophers, ever since the owner of it (for Jack
is no gentleman) threatened once upon a time to kick me out
of doors for wanting a mutton-chop at his hospitable board,
when the conqueror in thirteen battles was more full of *blue
ruin* than of good manners. I was the more mortified at this

repulse, inasmuch as I had heard Mr James Simpkins, hosier in the Strand, one day when the character of the *Hole in the Wall* was brought in question, observe—'The house is a very good house, and the company quite genteel: I have been there myself!' Remembering this unkind treatment of mine host, to which mine hostess was also a party, and not wishing to put her in unquiet thoughts at a time jubilant like the present, I waited at the door, when, who should issue forth but my friend Jo. Toms, and turning suddenly up Chancery-lane with that quick jerk and impatient stride which distinguishes a lover of the FANCY, I said, 'I'll be hanged if that fellow is not going to the fight, and is on his way to get me to go with him.' So it proved in effect, and we agreed to adjourn to my lodgings to discuss measures with that cordiality which makes old friends like new, and new friends like old, on great occasions. We are cold to others only when we are dull in ourselves, and have neither thoughts nor feelings to impart to them. Give a man a topic in his head, a throb of pleasure in his heart, and he will be glad to share it with the first person he meets. Toms and I, though we seldom meet, were an *alter idem* on this memorable occasion, and had not an idea that we did not candidly impart; and 'so carelessly did we fleet the time,' that I wish no better, when there is another fight, than to have him for a companion on my journey down, and to return with my friend Jack Pigott, talking of what was to happen or of what did happen, with a noble subject always at hand, and liberty to digress to others whenever they offered. Indeed, on my repeating the lines from Spenser in an involuntary fit of enthusiasm,

> What more felicity can fall to creature,
> Than to enjoy delight with liberty?

my last-named ingenious friend stopped me by saying that this, translated into the vulgate, meant '*Going to see a fight.*'

Jo. Toms and I could not settle about the method of going down. He said there was a caravan, he understood, to start from Tom Belcher's at two, which would go there *right out* and back again the next day. Now I never travel all night, and said I should get a cast to Newbury by one of the mails. Jo. swore the thing was impossible, and I could only answer that I had made up my mind to it. In short, he seemed to me to waver, said he only came to see if I was going, had letters to write, a cause coming on the day after, and faintly said at parting (for I was bent on setting out that moment)—'Well, we meet at Philippi!' I made the best of my way to Piccadilly. The mail coach stand was bare. 'They are all gone,' said I—'this is always the way with me—in the instant I lose the future—if I had not stayed to pour out that last cup of tea, I should have been just in time'—and cursing my folly and ill-luck together, without inquiring at the coach-office whether the mails were gone or not, I walked on in despite, and to punish my own dilatoriness and want of determination. At any rate, I would not turn back: I might get to Hounslow, or perhaps farther, to be on my road the next morning. I passed Hyde Park Corner (my Rubicon), and trusted to fortune. Suddenly I heard the clattering of a Brentford stage, and the fight rushed full upon my fancy. I argued (not unwisely) that even a Brentford coachman was better company than my own thoughts (such as they were just then), and at his invitation mounted the box with him. I immediately stated my case to him—namely, my quarrel with myself for missing the Bath or Bristol mail, and my determination to get on in consequence as well as I could, without any disparagement or insulting comparison between longer or shorter stages. It is a maxim with me that stage-coaches, and consequently stage-coachmen, are respectable in proportion to the distance they have to travel: so I said nothing on that subject to my Brentford friend. Any incipient tendency to an abstract proposition, or (as he might have construed it) to a personal reflection of this kind, was however nipped in the bud; for I had no sooner declared indignantly that I had missed the mails, than he flatly denied that they were gone along, and lo! at the instant three of them drove by in rapid, provoking, orderly succession, as if they would devour the ground before them. Here again I seemed in the contradictory situation of the man in Dryden who exclaims,

I follow Fate, which does too hard pursue!

If I had stopped to inquire at the White Horse Cellar, which would not have taken me a minute, I should now have been driving down the road in all the dignified unconcern and *ideal* perfection of mechanical conveyance. The Bath mail I had set my mind upon, and I had missed it, as I missed every thing else, by my own absurdity, in putting the will for the deed, and aiming at ends without employing means. 'Sir,' said he of the Brentford, 'the Bath mail will be up presently, my brother-in-law drives it, and I will engage to stop him if there is a place empty.' I almost doubted my good genius; but, sure enough, up it drove like lightning, and stopped directly at the call of the Brentford Jehu. I would not have believed this possible, but the brother-in-law of a mail-coach driver is himself no mean man. I was transferred without loss of time from the top of one coach to that of the other, desired the guard to pay my fare to the Brentford coachman for me as I had no change, was accommodated with a great coat, put up my umbrella to keep off a drizzling mist, and we began to cut through the air like an arrow. The mile-stones disappeared one after another, the rain kept off; Tom Turtle, the trainer, sat before me on the coach-box, with whom I exchanged civilities as a gentleman going to the fight; the passion that had transported me an hour before was subdued to pensive regret and conjectural musing on the next day's battle; I was promised a place inside at Reading, and upon the whole, I thought myself a lucky fellow. Such is the force of imagination! On the outside of any other coach on the 10th of December, with a Scotch mist drizzling through the cloudy moonlight air, I should have been cold, comfortless, impatient, and, no doubt, wet through; but seated on the Royal mail, I felt warm and comfortable, the air did me good, the ride did me good, I was pleased with the progress we had made, and confident that all would go well through the journey. When I got inside at Reading, I found Turtle and a stout valetudinarian, whose costume bespoke him one of the FANCY, and who had risen from a three months' sick bed to get into the mail to see the fight. They were intimate, and we fell into a lively discourse. My friend the trainer was confined in his topics to fighting dogs and men, to bears and badgers; beyond this he was 'quite chap-fallen,' had not a word to throw at a dog, or indeed very wisely fell asleep, when any other game was started. The whole art of training (I, however, learnt from him,) consists in two things, exercise and abstinence, abstinence and exercise, repeated alternately and without end. A yolk of an egg with a spoonful of rum in it is the first thing in a morning, and then a walk of six miles till breakfast. This meal consists of a plentiful supply of tea and toast and beef-steaks. Then another six or seven miles till dinner-time, and another supply of solid beef or mutton with a pint of porter, and perhaps, at the utmost, a couple of glasses of sherry. Martin trains on water, but this increases his infirmity on another very dangerous side. The Gas-man takes now and then a chirping glass (under the rose) to console him, during a six weeks' probation, for the absence of Mrs Hickman —an agreeable woman, with (I understand) a pretty fortune of two hundred pounds. How matter presses on me! What stubborn things are facts! How inexhaustible is nature and art! 'It is well,' as I once heard Mr Richmond observe, 'to see a variety.' He was speaking of cock-fighting as an edifying spectacle. I cannot deny but that one learns more of what *is* (I do not say of what *ought to be*) in this desultory mode of practical study, than from reading the same book twice over, even though it should be a moral treatise. Where was I? I was sitting at dinner with the candidate for the honours of the ring, 'where good digestion waits on appetite, and health on both.' Then follows an hour of social chat and native glee; and afterwards, to another breathing over heathy hill or dale. Back to supper, and then to bed, and up by six again—-Our hero

> Follows so the ever-running sun
> With profitable *ardour*—

to the day that brings him victory or defeat in the green fairy circle. Is not this life more sweet than mine? I was going to say; but I will not libel any life by comparing it to mine, which is (at the date of these presents) bitter as colo-quintida and the dregs of aconitum!

The invalid in the Bath mail soared a pitch above the trainer, and did not sleep so sound, because he had 'more figures and more fantasies.' We talked the hours away merrily. He had faith in surgery, for he had had three ribs set right, that had been broken in a *turn-up* at Belcher's, but thought physicians old women, for they had no antidote in their catalogue for brandy.   An indigestion is an excellent common-place for two people that never met before.   By way of ingratiating myself, I told him the story of my doctor, who, on my earnestly representing to him that I thought his regimen had done me harm, assured me that the whole pharmacopeia contained nothing comparable to the prescription he had given me; and, as a proof of its undoubted efficacy, said, that, 'he had had one gentleman with my complaint under his hands for the last fifteen years.'   This anecdote made my companion shake the rough sides of his three great coats with boisterous laughter; and Turtle, starting out of his sleep, swore he knew how the fight would go, for he had had a dream about it.   Sure enough the rascal told us how the three first rounds went off, but 'his dream,' like others, 'denoted a foregone conclusion.'   He knew his men.   The moon now rose in silver state, and I ventured, with some hesitation, to point out this object of placid beauty, with the blue serene beyond, to the man of science, to which his ear he 'seriously inclined,' the more as it gave promise *d'un beau jour* for the morrow, and showed the ring undrenched by envious showers, arrayed in sunny smiles.   Just then, all going on well, I thought on my friend Toms, whom I had left behind, and said innocently, 'There was a blockhead of a fellow I left in town, who said there was no possibility of getting down by the mail, and talked of going by a caravan from Belcher's at two in the morning, after he had written some letters.'   'Why,' said he of the lapells, 'I should not wonder if that was the very person we saw running about like mad from one coach-door to another, and asking if any one had seen a friend of his, a gentleman going to the fight, whom he had missed stupidly enough by staying to write a note.'   'Pray, Sir,' said my fellow-traveller, 'had he a plaid-cloak on?'—'Why, no,' said I, 'not at the time I left him, but he very well might afterwards, for he offered to lend me one.'   The plaid-cloak and the letter decided the thing.   Joe, sure enough, was in the Bristol mail, which preceded us by about fifty yards. This was droll enough.   We had now but a few miles to our place of destination, and the first thing I did on alighting at Newbury, both coaches stopping at the same time, was to call out, 'Pray, is there a gentleman in that mail of the name of Toms?' 'No,' said Joe, borrowing something of the vein of Gilpin, 'for I have just got out.' 'Well!' says he, 'this is lucky; but you don't know how vexed I was to miss you; for,' added he, lowering his voice, 'do you know when I left you I went to Belcher's to ask about the caravan, and Mrs Belcher said very obligingly, she couldn't tell about that, but there were two gentlemen who had taken places by the mail and were gone on in a landau, and she could frank us. It's a pity I didn't meet with you; we could then have got down for nothing. But *mum's the word*.' It's the devil for any one to tell me a secret, for it's sure to come out in print. I do not care so much to gratify a friend, but the public ear is too great a temptation to me.

Our present business was to get beds and a supper at an inn; but this was no easy task. The public-houses were full, and where you saw a light at a private house, and people poking their heads out of the casement to see what was going on, they instantly put them in and shut the window, the moment you seemed advancing with a suspicious overture for accommodation. Our guard and coachman thundered away at the outer gate of the Crown for some time without effect—such was the greater noise within;—and when the doors were unbarred, and we got admittance, we found a party assembled in the kitchen round a good hospitable fire, some sleeping, others drinking, others talking on politics and on the fight. A tall English yeoman (something like Matthews in the face, and quite as great a wag)—

A lusty man to ben an abbot able,—

was making such a prodigious noise about rent and taxes, and the price of corn now and formerly, that he had prevented us from being heard at the gate. The first thing I heard him say was to a shuffling fellow who wanted to be off a bet for a shilling glass of brandy and water—'Confound it, man, don't be *insipid*!' Thinks I, that is a good phrase. It was a good omen. He kept it up so all night, nor flinched with the approach of morning. He was a fine fellow, with sense, wit, and spirit, a hearty body and a joyous mind, free-spoken, frank, convivial—one of that true English breed that went with Harry the Fifth to the siege of Harfleur—'standing like greyhounds in the slips,' &c. We ordered tea and eggs (beds were soon found to be out of the question) and this fellow's conversation was *sauce piquante*. It did one's heart good to see him brandish his oaken towel and to hear him talk. He made mince-meat of a drunken, stupid, red-faced, quarrelsome, *frowsy* farmer, whose nose 'he moralized into a thousand similes', making it out a firebrand like Bardolph's. 'I'll tell you what my friend,' says he, 'the landlady has only to keep you here to save fire and candle. If one was to touch your nose, it would go off like a piece of charcoal.' At this the other only grinned like an idiot, the sole variety in his purple face being his little peering grey eyes and yellow teeth; called for another glass, swore he would not stand it; and after many attempts to provoke his humourous antagonist to single combat, which the other turned off (after working him up to a ludicrous pitch of choler) with great adroitness, he fell quietly asleep with a glass of liquor in his hand, which he could not lift to his head. His laughing persecutor made a speech over him, and turning to the opposite side of the room, where they were all sleeping in the midst of this 'loud and furious fun,' said, 'There's a scene, by G—d, for Hogarth to paint. I think he and Shakspeare were our two best men at copying life.' This confirmed me in my good opinion of him. Hogarth, Shakspeare, and Nature, were just enough for him (indeed for any man) to know. I said, 'You read Cobbett, don't you? At least,' says I, 'you talk just as well as he writes.' He seemed to doubt this. But I said, 'We have an hour to spare: if you'll get pen, ink, and paper, and keep on talking, I'll write down what you say; and if it doesn't make a capital 'Political Register,' I'll forfeit my head. You have kept me alive to-night, however. I don't know what I should have done without you.' He did not dislike this view of the thing, nor my asking if he was not about the size of Jem Belcher; and told me soon afterwards, in the confidence of friendship, that 'the circumstance which had given him nearly the greatest concern in his life, was Cribb's beating Jem after he had lost his eye by racket-playing.'—The morning dawns; that dim but yet clear light appears, which weighs like solid bars of metal on the sleepless eyelids; the guests drop down from their chambers one by one—but it was too late to think of going to bed now (the clock was on the stroke of seven), we had nothing for it but to find a barber's (the pole that glittered in the morning sun lighted us to his shop), and then a nine miles' march to Hungerford. The day was fine, the sky was blue, the mists were retiring from the marshy ground, the path was tolerably dry, the sitting-up all night had not done us much harm—at least the cause was good; we talked of this and that with amicable difference, roving and sipping of many subjects, but still invariably we returned to the fight. At length, a mile to the left of Hungerford, on a gentle eminence, we saw the ring surrounded by covered carts, gigs, and carriages, of which hundreds had passed us on the road; Toms gave a youthful shout, and we hastened down a narrow lane to the scene of action.

Reader, have you ever seen a fight? If not, you have a pleasure to come, at least if it is a fight like that between the Gas-man and Bill Neate. The crowd was very great when we arrived on the spot; open carriages were coming up, with streamers flying and music playing, and the country-people were pouring in over hedge and ditch in all directions, to see their hero beat or be beaten. The odds were still on Gas, but only about five to four. Gully had been down to try Neate, and had backed him considerably, which was a damper to the sanguine confidence of the adverse party. About two hundred thousand pounds were pending. The Gas says, he has lost 3000*l.* which were promised him by different gentlemen if he had won. He had presumed too much on himself, which had made others presume on him. This spirited and formidable young fellow seems to have taken for his motto the old maxim, that 'there are three things necessary to success in life—*Impudence! Impudence! Impudence!*' It is so in matters of opinion, but not in the *Fancy*, which is the most practical of all things, though even here confidence is half the battle, but only half. Our friend had vapoured and swaggered too much, as if he wanted to grin and bully his adversary out of the fight. 'Alas! the Bristol man was not so tamed!'—'This is *the grave-digger*' (would Tom Hickman exclaim in the moments of intoxication from gin and success, shewing his tremendous right hand), 'this will send many of them to their long homes; I haven't done with them yet!' Why should he—though he had licked four of the best men within the hour, yet why should he threaten to inflict dishonourable chastisement on my old master Richmond, a veteran going off the stage, and who has borne his sable honours meekly? Magnanimity, my dear Tom, and bravery, should be inseparable. Or why should he go up to his antagonist, the first time he ever saw him at the Fives Court, and measuring him from head to foot with a glance of contempt, as Achilles surveyed Hector, say to him, 'What, are you Bill Neate? I'll knock more blood out of that great carcase of thine, this day fortnight, than you ever knock'd out of a bullock's!' It was not manly, 'twas not fighter-like. If he was sure of the victory (as he was not), the less said about it the better. Modesty should accompany the *Fancy* as its shadow. The best men were always the best behaved. Jem Belcher, the Game Chicken (before whom the Gas-man could not have lived), were civil, silent men. So is Cribb, so is Tom Belcher, the most elegant of sparrers, and not a man for every one to take by the nose. I enlarged on this topic in the mail (while Turtle was asleep), and said very wisely (as I thought) that impertinence was a part of no profession. A boxer was bound to beat his man, but not to thrust his fist, either actually or by implication, in every one's face. Even a highwayman, in the way of trade, may blow out your brains, but if he uses foul language at the same time, I should say he was no gentleman. A boxer, I would infer, need not be a blackguard or a coxcomb, more than another. Perhaps I press this point too much on a fallen man—Mr Thomas Hickman has by this time learnt that first of all lessons, 'That man was made to mourn.' He has lost nothing by the late fight but his presumption; and that every man may do as well without! By an over-display of this quality, however, the public had been prejudiced against him, and the *knowing-ones* were taken in. Few but those who had bet on him wished Gas to win. With my own prepossessions on the subject, the result of the 11th of December appeared to me as fine a piece of poetical justice as I had ever witnessed. The difference of weight between the two combatants (14 stone to 12) was nothing to the sporting men. Great, heavy, clumsy, long-armed Bill

Neate kicked the beam in the scale of the Gas-man's vanity.
The amateurs were frightened at his big words, and thought
that they would make up for the difference of six feet and
five feet nine. Truly, the FANCY are not men of imagination.
They judge of what has been, and cannot conceive of any thing
that is to be. The Gas-man had won hitherto; therefore he
must beat a man half as big again as himself—and that to
a certainty. Besides, there are as many feuds, factions,
prejudices, pedantic notions in the FANCY as in the state or
in the schools. Mr Gully is almost the only cool, sensible
man among them, who exercises an unbiassed discretion, and
is not a slave to his passions in these matters. But enough
of reflections, and to our tale. The day, as I have said, was
fine for a December morning. The grass was wet, and the
ground miry, and ploughed up with multitudinous feet, except
that, within the ring itself, there was a spot of virgin-green
closed in and unprofaned by vulgar tread, that shone with
dazzling brightness in the mid-day sun. For it was now
noon, and we had an hour to wait. This is the trying time.
It is then the heart sickens, as you think what the two champions
are about, and how short a time will determine their fate.
After the first blow is struck, there is no opportunity for
nervous apprehensions; you are swallowed up in the immediate
interest of the scene—but

> Between the acting of a dreadful thing
> And the first motion, all the interim is
> Like a phantasma, or a hideous dream.

I found it so as I felt the sun's rays clinging to my back, and
saw the white wintry clouds sink below the verge of the
horizon. 'So, I thought, my fairest hopes have faded from
my sight!—so will the Gas-man's glory, or that of his adversary,
vanish in an hour.' The *swells* were parading in their white
box-coats, the outer ring was cleared with some bruises on
the heads and shins of the rustic assembly (for the *cockneys*
had been distanced by the sixty-six miles); the time drew
near, I had got a good stand; a bustle, a buzz, ran through
the crowd, and from the opposite side entered Neate, between
his second and bottle-holder. He rolled along, swathed in
his loose great coat, his knock-knees bending under his huge
bulk; and, with a modest cheerful air, threw his hat into the

ring.   He then just looked round, and began quietly to undress; when from the other side there was a similar rush and an opening made, and the Gas-man came forward with a conscious air of anticipated triumph, too much like the cock-of-the walk. He strutted about more than became a hero, sucked oranges with a supercilious air, and threw away the skin with a toss of his head, and went up and looked at Neate, which was an act of supererogation.   The only sensible thing he did was, as he strode away from the modern Ajax, to fling out his arms, as if he wanted to try whether they would do their work that day.   By this time they had stripped, and presented a strong contrast in appearance.   If Neate was like Ajax, 'with Atlantean shoulders, fit to bear' the pugilistic reputation of all Bristol, Hickman might be compared to Diomed, light, vigorous, elastic, and his back glistened in the sun, as he moved about, like a panther's hide.   There was now a dead pause— attention was awe-struck.   Who at that moment, big with a great event, did not draw his breath short—did not feel his heart throb?   All was ready.   They tossed up for the sun, and the Gas-man won.   They were led up to the *scratch*— shook hands, and went at it.

In the first round every one thought it was all over.   After making play a short time, the Gas-man flew at his adversary like a tiger, struck five blows in as many seconds, three first, and then following him as he staggered back, two more, right and left, and down he fell, a mighty ruin.   There was a shout, and I said, 'There is no standing this.'   Neate seemed like a lifeless lump of flesh and bone, round which the Gas-man's blows played with the rapidity of electricity or lightning, and you imagined he would only be lifted up to be knocked down again.   It was as if Hickman held a sword or a fire in that right hand of his, and directed it against an unarmed body. They met again, and Neate seemed, not cowed, but particularly cautious.   I saw his teeth clenched together and his brows knit close against the sun.   He held out both his arms at full length straight before him, like two sledge-hammers, and raised his left an inch or two higher.   The Gas-man could not get over this guard—they struck mutually and fell, but without advantage on either side.   It was the same in the next round; but the balance of power was thus restored—the fate of the battle was suspended. No one could tell how it would end. This was the only moment in which opinion was divided; for, in the next, the Gas-man aiming a mortal blow at his adversary's neck, with his right hand, and failing from the length he had to reach, the other returned it with his left at full swing, planted a tremendous blow on his cheek-bone and eyebrow, and made a red ruin of that side of his face. The Gas-man went down, and there was another shout—a roar of triumph as the waves of fortune rolled tumultuously from side to side. This was a settler. Hickman got up, and 'grinned horrible a ghastly smile,' yet he was evidently dashed in his opinion of himself; it was the first time he had ever been so punished; all one side of his face was perfect scarlet, and his right eye was closed in dingy blackness, as he advanced to the fight, less confident, but still determined. After one or two rounds, not receiving another such remembrancer, he rallied and went at it with his former impetuosity. But in vain. His strength had been weakened,—his blows could not tell at such a distance,—he was obliged to fling himself at his adversary, and could not strike from his feet; and almost as regularly as he flew at him with his right hand, Neate warded the blow, or drew back out of its reach, and felled him with the return of his left. There was little cautious sparring—no half-hits—no tapping and trifling, none of the *petit-maitreship* of the art—they were almost all knock-down blows:—the fight was a good stand-up fight. The wonder was the half-minute time. If there had been a minute or more allowed between each round, it would have been intelligible how they should by degrees recover strength and resolution; but to see two men smashed to the ground, smeared with gore, stunned, senseless, the breath beaten out of their bodies; and then, before you recover from the shock, to see them rise up with new strength and courage, stand steady to inflict or receive mortal offence, and rush upon each other 'like two clouds over the Caspian'—this is the most astonishing thing of all:—this is the high and heroic state of man! From this time forward the event became more certain every round; and about the twelfth it seemed as if it must have been over. Hickman generally stood with his back to me; but in the scuffle, he had changed positions, and

Neate just then made a tremendous lunge at him, and hit him full in the face. It was doubtful whether he would fall backwards or forwards; he hung suspended for a second or two, and then fell back, throwing his hands in the air, and with his face lifted up to the sky. I never saw any thing more terrific than his aspect just before he fell. All traces of life, of natural expression, were gone from him. His face was like a human skull, a death's head, spouting blood. The eyes were filled with blood, the nose streamed with blood, the mouth gaped blood. He was not like an actual man, but like a preternatural, spectral appearance, or like one of the figures in Dante's *Inferno*. Yet he fought on after this for several rounds, still striking the first desperate blow, and Neate standing on the defensive, and using the same cautious guard to the last, as if he had still all his work to do; and it was not till the Gas-man was so stunned in the seventeenth or eighteenth round, that his senses forsook him, and he could not come to time, that the battle was declared over[1]. Ye who despise the Fancy, do something to shew as much *pluck*, or as much self-possession as this, before you assume a superiority which you have never given a single proof of by any one action in the whole course of your lives!—When the Gas-man came to himself, the first words he uttered were, 'Where am I? What is the matter?' 'Nothing is the matter, Tom,—you have lost the battle, but you are the bravest man alive.' And Jackson whispered to him, 'I am collecting a purse for you, Tom.'—Vain sounds, and unheard at that moment! Neate instantly went up and shook him cordially by the hand, and seeing some old acquaintance, began to flourish with his fists, calling out, 'Ah you always said I couldn't fight—What do you think now?' But all in good humour, and without any appearance of arrogance; only it was evident Bill Neate was pleased that he had won the fight. When it was over, I asked Cribb if he did not think it was a good one? He said,

---

[1] Scroggins said of the Gas-man, that he thought he was a man of that courage, that if his hands were cut off, he would still fight on with the stumps—like that of Widrington,—

> ——In doleful dumps,
> Who, when his legs were smitten off,
> Still fought upon his stumps.

'*Pretty well!*' The carrier-pigeons now mounted into the air, and one of them flew with the news of her husband's victory to the bosom of Mrs Neate. Alas, for Mrs Hickman!

Mais au revoir, as Sir Fopling Flutter says. I went down with Toms; I returned with Jack Pigott, whom I met on the ground. Toms is a rattle brain; Pigott is a sentimentalist. Now, under favour, I am a sentimentalist too—therefore I say nothing, but that the interest of the excursion did not flag as I came back. Pigott and I marched along the causeway leading from Hungerford to Newbury, now observing the effect of a brilliant sun on the tawny meads or moss-coloured cottages, now exulting in the fight, now digressing to some topic of general and elegant literature. My friend was dressed in character for the occasion, or like one of the FANCY; that is, with a double portion of great coats, clogs, and overhauls: and just as we had agreed with a couple of country-lads to carry his superfluous wearing-apparel to the next town, we were overtaken by a return post-chaise, into which I got, Pigott preferring a seat on the bar. There were two strangers already in the chaise, and on their observing they supposed I had been to the fight, I said I had, and concluded they had done the same. They appeared, however, a little shy and sore on the subject; and it was not till after several hints dropped, and questions put, that it turned out that they had missed it. One of these friends had undertaken to drive the other there in his gig: they had set out, to make sure work, the day before at three in the afternoon. The owner of the one-horse vehicle scorned to ask his way, and drove right on to Bagshot, instead of turning off at Hounslow: there they stopped all night, and set off the next day across the country to Reading, from whence they took coach, and got down within a mile or two of Hungerford, just half an hour after the fight was over. This might be safely set down as one of the miseries of human life. We parted with these two gentlemen who had been to see the fight, but had returned as they went, at Wolhampton, where we were promised beds (an irresistible temptation, for Pigott had passed the preceding night at Hungerford as we had done at Newbury), and we turned into an old bow-windowed parlour with a carpet and a snug fire; and after devouring a quantity of tea, toast, and eggs, sat down to consider, during an hour of philosophic leisure, what we should have for supper. In the midst of an Epicurean deliberation between a roasted fowl and mutton chops with mashed potatoes, we were interrupted by an inroad of Goths and Vandals—*O procul este profani*—not real flash-men, but interlopers, noisy pretenders, butchers from Tothill-fields, brokers from Whitechapel, who called immediately for pipes and tobacco, hoping it would not be disagreeable to the gentlemen, and began to insist that it was *a cross*. Pigott withdrew from the smoke and noise into another room, and left me to dispute the point with them for a couple of hours *sans intermission* by the dial. The next morning we rose refreshed; and on observing that Jack had a pocket volume in his hand, in which he read in the intervals of our discourse, I inquired what it was, and learned to my particular satisfaction that it was a volume of the New Eloise. Ladies, after this, will you contend that a love for the FANCY is incompatible with the cultivation of sentiment?—We jogged on as before, my friend setting me up in a genteel drab great coat and green silk handkerchief (which I must say became me exceedingly), and after stretching our legs for a few miles, and seeing Jack Randall, Ned Turner, and Scroggins, pass on the top of one of the Bath coaches, we engaged with the driver of the second to take us to London for the usual fee. I got inside, and found three other passengers. One of them was an old gentleman with an aquiline nose, powdered hair, and a pigtail, and who looked as if he had played many a rubber at the Bath rooms. I said to myself, he is very like Mr Windham; I wish he would enter into conversation, that I might hear what fine observations would come from those finely-turned features. However, nothing passed, till, stopping to dine at Reading, some inquiry was made by the company about the fight, and I gave (as the reader may believe) an eloquent and animated description of it. When we got into the coach again, the old gentleman, after a graceful exordium, said, he had, when a boy, been to a fight between the famous Broughton and George Stevenson, who was called the *Fighting Coachman*, in the year 1770, with the late Mr Windham. This beginning flattered the spirit of prophecy within me and rivetted my attention. He went on—'George Stevenson was coachman to a friend of my father's. He was an old man when I saw him some years afterwards. He took hold of his own arm and said, "there was muscle here once, but now it is no more than this young gentleman's." He added, "well, no matter; I have been here long, I am willing to go hence, and I hope I have done no more harm than another man." Once,' said my unknown companion, 'I asked him if he had ever beat Broughton? He said Yes; that he had fought with him three times, and the last time he fairly beat him, though the world did not allow it. "I'll tell you how it was, master. When the seconds lifted us up in the last round, we were so exhausted that neither of us could stand, and we fell upon one another, and as Master Broughton fell uppermost, the mob gave it in his favour, and he was said to have won the battle. But," says he, "the fact was, that as his second (John Cuthbert) lifted him up, he said to him, 'I'll fight no more, I've had enough'; "which," says Stevenson, "you know gave me the victory. And to prove to you that this was the case, when John Cuthbert was on his death-bed, and they asked him if there was any thing on his mind which he wished to confess, he answered, 'Yes, that there was one thing he wished to set right, for that certainly Master Stevenson won that last fight with Master Broughton; for he whispered him as he lifted him up in the last round of all, that he had had enough.'"' 'This,' said the Bath gentleman, 'was a bit of human nature'; and I have written this account of the fight on purpose that it might not be lost to the world. He also stated as a proof of the candour of mind in this class of men, that Stevenson acknowledged that Broughton could have beat him in his best day; but that he (Broughton) was getting old in their last rencounter. When we stopped in Piccadilly, I wanted to ask the gentleman some questions about the late Mr Windham, but had not courage. I got out, resigned my coat and green silk handkerchief to Pigott (loth to part with these ornaments of life), and walked home in high spirits.

P.S. Toms called upon me the next day, to ask me if I did not think the fight was a complete thing? I said I thought it was. I hope he will relish my account of it.

THE INDIAN JUGGLERS

Coming forward and seating himself on the ground in his white dress and tightened turban, the chief of the Indian Jugglers begins with tossing up two brass balls, which is what any of us could do, and concludes with keeping up four at the same time, which is what none of us could do to save our lives, nor if we were to take our whole lives to do it in. Is it then a trifling power we see at work, or is it not something next to miraculous? It is the utmost stretch of human ingenuity, which nothing but the bending the faculties of body and mind to it from the tenderest infancy with incessant, ever-anxious application up to manhood, can accomplish or make even a slight approach to. Man, thou art a wonderful animal, and thy ways past finding out! Thou canst do strange things, but thou turnest them to little account!—To conceive of this effort of extraordinary dexterity distracts the imagination and makes admiration breathless. Yet it costs nothing to the performer, any more than if it were a mere mechanical deception with which he had nothing to do but to watch and laugh at the astonishment of the spectators. A single error of a hair's-breadth, of the smallest conceivable portion of time, would be fatal: the precision of the movements must be like a mathematical truth, their rapidity is like lightning. To catch four balls in succession in less than a second of time, and deliver them back so as to return with seeming consciousness to the hand again, to make them revolve round him at certain intervals, like the planets in their spheres, to make them chase one another like sparkles of fire, or shoot up like flowers or meteors, to throw them behind his back and twine them round his neck like ribbons or like serpents, to do what appears an impossibility, and to do it with all the ease, the grace, the carelessness imaginable, to laugh at, to play with the glittering mockeries, to follow them with his eye as if he could fascinate them with its lambent fire, or as if he had only to see that they kept time with the music on the stage—there is something in all this which he who does not admire may be quite sure he never really admired any thing in the whole course of his life. It is skill surmounting difficulty, and beauty triumphing over skill. It seems as if the difficulty once mastered naturally resolved itself into ease and grace, and as if to be overcome at all, it must be overcome without an effort. The smallest awkwardness or want of pliancy or self-possession would stop the whole process. It is the work of witchcraft, and yet sport for children. Some of the other feats are quite as curious and wonderful, such as the balancing the artificial tree and shooting a bird from each branch through a quill; though none of them have the elegance or facility of the keeping up of the brass balls. You are in pain for the result, and glad when the experiment is over; they are not accompanied with the same unmixed, unchecked delight as the former; and I would not give much to be merely astonished without being pleased at the same time. As to the swallowing of the sword, the police ought to interfere to prevent it. When I saw the Indian Juggler do the same things before, his feet were bare, and he had large rings on the toes, which kept turning round all the time of the performance, as if they moved of themselves. —The hearing a speech in Parliament, drawled or stammered out by the Honourable Member or the Noble Lord, the ringing the changes on their common-places, which any one could repeat after them as well as they, stirs me not a jot, shakes not my good opinion of myself: but the seeing the Indian Jugglers does. It makes me ashamed of myself. I ask what there is that I can do as well as this? Nothing. What have I been doing all my life? Have I been idle, or have I nothing to shew for all my labour and pains? Or have I passed my time in pouring words like water into empty sieves, rolling a stone up a hill and then down again, trying to prove an argument in the teeth of facts, and looking for causes in the dark, and not finding them? Is there no one thing in which I can challenge competition, that I can bring as an instance of exact perfection, in which others cannot find a flaw? The utmost I can pretend to is to write a description of what this fellow can do. I can write a book: so can many others who have not even learned to spell. What abortions are these Essays! What errors, what ill-pieced transitions, what crooked reasons, what lame conclusions! How little is made out, and that little how ill! Yet they are the best I can do. I endeavour to recollect all I have ever observed or thought upon a subject, and to express it as nearly as I can. Instead of writing on four subjects at a time, it is as much as I can manage to keep the thread of one discourse clear and un-entangled. I have also time on my hands to correct my opinions, and polish my periods: but the one I cannot, and the other I will not do. I am fond of arguing: yet with a good deal of pains and practice it is often as much as I can do to beat my man; though he may be a very indifferent hand. A common fencer would disarm his adversary in the twinkling of an eye, unless he were a professor like himself. A stroke of wit will sometimes produce this effect, but there is no such power or superiority in sense or reasoning. There is no complete mastery of execution to be shewn there: and you hardly know the professor from the impudent pretender or the mere clown[1].

I have always had this feeling of the inefficacy and slow progress of intellectual compared to mechanical excellence, and it has always made me somewhat dissatisfied. It is a great many years since I saw Richer, the famous rope-dancer, perform at Sadler's Wells. He was matchless in his art, and added to his extraordinary skill exquisite ease, and unaffected natural grace. I was at that time employed in copying a half-length picture of Sir Joshua Reynolds's; and it put me out of conceit with it. How ill this part was made out in

---

[1] The celebrated Peter Pindar (Dr Wolcot) first discovered and brought out the talents of the late Mr Opie, the painter. He was a poor Cornish boy, and was out at work in the fields, when the poet went in search of him. 'Well, my lad, can you go and bring me your very best picture?' The other flew like lightning, and soon came back with what he considered as his master-piece. The stranger looked at it, and the young artist, after waiting for some time without his giving any opinion, at length exclaimed eagerly, 'Well, what do you think of it?'—'Think of it?' said Wolcot, 'why I think you ought to be ashamed of it—that you who might do so well, do no better!' The same answer would have applied to this artist's latest performances, that had been suggested by one of his earliest efforts.

the drawing! How heavy, how slovenly this other was painted! I could not help saying to myself, 'If the rope-dancer had performed his task in this manner, leaving so many gaps and botches in his work, he would have broke his neck long ago; I should never have seen that vigorous elasticity of nerve and precision of movement!'—Is it then so easy an undertaking (comparatively) to dance on a tight-rope? Let any one, who thinks so, get up and try. There is the thing. It is that which at first we cannot do at all, which in the end is done to such perfection. To account for this in some degree, I might observe that mechanical dexterity is confined to doing some one particular thing, which you can repeat as often as you please, in which you know whether you succeed or fail, and where the point of perfection consists in succeeding in a given undertaking.—In mechanical efforts, you improve by perpetual practice, and you do so infallibly, because the object to be attained is not a matter of taste or fancy or opinion, but of actual experiment, in which you must either do the thing or not do it. If a man is put to aim at a mark with a bow and arrow, he must hit it or miss it, that's certain. He cannot deceive himself, and go on shooting wide or falling short, and still fancy that he is making progress. The distinction between right and wrong, between true and false, is here palpable; and he must either correct his aim or persevere in his error with his eyes open, for which there is neither excuse nor temptation. If a man is learning to dance on a rope, if he does not mind what he is about, he will break his neck. After that, it will be in vain for him to argue that he did not make a false step. His situation is not like that of Goldsmith's pedagogue.—

> In argument they own'd his wondrous skill,
> And e'en though vanquish'd, he could argue still.

Danger is a good teacher, and makes apt scholars. So are disgrace, defeat, exposure to immediate scorn and laughter. There is no opportunity in such cases for self-delusion, no idling time away, no being off your guard (or you must take the consequences)—neither is there any room for humour or caprice or prejudice. If the Indian Juggler were to play tricks in throwing up the three case-knives, which keep their positions likes the leaves of a crocus in the air, he would cut his fingers.

I can make a very bad antithesis without cutting my fingers. The tact of style is more ambiguous than that of double-edged instruments. If the Juggler were told that by flinging himself under the wheels of the Jaggernaut, when the idol issues forth on a gaudy day, he would immediately be transported into Paradise, he might believe it, and nobody could disprove it. So the Brahmins may say what they please on that subject, may build up dogmas and mysteries without end, and not be detected: but their ingenious countryman cannot persuade the frequenters of the Olympic Theatre that he performs a number of astonishing feats without actually giving proofs of what he says.—There is then in this sort of manual dexterity, first a gradual aptitude acquired to a given exertion of muscular power, from constant repetition, and in the next place, an exact knowledge how much is still wanting and necessary to be supplied. The obvious test is to increase the effort or nicety of the operation, and still to find it come true. The muscles ply instinctively to the dictates of habit. Certain movements and impressions of the hand and eye, having been repeated together an infinite number of times, are unconsciously but unavoidably cemented into closer and closer union; the limbs require little more than to be put in motion for them to follow a regular track with ease and certainty; so that the mere intention of the will acts mathematically, like touching the spring of a machine, and you come with Locksley in Ivanhoe, in shooting at a mark, 'to allow for the wind.'

Farther, what is meant by perfection in mechanical exercises is the performing certain feats to a uniform nicety, that is, in fact, undertaking no more than you can perform. You task yourself, the limit you fix is optional, and no more than human industry and skill can attain to: but you have no abstract, independent standard of difficulty or excellence (other than the extent of your own powers). Thus he who can keep up four brass balls does this *to perfection*; but he cannot keep up five at the same instant, and would fail every time he attempted it. That is, the mechanical performer undertakes to emulate himself, not to equal another[1]. But the artist

---

[1] If two persons play against each other at any game, one of them necessarily fails.

undertakes to imitate another, or to do what nature has done, and this it appears is more difficult, *viz.* to copy what she has set before us in the face of nature or 'human face divine,' entire and without a blemish, than to keep up four brass balls at the same instant; for the one is done by the power of human skill and industry, and the other never was nor will be. Upon the whole, therefore, I have more respect for Reynolds, than I have for Richer; for, happen how it will, there have been more people in the world who could dance on a rope like the one than who could paint like Sir Joshua The latter was but a bungler in his profession to the other, it is true; but then he had a harder task-master to obey, whose will was more wayward and obscure, and whose instructions it was more difficult to practise. You can put a child apprentice to a tumbler or rope-dancer with a comfortable prospect of success, if they are but sound of wind and limb: but you cannot do the same thing in painting. The odds are a million to one. You may make indeed as many H——s and H——s, as you put into that sort of machine, but not one Reynolds amongst them all, with his grace, his grandeur, his blandness of *gusto*, 'in tones and gestures hit,' unless you could make the man over again. To snatch this grace beyond the reach of art is then the height of art—where fine art begins, and where mechanical skill ends. The soft suffusion of the soul, the speechless breathing eloquence, the looks 'commercing with the skies,' the ever-shifting forms of an eternal principle, that which is seen but for a moment, but dwells in the heart always, and is only seized as it passes by strong and secret sympathy, must be taught by nature and genius, not by rules or study. It is suggested by feeling, not by laborious microscopic inspection: in seeking for it without, we lose the harmonious clue to it within: and in aiming to grasp the substance, we let the very spirit of art evaporate. In a word, the objects of fine art are not the objects of sight but as these last are the objects of taste and imagination, that is, as they appeal to the sense of beauty, of pleasure, and of power in the human breast, and are explained by that finer sense, and revealed in their inner structure to the eye in return. Nature is also a language. Objects, like words, have a meaning; and the true artist is the interpreter of this language, which he can only do by knowing its application to a thousand other objects in a thousand other situations. Thus the eye is too blind a guide of itself to distinguish between the warm or cold tone of a deep blue sky, but another sense acts as a monitor to it, and does not err. The colour of the leaves in autumn would be nothing without the feeling that accompanies it; but it is that feeling that stamps them on the canvas, faded, seared, blighted, shrinking from the winter's flaw, and makes the sight as true as touch—

> And visions, as poetic eyes avow,
> Cling to each leaf and hang on every bough.

The more ethereal, evanescent, more refined and sublime part of art is the seeing nature through the medium of sentiment and passion, as each object is a symbol of the affections and a link in the chain of our endless being. But the unravelling this mysterious web of thought and feeling is alone in the Muse's gift, namely, in the power of that trembling sensibility which is awake to every change and every modification of its ever-varying impressions, that

> Thrills in each nerve, and lives along the line.

This power is indifferently called genius, imagination, feeling, taste; but the manner in which it acts upon the mind can neither be defined by abstract rules, as is the case in science, nor verified by continual unvarying experiments, as is the case in mechanical performances. The mechanical excellence of the Dutch painters in colouring and handling is that which comes the nearest in fine art to the perfection of certain manual exhibitions of skill. The truth of the effect and the facility with which it is produced are equally admirable. Up to a certain point, every thing is faultless. The hand and eye have done their part. There is only a want of taste and genius. It is after we enter upon that enchanted ground that the human mind begins to droop and flag as in a strange road, or in a thick mist, benighted and making little way with many attempts and many faiiures, and that the best of us only escape with half a triumph. The undefined and the imaginary are the regions that we must pass like Satan, difficult and doubtful, 'half flying, half on foot.' The object in sense is a positive thing, and execution comes with practice.

Cleverness is a certain *knack* or aptitude at doing certain things, which depend more on a particular adroitness and off-hand readiness than on force or perseverance, such as making puns, making epigrams, making extempore verses, mimicking the company, mimicking a style, &c. Cleverness is either liveliness and smartness, or something answering to *sleight of hand*, like letting a glass fall sideways off a table, or else a trick, like knowing the secret spring of a watch. Accomplishments are certain external graces, which are to be learnt from others, and which are easily displayed to the admiration of the beholder, *viz.* dancing, riding, fencing, music, and so on. These ornamental acquirements are only proper to those who are at ease in mind and fortune. I know an individual who if he had been born to an estate of five thousand a year, would have been the most accomplished gentleman of the age. He would have been the delight and envy of the circle in which he moved—would have graced by his manners the liberality flowing from the openness of his heart, would have laughed with the women, have argued with the men, have said good things and written agreeable ones, have taken a hand at piquet or the lead at the harpsichord, and have set and sung his own verses—*nugæ canoræ*—with tenderness and spirit; a Rochester without the vice, a modern Surrey! As it is, all these capabilities of excellence stand in his way. He is too versatile for a professional man, not dull enough for a political drudge, too gay to be happy, too thoughtless to be rich. He wants the enthusiasm of the poet, the severity of the prose-writer, and the application of the man of business. —Talent is the capacity of doing any thing that depends on application and industry, such as writing a criticism, making a speech, studying the law. Talent differs from genius, as voluntary differs from involuntary power. Ingenuity is genius in trifles, greatness is genius in undertakings of much pith and moment. A clever or ingenious man is one who can do any thing well, whether it is worth doing or not: a great man is one who can do that which when done is of the highest importance. Themistocles said he could not play on the flute, but that he could make of a small city a great one. This gives one a pretty good idea of the distinction in question.

Greatness is great power, producing great effects. It is

not enough that a man has great power in himself, he must shew it to all the world, in a way that cannot be hid or gainsaid. He must fill up a certain idea in the public mind. I have no other notion of greatness than this two-fold definition, great results springing from great inherent energy. The great in visible objects has relation to that which extends over space: the great in mental ones has to do with space and time. No man is truly great, who is great only in his life-time. The test of greatness is the page of history. Nothing can be said to be great that has a distinct limit, or that borders on something evidently greater than itself. Besides, what is short-lived and pampered into mere notoriety, is of a gross and vulgar quality in itself. A Lord Mayor is hardly a great man. A city orator or patriot of the day only shew, by reaching the height of their wishes, the distance they are at from any true ambition. Popularity is neither fame nor greatness. A king (as such) is not a great man. He has great power, but it is not his own. He merely wields the lever of the state, which a child, an idiot, or a madman can do. It is the office, not the man we gaze at. Any one else in the same situation would be just as much an object of abject curiosity. We laugh at the country girl who having seen a king expressed her disappointment by saying, 'Why, he is only a man!' Yet, knowing this, we run to see a king as if he was something more than a man.— To display the greatest powers, unless they are applied to great purposes, makes nothing for the character of greatness. To throw a barley-corn through the eye of a needle, to multiply nine figures by nine in the memory, argues infinite dexterity of body and capacity of mind, but nothing comes of either. There is a surprising power at work, but the effects are not proportionate, or such as take hold of the imagination. To impress the idea of power on others, they must be made in some way to feel it. It must be communicated to their understandings in the shape of an increase of knowledge, or it must subdue and overawe them by subjecting their wills. Admiration, to be solid and lasting, must be founded on proofs from which we have no means of escaping; it is neither a slight nor a voluntary gift. A mathematician who solves a profound problem, a poet who creates an image of beauty in the mind that was not there before, imparts knowledge and power to others, in which his greatness and his fame consists, and on which it reposes. Jedediah Buxton will be forgotten; but Napier's bones will live. Lawgivers, philosophers, founders of religion, conquerors and heroes, inventors and great geniuses in arts and sciences, are great men; for they are great public benefactors, or formidable scourges to mankind. Among ourselves, Shakespear, Newton, Bacon, Milton, Cromwell, were great men; for they shewed great power by acts and thoughts, which have not yet been consigned to oblivion. They must needs be men of lofty stature, whose shadows lengthen out to remote posterity. A great farce-writer may be a great man; for Molière was but a great farce-writer. In my mind, the author of Don Quixote was a great man. So have there been many others. A great chess-player is not a great man, for he leaves the world as he found it. No act terminating in itself constitutes greatness. This will apply to all displays of power or trials of skill, which are confined to the momentary, individual effort, and construct no permanent image or trophy of themselves without them. Is not an actor then a great man, because 'he dies and leaves the world no copy'? I must make an exception for Mrs Siddons, or else give up my definition of greatness for her sake. A man at the top of his profession is not therefore a great man. He is great in his way, but that is all, unless he shews the marks of a great moving intellect, so that we trace the master-mind, and can sympathise with the springs that urge him on. The rest is but a craft or *mystery*. John Hunter was a great man—*that* any one might see without the smallest skill in surgery. His style and manner shewed the man. He would set about cutting up the carcase of a whale with the same greatness of *gusto* that Michael Angelo would have hewn a block of marble. Lord Nelson was a great naval commander; but for myself, I have not much opinion of a sea-faring life. Sir Humphry Davy is a great chemist, but I am not sure that he is a great man. I am not a bit the wiser for any of his discoveries, nor I never met with any one that was. But it is in the nature of greatness to propagate an idea of itself, as wave impels wave, circle without circle. It is a contradiction in terms for a coxcomb to be a great man. A really great man has always an idea of something greater than himself. I have observed that certain sectaries and polemical writers have no higher compliment to pay their most shining lights than to say that 'Such a one was a considerable man in his day.' Some new elucidation of a text sets aside the authority of the old interpretation, and a 'great scholar's memory outlives him half a century,' at the utmost. A rich man is not a great man, except to his dependants and his steward. A lord is a great man in the idea we have of his ancestry, and probably of himself, if we know nothing of him but his title. I have heard a story of two bishops, one of whom said (speaking of St Peter's at Rome) that when he first entered it, he was rather awe-struck, but that as he walked up it, his mind seemed to swell and dilate with it, and at last to fill the whole building—the other said that as he saw more of it, he appeared to himself to grow less and less every step he took, and in the end to dwindle into nothing. This was in some respects a striking picture of a great and little mind—for greatness sympathises with greatness, and littleness shrinks into itself. The one might have become a Wolsey; the other was only fit to become a Mendicant Friar—or there might have been court-reasons for making him a bishop. The French have to me a character of littleness in all about them; but they have produced three great men that belong to every country, Molière, Rabelais, and Montaigne.

To return from this digression, and conclude the Essay. A singular instance of manual dexterity was shewn in the person of the late John Cavanagh, whom I have several times seen. His death was celebrated at the time in an article in the Examiner newspaper (Feb. 7, 1819), written apparently between jest and earnest: but as it is *pat* to our purpose, and falls in with my own way of considering such subjects, I shall here take leave to quote it.

'Died at his house in Burbage-street, St Giles's, John Cavanagh, the famous hand fives-player. When a person dies, who does any one thing better than any one else in the world, which so many others are trying to do well, it leaves a gap in society. It is not likely that any one will now see the game of fives played in its perfection for many years to come—for Cavanagh is dead, and has not left his peer behind him. It may be said that there are things of more importance

than striking a ball against a wall—there are things indeed
which make more noise and do as little good, such as making
war and peace, making speeches and answering them, making
verses and blotting them; making money and throwing it
away.   But the game of fives is what no one despises who has
ever played at it.   It is the finest exercise for the body, and
the best relaxation for the mind.   The Roman poet said that
"Care mounted behind the horseman and stuck to his skirts."
But this remark would not have applied to the fives-player.
He who takes to playing at fives is twice young.   He feels
neither the past nor future "in the instant."   Debts,
taxes, "domestic treason, foreign levy, nothing can touch
him further."   He has no other wish, no other thought,
from the moment the game begins, but that of striking the ball,
of placing it, of *making* it!   This Cavanagh was sure to do.
Whenever he touched the ball, there was an end of the chase.
His eye was certain, his hand fatal, his presence of mind
complete.   He could do what he pleased, and he always
knew exactly what to do.   He saw the whole game, and played
it; took instant advantage of his adversary's weakness, and
recovered balls, as if by a miracle and from sudden thought,
that every one gave for lost.   He had equal power and skill,
quickness, and judgment.   He could either out-wit his antagonist by finesse, or beat him by main strength.   Sometimes,
when he seemed preparing to send the ball with the full
swing of his arm, he would by a slight turn of his wrist drop
it within an inch of the line.   In general, the ball came from
his hand, as if from a racket, in a straight horizontal line;
so that it was in vain to attempt to overtake or stop it.   As it
was said of a great orator that he never was at a loss for a
word, and for the properest word, so Cavanagh always could
tell the degree of force necessary to be given to a ball, and
the precise direction in which it should be sent.   He did his
work with the greatest ease; never took more pains than was
necessary; and while others were fagging themselves to death,
was as cool and collected as if he had just entered the court.
His style of play was as remarkable as his power of execution.
He had no affectation, no trifling.   He did not throw away
the game to show off an attitude, or try an experiment.   He
was a fine, sensible, manly player, who did what he could,

but that was more than any one else could even affect to do. His blows were not undecided and ineffectual—lumbering like Mr Wordsworth's epic poetry, nor wavering like Mr Coleridge's lyric prose, nor short of the mark like Mr Brougham's speeches, nor wide of it like Mr Canning's wit, nor foul like the *Quarterly*, nor *let* balls like the *Edinburgh Review*. Cobbett and Junius together would have made a Cavanagh. He was the best *up-hill* player in the world; even when his adversary was fourteen, he would play on the same or better, and as he never flung away the game through carelessness and conceit, he never gave it up through laziness or want of heart. The only peculiarity of his play was that he never *volleyed*, but let the balls hop; but if they rose an inch from the ground, he never missed having them. There was not only nobody equal, but nobody second to him. It is supposed that he could give any other player half the game, or beat him with his left hand. His service was tremendous. He once played Woodward and Meredith together (two of the best players in England) in the Fives-court, St Martin's-street, and made seven and twenty aces following by services alone—a thing unheard of. He another time played Peru, who was considered a first-rate fives-player, a match of the best out of five games, and in the three first games, which of course decided the match, Peru got only one ace. Cavanagh was an Irishman by birth, and a house-painter by profession. He had once laid aside his working-dress, and walked up, in his smartest clothes, to the Rosemary Branch to have an afternoon's pleasure. A person accosted him, and asked him if he would have a game. So they agreed to play for half-a-crown a game, and a bottle of cider. The first game begun—it was seven, eight, ten, thirteen, fourteen, all. Cavanagh won it. The next was the same. They played on, and each game was hardly contested. "There," said the unconscious fives-player, "there was a stroke that Cavanagh could not take: I never played better in my life, and yet I can't win a game. I don't know how it is." However, they played on, Cavanagh winning every game, and the by-standers drinking the cider, and laughing all the time. In the twelfth game, when Cavanagh was only four, and the stranger thirteen, a person came in, and said, "What! are you here, Cavanagh?" The words

were no sooner pronounced than the astonished player let
the ball drop from his hand, and saying, "What! have I been
breaking my heart all this time to beat Cavanagh?" refused
to make another effort. "And yet, I give you my word,"
said Cavanagh, telling the story with some triumph, "I played
all the while with my clenched fist."—He used frequently to
play matches at Copenhagen-house for wagers and dinners.
The wall against which they play is the same that supports
the kitchen-chimney, and when the wall resounded louder
than usual, the cooks exclaimed, "Those are the Irishman's
balls," and the joints trembled on the spit!—Goldsmith
consoled himself that there were places where he too was
admired: and Cavanagh was the admiration of all the fives-
courts, where he ever played. Mr Powell, when he played
matches in the Court in St Martin's-street, used to fill his
gallery at half a crown a head, with amateurs and admirers
of talent in whatever department it is shown. He could
not have shown himself in any ground in England, but he
would have been immediately surrounded with inquisitive
gazers, trying to find out in what part of his frame his unrivalled
skill lay, as politicians wonder to see the balance of Europe
suspended in Lord Castlereagh's face, and admire the trophies
of the British Navy lurking under Mr Croker's hanging brow.
Now Cavanagh was as good-looking a man as the Noble
Lord, and much better looking than the Right Hon. Secretary.
He had a clear, open countenance, and did not look sideways
or down, like Mr Murray the bookseller. He was a young
fellow of sense, humour, and courage. He once had a quarrel
with a waterman at Hungerford-stairs, and, they say, served
him out in great style. In a word, there are hundreds at
this day, who cannot mention his name without admiration,
as the best fives-player that perhaps ever lived (the greatest
excellence of which they have any notion)—and the noisy
shout of the ring happily stood him in stead of the unheard
voice of posterity!—The only person who seems to have
excelled as much in another way as Cavanagh did in his, was
the late John Davies, the racket-player. It was remarked
of him that he did not seem to follow the ball, but the ball
seemed to follow him. Give him a foot of wall, and he was
sure to make the ball. The four best racket-players of that

day were Jack Spines, Jem. Harding, Armitage, and Church. Davies could give any one of these two hands a time, that is, half the game, and each of these, at their best, could give the best player now in London the same odds. Such are the gradations in all exertions of human skill and art. He once played four capital players together, and beat them. He was also a first-rate tennis-player, and an excellent fives-player. In the Fleet or King's Bench, he would have stood against Powell, who was reckoned the best open-ground player of his time. This last-mentioned player is at present the keeper of the Fives-court, and we might recommend to him for a motto over his door—"Who enters here, forgets himself, his country, and his friends." And the best of it is, that by the calculation of the odds, none of the three are worth remembering!—Cavanagh died from the bursting of a blood-vessel, which prevented him from playing for the last two or three years. This, he was often heard to say, he thought hard upon him. He was fast recovering, however, when he was suddenly carried off, to the regret of all who knew him. As Mr Peel made it a qualification of the present Speaker, Mr Manners Sutton, that he was an excellent moral character, so Jack Cavanagh was a zealous Catholic, and could not be persuaded to eat meat on a Friday, the day on which he died. We have paid this willing tribute to his memory.

> Let no rude hand deface it,
> And his forlorn "*Hic Jacet*".

ON GOING A JOURNEY

One of the pleasantest things in the world is going a journey; but I like to go by myself. I can enjoy society in a room; but out of doors, nature is company enough for me. I am then never less alone than when alone.

> The fields his study, nature was his book.

I cannot see the wit of walking and talking at the same time. When I am in the country, I wish to vegetate like the country. I am not for criticising hedge-rows and black cattle. I go out of town in order to forget the town and all that is in it. There are those who for this purpose go to watering-places, and carry the metropolis with them. I like more elbow-room, and fewer incumbrances. I like solitude, when I give myself up to it, for the sake of solitude; nor do I ask for

> ——a friend in my retreat,
> Whom I may whisper solitude is sweet.

The soul of a journey is liberty, perfect liberty, to think, feel, do just as one pleases. We go a journey chiefly to be free of all impediments and of all inconveniences; to leave ourselves behind, much more to get rid of others. It is because I want a little breathing-space to muse on indifferent matters, where Contemplation

> May plume her feathers and let grow her wings,
> That in the various bustle of resort
> Were all too ruffled, and sometimes impair'd,

that I absent myself from the town for awhile, without feeling at a loss the moment I am left by myself. Instead of a friend in a post-chaise or in a Tilbury, to exchange good things with, and vary the same stale topics over again, for once let me have a truce with impertinence. Give me the clear blue sky over my head, and the green turf beneath my feet, a winding road before me, and a three hours' march to dinner—and then to thinking! It is hard if I cannot start some game on these lone heaths. I laugh, I run, I leap, I sing for joy. From the point of yonder rolling cloud, I plunge into my past being, and revel there, as the sun-burnt Indian plunges headlong into the wave that wafts him to his native shore. Then long-forgotten things, like 'sunken wrack and sumless treasuries,' burst upon my eager sight, and I begin to feel, think, and be myself again. Instead of an awkward silence, broken by attempts at wit or dull common-places, mine is that undisturbed silence of the heart which alone is perfect eloquence. No one likes puns, alliterations, antitheses, argument, and analysis better than I do; but I sometimes had rather be without them. 'Leave, oh, leave me to my repose!' I have just now other business in hand, which would seem idle to you, but is with me 'very stuff of the conscience.' Is not this wild rose sweet without a comment? Does not this daisy leap to my heart set in its coat of emerald? Yet if I were to explain to you the circumstance that has so endeared it to me, you would only smile. Had I not better then keep it to myself, and let it serve me to brood over, from here to yonder craggy point and from thence onward to the far-distant horizon? I should be but bad company all that way, and therefore prefer being alone. I have heard it said that you may, when the moody fit comes on, walk or ride on by yourself, and indulge your reveries. But this looks like a breach of manners, a neglect of others, and you are thinking all the time that you ought to rejoin your party. 'Out upon such half-faced fellowship,' say I. I like to be either entirely to myself, or entirely at the disposal of others; to talk or be silent, to walk or sit still, to be sociable or solitary. I was pleased with an observa-tion of Mr Cobbett's, that 'he thought it a bad French custom to drink our wine with our meals, and that an Englishman ought to do only one thing at a time.' So I cannot talk and think, or indulge in melancholy musing and lively conversation by fits and starts. 'Let me have a companion of my way,' says Sterne, 'were it but to remark how the shadows lengthen as the sun declines.' It is beautifully said: but in my opinion, this continual comparing of notes interferes with the involuntary impression of things upon the mind, and hurts the sentiment.

If you only hint what you feel in a kind of dumb show, it is insipid: if you have to explain it, it is making a toil of a pleasure. You cannot read the book of nature, without being perpetually put to the trouble of translating it for the benefit of others. I am for the synthetical method on a journey, in preference to the analytical. I am content to lay in a stock of ideas then, and to examine and anatomise them afterwards. I want to see my vague notions float like the down of the thistle before the breeze, and not to have them entangled in the briars and thorns of controversy. For once, I like to have it all my own way; and this is impossible unless you are alone, or in such company as I do not covet. I have no objection to argue a point with any one for twenty miles of measured road, but not for pleasure. If you remark the scent of a beanfield crossing the road, perhaps your fellow-traveller has no smell. If you point to a distant object, perhaps he is short-sighted, and has to take out his glass to look at it. There is a feeling in the air, a tone in the colour of a cloud which hits your fancy, but the effect of which you are unable to account for. There is then no sympathy, but an uneasy craving after it, and a dissatisfaction which pursues you on the way, and in the end probably produces ill humour. Now I never quarrel with myself, and take all my own conclusions for granted till I find it necessary to defend them against objections. It is not merely that you may not be of accord on the objects and circumstances that present themselves before you—these may recal a number of objects, and lead to associations too delicate and refined to be possibly communicated to others. Yet these I love to cherish, and sometimes still fondly clutch them, when I can escape from the throng to do so. To give way to our feelings before company, seems extravagance or affectation; and on the other hand, to have to unravel this mystery of our being at every turn, and to make others take an equal interest in it (otherwise the end is not answered) is a task to which few are competent. We must 'give it an understanding, but no tongue.' My old friend C——, however, could do both. He could go on in the most delightful explanatory way over hill and dale, a summer's day, and convert a landscape into a didactic poem or a Pindaric ode. 'He talked far above singing.' If I could so clothe my ideas in sounding and flowing words, I might perhaps wish to have some one with me to admire the swelling theme; or I could be more content, were it possible for me still to hear his echoing voice in the woods of All-Foxden. They had 'that fine madness in them which our first poets had'; and if they could have been caught by some rare instrument, would have breathed such strains as the following.

> ——Here be woods as green
> As any, air likewise as fresh and sweet
> As when smooth Zephyrus plays on the fleet
> Face of the curled stream, with flow'rs as many
> As the young spring gives, and as choice as any;
> Here be all new delights, cool streams and wells,
> Arbours o'ergrown with woodbine, caves and dells;
> Choose where thou wilt, while I sit by and sing,
> Or gather rushes to make many a ring
> For thy long fingers; tell thee tales of love,
> How the pale Phœbe, hunting in a grove,
> First saw the boy Endymion, from whose eyes
> She took eternal fire that never dies;
> How she convey'd him softly in a sleep,
> His temples bound with poppy, to the steep
> Head of old Latmos, where she stoops each night,
> Gilding the mountain with her brother's light,
> To kiss her sweetest.——
>
>   Faithful Shepherdess.

Had I words and images at command like these, I would attempt to wake the thoughts that lie slumbering on golden ridges in the evening clouds: but at the sight of nature my fancy, poor as it is, droops and closes up its leaves, like flowers at sunset. I can make nothing out on the spot:—I must have time to collect myself.—

In general, a good thing spoils out-of-door prospects: it should be reserved for Table-talk. L—— is for this reason, I take it, the worst company in the world out of doors; because he is the best within. I grant, there is one subject on which it is pleasant to talk on a journey; and that is, what one shall have for supper when we get to our inn at night. The open air improves this sort of conversation or friendly altercation, by setting a keener edge on appetite. Every mile of the road heightens the flavour of the viands we expect at the end of it. How fine it is to enter some old town, walled and turreted, just at the approach of night-fall, or to come to some straggling

village, with the lights streaming through the surrounding
gloom; and then after inquiring for the best entertainment
that the place affords, to 'take one's ease at one's inn!' These
eventful moments in our lives' history are too precious, too
full of solid, heartfelt happiness to be frittered and dribbled
away in imperfect sympathy. I would have them all to
myself, and drain them to the last drop: they will do to talk
of or to write about afterwards. What a delicate speculation
it is, after drinking whole goblets of tea,

> The cups that cheer, but not inebriate,

and letting the fumes ascend into the brain, to sit considering
what we shall have for supper—eggs and a rasher, a rabbit
smothered in onions, or an excellent veal-cutlet! Sancho in
such a situation once fixed upon cow-heel; and his choice,
though he could not help it, is not to be disparaged. Then in
the intervals of pictured scenery and Shandean contemplation,
to catch the preparation and the stir in the kitchen—*Procul,
O procul este profani!* These hours are sacred to silence and
to musing, to be treasured up in the memory, and to feed
the source of smiling thoughts hereafter. I would not waste
them in idle talk; or if I must have the integrity of fancy
broken in upon, I would rather it were by a stranger than a
friend. A stranger takes his hue and character from the
time and place; he is a part of the furniture and costume of
an inn. If he is a Quaker, or from the West Riding of Yorkshire, so much the better. I do not even try to sympathise
with him, and he breaks no squares. I associate nothing with
my travelling companion but present objects and passing
events. In his ignorance of me and my affairs, I in a manner
forget myself. But a friend reminds one of other things,
rips up old grievances, and destroys the abstraction of the
scene. He comes in ungraciously between us and our imaginary character. Something is dropped in the course of
conversation that gives a hint of your profession and pursuits;
or from having some one with you that knows the less sublime
portions of your history, it seems that other people do. You
are no longer a citizen of the world: but your 'unhoused
free condition is put into circumscription and confine.' The
incognito of an inn is one of its striking privileges—'lord of

one's-self, uncumber'd with a name.'   Oh! it is great to shake
off the trammels of the world and of public opinion—to lose
our importunate, tormenting, everlasting personal identity in
the elements of nature, and become the creature of the moment,
clear of all ties—to hold to the universe only by a dish of
sweet-breads, and to owe nothing but the score of the evening
—and no longer seeking for applause and meeting with
contempt, to be known by no other title than *the Gentleman
in the parlour!*   One may take one's choice of all characters
in this romantic state of uncertainty as to one's real pretensions,
and become indefinitely respectable and negatively right-wor-
shipful.   We baffle prejudice and disappoint conjecture; and
from being so to others, begin to be objects of curiosity and
wonder even to ourselves.   We are no more those hackneyed
common-places that we appear in the world: an inn restores
us to the level of nature, and quits scores with society!   I have
certainly spent some enviable hours at inns—sometimes when
I have been left entirely to myself, and have tried to solve
some metaphysical problem, as once at Witham-common,
where I found out the proof that likeness is not a case of the
association of ideas—at other times, when there have been
pictures in the room, as at St Neot's (I think it was), where
I first met with Gribelin's engravings of the Cartoons, into
which I entered at once, and at a little inn on the borders
of Wales, where there happened to be hanging some of Westall's
drawings, which I compared triumphantly (for a theory that
I had, not for the admired artist) with the figure of a girl who
had ferried me over the Severn, standing up in the boat
between me and the twilight—at other times I might mention
luxuriating in books, with a peculiar interest in this way,
as I remember sitting up half the night to read Paul and
Virginia, which I picked up at an inn at Bridgewater, after
being drenched in the rain all day; and at the same place
I got through two volumes of Madame D'Arblay's Camilla.
It was on the tenth of April, 1798, that I sat down to a volume
of the New Eloise, at the inn at Llangollen, over a bottle of
sherry and a cold chicken.   The letter I chose was that in
which St Preux describes his feelings as he caught a glimpse
from the heights of the Jura of the Pays de Vaud, which I
had brought with me as a *bonne bouche* to crown the evening

with. It was my birth-day, and I had for the first time come
from a place in the neighbourhood to visit this delightful
spot. The road to Llangollen turns off between Chirk and
Wrexham; and on passing a certain point, you come all
at once upon the valley, which opens like an amphitheatre,
broad, barren hills rising in majestic state on either side,
with 'green upland swells that echo to the bleat of flocks'
below, and the river Dee babbling over its stony bed in the
midst of them. The valley at this time 'glittered green with
sunny showers,' and a budding ash-tree dipped its tender
branches in the chiding stream. How proud, how glad I was
to walk along the high road that overlooks the delicious
prospect, repeating the lines which I have just quoted from
Mr Coleridge's poems! But besides the prospect which opened
beneath my feet, another also opened to my inward sight,
a heavenly vision, on which were written, in letters large as
Hope could make them, these four words, LIBERTY, GENIUS,
LOVE, VIRTUE; which have since faded into the light of
common day, or mock my idle gaze.

> The beautiful is vanished, and returns not.

Still I would return some time or other to this enchanted
spot; but I would return to it alone. What other self could
I find to share that influx of thoughts, of regret, and delight,
the fragments of which I could hardly conjure up to myself,
so much have they been broken and defaced! I could stand
on some tall rock, and overlook the precipice of years that
separates me from what I then was. I was at that time going
shortly to visit the poet whom I have above named. Where
is he now? Not only I myself have changed; the world,
which was then new to me, has become old and incorrigible.
Yet will I turn to thee in thought, O sylvan Dee, in joy,
in youth and gladness as thou then wert; and thou shalt
always be to me the river of Paradise, where I will drink of
the waters of life freely!

There is hardly any thing that shows the short-sightedness
or capriciousness of the imagination more than travelling
does. With change of place we change our ideas; nay, our
opinions and feelings. We can by an effort indeed transport
ourselves to old and long-forgotten scenes, and then the

picture of the mind revives again; but we forget those that we have just left. It seems that we can think but of one place at a time. The canvas of the fancy is but of a certain extent, and if we paint one set of objects upon it, they immediately efface every other. We cannot enlarge our conceptions, we only shift our point of view. The landscape bares its bosom to the enraptured eye, we take our fill of it, and seem as if we could form no other image of beauty or grandeur. We pass on, and think no more of it: the horizon that shuts it from our sight, also blots it from our memory like a dream. In travelling through a wild barren country, I can form no idea of a woody and cultivated one. It appears to me that all the world must be barren, like what I see of it. In the country we forget the town, and in town we despise the country. 'Beyond Hyde Park,' says Sir Fopling Flutter, 'all is a desert.' All that part of the map that we do not see before us is a blank. The world in our conceit of it is not much bigger than a nutshell. It is not one prospect expanded into another, county joined to county, kingdom to kingdom, lands to seas, making an image voluminous and vast;—the mind can form no larger idea of space than the eye can take in at a single glance. The rest is a name written in a map, a calculation of arithmetic. For instance, what is the true signification of that immense mass of territory and population, known by the name of China to us? An inch of paste-board on a wooden globe, of no more account than a China orange! Things near us are seen of the size of life: things at a distance are diminished to the size of the understanding. We measure the universe by ourselves, and even comprehend the texture of our own being only piece-meal. In this way, however, we remember an infinity of things and places. The mind is like a mechanical instrument that plays a great variety of tunes, but it must play them in succession. One idea recalls another, but it at the same time excludes all others. In trying to renew old recollections, we cannot as it were unfold the whole web of our existence; we must pick out the single threads. So in coming to a place where we have formerly lived and with which we have intimate associations, every one must have found that the feeling grows more vivid the nearer we approach the spot, from the mere anticipation of the actual impression:

we remember circumstances, feelings, persons, faces, names, that we had not thought of for years; but for the time all the rest of the world is forgotten!—To return to the question I have quitted above.

I have no objection to go to see ruins, aqueducts, pictures, in company with a friend or a party, but rather the contrary, for the former reason reversed. They are intelligible matters, and will bear talking about. The sentiment here is not tacit, but communicable and overt. Salisbury Plain is barren of criticism, but Stonehenge will bear a discussion antiquarian, picturesque, and philosophical. In setting out on a party of pleasure, the first consideration always is where we shall go to: in taking a solitary ramble, the question is what we shall meet with by the way. 'The mind is its own place ; nor are we anxious to arrive at the end of our journey. I can myself do the honours indifferently well to works of art and curiosity. I once took a party to Oxford with no mean *éclat*— shewed them that seat of the Muses at a distance,

With glistering spires and pinnacles adorn'd—

descanted on the learned air that breathes from the grassy quadrangles and stone walls of halls and colleges—was at home in the Bodleian; and at Blenheim quite superseded the powdered Cicerone that attended us, and that pointed in vain with his wand to common-place beauties in matchless pictures.—As another exception to the above reasoning, I should not feel confident in venturing on a journey in a foreign country without a companion. I should want at intervals to hear the sound of my own language. There is an involuntary antipathy in the mind of an Englishman to foreign manners and notions that requires the assistance of social sympathy to carry it off. As the distance from home increases, this relief, which was at first a luxury, becomes a passion and an appetite. A person would almost feel stifled to find himself in the deserts of Arabia without friends and countrymen: there must be allowed to be something in the view of Athens or old Rome that claims the utterance of speech; and I own that the Pyramids are too mighty for any single contemplation. In such situations, so opposite to all one's ordinary train of ideas, one seems a species by one's-self, a limb torn off from society, unless one can meet with instant fellowship and support.—Yet I did not feel this want or craving very pressing once, when I first set my foot on the laughing shores of France. Calais was peopled with novelty and delight. The confused, busy murmur of the place was like oil and wine poured into my ears; nor did the mariners' hymn, which was sung from the top of an old crazy vessel in the harbour, as the sun went down, send an alien sound into my soul. I only breathed the air of general humanity. I walked over 'the vine-covered hills and gay regions of France,' erect and satisfied; for the image of man was not cast down and chained to the foot of arbitrary thrones: I was at no loss for language, for that of all the great schools of painting was open to me. The whole is vanished like a shade. Pictures, heroes, glory, freedom, all are fled: nothing remains but the Bourbons and the French people!—There is undoubtedly a sensation in travelling into foreign parts that is to be had nowhere else: but it is more pleasing at the time than lasting. It is too remote from our habitual associations to be a common topic of discourse or reference, and, like a dream or another state of existence, does not piece into our daily modes of life. It is an animated but a momentary hallucination. It demands an effort to exchange our actual for our ideal identity; and to feel the pulse of our old transports revive very keenly, we must 'jump' all our present comforts and connexions. Our romantic and itinerant character is not to be domesticated. Dr Johnson remarked how little foreign travel added to the facilities of conversation in those who had been abroad. In fact, the time we have spent there is both delightful and in one sense instructive; but it appears to be cut out of our substantial, downright existence, and never to join kindly on to it. We are not the same, but another, and perhaps more enviable individual, all the time we are out of our own country. We are lost to ourselves, as well as our friends. So the poet somewhat quaintly sings,

> Out of my country and myself I go.

Those who wish to forget painful thoughts, do well to absent themselves for a while from the ties and objects that recal them: but we can be said only to fulfil our destiny in the place that gave us birth. I should on this account like well enough to spend the whole of my life in travelling abroad, if I could any where borrow another life to spend afterwards at home!—

NOTES

MY FIRST ACQUAINTANCE WITH POETS

First published in *The Liberal*, 1823, and included in the *Literary Remains* and the *Winterslow* volume. One paragraph, that beginning "It was in January 1798" and ending with the quotation "Like to that sanguine flower inscribed with woe" had appeared in 1817 in the form of a letter to Leigh Hunt's paper *The Examiner*. See below (the note on "Jus Divinum") for a further account of this letter.

p. 1, l. 1. **W——m.** Wem.

p. 1, l. 3. **dreaded name of Demogorgon.** *Paradise Lost*, II, 964–5:

> With him enthroned
> Sat sable-vested Night, eldest of things,
> The consort of his reign; and by them stood
> Orcus and Ades, and the dreaded name
> Of Demogorgon.

Demorgorgon, oldest of the gods, the fabled ruler of Chaos, had so "dreaded" a name, that the world trembled at its sound. Compare Spenser, *Faerie Queene*, I, i, 37:

> A bold bad man, that dar'd to call by name
> Great Gorgon, prince of darkness and dead night;
> At which Cocytus quakes, and Styx is put to flight.

It is Demorgorgon who, in Shelley's *Prometheus Unbound*, dethrones Jupiter and secures the release of Prometheus.

p. 1, l. 10. **a round-faced man.** Hazlitt's description of Coleridge as "a round-faced man in a short black coat" may be compared with De Quincey's first impression nine years later: "I immediately took my leave of Mr Poole, and went over to Bridgewater. I had received directions for finding out the house where Coleridge was visiting; and, in riding down a main street of Bridgewater, I noticed a gateway corresponding to the description given me. Under this was standing, and gazing about him, a man whom I will describe. In height he might seem to be about five feet eight (he was, in reality, about an inch and a half taller, but his figure was of an order which drowns the height); his person was broad and full, and tended even to corpulence; his complexion was fair, though not what painters technically style fair, because it was associated with black hair; his eyes were large, and soft in their expression; and it was from the peculiar appearance of haze or dreaminess which mixed with their light that I recognised my object. This was Coleridge" (*Literary Reminiscences*, Works, Vol. II, p. 150).

p. 1, l. 16. He did not cease. Hazlitt's witty gibe at Coleridge's power of monologue matches the anecdote related of Lamb, to whom Coleridge said, "Did you ever hear me preach, Charles?" "I n-never heard you d-do anything else," stuttered Lamb, in reply.

p. 1, l. 19. fluttering the proud, etc. An adaptation of *Coriolanus*, v, vi, 114–115 :

> If you have writ your annals true, 'tis there
> That, like an eagle in a dovecote, I
> Fluttered your Volscians in Corioli ;
> Alone I did it.

p. 1, l. 23. High-born Hoel's harp, etc. Gray, *The Bard*, l. 28. Hoel and Llewelyn were traditional Welsh bards.

p. 2, l. 7. With Styx, etc. Pope, *Ode on St Cecilia's Day* :

> Though fate had fast bound her
> With Styx nine times round her,
> Yet music and love were victorious.

—the reference being to Eurydice, and the conquest of the powers of the underworld by "Orpheus with his lute."

p. 2, l. 24. the fires in the Agamemnon. A reference to the speech of Clytemnestra in the *Agamemnon* of Aeschylus, describing how beacon after beacon flashed the news of the fall of Troy—just as, in Macaulay's familiar lines, the blazing hill-tops of England signalled the approach of the Armada.

p. 2, l. 38. Il y a des impressions, etc., "There are some impressions that neither time nor circumstances can obliterate. Were I to live whole centuries, the sweet days of my youth could never return and never fade from my recollection." The passage resembles several sentences in Rousseau's *Confessions* and *La Nouvelle Héloïse.*

p. 3, l. 5. And he went up, etc. Gospel of St John, vi, 15.

p. 3, l. 6. rose like a steam, etc. *Comus*, l. 556 :

> At last a soft and solemn-breathing sound
> Rose, like a steam of rich distilled perfumes,
> And stole upon the air.

For another impressionable young listener's description of a great man in the pulpit, see Matthew Arnold's exquisite vignette of Newman : "Who could resist the charm of that spiritual apparition, gliding in the dim afternoon light through the aisles of St Mary's, rising into the pulpit, and then, in the most entrancing of voices, breaking the silence with words and thoughts which were a religious music—subtle, sweet, mournful? I seem to hear him still, saying : 'After the fever of life, after wearinesses and sicknesses, fightings and despondings, languor and fretfulness, struggling and succeeding ; after all the changes and chances of this troubled, unhealthy state—at length comes death, at length the white throne of God, at length the beatific vision'."

p. 3, l. 12. of one crying, etc. Gospel of St Matthew, iii, 3–4.

p. 3, l. 15. The sermon was upon, etc. See note below on "Jus Divinum."

p. 3, l. 28. cue. We should spell it now in its French form—"queue," a pig-tail.

p. 3, l. 30. **Such were the notes,** etc. Pope, *Epistle to Robert Earl of Oxford*, etc.—the opening lines:

> Such were the notes thy once-loved Poet sung,
> Till Death untimely stopped his tuneful tongue.

Harley's "once-loved poet" was Parnell, author of *The Hermit.*

p. 4, l. 3. **Jus Divinum,** Divine Right. This allusion needs some explanation. As I have noted above, the present paragraph of this essay appeared in *The Examiner* of 12 Jan. 1817, in the form of a letter to the editor. *The Examiner* of 29 December 1816, had published from the pen of Hazlitt a long anonymous review of Coleridge's pamphlet *The Statesman's Manual; or The Bible the best Guide to Political Skill and Foresight, A Lay Sermon addressed to the Higher Classes of Society.* Coleridge, who had begun political life as a revolutionist and religious life as a unitarian, had come round to a conservative view both of state and church. Hazlitt, with all the fervour of a consistent revolutionist, hated Coleridge for his apostasy. In *The Statesman's Manual* occurs a sentence which Hazlitt seized upon as proof that Coleridge was now prepared even to uphold the Stewart theory of "Divine Right." Hazlitt devotes several passages of his article to comments upon " Jus Divinum"; and so a reference to it in a letter published a fortnight later was quite intelligible to readers of *The Examiner*. But by 1823 when this paragraph was incorporated into the long essay as we now have it, the allusion had become obscure. The point is this: the Coleridge of 1798 abhorred the doctrine of "Jus Divinum" which the Coleridge of 1816 was prepared to bless. The whole description of the sermon at Wem is plainly written with the intention of emphasising Coleridge's change of political faith. In *The Examiner* the sentence appears thus: "*That* sermon, like *this* Sermon, was upon peace and war; upon church and state—not their alliance, but their separation," etc. And at the conclusion of his letter Hazlitt writes: "Again, Sir, I ask Mr Coleridge, why, having preached such a sermon as I have described [i.e. the sermon of 1798 at Wem], he has published such a sermon as you have described" [i.e. the *Lay Sermon* of 1816]. The letter in *The Examiner* was signed "Semper Ego Auditor" and was couched in such terms as to imply that the writer was not the author of the article on Coleridge's volume. See *Works,* Vol. III, for the article in question.

p. 4, l. 4. **Like to that sanguine flower.** *Lycidas*, l. 106.

p. 4, l. 17. **As are the children,** etc. Thomson, *The Castle of Indolence*, Canto II, St. 33:

> He came, the Bard, a little Druid wight
> Of withered aspect; but his eye was keen,
> With sweetness mixed. In russet brown bedight,
> As is his sister of the copses green,
> He crept along, unpromising of mien.
> Gross he who judges so. His soul was fair,
> Bright as the children of yon azure sheen!
> True comeliness, which nothing can impair,
> Dwells in the mind: all else is vanity and glare.

p. 4, l. 20. **A certain tender bloom,** etc. Thomson, *The Castle of Indolence,* Canto I, St. 57:

Of all the gentle tenants of the place,
There was a man of special grave remark;
A certain tender bloom o'erspread his face,
Pensive, not sad.

p. 4, l. 23. **Murillo and Velasquez.** Bartolomé Esteban Murillo (1618–1682), a very popular Spanish painter, whose work falls roughly into two main groups,—vigorous and realistic sketches of Spanish beggar children, and rather sentimental religious pictures with the Virgin Mary as the central figure. Murillo is fairly well represented at the National Gallery and at Dulwich. His portraits are extremely few and not generally known. On the other hand, Don Diego de Silva y Velasquez (1599–1660), the greatest of Spanish painters and one of the supreme artists of the world, is specially renowned for his portraits of princes, nobles, ladies and buffoons of the Spanish court. There are a few important pictures by Velasquez in the National Gallery and the Wallace collection; but the bulk of his work has to be sought in Spain.

p. 4, l. 26. **like what he has done.** Coleridge's work is, for the most part, fragmentary—mere beginnings of things that he had not will enough to finish.

p. 4, l. 34. **inclining to the corpulent.** Coleridge's own poem *Youth and Age* contains allusions to his personal appearance, e.g.:

This body that does me grievous wrong,

and,

I see these locks in silvery slips,
This drooping gait, this altered size.

Hazlitt's description should be compared with the portraits of Coleridge by Peter Vandyke (1795) and by Robert Hancock (1796), both in the National Portrait Gallery. One of Coleridge's letters belonging to this period contains a remarkable self-portrait: "Your portrait of yourself interested me. As to me, my face, unless when animated by immediate eloquence, expresses great sloth, and great, indeed, almost idiotic good-nature. Tis a mere carcass of a face; fat, flabby, and expressive chiefly of inexpression. Yet I am told that my eyes, eyebrows and forehead are physiognomically good; but of this the deponent knoweth not. As to my shape, tis a good shape enough if measured, but my gait is awkward, and the walk of the whole man indicates *indolence capable of energies*....I cannot breathe through my nose, so my mouth, with sensual thick lips, is almost always open... (Letter to John Thelwall, Nov. 19, 1796).

p. 4, l. 35. **somewhat fat and pursy.** A confusion of two entirely unconnected phrases in *Hamlet*; first, the queen's exclamation in the duel scene (Act v, Sc. ii, l. 298), "He's fat, and scant of breath," and next, Hamlet's speech to his mother (Act III, Sc. iv, l. 153):

Forgive me this my virtue;
For in the fatness of these pursy times
Virtue itself of vice must pardon beg.

p. 5, l. 8. **Adam Smith.** Adam Smith (1723–1790), the author of *The Wealth of Nations.* From 1751 to 1763 he was professor of philosophy at Glasgow.   For an account of Adam Smith see Bagehot's essay *Adam Smith as a Person*.

p. 5, l. 29.   **no figures,** etc.   *Julius Caesar*, II, ii, 231:

> Enjoy the honey-heavy dew of slumber:
> Thou hast no figures nor no fantasies
> Which busy care draws in the brains of men.

p. 6, l. 27.   **Mary Wolstonecraft and Mackintosh.**   The attempts of the revolutionists to draw up a workable constitution for France were regarded in England with much sympathy by some and much contempt by others.   The first serious attack on the reformers came in 1790 from the famous political philosopher Edmund Burke (1729–1797) who, in his *Reflections on the Revolution in France,* ridiculed unsparingly the proposals of the constitutionalists, and appealed with eloquent and rhetorical fervour to prejudice and sentiment on behalf of the old order. Burke's pamphlet incurred the admiration of George III and the opposition of English liberals.   Several replies were written, among them being *The Rights of Man* by Tom Paine (for whom see note on p. 157), the *Vindiciae Gallicae* of Sir James Mackintosh, and the *Answer to Burke's Reflections on the French Revolution* by Mary Wollstonecraft. Mackintosh (1765–1832), a writer on philosophy, law and history, was also famous as an Indian judge.   See Macaulay's essay, and Hazlitt's sketch in *The Spirit of the Age.*   Mary Wollstonecraft (1759–1797) was a pioneer of the movement which has given to women many rights in society, law and education formerly denied them.   Her *Vindication of the Rights of Women* (1792) is a landmark of social progress.   She married William Godwin, famous in his day as a philosopher, but remembered now almost solely for his connection with such men as Wordsworth, Shelley and Lamb.   The daughter of Godwin and Mary Wollstonecraft became the second wife of Shelley.

p. 7, l. 4.   **a great opinion of Burke.**   Hazlitt had every reason for hating Burke the apostle of reaction, and accordingly he says many hard things of the great politician.   But on the other hand Hazlitt had the deepest admiration for Burke's rich power of mind and mastery of prose eloquence.   Scattered up and down the essays are many glowing tributes to Burke, the more sincere as coming from an avowed opponent.   See, for instance, "The Prose Style of Poets" (*Plain Speaker*), the "Character of Mr Burke" (*Political Essays*) and a reference on p. 69 of the present volume.

p. 7, l. 11.   **Tom Wedgwood.**   Thomas and Josiah Wedgwood were sons of the great potter, founder of the famous works at Etruria, and maker of the celebrated Wedgwood ware.   They were both greatly interested in Coleridge, and hearing that he proposed to accept the post of unitarian minister for a stipend of £150 a year, they offered him a present of £100 if he abandoned his intention and devoted himself to poetry and philosophy.   Coleridge refused on the ground that £100 would soon be consumed and he would be as badly off as before. Whereupon Josiah (not Tom) wrote a letter on behalf of himself and his brother offering Coleridge an annuity of £150 without any conditions. The annuity was regularly paid until 1812 when Josiah Wedgwood withdrew his half of the contribution.

p. 7, l. 28.   **Holcroft.**   Thomas Holcroft (1745–1809), a playwright and novelist of importance in his day, now remembered as author of the comedy *The Road to Ruin* and as the subject of a biography written partly by Hazlitt. See also the next note.

p. 7, l. 28. **He had been asked,** etc. This is rather tangled. "He" and "him" are Coleridge and Holcroft respectively, i.e. "He (Coleridge) had been asked if he was not much struck with him (Holcroft), and he (Coleridge) said he thought himself in more danger of being struck by him (Holcroft). I (Hazlitt) complained that he (Holcroft) would not let me get on," etc. Hazlitt had met Holcroft and the Godwins in London about 1798. Holcroft was something of a philosophical politician and was one of those people who were tried in 1794 for high treason under Pitt's measures against free speech and public discussion.

p. 8, l. 11. **the shores of old romance.** A phrase from Wordsworth's *Poems on the Naming of Places*—the fourth, that beginning "A narrow girdle of rough stones," etc.:

> Many such there are,
> Fair ferns and flowers, and chiefly that tall fern,
> So stately, of the Queen Osmunda named;
> Plant lovelier, in its own retired abode
> On Grasmere's beach, than Naiad by the side
> Of Grecian brook, or Lady of the Mere
> Sole-sitting by the shores of old romance.

p. 8, l. 14. **the Delectable Mountains.** See *The Pilgrim's Progress.*

p. 8, l. 24. **in Cassandra.** *Cassandra* is a romance by Gautier de Costes, Seigneur de La Calprenède, who was born in Gascony early in the seventeenth century and died in 1663. He wrote lengthy romances, the chief being *Cassandra* (10 volumes, 1642) and *Cleopatra* (10 volumes, 1647), and also tragedies, among them being *La Mort de Mithridate* (1637), *Jeanne, Reine d'Angleterre* (1637) and *Le Comte d'Essex*, the last of which was very successful. Few modern readers have any direct acquaintance with the works of La Calprenède; a reference in Boileau's *Art of Poetry* and others in the Letters of Mme de Sévigné usually satisfy most people's curiosity about this once popular writer. Hazlitt had doubtless read *Cassandra* in the translation of Sir George Cotterill, published in 1676 and several times reprinted. The exact allusion is as follows: "Never did Thunderbolt, falling at the foot of some young Shepherd, strike him with so strange a surprise as that did the Prince of Scythia, when he heard pronounced that hated, detested name of Perdiccas." Part 2, Book v.

p. 8, l. 32. **Sounding on his way.** What Chaucer said of the Clerk of Oxenford is quite different:

> Sownynge in moral vertu was his speche,
> And gladly wolde he lerne and gladly teche.

—"sownynge in" meaning "tending towards." There is no doubt that Hazlitt's memory confused these lines with another, and much later passage:

> By pain of heart—now checked—and now impelled—
> The intellectual power, through words and things,
> Went sounding on, a dim and perilous way!

(Wordsworth, *The Excursion*, Bk III, ll. 699–701.)

p. 9, l. 7. **Hume.** David Hume (1711–1776), the famous philosopher and historian. His chief works are the *Treatise on Human Nature* (1739), *Essays Moral and Political* (1741–42), *Inquiry into the Principles of Morals* (1751) and *Political Discourses* (1752).

p. 9, l. 8. **South's sermons.** Robert South (1633–1716), a Restoration divine, is remembered for the racy vigour of his published sermons. Specimens of South can be found in all the usual books containing prose quotations. There is no obvious resemblance between Hume's *Essay on Miracles* and any of South's sermons; but Coleridge was rather given to discovering such imagined and always far-fetched resemblances.

p. 9, l. 8. **Credat**, etc. Horace, *Satires*, I, v, 100:

> credat Judaeus Apella,
>
> Non ego.

"Let the Jew Apella believe it; I don't." The Jews were regarded by the Romans as very credulous, and ready to believe any improbable story. The saying is thus roughly equivalent to our "Tell that to the Marines." The name Apella stands for any Jew, and does not refer to a particular individual.

p. 9, l. 11. **choke-pears.** Literally a fruit difficult to swallow because of its rough, astringent nature, and so, metaphorically, anything hard to understand. Hume's *Treatise* is, in point of style at least, much less "hard to swallow" than Hazlitt would make out. It may be noted here that Hazlitt was in the habit of italicising any of his words or phrases that seemed to depart from standard literary English.

p. 9, l. 17. **Berkeley.** George Berkeley (1685–1753), the bishop of Cloyne, famous as a philosophical writer. His chief works are *An Essay towards a New Theory of Vision* (1709), *A Treatise concerning the Principles of Human Knowledge* (1710), *Alciphron* (1732), and *Siris* (1744). His chief doctrine is that matter is not independent of mind—that we can know only what the mind perceives, and that what the mind does not perceive has no existence for us. The "refutation" by Johnson is given in Boswell under date 1763: "After we came out of the church, we stood talking for some time together of Bishop Berkeley's ingenious sophistry to prove the non-existence of matter, and that everything in the universe is merely ideal. I observed, that though we are satisfied his doctrine is not true, it is impossible to refute it. I never shall forget the alacrity with which Johnson answered, striking his foot with mighty force against a large stone, till he rebounded from it, 'I refute it *thus*.'" Johnson's supposed "refutation" is quite inconclusive. The act of kicking the stone gave him a perception (or "idea," in Berkeley's language) of its solidity, and its solidity thus came into existence for him.

p. 9, l. 24. **Tom Paine.** Thomas Paine (1737–1809) was a writer on politics and religion. He went to America in 1774 and took the side of the rebellious colonies in his pamphlet *Common Sense*—one of the earliest publications to advocate complete separation of the colonies from England. He fought on the American side and held a post in the rebel government. He returned to England and published in 1791–92 his *Rights of Man*, an answer to Burke's *Reflections on the French*

Revolution. The book was prosecuted by the English government, and Paine escaped to France, where he was elected to the Convention and was imprisoned by Robespierre for advocating clemency to Louis XVI. After his release he went to America, where he died. His last important work was *The Age of Reason*, an attack on orthodox religion.

p. 9, l. 28. **Bishop Butler.** Joseph Butler (1692–1750), Bishop of Durham, is one of the greatest of English theologians. In 1718 he was appointed preacher at the Rolls chapel (on the site of which the Record office now stands) and delivered there the *Sermons* (published in 1726) to which Coleridge refers. Ten years later he published his most famous work, *The Analogy of Religion, Natural and Revealed, to the Constitution and Course of Nature.* The *Sermons* are indeed excellent; but it is difficult to follow Hazlitt's (and Coleridge's) very pronounced preference of them to *The Analogy*, as the latter is very largely an extension and development of the thought expounded in the *Sermons*—notably in the first three, "Upon Human Nature," and the fifteenth, "The Ignorance of Man."

p. 9, l. 38. **I had written a few remarks,** etc. A reference to Hazlitt's metaphysical essay published in 1805 as *An Essay on the Principles of Human Action: being an Argument in Favour of the Natural Disinterestedness of the Human Mind.* Hazlitt's "discovery" was that the doctrine of the innate and necessary selfishness of the human mind, which he supposed to have been taught by philosophers like Hobbes, was quite untrue. Hazlitt alleged that disinterestedness was innate and that self-interest arose later out of habit and convenience. The "discovery" is hardly valid, and in any case it is of no practical importance. To speak unphilosophically, the qualities that men may be born with are much less important, practically, than the qualities that they undoubtedly live by.

p. 10, l. 18. **the quaint Muse of Sir Philip Sidney.** No doubt Hazlitt had in mind Sonnet LXXXIV in *Astrophel and Stella*:

> Highway! since you my chief Parnassus be,
> And that my Muse, to some ears not unsweet,
> Tempers her words to trampling horses' feet
> More oft than to a chamber melody:
> Now, blessed you! bear onward blessed me
> To her, where I my heart safeliest shall meet.
> My Muse and I must you of duty greet
> With thanks and wishes, wishing thankfully.
> Be you still fair! honoured by public heed!
> By no encroachment wronged! nor time forgot!
> Nor blamed for blood, nor shamed for sinful deed!
> And that you know I envy you no lot
> Of highest wish, I wish you so much bliss:
> Hundreds of years you STELLA's feet may kiss!

p. 10, l. 25. **Paley.** William Paley (1743–1805), a theological writer. His chief works are, *Principles of Moral and Political Philosophy* (1785), *Horae Paulinae* (1790), *Evidences of Christianity* (1794) and *Natural Theology* (1802).

p. 10, l. 33. **Kind and affable**, etc. A reminiscence of Adam's thanks to the archangel Raphael, *Paradise Lost*, VIII, 646–650:

> Go, Heavenly Guest, Ethereal Messenger,
> Sent from whose sovran goodness I adore!
> Gentle to me and affable hath been
> Thy condescension and shall be honoured ever
> With grateful memory.

p. 11, l 3. **another story**. In chapter X of *Biographia Literaria*, Coleridge describes, with somewhat heavy-handed humour, how he went to sleep after being made ill by smoking; but his recorded remarks on awaking have nothing to do with the third or any other heaven: "Here and thus I lay, my face like a wall that is whitewashing, deathly pale, and with the cold drops of perspiration running down it from my forehead, while one after another there dropped in the different gentlemen who had been invited to meet and spend the evening with me, to the number of from fifteen to twenty. As the poison of tobacco acts but for a short time, I at length awoke from insensibility, and looked round on the party, my eyes dazzled by the candles which had been lighted in the interim. By way of relieving my embarrassment, one of the gentlemen began the conversation with, "Have you seen a paper to-day, Mr Coleridge?" "Sir," I replied, rubbing my eyes, "I am far from convinced that a Christian is permitted to read either newspapers or any other works of merely political and temporary interest." The humour of the situation lies in the fact that the purpose of Coleridge's visit was to further the sale of his own periodical or newspaper, *The Friend*.

p. 11, l. 10. **Vision of Judgment**. Southey's *Vision of Judgment* (1821) was a poem written in his capacity as Laureate, praising George III, who had died in the preceding year. It is introduced by an obsequious preface to George IV in which that monarch is credited with all the success of British arms during the late war. The poem is written in a sort of hexameter rhythm and has twelve short sections or cantos. It is a vision in which George III is seen at the gate of Heaven seeking admission. An angel summons all who wish to accuse him of misdeeds; but only two appear—Wilkes and Junius, and they are abashed to silence. Washington arrives and pleads for the king, who is thereupon admitted to Heaven, where he sees the glorious forms of other British monarchs surrounded by immortal spirits having the forms of Wolfe, Hogarth, Wesley, Mansfield, Burke and other famous persons. This painful absurdity of plan is relieved by no merit of execution, and the piece may be pronounced the worst of all Southey's attempts at the sublime. The other *Vision of Judgment* was Byron's, first published in *The Liberal*—the magazine in which Hazlitt's present essay appeared—and republished in book form by John Murray. "The Bridge Street Junto" was "The Constitutional Association" founded in 1821, "to support the laws for suppressing seditious publications, and for defending the country from the fatal influence of disloyalty and sedition." It was commonly known as "The Bridge Street Gang" ("junto" means "gang") from the situation of its office. As may be gathered from the statement of its aims, the Association was a thoroughly illiberal and repressive body. The point of Hazlitt's gibe about the connection of John Murray with the "gang" lies in the fact that Byron's poem, which Murray published, was not merely a savage satire on Southey's latter-day loyalty, but a violent attack on the deceased George III. Thus Murray the publisher had actually issued one of the "disloyal and seditious publications" which Murray the "Constitutionalist" was solemnly pledged to suppress.

p. 11, l. 20. **Llangollen.** See the essay "On Going a Journey" (p 146, l. 35) for the passage in which Hazlitt describes how he celebrated his birthday in this year.

p. 11, l. 22. **Coleridge's description of England.** *Ode on the Departing Year*, VII:

> Not yet enslaved, not wholly vile,
> O Albion! O my mother isle!
> Thy valleys, fair as Eden's bowers,
> Glitter green with sunny showers;
> Thy grassy uplands' gentle swells
> 　Echo to the bleat of flocks;
> (Those grassy hills, those glittering dells
> 　Proudly ramparted with rocks)
> And Ocean mid his uproar wild
> Speaks safety to his Island-child!

p. 11, l. 40. **Tom Jones.** The adventures of Tom Jones at the Upton inn occupy several chapters in books IX and X of Fielding's novel. In chapter V of book X Sophia Western, also at Upton, sends Tom Jones her muff, hallowed to him by many sentimental associations, to reproach him for his supposed infidelity to her.

p. 12, l. 2. **at Tewkesbury.** See the essay "On Going a Journey," where the reading of *Paul and Virginia* is placed at Bridgwater. *Paul and Virginia* is the romance by Bernardin de Saint-Pierre (1737–1814) whose Rousseau-like simplicity of sentiment was more popular in the eighteenth century than it is to-day.

p. 12, l. 13. **Wordsworth...Poems on the Naming of Places.** A set of five poems first published in vol. II of *Lyrical Ballads* (1800). The inscriptions in *Paul and Virginia* are certainly similar in idea, but the similarity implies no borrowing. Numbers of people have named familiar spots from personal and sentimental associations, as Wordsworth did, when he called one place "Emma's Dell," another " Joanna's Rock" and a third "Point Rash-Judgment."

p. 12, l. 26. **Camilla.** Frances Burney (1752–1840), daughter of Dr Johnson's friend the musician Dr Burney, wrote a very successful novel *Evelina* (published in 1778), and, nearly twenty years after, a much less successful story, *Camilla*. She held a court appointment, and her letters and diaries give valuable sketches of the period. She married a French refugee, general D'Arblay. See also the essay "On Going a Journey."

p. 12, l. 36. **Alfoxden.** In 1797 Wordsworth, who, although he had by then written some of his early pieces, was only at the threshold of his poetic career, moved from Racedown in Dorset to Alfoxden, about three miles from Nether Stowey, where Coleridge was living. This was the richest and probably the happiest period of Wordsworth's life. The two poets met often, and their many talks about the essentials of poetic art resulted in the appearance, not merely of a new volume,

Lyrical Ballads (1798), but also of a new and wonderful spirit in English poetry. See the latter part of Coleridge's *Biographia Literaria*, beginning at chapter XIV. Wordsworth did not have "free use" of Alfoxden. It was tenanted by one John Bartholomew, during the minority of the St Aubin heir, and sub-let to the poet for a rental of £23 per annum. No doubt the "friend of the poet" was Thomas Poole, a tanner and leather merchant of Nether Stowey, who proved a most valuable friend to both Wordsworth and Coleridge. Poole was not in possession of the house, but he probably facilitated the business connected with Wordsworth's tenancy.

p. 13, l. 2. **the scales that fence**. This is an allusion to a passage quoted by Hazlitt in the first of his *Lectures on the Dramatic Literature of the Age of Elizabeth*: "But in the Christian religion 'we perceive a softness coming over the heart of a nation, and the iron scales that fence and harden it, melt and drop off.'"

p. 13, l. 3. **his sister**. Dorothy, whose deep creative influence on her brother is gratefully acknowledged by Wordsworth, especially in the latter part of the wonderful *Tintern Abbey* lines.

p. 13, l. 6. **Sibylline Leaves**. The sibyl or prophetess Amalthea of Cumae offered to sell her nine books of wisdom to Tarquin the Proud, king of Rome. He refused, whereupon she burned three and, a year later, offered the rest at the same price. He still refused, and again she burned three and offered the remainder at the same price. The surviving three were then purchased and carefully guarded in the temple of Jupiter, where also were kept the Sibylline verses or various utterances of the prophetesses. Coleridge published a collection of his scattered poems under the title *Sibylline Leaves*. Hazlitt glances at this title in the present phrase, though what he actually meant was that he saw the manuscript of *Lyrical Ballads* in loose sheets.

p. 13, l. 13. **hear the loud stag speak**. Ben Jonson, *The Forest*. III ; To Sir Robert Wroth :

> Or, if thou list the night in watch to breake,
> A-bed canst heare the loud stag speake.

p. 13, l. 32. **Betty Foy**. This is Wordsworth's poem *The Idiot Boy*, which, with the other poems named, appeared in the *Lyrical Ballads* of 1798.

p. 13, l. 38. **In spite of pride**. Pope, *The Essay on Man*, I, 293 :

> And, spite of Pride, in erring Reason's spite,
> One truth is clear, WHATEVER IS, IS RIGHT.

p. 14, l. 4. **While yet the trembling year**, etc. Thomson, *The Seasons*, Spring, l. 18 :

> As yet the trembling year is unconfirmed,
> And Winter oft at eve resumes the breeze,
> Chills the pale morn, and bids his driving sleets
> Deform the day delightless.

p. 14, l. 7. **Of Providence**, etc. *Paradise Lost*, II, 559–560 :

> Others apart sat on a hill retired
> I thoughts more elevate, and reasoned high
> Of Providence, Foreknowledge, Will and Fate,
> Fixed fate, free will, foreknowledge absolute,
> And found no end, in wandering mazes lost.

p. 14, l. 29. **Peter Bell.** The potter, or pedlar of crockery-ware, "hero" (if he may be so called) of Wordsworth's poem bearing his name:

> He had a dark and sidelong walk,
> And long and slouching was his gait.

p. 14, l. 36. **Chantry's bust.** Sir Francis Chantrey (1781–1841), a poor boy who became a very distinguished sculptor. He left to the Royal Academy a very large sum of money, the interest on which was to be spent in purchasing native works of art. The purchases made under the Chantrey bequest are housed in the Tate gallery. Chantrey's bust of Wordsworth is at Coleorton, formerly the residence of Wordsworth's friend Sir George Beaumont.

p. 14, l. 37. **Haydon's head.** Benjamin Haydon (1786–1846), the painter of historical pictures. The ultimate failure of his work, financially, led him to commit suicide. His most certain claim on the interest of posterity is based on his friendship and correspondence with John Keats. The picture "Christ entering Jerusalem," in which Wordsworth's head appears, is now in the Roman Catholic cathedral at Cincinnati.

p. 15, l. 9. **Monk Lewis.** Matthew Gregory Lewis (1775–1818), called "Monk" from his romance, *Ambrosio, or the Monk*, was the writer of many now forgotten romances and plays. *The Castle Spectre* was "a dramatic romance" in five acts interspersed with occasional songs and choruses.

p. 15, l. 24. **his face**, etc. *Macbeth*, Act I, Sc. v, l. 63–64:

> Your face, my thane, is as a book where men
> May read strange matters.

p. 16, l. 8. **flip.** A drink compounded of sugar and hot cider, wine, spirits or beer. Sometimes an egg was added, making what was called "egg-flip" or "egg-hot." This compound is endeared to all good readers by the frequent references to it in Lamb's letters. For instance: "That sonnet, Coleridge, brings afresh to my mind the time when you wrote those on Bowles, Priestley, Burke;—'twas two Christmases ago, and in that nice little smoky room at the *Salutation*, which is even now continually presenting itself to my recollection with all its associated train of pipes, tobacco, egg-hot, welsh-rabbit, metaphysics and poetry.—Are we never to meet again?" "The Salutation and the Cat" was a hostelry in Newgate Street.

p. 16, l. 10. **John Chester.** Very little can be discovered of Chester beyond the facts that he was a very faithful and good-natured young man living at Nether Stowey, that he was fascinated by Coleridge's genius and that he accompanied Coleridge to Germany. Coleridge's references to him in the letters written from Germany are very brief and give no clue to the nature of their relations.

p. 16, l. 14. **followed**, etc. An inversion of *Othello*, Act II, Sc. iii, l. 379, etc.: "I do follow here in the chase, not like a hound that hunts, but one that fills up the cry." A "cry" is a "pack." The point is that Chester was assiduous in following Coleridge, and was not content to be merely one of the crowd around him.

p. 16, l. 26. **the Kantean philosophers.** Immanuel Kant (1724–1804), one of the greatest of modern philosophers, was first made known to English people by men like Coleridge and De Quincey. To be familiar with Kant in 1798 was to be very "advanced" in thought, and there is not wanting evidence that certain of his English disciples were inclined to parade their knowledge of him. Hence the faint sneer in Hazlitt's reference. The greatest work of Kant is the *Critique of Pure Reason* (1781). In this work he divides the fundamental concepts of the human understanding into twelve "categories" or orders—categories of quantity (unity, plurality, totality), categories of quality (reality, negation, limitation), categories of relation (substance, causality, reciprocity), categories of modality (possibility, actuality, necessity). Hence the allusion lower down to the "categories" of the Kanteans.

p. 16, l. 28. **Sir Walter Scott's, or Mr Blackwood's.** William Blackwood (1776–1834), the famous Edinburgh publisher. The reference is doubtless to the banquet given to George IV at Edinburgh in 1822.

p. 16, l. 35. **Gaspar Poussin's or Domenichino's.** For Gaspard Poussin see p. 219. Domenichino, or "little Dominic," is the popular name of Domenico Zampieri (1581–1641), a painter of the same order as the Carracci, for whom see p. 223. Domenichino, once overpraised, is now much less highly esteemed. He specialised in dramatic landscapes, and is represented in the National Gallery by four fair pictures.

p. 17, l. 12. **the Ancient Mariner.** An allusion to the lines:

> The western wave was all a-flame,
>   The day was well nigh done!
> Almost upon the western wave
>   Rested the broad bright Sun;
> When that strange shape drove suddenly
>   Betwixt us and the Sun.

> And strait the Sun was fleck'd with bars,
>   (Heaven's mother send us grace)
> As if thro' a dungeon grate he peer'd
>   With broad and burning face.

p. 17, l. 14. **the Valley of Rocks.** This now very familiar spot is impressive enough, but rather less awe-inspiring than Hazlitt's description would suggest.

p. 17, l. 27. **a prose-tale.** This is *The Wanderings of Cain*, of which a fragment exists, usually included in collections of Coleridge's verse. Such a passage as the following applies very exactly to the Valley of the Rocks: "The pointed and shattered summits of the ridges of the rocks made a rude mimicry of human concerns, and seemed to prophesy mutely of things that then were not; steeples, and battlements, and ships with naked masts." It is worth notice that the scenery of Wordsworth's *Peter Bell*, though supposed to represent the district of the Swale in Yorkshire, is really derived from Lynton, near and familiar to Wordsworth at the time when he was writing the poem.

p. 17, l. 28. **the Death of Abel.** A sort of prose poem, once popular, but now almost forgotten, written by Solomon Gessner (1730–88) a native of Zurich.

p. 18, l. 24. **Caleb Williams.** A novel written by William Godwin. It is a study of social injustice in the "age of chivalry" at the end of the eighteenth century.

p. 18, l. 28. **the ribbed sea-sands.** *Ancient Mariner*:

> And thou art long and lank and brown
> As is the ribbed sea-sand.

p. 18, l. 31. **A fisherman,** etc. This sentence as it stands is quite bad. The first "that" clause is adjectival, qualifying "boy," the second "that" clause is noun object ungoverned by any verb or preposition. The insertion of "said" between "and" and "that" in line 32 provides the necessary governing verb. Hazlitt did not reprint this essay himself in any volume, so we have only the magazine text as our authority.

p. 18 note. **Buffamalco.** Buonamico di Cristofano, called Buffalmacco (not Buffamalco) was a Florentine painter living between 1262 and 1351. Most of the works formerly attributed to this almost mythical artist are now assigned to other hands. Vasari and Boccaccio are the main sources of anecdotes about Buffalmacco, whose very existence has been questioned by modern criticism. It might be observed that Coleridge's ability to appreciate the moral conveyed by a picture implies no ability to appreciate the picture. Quite good morals may be conveyed by hopelessly bad works of art. As Lamb points out, the moral of *George Barnwell* is much more obvious than the moral of *Othello*.

p. 19, l. 11. **explained at length elsewhere.** In the *Essay on the Principles of Human Action*.

p. 19, l. 20. **for Germany.** Coleridge went to Germany in September 1798, and returned in July 1799.

p. 19, l. 29. **his tragedy.** Coleridge's *Remorse* was performed at Drury Lane in 1813 and ran for twenty nights,—quite a success in those days. The part of Don Alvar was taken by Robert William Elliston (1774–1831), the egregious and excessive actor immortalised by Lamb in the *Essays of Elia*.

p. 20, l. 9. **But there is matter,** etc. The last lines of Wordsworth's *Hart Leap Well*, Pt I:

> The Knight, Sir Walter, died in course of time,
> And his bones lie in his paternal vale.—
> But there is matter for a second rhyme,
> And I to this would add another tale.

ON THE CONVERSATION OF AUTHORS. I

Essay III in *The Plain Speaker*. First published in *The London Magazine*, September 1820.

p. 21, l. 15. **mum-chance.** "Mumchance" or "mumbudget" was a game in which strict silence had to be kept. "Mum's the word" is a very old phrase for silence, originating from the fact that "mum" is a rough representation of all we can say when the lips are closed.

p. 21, l. 19. **And of his port,** etc. Chaucer, *Prologue to the Canterbury Tales*, l. 69, part of the description of the knight:

> And though that he were worthy, he was wys,
> And of his port as meeke as is a mayde.

p. 21, l. 24. **he is one that cannot,** etc. From *The Return from Parnassus*, Act II, Sc. 6, part of the description of a scholar. This very interesting play (1606) was first publicly acted by "the Students in St John's College in Cambridge," and is remarkable for its criticisms of many contemporary or lately dead writers, such as Spenser, Daniel, Drayton, Marston, Marlowe and Shakespeare. It sketches the unhappiness of a poor scholar's life in terms that recall Dr Johnson's indictment:

> There mark what ills the scholar's life assail,
> Toil, envy, want, the patron, and the jail.

Hazlitt gives an account of *The Return from Parnassus* in the fifth of his *Lectures on the Dramatic Literature of the Age of Elizabeth*; but all discussions of it have been superseded by the passages devoted to it in *University Drama in Tudor Times* by Dr F. S. Boas. The author of the play has not been identified.

p. 21, l. 30. **He knows nothing,** etc. This same charge has been brought against the mere author in an essay *Shakespeare the Man* by Walter Bagehot, whose work, generally, shows many signs of Hazlitt's influence: "The reason why so few good books are written, is that so few people that can write know anything. In general an author has always lived in a room, has read books, has cultivated science, is acquainted with the style and sentiments of the best authors, but he is out of the way of employing his own eyes and ears. He has nothing to hear and nothing to see. His life is a vacuum....Now, what can any one think of such a life—except how clearly it shows that the habits best fitted for communicating information...are exactly the habits which are likely to afford a man the least information to communicate."

p. 22, l. 1. **Quidnunc.** A quidnunc is a busybody who makes it his business to hear all the gossip. The name comes from the Latin interrogative *quid*, what, *nunc*, now. An inveterate gossip named Quidnunc is the chief character in a farce *The Upholsterer, or What News?* by Arthur Murphy (1727–1805).

p. 22, l. 3. **Tull's Husbandry.** A book on practical farming (1733) by Jethro Tull. An introduction was written for a later edition by William Cobbett, "the philosopher of Botley." **William Cobbett** (1762–1835), son of a Hampshire farmer, led a varied life, first as a farmer's boy, then as a soldier, then as a political refugee in America, and nearly all the time as a bold and vigorous pamphleteer, denouncing fearlessly the social and political abuses of the day. Cobbett, ardent reformer as he was, belonged in spirit to an older time—to a "Merrie England" of friendly (and possibly quite imaginary) feudalism, when England produced its own necessaries, when there was plenty in moderation for all, when labour dwelt on its own land, cultivated its own fields, fed its own beasts on unenclosed commons, and knew nothing of industrial slavery in the factories of vast and sordid slum-cities. Cobbett fought very vigorously against the coming invasion of commercialism with all its attendant evils of competitive wages, factories, huge and unwholesome towns, stock-jobbing and paper-money. His "Tory democracy" resembles, as it doubtless suggested, much in the "Young England" visions of Disraeli as set forth in *Coningsby, Sybil* and *Tancred*. Cobbett's strong, homely, powerful English is excellent. His *Weekly Register* (1802–1835) was a highly popular organ of public opinion. His innumerable works include *Advice to Young Men*, a very readable *English Grammar*, a *History of the Reformation*, and *Rural Rides*, a most valuable account of agricultural England in the early years of the nineteenth century—when, indeed, agricultural England was passing away before the new England of commerce. Cobbett lived for many years at Botley in Hampshire, hence Hazlitt's reference to "the philosopher of Botley." For Hazlitt's view of Cobbett see *The Spirit of the Age*, or *Table-Talk*—the essay appears in both books.

p. 23, l. 1. **Montaigne's Essays.** Michel de Montaigne (1533–1592), a French nobleman, immortal as the author of essays that are delightful in themselves and important as being the original from which many other personal essays have descended. A translation of Montaigne into English by John Florio was known to and used by Shakespeare.

p. 23, l. 2. **Dilworth's Spelling Book.** A well-known eighteenth century primer.

p. 23, l. 2. **Fearne's Treatise.** A law-book (1772) that was for a long while an authority on its subject.

p. 23, l. 20. **etherial mould, sky-tinctured.** A reminiscence of two passages in *Paradise Lost*:

> our great Enemy
> All incorruptible, would on his throne
> Sit unpolluted, and the ethereal mould,
> Incapable of stain, would soon expel
> Her mischief. (II, 139.)

> Six wings he wore, to shade
> His lineaments divine: the pair that clad
> Each shoulder broad came mantling o'er his breast
> With regal ornament; the middle pair
> Girt like a starry zone his waist, and round
> Skirted his loins and thighs with downy gold
> And colours dipt in Heaven; the third his feet
> Shadowed from either heel with feathered mail,
> Sky-tinctured grain. (V, 285.)

p. 23, l. 29. **breathe in other air.** *Paradise Lost*, XI, 284–285:

> How shall we breathe in other air
> Less pure, accustomed to immortal fruits?

p. 23, l. 32. **confined and cabin'd in.** *Macbeth*, Act III, Sc. iv, l. 24:

> But now I am cabined, cribbed, confined, bound in
> To saucy doubts and fears.

p. 24, l. 2. **to cozen fortune.** *Merchant of Venice*, Act II, Sc. ix, 37–39:

> for who shall go about
> To cozen fortune and be honourable
> Without the stamp of merit?

p. 24, l. 3. **because we are scholars,** etc. *Twelfth Night*, Act II, Sc. iii, 123, etc.: "Art any more than a steward? Dost thou think, because thou art virtuous, there shall be no more cakes and ale?"

p. 24, l. 28. **where I write this.** Winterslow Hut, Salisbury Plain.

p. 24, l. 35. **The wretched slave.** *Henry V*, Act IV, Sc. i, ll. 285–294. Hazlitt has abbreviated the passage:

> The wretched slave
> Who, with a body filled and vacant mind,
> Gets him to rest, crammed with distressful bread,
> Never sees horrid Night, the child of Hell,
> But, like a lackey, from the rise to set,
> Sweats, etc.

Hyperion the Titan was the predecessor of Phoebus in driving the horses that drew the sun on its daily journey.

p. 25, l. 1. **Ephemerides.** Plural of "ephemeris," a diary, and so an account of one's own life. Possibly Hazlitt is casting a hint at Coleridge's *Biographia Literaria*.

p. 25, l. 15. **Congreve.** William Congreve (1670–1729), author of *The Way of the World, Love for Love, The Double Dealer,* etc. The first named is one of the most brilliant of English prose comedies. Congreve's verse tragedy *The Mourning Bride* gives us, in its first line, the familiar quotation:

> Music has charms to soothe the savage breast.

p. 25, l. 19. **Machiavel.** Niccolò Machiavelli (1469–1527), the Florentine historian, statesman and political philosopher, author of *The Prince*, a treatise on government, long supposed (rather stupidly) to represent the limit of devilish cunning in its teaching.

p. 25, l. 21. **the New Eloise.** The famous novel by Jean-Jacques Rousseau (1712–1778). Rousseau, who was born in Geneva, led a varied and harassed life. His writings—chief among them *The Social Contract, Émile, La Nouvelle Héloïse* and the *Confessions*—represent a revolt from the artificialities of civilisation in the direction of a simple, natural scheme of life and social relations. Their influence was very great; in fact, Rousseau was one of the great educators of the generation that succeeded him, and the doctrines of liberty, equality, fraternity and the rights of man, dominant in the Revolution, were derived mainly from his teaching. The effect of Rousseau upon the life and thought of the time was somewhat similar to that of Tolstoy upon the present; but the two men were quite dissimilar in personal character.

p. 26, l. 1. **the Viscount of St Albans.** Francis Bacon (1561–1626), the great lawyer, philosopher and essay writer.

p. 26, l. 8. **stocks and stones.** *Julius Caesar*, Act I, Sc. i, l. 40:

> You blocks, you stones, you worse than senseless things!
> Oh you hard hearts, you cruel men of Rome!

Probably the "stocks" came from Milton's sonnet *On the Late Massacre in Piedmont*:

> Avenge, O Lord, thy slaughtered saints, whose bones
> Lie scattered on the Alpine mountains cold;
> Even them who kept thy truth so pure of old,
> When all our fathers worshipped stocks and stones.

p. 26, l. 10. **a person of this class.** Godwin.

p. 26, l. 11. **a celebrated authoress.** It has been suggested that this refers to Fanny Burney, for whom see p. 160. Hazlitt had met captain James Burney, brother of the novelist, at the Lambs', and his daughter was, of course, Fanny Burney's niece.

p. 26, l. 36. **Whose is the superscription?** St Matthew's Gospel, xxii, 20.

p. 26, l. 39. **G——.** Godwin, as elsewhere in this and the following essay.

p. 26, l. 40. **C——.** Coleridge. In the preceding essay Hazlitt has remarked upon Coleridge's tendency to prefer the unknown to the known.

p. 27, l. 11. **Prometheus.** Prometheus the Titan brought fire from heaven to mankind and first taught the human race the arts and sciences. The angry immortals, fearing that man would become as the gods, knowing good and evil, punished Prometheus by chaining him to a rock in the Caucasus where an eagle preyed upon his vitals. *Prometheus Bound* is a drama by the Greek poet Aeschylus, *Prometheus Unbound* a drama by the English poet Shelley.

p. 27, l. 27. **virtù.** An Italian word meaning taste in the fine arts, much used in England about Hazlitt's time and earlier, but now far less frequently heard than its derivative "virtuoso," meaning one possessed of talent in the arts, especially great executive skill in music. This last limitation of its meaning seems now becoming definite.

p. 27, l. 39. **flat, insipid,** etc. A reminiscence of *Hamlet*, Act I, Sc. ii, 133 etc.:

> Oh God! God!
> How weary, stale, flat and unprofitable
> Seem to me all the uses of this world.

p. 28, l. 36. **subjects of fancy.** Prize-fighting.

p. 29, l. 2. **double entendre.** The usual version in England of *double entente*—double meaning.

p. 29, note. **The French...are a more sensible,** etc. Such an assertion, which would pass nowadays almost unchallenged, required considerable courage to maintain in Hazlitt's day, when France was the hereditary enemy.

p. 30, l. 7. **The fear of being silent**, etc. A reminiscence of Cowper, *Conversation*, 352:

> Our sensibilities are so acute,
> The fear of being silent makes us mute.

p. 30, l. 39. **a remark of Rousseau's**. That the proper study of mankind is not only man, but all the other facts of nature, and that a merely bookish knowledge is useless, and even dangerous, may be called the general theme of Rousseau's *Émile, or Education*, a treatise which, published in 1762, anticipates almost every recent development of educational theory.

p. 31, l. 15. **Grimm's Memoirs**. Friedrich Melchior Grimm (1723–1807) was a German who made himself prominent by attaching himself to various French notabilities, thus getting into the main current of French life and literature. He was for a short time friendly with Rousseau, and for much longer with Diderot, to whom he addressed a voluminous literary and philosophical correspondence. He became secretary to the duke of Orleans and, until the Revolution, was a minister at the French court. An English version of his *Memoirs* published in 1814 is noticed by Hazlitt in his *Round Table* essay *On the literary Character*, a paper that, in its general subject, should be compared with the present essay. Grimm's references to Rousseau are quite untrustworthy.

p, 31 l. 28. **We had good talk**. See Boswell, under date 1768: "When I called upon Dr Johnson next morning, I found him highly satisfied with his colloquial prowess the preceding evening. 'Well (said he) we had good talk.' *Boswell* 'Yes, Sir; you tossed and gored several persons.'"

p. 31, l. 39. **Gil Blas**. The celebrated novel by Le Sage (1668–1747). There is no one set dispute in *Gil Blas*. In the first chapter young Gil is described as so fond of disputes that he stopped passers-by to argue with them. These discussions ended in grimaces, violent gestures, furious eyes and foaming mouths, till the disputants looked more like maniacs than philosophers. Another dispute, briefly described, is that of the wits and authors, friends of Nunnez. This ends in fisticuffs, the apostles of culture having to be violently parted by Gil Blas, Nunnez, Scipio and the lackeys. A third dispute is again that among critics and authors, friends of Nunnez, who are found discussing which is the chief character in the *Iphigenia* of Euripides. The bachelor Melchior de Villegas maintains that the chief character is the wind. He is violently opposed, but after mutual revilings, the disputants settle down to eating and drinking amicably together.

p. 31, l. 40. **a very ingenious man**. Sir John Stoddart, brother of Sarah Stoddart to whom Hazlitt was married. He was editor of *The New Times* for some years, and was very strong on the necessity for destroying Napoleon and restoring the Bourbons.

p. 32, l. 6. **the chapter in Sterne**. See *A Sentimental Journey*, second of the chapters entitled, "The Passport, Versailles."

p. 33, l. 13. **villainous, and shews**, etc. *Hamlet*, Act III, Sc. ii, l. 48: "And let those that play your clowns speak no more than is set down for them; for there be of them that will themselves laugh, to set on some quantity of barren spectators to laugh too; though, in the mean time, some necessary question of the play be then to be considered: that's villainous, and shows a most pitiful ambition in the fool that uses it.''

p. 33, l. 17. **When Greek meets Greek**, etc. The usual mis-quotation of a line from the play *The Rival Queens, or Alexander the Great*, by Nathaniel Lee (1653–1692). It occurs in Act IV, sc. ii:

> Your father, Philip. I have seen him march,
> And fought beneath his dreadful banner, where
> The boldest at this table would have trembled.
> Nay, frown not, sir, you cannot look me dead.
> When Greeks joined Greeks, then was the tug of war,
> The laboured battle sweat, and conquest bled.

p. 34, l. 3. **the pearls in the adage.** In the ''text,'' Hazlitt should have said, for the reference is to St Matthew, vii, 6. No doubt Hazlitt had in his mind Lady Macbeth's ''cat i' the adage.''

p. 34, l. 8. **of adepts, of illuminati.** These words were specially applied to the initiated members of secret masonic societies that flourished on the continent during the eighteenth century.

ON THE CONVERSATION OF AUTHORS. II

Essay IV in *The Plain Speaker*.

p. 35, l. 1. **L——'s.** Lamb's.

p. 35, l. 3. **the Small-coal man's musical parties.** Thomas Britton (1654–1714) was a Northampton man who came up to London as a boy and learned the coal-trade. He afterwards set up for himself in a stable which he divided into two storeys, the lower being devoted to the sale of coal, and the upper to loftier purposes, for here he established in 1678 a sort of musical club or assembly, and for thirty-six years there were held, every Thursday, concerts of chamber music, both vocal and instrumental, attended by a mixed audience ranging from genuine musical amateurs to fashionable people who came out of curiosity. The greatest performers of the day could be heard in Britton's upper room, no less a person than Handel, for instance, appearing there as an organist. Britton was also a notable book-collector, and in his coal-seller's dress joined such noble lords as Harley, Sunderland, Pembroke and Devonshire in book-hunting expeditions. His death was as remarkable as his life; for a ventriloquist, by way of a practical joke, having announced in a mysterious voice that he would shortly die, Britton received such a shock that he actually died a few days afterwards.

p. 35, l. 4. **John Buncle.** Thomas Amory (1691–1788), ''the English Rabelais,'' was a very eccentric author, who produced various compilations, now forgotten, but wrote, as well, the *Life of John Buncle*, a kind of novel, part fact, part fancy, a curious blend of autobiography, theology and rhapsodical descriptions of impossible places. The wild scenes may be called without exaggeration the landscapes of a madman, and there is no doubt that Amory was not quite sane. One form of his eccentricity was a refusal to go out by day. He emerged at night-time and crept shyly and silently about the streets. For an enthusiastic account of *John Buncle* see Hazlitt's essay on that subject in *The Round Table.*

p. 35, l. 18. **And, in our flowing cups,** etc. An adaptation of *Henry V*, Act IV, Sc. iii, ll. 51–55:

> then shall our names,
> Familiar in his mouth as household words,
> Harry the King, Bedford and Exeter,
> Warwick and Talbot, Salisbury and Gloucester,
> Be in their flowing cups freshly remembered.

p. 35, l. 21. **the old everlasting set.** Most of the allusions here need no annotation. Others will be found explained elsewhere. **John Gay** (1685–1732), a prolific author and wit, is now remembered mainly by his *Fables*, by such songs as *Black-eyed Susan*, and by *The Beggar's Opera*, a comedy interspersed with popular songs—the greatest theatrical success of its day. **William Hogarth** (1697–1764), the most English of painters, is well represented in the national collections, "Marriage à la Mode" being at the National Gallery, "The Election", and "The Rake's Progress" at the Soane Museum. His pictures were all engraved and published, hence the reference to prints. Lamb has an excellent essay on Hogarth. **Claude's landscapes.** Claude Gelée (1600–1682), often called Claude Lorrain from his birthplace, was a famous landscape painter. He spent much of his time in Italy, and was tireless in drawing and sketching from nature. The effect of this direct study can be seen in his painted pictures, which show a distinct leaning towards the modern, natural type of landscape. The National Gallery has several good Claudes. **The Cartoons.** The famous Raphael (1483–1520) drew, as designs for tapestry to be hung in the Sistine chapel at Rome, ten very large cartoons upon subjects from *The Acts of the Apostles*. Three of these are lost, but the other seven exist and are now at South Kensington. In Hazlitt's time they were at Hampton Court.

p. 35, l. 25. **The Scotch Novels.** The novels of Sir Walter Scott, published anonymously. The authorship of these novels was not publicly acknowledged by Sir Walter until 1827, though for some time he had been generally accepted as the writer.

p. 35, l. 27. **The author of the Rambler.** Dr Johnson. *The Rambler* was a periodical issue of little essays on the model of *The Spectator*. It ran from 1749 to 1752. In the *Rambler* essays Johnson's style reaches its limit of ponderosity: hence the preference in the text for his spoken words as recorded in Boswell's ever delightful *Life*.

p. 35, l. 30. **Junius.** From 1769 to 1772 a series of letters signed "Junius" appeared in *The Public Advertiser* attacking with polished ease and deadly skill the personal rule of George III and its political instruments. These letters, with their command of facts, their outspoken directness, and their calm and merciless style, were an altogether new thing in English political literature, and their fame has therefore endured to our time. The identity of "Junius" has never been conclusively established.

p. 36, l. 2. **a list of persons famous in history.** See in the present volume the essay *Of Persons one would wish to have seen.*

p. 36, l. 3. **Sir Thomas Browne.** Sir Thomas Browne (1605–1682), the Norwich physician, author of *Religio Medici*, *Hydriotaphia (or Urn Burial)*, *The Garden of Cyrus* and other works, has written the richest, most solemn and organ-like prose in our language.

p. 36, l. 4. **Dr Faustus**. The mythical person whose bargain with the devil forms the subject of several medieval legends, and of two famous dramas, the *Dr Faustus* of Marlowe and the *Faust* of Goethe.

p. 36, l. 6. **Donne**. John Donne (1573–1631), dean of St Paul's and English poet. He is the subject of a delightful little biography by Izaak Walton.

p. 36, l. 6. **Sir Philip Sidney**. Sir Philip Sidney (1554–1586), the famous Elizabethan courtier, scholar, poet and soldier, whose relinquishing of a glass of water, when he was wounded, to the greater necessity of a dying soldier, is an imperishable legend. He wrote a romance *Arcadia* which is very little read, an *Apology for Poetry* and a sonnet sequence *Astrophel and Stella*. One of these sonnets is quoted on page 158.

p. 36, l. 11. **the sumptuous banquet**. The feast with which Satan tempted Jesus after the forty days' fast in the wilderness. *Paradise Regained*, II, 338–361:

> Our Saviour, lifting up his eyes, beheld,
> In ample space under the broadest shade,
> A table richly spread in regal mode,
> With dishes piled and meats of noblest sort
> And savour—beasts of chase, or fowl of game,
> In pastry built, or from the spit, or boiled,
> Grisamber-steamed; all fish, from sea or shore,
> Freshet or purling brook, of shell or fin,
> And exquisitest name, for which was drained
> Pontus, and Lucrine bay, and Afric coast.
> Alas! how simple, to these cates compared,
> Was that crude apple that diverted Eve!
> And at a stately sideboard, by the wine,
> That fragrant smell diffused, in order stood
> Tall stripling youths rich-clad, of fairer hue
> Than Ganymed or Hylas; distant more,
> Under trees now tripped, now solemn stood,
> Nymphs of Diana's train, and Naiades
> With fruits and flowers from Amalthea's horn,
> And ladies of the Hesperides, that seemed
> Fairer than feigned of old, or fabled since
> Of faery damsels met in forest wide
> By knights of Logres, or of Lyones,
> Lancelot, or Pelleas, or Pellenore.

p. 36, l. 24. **piquet**. A once popular card game.

p. 36, l. 27. **Irish blackguard**. This and Scotch rappee were varieties of snuff.

p. 36, l. 31. **no mean person**. It will be remembered that, in Lamb's immortal essay, Mrs Battle would lose a game rather than soil her lips with the ungenteel phrases demanded in the game of cribbage.

p. 36, l. 31. **Ned P——**. Edward Phillips, who cannot be better described than in the words of one of Lamb's letters to Coleridge: "One piece of news I know will give you pleasure—Rickman is made Clerk to the House of Commons, £2000 a year with greater expectations

—but that is not the news—it is that poor card-playing Phillips, that has felt himself for so many years the outcast of Fortune,...has strangely stepped into Rickman's Secretaryship—sword, bag, house and all—from a hopeless £100 a year eaten up beforehand with desperate debts, to a clear £400 or £500—it almost reconciles me to the belief of a moral government of the world—the man stares and gapes and seems to be always wondering at what has befallen him—he tries to be eager at Cribbage, but alas! the source of that Interest is dried up for ever, he no longer plays for his next day's meal, or to determine whether he shall have a half dinner or a whole dinner, whether he shall buy a pair of black silk stockings, or wax his old ones a week or two longer, the poor man's relish of a Trump, the Four Honours is gone—and I do not know whether, if we could get at the bottom of things, poor star-doomed Phillips with his hair staring with despair was not a happier being than the sleek well-combed oily-pated Secretary that has succeeded."

p. 36, l. 36. **Baron Munchausen.** Everyone is familiar with the staggering unveracity of Baron Münchhausen's recorded deeds. There was a real Baron von Münchhausen (1720–1797) who fought with the Russians against the Turks. A grotesque history of the Baron's prowess was written by a certain Rudolf Raspe a clever but rascally author, whose dishonesty suggested the character of the swindling German Dousterswivel in Scott's delightful novel *The Antiquary.*

p. 36, l. 37. **Captain——.** Captain James Burney, son of Johnson's old friend Dr Burney, and brother of Madame D'Arblay. He was a distinguished sailor who had served under Captain Cook.

p. 36, l. 38. **Jem White.** James White (1775–1820) was a schoolfellow of Lamb at Christ's Hospital, and is immortalised in Lamb's essay *The Praise of Chimney-Sweepers.* He wrote, possibly with the help of Lamb, a volume of what were alleged to be *Original Letters, etc., of Sir John Falstaff and His Friends, now first made public by a Gentleman, a Descendant of Dame Quickly* (1796). The best available account of this odd volume is Lamb's review of it reprinted in Vol. I of Lucas's edition of Lamb.

p. 36, l. 40. **turning like the latter end,** etc. A quotation from *Falstaff's Letters* referred to above. It is from a letter supposed to be written to Justice Shallow by his servant Davy (for whom see *King Henry IV, Part II*): "Master Abram is dead, gone, your Worship, dead! Master Abram! Oh! good your Worship a's gone. A' never throve, since a' came from Windsor—'twas his death. I called him rebel, your Worship—but a' was all subject—a' was subject to any babe, as much as a King—a' turned, like as it were the latter end of a lover's lute—a' was all peace and resignment—a' took delight in nothing but his Book of Songs and Sonnets—a' would go to the Stroud side under the large beech tree, and sing, till 'twas quite pity of our lives to mark him, etc."

p. 37, l. 1. **A——.** William Ayrton (1777–1858), a musical friend of Lamb, director of the King's theatre in the Haymarket, where *Don Giovanni* had been produced in 1817. An amusing rimed epistle of Lamb to Ayrton asking for orders to see *Don Giovanni* is included in Lamb's letters.

p. 37, l. 2.　**the Will Honeycomb.**　Will Honeycomb is a character described in the "Sir Roger de Coverley" essays of Steele and Addison. The set description of Will Honeycomb appears in Steele's essay called *The Spectator Club*: "But that our society may not appear a set of humorists, unacquainted with the gallantries and pleasures of the age, we have amongst us the gallant Will Honeycomb, a gentleman who, according to his years, should be in the decline of his life, but having been very careful of his person, and always had a very easy fortune, time has made but very little impression, either by wrinkles on his forehead, or traces on his brain.　His person is well-turned, and of a good height.　He is very ready at that sort of discourse with which men usually entertain women.　He has all his life dressed very well, and remembers habits as others do men.　He can smile when one speaks to him, and laughs easily.　He knows the history of every mode....In a word, all his conversation and knowledge has been in the female world."

p. 37, l. 2.　**Mrs R——.**　Mrs Reynolds, who had been Lamb's schoolmistress in his earliest days, and to whom in later life he paid, with characteristic generosity, an annuity of £30 or £32.

p. 37, l. 7.　**P——.**　Edward Phillips, for whom see note on p. 3 6, l. 31.

p. 37, l. 8.　**M.B.**　Martin Burney, one of Lamb's most attached friends, frequently mentioned in the letters.　He was a son of Captain James Burney.

p. 37, l. 12.　**the author of "The Road to Ruin."**　Holcroft, for whom see p. 156.

p. 37, l. 35.　**the Biographia Literaria.**　Coleridge's desultory and unfinished autobiography, published in 1817.

p. 37, l. 37.　**An event.**　It is not immediately clear what Hazlitt means by this.　Obviously something more is implied than a mere personal difference between him and Lamb, such as happened in 1814. The last paragraph of the essay called *Of Persons One Would Wish to Have Seen* (p. 59 of this volume) intimates that Hazlitt is referring to the downfall of Napoleon as the event that destroyed the friendly intercourse he has been describing.　Hazlitt's intense sympathy with Napoleon is dealt with in the introduction and needs no further discussion here.　The only difficulty in this explanation is one of chronology.　Hazlitt is describing assemblies that took place in Mitre Court Buildings where Lamb lived from 1801 to 1809.　Obviously the downfall of Napoleon in 1814–1815 could hardly break up a party that had already broken up in 1809.　Hazlitt, however, is notoriously bad in matters of chronology, and it is plain that, writing several years later, he simply forgot how much time separated Mitre Court from Elba and Waterloo.　See, too, the Advertisement to *The Round Table*, describing his association with Leigh Hunt, and their proposed joint contribution of essays to *The Examiner*: "Our plan had been no sooner arranged and entered upon, than Buonaparte landed at Fréjus, *et voilà la Table Ronde dessoûte*.　Our little congress was broken up as well as the great one."

p. 37, l. 40.　**Like angels' visits,** etc.　A blend of two quotations. The ultimate origin is *The Grave* by Robert Blair (1699–1746), a poem the best parts of which are those that do not immediately recall *Hamlet* and Gray's *Elegy*. *The Grave* is further commended to people of taste by the fact that Blake illustrated it with some striking designs. Thus writes Blair:

> the good he scorned
> Stalked off reluctant, like an ill-used ghost,
> Not to return; or, if it did, its visits,
> Like those of angels, short, and far between.

Thomas Campbell (1777–1844), author of *Ye Mariners of England, The Battle of the Baltic* and *Hohenlinden,* consciously or unconsciously borrowed Blair's simile for a passage in *The Pleasures of Hope:*

> What though my winged hours of bliss have been
> Like angel-visits, few and far between?

Hazlitt pointed out the similarity, and added that, in altering Blair's line, Campbell had spoiled it, as "few" and "far between" are the same thing, whereas "short" and "far between" are not.

p. 38, l. 7. **Mr Douce.** Francis Douce (1757–1834) was a very eccentric antiquary who was, for a short time, Keeper of Manuscripts at the British Museum. He is best remembered by his *Illustrations of Shakespeare* (2 vols.), a valuable work. He affected a singularity of manner and costume, and seems to have been a "difficult" man to all but a few bibliomaniacs like himself.

p. 38, l. 9. **L. H.** Leigh Hunt (1784–1859), the essayist and miscellaneous writer, friend of Lamb, Keats, Shelley and Byron, had a gay, light-hearted, companionable disposition; but it is necessary to remind ourselves that he also had courage enough to hold political opinions unpalatable to a corrupt court and to endure two years' imprisonment for asserting them. His father was a Barbadian, hence the allusion to tropical blood. Hazlitt's criticism is very sound. Leigh Hunt's work can scarcely be said to survive. It lacks character and personality. Hunt is described at full length in *The Spirit of the Age.*

p. 38, l. 18. **aliquando sufflaminandus erat.** "He sometimes needed to be checked." Hazlitt no doubt got this phrase from Ben Jonson's *Timber, or Discoveries made upon Men and Matters as they have flowed out of his Daily Readings or had their Reflux to his Peculiar Notions of the Times*—a collection of prose miscellanies, ranging from mere sentences to essays, first published posthumously in 1641. The phrase occurs in the section called *De Shakespeare nostrati,* where Ben, in terms now familiar, speaks of Shakespeare's never having blotted a line. "He was indeed, honest, and of an open and free nature, had an excellent fancy, brave notions, and gentle expressions, wherein he flowed with that facility that sometime it was necessary he should be stopped. *Sufflaminandus erat,* as Augustus said of Haterius." This last allusion is to an anecdote related in Seneca's *Excerpta Controversiarum,* Bk IV, Proem, par. 7.

p. 39, l. 4. **slubber over.** A Shakespearean reminiscence. See *The Merchant of Venice,* Act II, Sc. viii, l. 39:

> Slubber not business for my sake, Bassanio,
> But stay the very riping of the time.

"To slubber" means "to slur over." Shakespeare uses it in the sense of doing something carelessly, Hazlitt rather in the sense of concealing or disguising.

p. 39, l. 8. **the Indicator.** A periodical edited by Leigh Hunt from 1819 to 1821. His editorship ceased a little before the paper came to an end. Of the title Hunt himself says: "It is to be called the *Indicator*, after a bird of that name, who shows people where to find honey."

p. 39, l. 19. **Mr Northcote, the painter.** James Northcote (1746–1831), a painter of some note in his day, was a pupil of Sir Joshua, and produced portraits and historical pictures; but he is remembered now almost solely for *The Conversations of John Northcote, Esq. R.A.* published by Hazlitt in 1826 and 1827, six years after the date of the present essay.

p. 39, l. 29. **His face is as a book.** *Macbeth*, Act I, Sc. v, l. 63:
> Your face, my thane, is as a book where men
> May read strange matters.

p. 40, l. 2. **the Catalogue Raisonné.** The *Catalogue Raisonné*, of pictures exhibited at the British Institution, was vigorously criticised by Hazlitt in three essays, two of which are included in *The Round Table*. A *catalogue raisonné* is a list compiled on systematic principles.

p. 40, l. 11. **I never ate or drank with Mr Northcote.** Few people did. Northcote was very miserly and not given to hospitality that cost money.

p. 40, l. 16. **he cannot write himself.** He was, nevertheless, the author of certain fables and criticisms, together with lives of Reynolds and Titian.

p. 40, l. 36. **Montesquieu.** A French nobleman (1689–1755) who criticised adversely the political conditions of his time, and in his most famous work, *De l'Esprit des Lois*, discussed a free constitution on the English model. Montesquieu's work was one of the undercurrents in the flood of the Revolution. Hazlitt is rather hard on Montesquieu, who long suffered from defective sight and died totally blind. That dictation is not incompatible with supreme literary art is triumphantly proved by the case of Milton.

p. 40, l. 39. **Horne Tooke.** John Horne (1736–1812), who took his more familiar name from that of a rich benefactor, Mr Tooke of Purley, was a very prominent figure on the liberal side of English politics in the years of the French Revolution, when freedom of thought and speech were persecuted as offences. He suffered considerably for his opinions. His once famous work, *The Diversions of Purley*, a curious blend of grammar, literary criticism and politics, is now forgotten by most people. Hazlitt gives a very interesting sketch of Horne Tooke in *The Spirit of the Age* and a long account of *The Diversions of Purley* in a lecture published among his fugitive writings (*Works*, Vol. XI).

p. 41, l. 3. **no one could relish a good style.** etc. There is something in this assertion, as Hazlitt himself admits lower down. Charles Lamb is emphatic on the point: "Anything high may, nay, must, be read out; you read it to yourself with an imaginary auditor." (Letter to Wordsworth, 22 Jan. 1830.) The French novelist Flaubert, who aimed at perfection in his prose, attached special importance to an oral test of his work: "He had an excellent method which can be recommended to every writer; he read aloud what he had written, carefully listening for any break in the rhythm, any dull sounds, or any beating of the words against each other.   Maupassant tells us that he took up his sheet of paper and raised it to his line of sight, then, leaning on his elbow, declaimed it in a slow incisive voice...conscientiously placing his commas like halts on a long road....He himself said: 'A phrase can only live when it corresponds to all the necessities of respiration. I know it to be good when it can be read aloud easily.'" (*Flaubert*, by Emile Faguet.)

p. 41, l. 7. **hear a sound so fine.** From Act v, Sc. ii, of the tragedy *Virginius* by James Sheridan Knowles (1784–1862):

> Is it a voice, or nothing, answers me?
> I hear a sound so fine, there's nothing lives
> Twixt it and silence.

p. 41, l. 17. **classical centos.** A cento is a sort of patchwork composition made by stringing together words and phrases borrowed from the works of different writers. An unoriginal person who tries to produce an elaborate composition usually manages to bring forth nothing but scraps from his remembered reading. A cento purposely made up may be very amusing. "Hamlet's Soliloquy" as rendered by the rascally barn-stormer in *Huckleberry Finn* is a delightful cento of Shakespearean quotations joined together with ludicrous inappropriateness.

p. 41, l. 35. **a learned professor.** Dr Samuel Parr (1747–1825), once famous as a Greek scholar, schoolmaster, and imitator of Dr Johnson's mighty conversational manner. De Quincey has a long essay on Parr.

p. 41, l. 39. **Fuseli's fantastic hieroglyphics.** Johann Heinrich Fuessli (1742–1825) was a Swiss of very eccentric habits who settled in London and became famous as a painter in the style of exaggerated sublimity then fashionable. He Italianised his name into the form now familiar. Many of his works were painted in illustration of Shakespeare and Milton, but, as in the case of Blake, with whom he has some affinity, his conceptions were beyond the power of his technique to express. His "fantastic hieroglyphics" may mean his illegible handwriting—a fault strangely common among famous artists; but possibly Hazlitt is using the word metaphorically for Fuseli's quaint forms of speech and his bad pronunciation. The excellent character of him given in the essay *On the Old Age of Artists* (*The Plain Speaker*) seems to indicate this. Fuseli was ambidextrous and could write as well (or ill) with one hand as with the other. "Hieroglyphics" were, strictly speaking, the sacred picture-writing of the ancient Egyptians, and so, writing that could be deciphered only by the learned and initiated. The word, by degradation, has now come to mean any oddly illegible handwriting.

p. 41, l. 40. **Curran.** John Philpot Curran (1750-1817), the famous Irish lawyer and political orator. Curran, though a Protestant, was a strong opponent of the Catholic disabilities, and, after the rebellion of 1798, defended most eloquently the leaders who were tried for treason.

p. 42, l. 8. **Sheridan.** Richard Brinsley Sheridan (1751–1816), the famous Whig politician and orator, friend of Burke and Fox. He is, however, more generally remembered as the author of three immortal prose comedies, *The Rivals*, *The Critic* and *The School for Scandal*.

p. 42, l. 8. **John Kemble.** John Philip Kemble (1757–1823), a tragic actor in the grand style, the leading male figure on the English stage of his time till his classic fame was challenged by the new intense realism of Edmund Kean. Kemble was the brother of Mrs Siddons.

p. 42, l. 9. **Mrs Inchbald.** Elizabeth Inchbald, born Thompson (1753–1821), gained some fame as actress, play-writer and novelist.

p. 42, l. 10. **from noon to dewy eve.** *Paradise Lost*, i, 743–4:

> Nor was his name unheard or unadored
> In ancient Greece; and in Ausonian land
> Men called him Mulciber; and how he fell
> From Heaven they fabled, thrown by angry Jove
> Sheer o'er the crystal battlements: from morn
> To noon he fell, from noon to dewy eve,
> A summer's day, and with the setting sun
> Dropt from the zenith, like a falling star,
> On Lemnos, the Aegaean isle.

p. 42, l. 14. **a Table-talk.** Hazlitt did not carry out this intention.

p. 42, l. 14. **Peter Pindar.** John Wolcot (1738–1819), a Devonshire physician, who, after some time in Jamaica, practised his profession at Truro. In later years he came to London and wrote much in the form of topical and would-be humorous verse under the name Peter Pindar. His work was often very coarse and brutal in manner, and nothing of it can be said to survive, with the possible exception of a piece, occasionally met with in some collections, recording the curiosity of George III to know how apples got inside dumplings.

p. 42, l. 20. **Mrs M——.** Mrs Montagu, third wife of Basil Montagu, who played a part of some importance in the life of Coleridge. Mrs Montagu, formerly Mrs Skepper, was a woman of fine character. She had known Burns, fascinated the celebrated preacher Edward Irving, who called her his "noble lady," and attracted Carlyle, who wrote many letters to her.

p. 42, l. 22. **H—t's**, etc. H—t is Hunt, N, Northcote and H, Haydon.

p. 42, l. 36. **Tronchin.** Theodore Tronchin (1709–81), a physician of Geneva, at first the friend and afterwards the enemy of Rousseau. The reference is no doubt to Bk XII of *The Confessions*; but it is not Tronchin who utters the words. "A certain village mayor, who had been dismissed for malversation, remarked to the lieutenant of the Val de Travers...'It is said that this Rousseau has plenty of wit; bring him to me, that I may see if it is true'."

p. 43, l. 4. **Sir Fopling Flutter.** A character in *The Man of Mode, or Sir Fopling Flutter*, a comedy by "the gay Sir George Etherege" (1634?–1691) who had lived in France, and imported into England the spirit of French comedy as embodied in the work of his great contemporary Molière. Etherege may be called the father of English prose comedy, as he represents the first real departure from the formal verse drama of the Elizabethan and Jacobean period. He wrote two other plays, *The Comical Revenge, or Love in a Tub*, and *She would if she could*. The sentiment about tennis attributed to Sir Fopling Flutter is not to be found in the play. The only allusion to the game is the following. Sir Fopling, a foolish and vainglorious beau, has been boasting of his success with the ladies, and this conversation ensues:

Medley. For all this smattering of the mathematics you may be out in your judgment at tennis.

Fopling. What a *coq-à-l'âne* is this! I talk of women, and thou answerest tennis.

p. 43, l. 6. **For wit is like a rest,** etc. From Francis Beaumont's *Letter to Ben Jonson, written before he and Mr Fletcher came to London, with two of the precedent comedies then not finished, which deferred their merry meetings at the Mermaid*:

> Methinks the little wit I had is lost
> Since I saw you, for wit is like a rest
> Held up at tennis, which men do the best
> With the best gamesters: what things have we seen
> Done at the Mermaid!

p. 43, l. 15. **L—— once came down.** The Lambs visited the Hazlitts at Winterslow in the summer of 1810. Lamb's visit to Oxford resulted in the essay *Oxford in the Vacation*. See further the essay *On going a Journey* (p. 149) and the notes thereto.

p. 43, l. 16. **like the most capricious poet,** etc. *As You Like It*, Act III, Sc. iii, l. 8: "I am here with thee and thy goats as the most capricious poet, honest Ovid, was among the Goths." Ovid, the famous Latin poet, was banished to the shores of the Black Sea. In Shakespeare's time "goats" and "Goths" were pronounced almost alike, the pun (if it may be so called) being emphasised by the fact that "capricious" is derived from the Latin word for "goat."

p. 43, l. 22. **walked gowned.** From Lamb's sonnet, *Written at Cambridge, Aug. 15, 1819*":

> I was not trained in Academic bowers,
>
> *   *   *   *   *   *
>
> Yet can I fancy, wandering 'mid thy towers,
> Myself a nursling, Granta, of thy lap;
> My brow seems tightening with the Doctor's cap,
> And I walk gowned.

p. 44, l. 16. **one such instance.** This must be George Dyer, immortalised in many passages of Lamb's essays and letters. See especially *Oxford in the Vacation* and *Amicus Redivivus* among the Elia essays.

p. 44, l. 31. **The legend of good women.** Chaucer planned a long poem to embody twenty famous instances of women faithful in love. The poem as we have it contains only nine of the promised twenty.

p. 44, l. 35. **camera obscura.** Literally "a dark room." The "camera obscura" was a sort of optical show. A large lens, fitted into one of the walls of a dark room, focussed an image which was then reflected on a table or screen in the room, so that those within saw a picture in little of what was happening without. The picture was like that seen on the focussing screen of a photographic camera, but of course on a vastly greater scale—and the right way up.

p. 44, l. 39. **dog Tray.** An allusion to the *Irish Harper*, a poem by Campbell describing the affection of a poor Irish beggar for his faithful true-hearted dog. The sentiment of the piece is much better than the verse.

OF PERSONS ONE WOULD WISH TO HAVE SEEN

First published in *The New Monthly Magazine*, January, 1826. Reprinted in *Literary Remains* and *Winterslow*. This essay, like the second *On the Conversation of Authors*, seeks to reproduce the wit and wisdom of the Lamb circle. The subject is mentioned in the last essay as the theme of an evening's talk at Mitre Court Buildings. B—— stands for Lamb throughout the whole piece. Most of the other speakers have been identified in the preceding essay, to the notes on which the reader may be generally referred.

p. 46, l. 1. **Come like shadows.** *Macbeth*, Act IV. Sc. i, 110–111:
> Show his eyes and grieve his heart;
> Come like shadows, so depart!

p. 46, l. 3. **Guy Faux.** Hazlitt defended Guy Fawkes in three essays published in *The Examiner* during November 1821. As a matter of fact Lamb had touched upon the topic in an essay written ten years earlier and entitled *On the Probable Effects of the Gunpowder Treason in this Country if the Conspirators had accomplished their Object.* In 1823 Lamb returned to the subject and contributed to *The London Magazine* a long essay on Guy Fawkes in which he incorporates most of his earlier article and refers humorously to Hazlitt's three papers—Hazlitt himself being preposterously described as an ex-Jesuit, not unknown at Douay!

p. 46, l. 7. **Never so sure,** etc. Pope, *Moral Essays: Ep. II to a Lady, Of the Character of Women,* 51–52:
> Strange graces still, and stranger flights she had,
> Was just not ugly, and was just not mad;
> Yet ne'er so sure our passion to create,
> As when she touched the brink of all we hate.

p. 46, l. 17. **A——.** Ayrton. See p. 173.

p. 46, l. 19. **Sir Isaac Newton.** The greatest of English natural philosophers (1642–1727), discoverer of many principles upon which physical investigation is still based. His views on universal gravitation and other astronomical phenomena were published in *Philosophiae Naturalis Principia Mathematica* (1687), generally known briefly as "Principia."

p. 46, l. 20. **Locke.** John Locke (1632–1704), one of the chief English philosophical writers, was the author of *An Essay concerning Human Understanding* (1690), *Thoughts on Education* (1693), *Of the Conduct of the Understanding* and many minor works. The writings

of Locke were very influential both in England and on the Continent.
Rousseau represents a point of abrupt departure from Locke both in
educational theory and in political philosophy. A very long and severely
critical discussion of Locke in general, and a shorter paper on *Locke
as a Plagiarist*, are included among Hazlitt's fugitive writings (*Works*,
Vol. XI).

p. 47, l. 13. **in his habit as he lived.** *Hamlet*, Act III, Sc. iv, l. 135.

p. 47, l. 15. **Fulke Greville.** Lord Brooke (1554–1628) was
the author of two strange tragedies, *Alaham* and *Mustapha*,
a collection of rather angular and sometimes beautiful poems called
Caelica, and a very characteristic life of his friend and schoolfellow
Sir Philip Sidney. There is a curiously attractive quality in Lord
Brooke's work, quaint and uncouth as much of it appears.

p. 47, l. 37. **And call up him.** *Il Penseroso*, 109–115 :

> Or call up him that left half-told
> The story of Cambuscan bold,
> Of Camball, and of Algarsife,
> And who had Canace to wife,
> That own'd the virtuous ring and glass,
> And of the wondrous horse of brass
> On which the Tartar king did ride.

The allusion is to Chaucer's unfinished *Squire's Tale*.

p. 48, l. 6. **wished that mankind,** etc. "The whole World
was made for man, but the twelfth part of man for woman : Man is
the whole World and the Breath of GOD ; Woman the Rib and crooked
piece of man. I could be content that we might procreate like trees,
without conjunction, or that there were any way to perpetuate the
World without this trivial and vulgar way of union." (*Religio Medici*,
Part II, Sect. IX.)

p. 48, l. 8. **old king of Ormus.** Lamb quoted from *Alaham*
and *Mustapha* in his *Specimens of the English Dramatic Poets*. His
introductory notes will explain the allusion in the text: "Alaham,
second Son to the King of Ormus, deposes his Father: whose Eyes,
and the Eyes of his elder Brother Zophi (acting upon a maxim of
Oriental Policy) he causes to be put out....A Nuntius relates to Alaham
the manner of his Father's Brother's and Sister's deaths ; and the
popular discontents which followed. Alaham by the sudden working
of Remorse is distracted, and imagines he sees their Ghosts." Hazlitt's
representation of Lamb's talk on this subject may be compared with
the final passage of Lamb's concluding note in *Specimens*: "The
finest movements of the human heart, the utmost grandeur of which
the soul is capable, are essentially comprised in the actions and speeches
of Caelica and Camena. Shakespeare, who seems to have had a peculiar
delight in contemplating womanly perfection, whom for his many
sweet images of female excellence all women in an especial manner
are bound to love, has not raised the *ideal* of the female character
higher than Lord Brooke in these two women has done. But it requires
a study equivalent to the learning of a new language to understand
their meaning when they speak. It is indeed hard to hit:

> Much like thy riddle, Samson, in one day
> Or seven though one should musing sit.

It is as if a being of pure intellect should take upon him to express the emotions of our sensitive natures. There would be all knowledge, but sympathetic expression would be wanting."

p. 48, l. 9. **apocalyptical, cabalistical.** "Apocalyptical," full of high mysticism and similitude, like the Apocalypse, or Revelation of St John the Divine. "Cabalistical," derived from "Cabbala," the secret interpretation of the Jewish scriptures by rabbis instructed in the hidden meanings handed down by tradition, signifies anything with a secret meaning known only to the initiated.

p. 48, l. 17. **Dr Donne.** The old edition referred to is that of 1669. The lines beginning "Here lies a She-Sun" are from his *Epithalamion on the Lady Elizabeth and the Count Palatine*—the Lady Elizabeth being the daughter of James I, married to the Elector Palatine, the choice of whom as King of Bohemia precipitated the Thirty Years' War. The same princess is celebrated in Sir Henry Wotton's familiar lines beginning "Ye meaner beauties of the night." The *Elegy to his Mistress* is quoted in full.

p. 49, l. 13. **wild Boreas' harshness.** Boreas, the North Wind, carried off Orithyia, daughter of Erechtheus, King of Attica, and had as sons, Zetes and Calais, the winged brothers who delivered King Phineus of Salmydessa from the Harpies.

p. 49, l. 26. **Spittles.** Hospitals—here used figuratively.

p. 49, l. 44. **the Temple-walk.** The connection of Chaucer with the Temple is very doubtful. The tradition derives from an uncorroborated anecdote related in the life of Chaucer contained in the folio edition of 1602.

p. 49, l. 47. **ruggedness of the metre.** That the verse of Chaucer was rough and inharmonious was a superstition of the "polite and courtly" age of English literature. Thus Dryden, who published in 1700 some versions of Homer, Ovid and Boccaccio, included translations of Chaucer as if that most English of poets were a foreign writer. "The verse of Chaucer," says Dryden, "is not harmonious to us...they who lived with him, and some time after, thought it musical;...there is the rude sweetness of a Scotch tune in it, which is natural and pleasing, though not perfect." And he goes on to assert that many of Chaucer's lines are "lame for want of half a foot." The simple fact is that Dryden and his contemporaries could not read Chaucer correctly. The final "e," so often sounded in Chaucer's verse, was treated as a mute, with the effect of clipping many a line half a foot or more short. That Chaucer, who was an English Court official twice employed on foreign diplomatic missions, who had eagerly studied the language and literature of France and Italy and had perhaps discussed poetry with Petrarch, was a sort of peasant poet incapable of rhythm is altogether too absurd a proposition. In reality, Chaucer's verse is much more smooth and harmonious than that of many later poets. Here, for instance, are the opening lines of the *Knight's Tale*:

> Whilom, as oldé stories tellen us
> Ther was a duc that highté Thesëus;
> Of Atthenes he was lord and governour,
> And in his tymé swich a conquerour
> That gretter was ther noon under the sonne.

This is Dryden's version:

> In days of old, there lived, of mighty fame
> A valiant Prince, and Theseus was his name;
> A chief who more in feats of arms excelled
> The rising nor the setting sun beheld.

It can scarcely be claimed that Dryden has the advantage in smoothness or harmony. However, Dryden had a manly admiration for Chaucer's humour and humanity, and his "translations" certainly contributed to maintain an interest in the older poet. The opinion of Ayrton (half assented to by Hazlitt) is therefore no more than an echo of the patronising and incorrect sentiments about Chaucer that prevailed in the elegant seventeen-hundreds.

p. 50, l. 9. **lisped in numbers.** Pope's *Prologue to the Satires—Epistle to Dr Arbuthnot*: l. 128:

> Why did I write? what sin to me unknown
> Dipped me in ink, my parents', or my own?
> As yet a child, nor yet a fool to fame,
> I lisped in numbers, for the numbers came.

p. 50, l. 17. **Mine Host of Tabard.** Chaucer's Canterbury Pilgrims assembled at the Tabard Inn in the Borough, to the south of London Bridge. The Host is described by Chaucer as:

> Boold of his speche, and wys and well y-taught,
> And of manhod hym lakkedé right naught.
> Eek therto he was right a myrie man.
> And after soper pleyen he bigan,
> And spak of myrthe amongés othere thynges,
> Whan that we haddé maad our rekenynges.

It is the Host who suggests the telling of tales on the journey.

p. 50, l. 17. **His interview with Petrarch.** Francesco Petrarca (1304–1374), the great Italian poet, famous especially for his love sonnets, was greatly admired throughout France and Italy both for his own work and for his keen interest in all literary studies. Chaucer (1340–1400), who was in the royal service during the reigns of Edward III, Richard II and Henry IV, was in Italy on official business during several months of 1372 and 1373, and again in 1378–1379. He became familiar with the Italian language and its current literature, and being himself a poet, would no doubt endeavour to seek an interview with the admired Petrarch, who, in 1373, was at Arqua, near Padua, engaged in adapting from Boccaccio the story of Griselda, which Chaucer borrowed for the Clerk of Oxenford's tale. Thus, though there is no direct evidence that the English and Italian poets ever met, the probability is very strong. The words put by Chaucer in the mouth of the Oxford scholar strongly support the supposition:

> I wol you tell a talé which that I
> Lernéd in Padwé of a worthy clerk,
> As prevéd by his wordés and his werk...
> Fraunceys Petrak, the lauriat poéte
> Highté this clerk whos rhetoriké sweete
> Enlumyned all Ytaille of poetrie.

p. 50, l. 19. **the author of the Decameron.** Giovanni Boccaccio

(1313–1375), next to Dante the greatest of Italian writers, famous for his stories in prose and verse, and above all for the *Decamerone*, a collection of tales supposed to be told in turn by ten ladies and gentlemen who have retreated to a secluded villa to escape the plague which ravaged Florence in 1348. Each person tells ten stories, and ten days are taken in the telling; hence the name "Decamerone," which means "The Ten Days." The stories of the *Decameron* (the name is usually thus shorn of a syllable in English) have been the source of many plays, poems and narratives in many languages ever since its composition. Chaucer borrowed nothing from the *Decameron*, and perhaps did not know more of that collection than the general idea, which he may have had in mind when he planned *The Canterbury Tales*. The marked likeness of *The Reeve's Tale* to Novel VI of the Ninth Day is due to a common origin rather than to any direct borrowing. However, from Boccaccio's other works Chaucer took materials for *Anelida and Arcyte*, *Troilus and Cressida*, *The Parlement of Foules*, *The Legend of Good Women* and *The Monk's Tale*. Hazlitt's desire to hear Chaucer and Boccaccio exchange stories was just possible of accomplishment, for Chaucer was in Italy during 1372-1373 and Boccaccio died in 1375; but it is highly improbable that they ever met. The other allusions can be briefly dismissed. *The Squire's Tale* is "the Story of Cambuscan bold" referred to in a previous note. The Wife of Bath is a much married lady who defends her matrimonial adventures in the prologue to the story she tells. Boccaccio's tale of the Hawk (Novel IX of the Fifth Day), a favourite with Hazlitt, and often referred to by him, will probably be best known to English readers from Tennyson's play *The Falcon* or Longfellow's "Falcon of Ser Federigo" in *Tales of a Wayside Inn*. The adventures of Friar Albert, who put on angel's wings to deceive an absurdly vain woman, are related in Novel II of the Fourth Day.

p. 50, l. 27. **Cadmuses.** Cadmus, a traditional hero of Greek legend, wandering to find his sister Europa, was told by an oracle to follow a certain cow and found a city where she should sink down with fatigue. When the beast had collapsed, Cadmus resolved to offer her as a sacrifice to Athene, and sent his companions to a neighbouring stream to find water. Here they were slain by a dragon, the offspring of Ares (Mars) the god of war. After a great struggle Cadmus killed the dragon, and, as directed by Athene, sowed its teeth over the ground. Armed men at once sprang up, and fought each other, leaving only five survivors. These five, with Cadmus, built the stronghold which developed into the famous city of Thebes.

p. 50, l. 30. **Dante.** Dante Alighieri (1265–1321), the greatest of Italian writers and one of the world's supreme poets, is specially famous for his *Divina Commedia*, or Vision of Hell, Purgatory and Paradise. His "lineaments" are, in fact, among the most familiar in the world; for a cast of his face was taken after death, and a record of the strong, haughty, ascetic features of the poet have thus been authentically transmitted through the ages. Other portraits, one by Giotto his contemporary, confirm the evidence of the death-mask.

The dreadful story of Ugolino is told in Cantos XXXII and XXXIII of the *Inferno*. Count Ugolino, a desperate and ambitious man who aspired to rule in Pisa, was accused by another competitor for power, the Archbishop Ruggieri, of betraying Pisa to the Florentines.

The infuriated Pisans attacked Ugolino in his palace, and cast him,
with two sons and grandsons, into prison. After some months, the
tower was locked up, the key was cast into the Arno, and the wretched
prisoners were left to perish of hunger and thirst in the Tower of Famine,
as it was afterwards called. Chaucer has adapted Dante's story of
Ugolino in a passage of the Monk's tale.

p. 50, l. 34. **fine portrait of Ariosto.** Ludovico Ariosto (1474–
1533), the Italian poet, famous for his epic *Orlando Furioso*, relating
the adventures of Roland the great paladin of Charlemagne. "Titian's
portrait of Ariosto," to which Hazlitt refers, is now in the National
Gallery. It is almost certainly not a portrait of Ariosto, and very
possibly not by Titian. Why Hazlitt calls it "Moorish" is difficult
to say—unless the luxuriant brown hair and beard of the sitter suggested
the epithet.

p. 50, l. 36. **Peter Aretine.** Pietro Aretino (1492–1557) was an
Italian writer of light poems and comedies. He died, very appropriately,
of laughing—so at least tradition says. A paroxysm of merriment
caused him to fall from his chair, and he was instantly killed. Titian's
portrait of Aretino is in the Pitti Gallery at Florence.

p. 50, l. 38. **the mighty dead.** Thomson, *The Seasons: Winter*,
l. 432:

> Where ruddy fire and beaming tapers join
> To cheer the gloom, there studious let me sit
> And hold high converse with the mighty Dead.

p. 51, l. 8. **a creature of the element.** *Comus*, 299–301:

> Their port was more than human as they stood;
> I took it for a faery vision
> Of some gay creatures of the element
> That in the colours of the rainbow live,
> And play i' the plighted clouds.

p. 51, l. 14. **That was Arion.** *Faerie Queene*, Bk IV, Canto XI,
Stanzas xxiii and xxiv:

> Then was there heard a most celestiall sound
> Of dainty musicke, which did next ensew
> Before the spouse: that was Arion crownd;
> Who, playing on his harpe, unto him drew
> The eares and hearts of all that goodly crew,
> That even yet the Dolphin, which him bore
> Through the Aegaean seas from Pirates vew,
> Stood still by him astonisht at his lore,
> And all the raging seas for joy forgot to rore.

> So went he playing on the watery plaine, etc.

Arion, according to the legend, was a celebrated bard who went from
Corinth to Sicily to take part in a contest of song. As he was returning
laden with prizes and gifts, the sailors resolved to murder him for the
spoil. Arion sang to his harp, and the dolphins, charmed by the sound,
gathered round the vessel; whereupon Arion cast himself into the
sea and was carried safe to shore on the back of a friendly fish.

p. 51, l. 17. **the Wandering Jew.** The Wandering Jew, in
medieval legend, was a man condemned by Jesus to wander without

rest through the world until the Saviour should come again.　According to one story the Wandering Jew is Khartaphilos the doorkeeper of Pilate's palace.　As Jesus was being dragged to crucifixion, Khartaphilos struck him, saying "Go more quickly!"　Jesus replied, "I go, but thou shalt tarry in the world without peace or rest until I come again." Another legend makes a cobbler, Ahasuerus, the Wandering Jew. The Saviour, stumbling under the weight of the cross, stayed to rest by the cobbler's door; but Ahasuerus spurned him away saying "You shall not rest here"; to which Jesus replied "Neither shalt thou rest again until I return."　In other stories the Wandering Jew appears under various names—Salathiel ben Sadi, Isaac Laquedem (or Lakedion), Johannes Buttadaeus, etc.　The Flying Dutchman is another example of this perpetual expiatory wandering, and yet another is Kundry in Wagner's so-called religious opera *Parsifal*.

p. 51, l. 19.　**Miss D——.**　Mrs Reynolds, for whom see p. 174.

p. 51, l. 20.　**Patty Blount.**　Martha Blount (1690–1762) is romantically connected with the life of Pope.　She was the daughter of a Roman Catholic gentleman living at Mapledurham.　Pope became acquainted with her in early life, and when her father's death led to a change of fortunes and consequent family quarrels, Pope took her under his protection.　She was then living at Petersham just opposite Twickenham, across the Thames, where Pope had his villa.　Pope seems to have been greatly attached to her.　He defended her in all her quarrels and left her much of his property.

p. 51, l. 23.　**Dr Johnson in the years 1745–6.**　The suggestion is that Dr Johnson was out in the '45, with other Tory adherents of the Jacobite cause, and that he wrote the Young Pretender's Proclamation!　Such a suggestion must of course not be taken seriously. Johnson certainly professed Jacobitism in a good-humoured and exaggerated way; but his devotion was so far unreal that he made no scruples about accepting a pension from the Hanoverian king. As to his occupation during the years 1745–1746, Boswell says: "It is somewhat curious that his literary career appears to have been almost totally suspended in the years 1745 and 1746, those years which were marked by a civil war in Great Britain, when a rash attempt was made to restore the House of Stuart to the throne.　That he had a tenderness for that unfortunate House, is well known; and some may fancifully imagine that a sympathetic anxiety impeded the exertion of his intellectual powers: but I am inclined to think that he was, during this time, sketching the outlines of his great philological work."　To which we may add that a time of war at home is not one in which such miscellaneous writings as Johnson was contributing to *The Gentleman's Magazine* about this date can be profitably produced or published. A reference to volumes of the Magazine for 1744–46 will show how much the Civil War had lessened the opportunities of the general contributor. Johnson's undoubted visit to Scotland, as recorded in the *Journey to the Western Islands*, took place much later, in 1773.

p. 51, l. 28.　**with lack-lustre eye.**　*As You Like It*, Act II, Sc. vii, l. 21:

> And then he drew a dial from his poke,
> And looking on it with lack-lustre eye,
> Says very wisely, "It is ten o'clock."

p. 51, l. 37. **the Lake School.** The term formerly applied to
Wordsworth, Coleridge and Southey, because of their connection by
residence with the Lake district. B——, i.e. Lamb, though a keen
and discriminating admirer of his Lake friends, was in no possible
sense of the term himself connected with the Lake school. By birth,
residence, sympathy and passionate attachment, Charles Lamb is the
complete Londoner.

p. 52, l. 8. **Despise low joys,** etc. This passage and the next
are taken from Pope's *Imitations of Horace, The Sixth Epistle of
the First Book, to Mr Murray*—i.e. William Murray (1705–1793), the
famous lawyer, successively Solicitor-General, Attorney-General, Chief
Justice of the King's Bench and Earl of Mansfield, famous in a rather
venal age for the strict impartiality of his decisions, and therefore
unpopular with court and mob alike. "Junius" attacked him in
four of the famous Letters and the Gordon rioters burned his house.
Pope's panegyric belongs to 1741 when Murray was on the threshold of
his career. Lord Cornbury, referred to in the first passage, was a
great-grandson of the famous Earl of Clarendon (the "Hyde" of the
second quotation). Cornbury (1710–1753) was universally admired
for his pleasant talents and his amiable character. Bolingbroke
addressed to him his *Letters on History*, and even the censorious
Horace Walpole speaks of him with enthusiasm and calls him "an
exceedingly honest man." Tully, in the next quotation, is Marcus
Tullius Cicero, the great Roman orator.

p. 52, l. 20. **Lord Bolingbroke.** Henry St John, Viscount
Bolingbroke, the brilliant statesman and orator of Queen Anne's reign,
to whom Pope addressed his *Essay on Man*, which is itself an embodiment of Bolingbroke's shallow philosophy.

p. 52, l. 21. **Why rail they...?** Pope, *Epilogue to the Satires,
Dialogue* II, 138–139.

p. 52, l. 25. **But why then publish...?** Pope, *Prologue to the
Satires, Epistle to Dr Arbuthnot*, 135–146. Arbuthnot (1675–1735),
doctor, wit, scholar and writer, is famous for his friendship with Swift,
Bolingbroke and other great men, as well as for his satire *The History
of John Bull*, in which the familiar personification of England makes
his first appearance. "Granville the Polite" is George Granville
(1667–1735), afterwards Lord Lansdowne, who was in his youth a
poet of good intentions and slight performance. "Knowing Walsh"
was a critic whom Dryden called the best of his age. "Well-natured
Garth" is Sir Samuel Garth (1661–1718), a distinguished physician,
author of *The Dispensary*, a satirical poem against rapacious doctors.
"If ever there was a good Christian without knowing himself to be so,
it was Dr Garth"—thus Pope in a later tribute to his friend. Garth
deserves special acknowledgment as the man who secured honourable
sepulture in Westminster Abbey for the great Dryden, who, at the time
of his death, had fallen (like Milton) upon evil days and evil tongues.
Congreve (1669–1728) is the famous dramatist. "Courtly Talbot"
was the Duke of Shrewsbury (1660–1718) who held many high offices
in Queen Anne's reign, and made the *coup d'état* which defeated the
Tory-Jacobite plots at the time of that monarch's celebrated and
unexpected death. Somers is the great Whig statesman (1652–1716)
who helped to bring about the Revolution of 1688. Sheffield is the

Duke of Buckinghamshire (1649–1722), statesman, and author of
an *Essay on Poetry*. "Mitred Rochester" is Francis Atterbury
(1663–1732), Bishop of Rochester, a keen Tory and avowed Jacobite
who was arrested at the death of Queen Anne and sentenced to perpetual
banishment.   Burnet is Gilbert Burnet (1643–1715), the Whig Bishop
of Salisbury, author of the *History of His Own Times*.   Oldmixon is
John Oldmixon (1673–1742), a bad critic and worse historian, pilloried
by Pope in *The Dunciad*.   Thomas Cooke (1703–56), another hack-
writer, translated Hesiod, but owes his immortality to Pope's contempt.
In the quoted lines Pope is referring to the kind reception accorded
by all the best judges to his early poems.

p. 53, l. 15.   **Gay's verses.**   *Epistle VI, To Mr Pope on his
having finished his translation of Homer's Iliad.*   An assembly of
notable English writers greets the poet after his supposed long sojourn
in Greece.   The piece is interesting as literary history, but possesses
no merit as poetry.

p. 53, l. 21.   **Lady Mary Wortley Montagu.**   The brilliant and
witty daughter (1689–1762) of the Duke of Kingston.   She married
Edward Wortley Montagu and accompanied him when he was appointed
ambassador at Constantinople, whence she wrote the *Letters* upon
which her fame depends.   She had been on friendly terms with Addison,
Pope and other literary notables of the day.   Pope was her neighbour
at Twickenham, but they quarrelled very soon.   Lady Mary was the
first to introduce into England the practice of inoculation for small-pox.

p. 53, l. 22.   **E——.**   Probably Edward Phillips referred to on p. 172.

p. 53, l. 28.   **Richardson.**   Samuel Richardson (1689–1761) was
a little printer who at fifty turned novelist almost by accident, and wrote
Pamela.   His next work *Clarissa*, a long and quietly tragic tale, told
(like *Pamela*) in a series of letters, is one of the masterpieces of English
fiction.   His third novel, *Sir Charles Grandison*, is longer, but less
readable.   The immediate success of Richardson was enormous, and
his influence on the European literature of his day quite remarkable.
His work, sentimental, yet sincere, struck a new note, which so echoed
in the hearts of his readers, that reams of letters were sent to the prim
little author by love-sick persons who regarded him as an oracle of
wisdom in all that concerned the passions.   Fielding's *Joseph Andrews*
was written, or at least begun, with the intention of ridiculing the very
politic honesty of *Pamela*.   Hence the allusion in the text.

p. 54, l. 1.   **one enthusiast.**   In older times, "enthusiast" meant
"visionary" or "fanatic."   The polite eighteenth century used it
frankly as a term of reproach.   Hazlitt applies it to Bunyan in its sense
of "visionary," but with admiration.   "Dreams would follow him"
because *The Pilgrim's Progress*, like many other great pieces, is narrated
as a dream.

p. 54, l. 4.   **nigh-sphered in heaven.**   Collins, *Ode on the
Poetical Character*:

> I view that oak, the fancied glades among,
> By which, as Milton lay, his evening ear,
> From many a cloud that dropped ethereal dew
> Nigh sphered in Heaven its native strains could hear.

p. 54, l. 5. **as any in Homer**. Perhaps the clouds that canopied Olympus, the abode of the gods.

p. 54, l. 6. **Garrick's name.** David Garrick (1717–1779), the most famous of English actors, was born at Hereford, but was educated at Lichfield, where he made the acquaintance of his life-long friend, Dr Johnson. His first London success was gained at an outlying theatre in the east of London, but he soon moved to Covent Garden and Drury Lane, at the latter of which he settled as joint manager. Garrick wrote many pieces for the theatre, none of which have any permanent interest. Among the adaptations which he made or countenanced may be mentioned the transformation of Wycherley's *Country Wife* into the *Country Girl*, and the most reprehensible altera- tion of *King Lear* into a play with an alleged "happy" ending. See Lamb's admirable essay *On the Tragedies of Shakespeare* for a sternly critical view of the liberties taken by Garrick with the text of Shake- speare. Boswell's *Life of Johnson* naturally contains many allusions to Garrick. The great Doctor paid a magnificent posthumous compli- ment to the actor in the *Lives of the English Poets* (life of Edward Smith). Referring to Gilbert Walmsley, who had supplied him with facts about Smith, Johnson says: "At this man's table I enjoyed many cheerful and instructive hours, with companions such as are not often found; with one who has lengthened and one who has gladdened life; with Dr James, whose skill in physic will be long remembered; and with David Garrick, whom I hoped to have gratified with this character of our common friend: but what are the hopes of man! I am dis- appointed by that stroke of death, which has eclipsed the gaiety of nations and impoverished the public stock of harmless pleasure." Goldsmith's mock epitaph in *Retaliation* hits off very admirably the excellence and the failings of the great actor:

> Here lies David Garrick, describe me who can,
> An abridgement of all that was pleasant in man;
> As an actor, confessed without rival to shine:
> As a wit, if not first, in the very first line:
> Yet, with talents like these, and an excellent heart,
> The man had his failings, a dupe to his art.
> Like an ill-judging beauty, his colours he spread,
> And beplastered with rouge his own natural red.
> On the stage he was natural, simple, affecting,
> 'Twas only that when he was off he was acting.
>
> *   *   *   *   *   *   *   *
>
> Of praise a mere glutton, he swallowed what came,
> And the puff of a dunce, he mistook it for fame;
> Till his relish grown callous, almost to disease,
> Who peppered the highest was surest to please....

The delightful account of Partridge at the play in Fielding's *Tom Jones* is a description of Garrick's performance as Hamlet.

p. 54, l. 8. **J. F.** Barron Field (1786–1846), a friend of Lamb, and, for a time, a Judge in New South Wales, where, in 1817, he was the recipient of a characteristic letter from Lamb, developed later into the Elia essay entitled *Distant Correspondents*. Field wrote certain verse published as *The First Fruits of Australian Poetry*, a volume of no great merit, yet specially interesting as the first book printed and published in Australia. Lamb's review of it is included in his miscellaneous pieces.

p. 54, l. 8. **Handel.** Georg Friedrich Händel, Anglicised into George Frideric Handel (1685–1759), the great musician, was born at Halle in Saxony, but was naturalised in 1726, and is so far English in spirit as to have become almost a national institution. He wrote many successful Italian operas and chamber pieces, but is most famous for the great series of sacred oratorios written to English words. It is a striking circumstance that many passages from the writings of the blind poet Milton were set to music by a composer who was himself, in later years, almost completely blind, the coincidence being pathetically complete in the case of *Samson,* in which the affecting tenor solo "Total Eclipse" is a lament for loss of sight. Handel was one of the few musicians whom Lamb's limited ear could appreciate.

p. 54, l. 11. **Wildair.** Sir Harry Wildair is a gay, profligate, yet good-hearted character in *The Constant Couple,* a comedy written by George Farquhar (1678–1707). The character proved so popular, that Farquhar wrote another play *Sir Harry Wildair* in which the dashing hero plays again the chief part.

p. 54, l. 11. **Abel Drugger.** A rather soft and foolish seller of tobacco in Ben Jonson's excellent comedy *The Alchemist.*

p. 54, l. 15. **what a troop**, etc. Spranger Barry (1719–1777), born in Ireland, was gifted with a fine figure and a perfect voice. He was the rival of Garrick in such parts as Othello, Macbeth and Romeo. In parts requiring beauty of face, figure and diction, Barry was held superior to Garrick; but Garrick beat him in parts that gave scope for intensity of genius and intellectual power. "Garrick, Madam, was no declaimer," said Johnson to Mrs Siddons; "there was not one of his own scene-schifters who could not have spoken *To be, or not to be* better than he did; yet he was the only actor I ever saw who could be called a master both in tragedy and comedy." James Quin (1693–1766) was the leading actor of the day till Garrick displaced him. He shone in such parts as Othello, Macbeth and Falstaff; his greatest impersonations being Brutus in *Julius Caesar* and Cato in Addison's tragedy. Edward Shuter (1728–1776) was called by Garrick the greatest comic genius he had ever seen. He was famous in such parts as Falstaff, and the 1st Grave-digger in *Hamlet,* but he acted chiefly in the prose comedies of Wycherley and his contemporaries. Thomas Weston (1737–1776) was a genuine comedian who won the praise—rare in such cases—of never clowning and never "gagging." His Abel Drugger was thought by some finer than Garrick's. Kitty Clive (1711–1785) was a sprightly actress of comedy. "Clive, Sir," said Johnson, "is a good thing to sit by; she always understands what you say." He added that in sprightliness of humour he had never seen her equalled. Hannah Pritchard (1711–1768) was specially great in such parts as Katherine and Lady Macbeth. She was an anticipation of Mrs Siddons in the grand manner. "Pritchard, in common life," said Johnson, "was a vulgar idiot; she would talk of her *gownd*; but, when she appeared on the stage, seemed to be inspired by gentility and understanding."

p. 54, l. 28. **a Bartlemy Fair actor.** On St Bartholomew's day (Aug. 24) a great fair used to be held at Smithfield in London. There were, of course, many "shows," the usual accompaniment of a fair, and among them booths in which bad performances of bad plays were given by bad actors. So a Bartlemy Fair actor was what we should call a "barn-stormer." The Fair, an institution of London for over seven hundred years, was finally stopped in 1855. One of Ben Jonson's comedies is called *Bartholomew Fair* and gives a lively picture of London and the Fair in 1614.

p. 54, l. 28. **to play Macbeth in a scarlet coat.** In Garrick's time, and earlier, no attempt was made to give historical illusion in the matter of costume. The actors wore garments of the current date, and depended on their art for dramatic effect. In Zoffany's picture of Garrick and Mrs Pritchard in *Macbeth* the actor wears elaborate gold-laced and scarlet faced garments of eighteenth century fashion. It may be urged that, if this state of things was rather undesirable, it is at least no worse than the modern method of smothering Shakespeare under elaborately correct scenery and accurate costumes and letting the arts of diction and interpretation take care of themselves.

p. 54, l. 32. **histrionic æstus.** Dramatic fire and energy.

p. 55, l. 5. **Roscius.** Quintus Roscius was an actor who flourished in Rome during the first century B.C. So excellent was he that his name has ever since been taken as the symbol of histrionic perfection. Roscius taught Cicero elocution and the orator defended the actor in one of his extant speeches. He was honoured by the dictator Sulla in a way that affords a kind of precedent for the modern custom of conferring titles upon distinguished actors.

p. 55, l. 13. **the author of Mustapha.** Lord Brooke. See p. 181.

p. 55, l. 15. **Kit Marlowe.** Christopher Marlowe (1564–1593), Shakespeare's famous predecessor and exemplar, had a short and wild life. His plays include *Tamburlaine the Great, The Tragical History of Dr Faustus, The Jew of Malta* and *Edward II.* The last, the most satisfying of his dramas, served Shakespeare as a model for *Richard II.* Marlowe was stabbed in a drunken quarrel at a Deptford tavern.

p. 55, l. 16. **the sexton of St Ann's.** John Webster the dramatist was traditionally supposed to have been parish clerk at St Andrew's, Holborn. Of his several plays, *The White Devil* and *The Duchess of Malfy* (1623) are the best known. The dramatic apparatus of the latter includes a dead man's hand, a coffin with its cords, a tolling bell, madmen who dance and sing and waxen images anticipating the posture of death! Charles Lamb's admiration for this play is expressed very finely in his *Specimens.* The Duchess, he says, "has lived among horrors till she is become 'native and endued unto that element.' She speaks the dialect of despair, her tongue has a smatch of Tartarus and the souls in bale….To move a horror skilfully, to touch a soul to the quick, to lay upon fear as much as it can bear, to wean and weary a life till it is ready to drop and then step in with mortal instruments to take its last forfeit: this only a Webster can do…."

p. 55, l. 17. **Deckar.** Thomas Dekker, a voluminous dramatist, wrote alone *The Shoemaker's Holiday* and *Old Fortunatus,* and many other plays in collaboration with Webster, Middleton and Massinger. His prose sketch or essay, *The Gull's Hornbook* (1609), is a lively and valuable sketch of how the contemporary gallant of fashion spent his days. Hazlitt is unnecessarily scornful of Dekker.

p. 55, l. 18. **Thomas Heywood.** This dramatist is best remembered for *A Woman Killed with Kindness* (1607). His title to the epithet "voluminous" is established by his own confession that he had "either an entire hand or at the least a main finger" in the composition of no less than 220 plays! Of these some two dozen survive. Lamb magnanimously calls him "a sort of *prose* Shakespeare."

p. 55, l. 18. **Beaumont and Fletcher.** Many fine plays, including *The Maid's Tragedy* and *Philaster*, were written in collaboration by Francis Beaumont (1584–1616) and John Fletcher (1579–1625). It is this pair of dramatists whom Keats addresses in his lines:

> Bards of Passion and of Mirth,
> Ye have left your souls on earth!
> Have ye souls in heaven, too,
> Double-lived in regions new?

p. 55, l. 22. **a vast species alone.** From *The Praise of Pindar, in Imitation of Horace's Second Ode, Bk IV*, by Abraham Cowley (1618–1667):

> Pindar is imitable by none;
> The phoenix Pindar is a vast species alone.

Cowley, a voluminous writer, considered in his own day among the greatest of poets, is now unread, save for a lyric or two in the anthologies, and for his *Essays*, a few graceful prose compositions with appended verse and translations. His epic *The Davideis* and his alleged *Pindarique Odes* are quite forgotten.

p. 55, l. 25. **Ben Jonson.** This dramatist (1573?–1637) is one of the few contemporaries of Shakespeare who approach that supreme master in power. His principal plays are *Every Man in His Humour, Cynthia's Revels, Sejanus, Volpone, Epicoene, The Alchemist, Catiline* and *Bartholomew Fair*. He is the writer of some exquisite songs (to be found in the anthologies) and of the prose *Timber*, referred to on p. 175. Jonson died in poverty and was buried in Westminster Abbey, where the slab over his grave is inscribed "O Rare Ben Johnson," which, says Aubrey, "was done at the charge of Jack Young, afterwards knighted, who, walking there when the grave was covering, gave the fellow eighteenpence to cut it."

p. 55, l. 29. **his romantic visit.** William Drummond of Hawthornden (1585–1649), a devoted adherent to the cause of Charles I, wrote many poems, but is remembered now almost solely for his sonnet on John the Baptist and his most interesting notes of conversations with Ben Jonson, when that sturdy dramatist visited him in 1618–19. This slim record of their talk is an invaluable collection of *obiter dicta* about many distinguished figures of Elizabethan and Jacobean times. Drummond died heart-broken after the execution of the king to whose cause he was so deeply attached.

p. 55, l. 33. **Eugene Aram.** This person (1704–1759) was the son of a Yorkshire gardener. He developed his considerable natural gifts by study and became a schoolmaster at Knaresborough. Here he was intimate with a certain Daniel Clark who disappeared in 1745 with mysterious suddenness at a time when he was in the possession of much valuable property dishonestly acquired. Aram was suspected of being concerned in Clark's dishonesty, but no evidence could be found against him. He left the neighbourhood and continued his studies in languages and his work as a teacher. He had really remarkable philological gifts and established the affinity of the Celtic with other European languages long before anyone else had discerned it. Several years later a confederate, Houseman, confessed that Clark was murdered, and implicated Aram. The bones of the murdered man were found, and Eugene Aram, then a schoolmaster at Lynn in Norfolk, was arrested, tried and hanged. Lytton has a novel with Eugene Aram as the chief figure, and Tom Hood's finely dramatic poem has made his name even more familiar.

p. 55, l. 34. **the Admirable Crichton.** James Crichton (1560– 1585?), called the Admirable Crichton from his brilliant gifts of mind and person, was the son of a Scottish judge. He was educated at St Andrews, served in the French army and spent his latest years in Italy, making a great figure at the academies and universities. He seems to have astonished everyone by his command of languages, his marvellous memory and his skill with the rapier. However, in spite of his swordsmanship he was killed in a brawl—so at least tradition says. The extravagant eulogies of his friends were taken seriously in a later generation and Crichton became a sort of mythical epitome of human perfection. The first to write of him was Urquhart, the famous seventeenth century translator of Rabelais. A later life was published in 1819 by Patrick Fraser Tytler the Scottish historian. Crichton is also the hero of a very poor novel by Harrison Ainsworth. It should be added that Sir J. M. Barrie's delightful comedy *The Admirable Crichton* has nothing to do with the subject of this note.

p. 56, l. 7. **Hobbes.** Thomas Hobbes (1588-1679), a very voluminous philosophical writer, is remembered now almost solely by his *Leviathan* (1651), a very interesting discussion of government and social rights. A striking sketch of "the Philosopher of Malmesbury" appears in Shorthouse's fine novel *John Inglesant*. Hazlitt has an essay on his writings.

p. 56, l. 8. **Leibnitz.** Gottfried Leibniz (1646–1716), a famous German philosopher, with sane and practical interests in many departments of life and learning. His optimistic philosophy, involving the view that this is the best of all possible worlds, is ridiculed by Voltaire in the person of Dr Pangloss, the arch-optimist in *Candide*. Leibniz is further interesting from the fact that Bolingbroke borrowed his views, which were in turn borrowed by Pope and distilled into the couplets of the *Essay on Man*.

p. 56, l. 9. **Jonathan Edwards.** The elder of two writers bearing this name is plainly meant. He was a Connecticut man (1703– 1758) but spent most of his life as a minister in Massachusetts and died shortly after being made President of Princeton College. His chief work is the *Inquiry into the Freedom of the Will* which competent critics say entitles him to be considered one of the greatest thinkers America has produced. Edwards held some of the views that we usually associate with Berkeley, and it is a curious coincidence that the Irish philosopher was living in Rhode Island at the very period when Edwards was beginning his career as a minister not far away. Sir Leslie Stephen has a very interesting essay on Jonathan Edwards in the first volume of his *Hours in a Library*.

p. 56, l. 21. **Dugald Stewart.** This Scottish philosopher (1753–1828) was the author of several works—*Elements of the Philosophy of the Human Mind, Outlines of Moral Philosophy, Philosophical Essays,* etc.

p. 56, l. 23. **scholiasts.** Hazlitt uses this word incorrectly—perhaps because his beloved Sir Walter uses it in the same sense in *The Monastery.* The scholiasts were the ancient commentators on the classics —unknown students who wrote "scholia" or marginal notes, often of inestimable value, on the manuscripts of the classical authors, explaining difficulties of vocabulary, grammar or interpretation. Thomas Aquinas and Duns Scotus were not "scholiasts"; they were "scholastic philosophers" or "schoolmen," that is, teachers of theology, in medieval times, according to the rules of Aristotle's philosophy. Thomas Aquinas (1226–1274), "the Angelic Doctor," born at Aquino in southern Italy, was the greatest philosopher of the Middle Ages. He was a close student of Aristotle, and in his *Summa Theologiae* codified all theological doctrine according to the rules of Aristotle's logic. It is worth noting that St Thomas wrote the sacramental hymn,

> Pange, lingua, gloriosi
> corporis mysterium,

resembling, in its opening words, the Good Friday hymn of Venantius Fortunatus (6th century),

> Pange, lingua, gloriosi
> proelium certaminis.

St Thomas stood for authority and fixity of doctrine. Within the limits of theology as set by the Church all human knowledge was contained, and any attempt to pass those bounds was unlawful. His chief opponent was "the Subtle Doctor," Duns Scotus (1265–1308), a native of these islands, who argued for greater freedom, urging that practical faith, not speculative theory, was the first consideration in theology. The Dominican order of friars followed St Thomas Aquinas; the Franciscans followed Duns Scotus. It might be mentioned that the term "dunce" originated from the abuse heaped upon Duns Scotus and his followers by later opponents.

p. 56, l. 31. **irritabile genus.** "Genus irritabile vatum," a quotation from Horace, *Epistles,* Book II, ii, line 102. It may be translated "the cantankerous race of poets."

p. 57, l. 2. **Gray.** Thomas Gray (1716–1771), the famous author of the *Elegy.* Gray "declined the invitation" no doubt because of his personal shyness and his love of studious retirement. "He had not yet been asked" presumably because there was a tendency in the Wordsworth-Coleridge circle to depreciate Gray. Hazlitt himself is a little hesitant. Thus he writes: "Gray's Pindaric Odes [i.e. *The Bard* and *The Progress of Poetry*] are, I believe, generally given up at present: they are stately and pedantic, a kind of methodical borrowed frenzy. But I cannot so easily give up, nor will the world be in any haste to part with his *Elegy in a Country Churchyard,* etc."; and then he goes on to praise this poem and the *Letters,* and to suggest faults in the *Eton College* ode. The whole of this passage in *Lectures on the English Poets* should be read as an instance of Hazlitt's own originality struggling against the influence of his surroundings. We may observe that the two "Pindaric Odes" are very far from being "generally given up at present." Certain ultra-fastidious critics have tried, and still try, to depreciate the *Elegy*. They seem to think that its outstanding popularity is a mark of suspicion against it. But we must be careful. The best poetry may appeal only to a few; but we must not assume that everything the many like is trash. The final answer to all objections is this, that the balanced opinion of all sincere lovers of poetry during a hundred and fifty years is solidly against any attempt to depreciate Gray in general and to disparage the *Elegy* in particular. It is this balance of opinion over a long range of time that gives or withholds immortality in any art, and the individual opinions of isolated critics cannot set aside that verdict.

p. 57, l. 4. **the Duchess of Bolton.** Lavinia Fenton (1708–1760), a vivacious actress who took the town by storm in the character of Polly Peachum, the heroine of Gay's musical comedy *The Beggar's Opera*. She fascinated the third Duke of Bolton (1685–1754) who married her in 1751 and thus initiated a matrimonial connection between the peerage and the stage, common enough now, but unheard of till then. One of Hogarth's best portraits is that of Lavinia Fenton as Polly. It is in the National Gallery.

p. 57, l. 5. **Captain Sentry and Sir Roger de Coverley.** A pair of simple-hearted, lovable gentlemen, members of the "Spectator Club," described in the delightful papers of Steele and Addison.

p. 57, l. 6. **Swift.** The great Dean of St Patrick's might very well behave in the manner suggested, for he was a masterful person, very terrible in his moods of silent anger and contempt, though normally pleasant and even amiable to his intimates.

p. 57, l. 7. **Otway and Chatterton.** Thomas Otway (1652–1685), a prolific dramatist, whose natural defects of character joined with an unhappy passion for the beautiful actress Mrs Barry to drive him to ruin, want, despair and a death—like his life—of abject misery. One of his tragedies, *Venice Preserved*, was long a favourite on the stage up to the beginning of the nineteenth century, the characters of Jaffier, Pierre and Belvidera being strong parts in the repertory of tragic actors and actresses. **Thomas Chatterton** (1752–1770) was a Bristol lad who began to write verses at a very early age. All his eagerness and energy centred in books, and, being specially attracted by certain old volumes and documents, he began to imitate the ancient style of hand and phrase, and at last to fabricate many manuscripts of prose and verse which he alleged were written in the fifteenth century by a certain monk, Thomas Rowley. These Rowley poems aroused much interest; and, elated with the hope of success, Chatterton came to London in 1770, wrote feverishly all day, and almost all night, only to find that London offered him neither fame nor fortune, not even recognition, not so much as a scanty living. A few weeks of despair ended in three days of complete starvation. Haughtily refusing food offered by his landlady, he shut himself in his garret at Brooke Street, Holborn, and, after destroying all his papers, took poison. He was then little more than seventeen and a half years of age.

> I thought of Chatterton, the marvellous boy,
> The sleepless soul that perished in his pride;

—so wrote Wordsworth, both finely and truly, for it is Chatterton's extraordinary life and tragic death, and not the poetical value of his work (frankly, not very great), to which his immortality of fame is due. See the conclusion of the sixth and the beginning of the seventh of Hazlitt's *Lectures on the English Poets* for a very sane discussion of Chatterton's merits. Thus in Hazlitt's assembly of poets, Otway and Chatterton appear as types of destitution so complete that they could not find the obolus (about three-half-pence) which, according to legend, was placed in the mouth of the dead as the fare of Charon, the boatman who ferried the departed across the river Styx into the realm of shades.

p. 57, l. 10. **Thomson.** James Thomson (1700–1748), author of *The Seasons* and *The Castle of Indolence*, and specially famous for the words of *Rule Britannia*, the song with Arne's music, in the *Masque of Alfred*, is represented as falling asleep because he was fat, good-natured, rather greedy and somewhat lazy. He must not be confused with a nineteenth century poet James Thomson, author of the gloomy *City of Dreadful Night*.

p. 57, l. 11. **John Barleycorn.** Barley is the grain from which malt liquor is brewed and whisky distilled. John Barleycorn, "the king's grain," is the subject of one poem by Burns and referred to in several others. His praise of Scotland's spirit was not based merely on report, hence the allusion in the text. In 1789 Burns was given an appointment in the Excise; that is why he is referred to as an exciseman.

p 57, l. 23. **Leonardo.** Leonardo da Vinci (1452–1519), a painter of peculiar attractiveness, was also architect, engineer, anatomist, botanist and inventor with views on the possibilities of flying-machines. That is why he is represented with a bust of Archimedes (3rd century B.C.), the most famous of ancient philosophers. Genuine pictures by Leonardo are very rare in England and far from plentiful anywhere. The most famous is the "Monna Lisa" or "La Gioconda" in the Louvre, remarkable for the mysterious theft and restoration of which it was recently the subject. There is a valuable cartoon at Burlington House.

p. 57, l. 25. **Raphael.** According to tradition, La Fornarina ("the baker's daughter") was Raphael's lover and model. A portrait called "La Fornarina" is in the Uffizi Gallery at Florence, and another in the Barberini Palace at Rome. Raphael did not paint a portrait of Lucrezia Borgia; but loose and inaccurate titles were often given, in Hazlitt's time, to pictures by the old masters. Hazlitt once saw a lock of golden hair alleged to be Lucrezia's, and refers to it several times.

p. 57, l. 27. **Michael Angelo.** This most masterful of artists (1475–1564) was one of the succession of architects employed in the erection of St Peter's, the present form of the building being largely his. Hence the allusion.

p. 57, l. 28. **Correggio.** Antonio Allegri (1494–1534), called Correggio from his birthplace, may not strike one specially as "the painter of angels." There are however many angels in his paintings in the Cathedral at Parma (which Hazlitt had visited), notably, "The Virgin Ascending," with a crowd of attendant angels and saints, painted in the cupola. There is a beautiful angel head in his "Madonna of St Jerome" (Parma Gallery) and two fine angel-musicians in the

"Madonna and Jesus with Angels" (Uffizi Gallery, Florence). Others occur in the church of St John the Evangelist at Parma, decorated by Correggio.

p. 57, l. 29. **Titian.** Tiziano Vecellio (1477–1576), a painter of superb power and range, is fairly well represented in England—the "Bacchus and Ariadne" in the National Gallery being one of his greatest productions. The picture Hazlitt calls his "Mistress" is in the Louvre. It is more accurately called "Laura de' Dianti" or "Alfonso da Ferrara and Laura de' Dianti."

p. 57, l. 30. **Giorgione.** Giorgio Barbarelli (1477–1510) was a fellow student in Venice with Titian. His influence in his own day was very great, but to us his fame is almost legendary, as very few existing pictures can be definitely assigned to him. Giorgione is the subject of a delightful essay in Walter Pater's volume *The Renaissance.*

p. 57, l. 30. **Guido.** The sentimental art of Guido Reni (1575–1642) is now less esteemed than formerly. "Aurora and the Hours," or "Aurora preceding the Chariot of Apollo," an elaborate ceiling painting in the Rospigliosi Palace at Rome, is considered by many to be his finest work. Guido was a spendthrift and gambler; hence Hazlitt's allusion to the dice box.

p. 57, l. 31. **Claude.** For this painter see p. 171. He is represented here with a mirror probably because his landscapes are faithful reflections of Nature's moods. The several hundred existing sketches and drawings, nearly all direct notes from nature, prove that he was a diligent observer, eager to draw nature as he actually saw it, and not nature rearranged on classical principles.

p. 57, l. 32. **Rubens.** Sir Peter Paul Rubens (1577–1640), the most flamboyant of Flemish painters, produced either alone, or with the help of assistants, many great pictures of historical scenes and classical legends, together with some admirable portraits, landscapes and religious pictures—the Antwerp "Descent from the Cross" being the most famous among the last-named group. He is well represented in England. His riotous pictures of mythological scenes abound in satyrs, panthers and other accompaniments of Bacchanalian revel—hence the allusion in the text. Rubens was an accomplished man of the world and was twice sent on diplomatic missions to the Court of Spain.

p. 57, l. 33. **Vandyke.** Sir Anthony van Dyck (1599—1641), the pattern of courtly painters, was born in Antwerp, and, after visiting Italy, spent several years in England, where he was pensioned and knighted by Charles I. His early work was influenced by Rubens; but he is specially renowned for his magnificent portraits of noble ladies and gentlemen, painted during the later development of his art. "His own Paris" is doubtless the portrait of himself as the shepherd Paris, now in the Wallace collection, London.

p. 57, l. 33. **Rembrandt.** Rembrandt Harmensz van Ryn (1606–1669), born at Leyden in Holland, is one of the supreme artists of the world. He has left almost innumerable portraits, subject-pieces, landscapes, etchings, drawings, etc., all remarkable for mastery of line, form and lighting, and for power of expression. Rembrandt was often his own model, and loved rendering the effect of furs, rich costumes, gold, gems and similar properties. Portraits "richly dressed" are of frequent occurrence in his work. That is why Hazlitt imagines him as appearing in the fashion described.

p. 58, l. 1. Giotto, Cimabue and Ghirlandaio. Cimabue (about 1240–1301) and his pupil Giotto (about 1266–1337), two Florentines, were the first to attempt the introduction of natural touches, based on direct observation, into the art of painting, which, till then, had been stiff, crude and expressionless, like work in mosaic. They may be regarded as the founders of modern painting. Certainly nothing like the sweet and appealing "St Francis preaching to the Birds" by Giotto had ever appeared before in European art. The work of Cimabue and Giotto (the names are pronounced Chee-ma-boo'-ay and Jotto) cannot be seen out of Italy, as it takes the form chiefly of frescoes on the walls of the upper and lower church at Assisi. Domenico del Ghirlandaio (1447–1494) is a painter of great charm and sincerity. Very little of his work can be seen out of Italy, as it is mainly in fresco. He is a much later artist, and it is not very critical of Hazlitt to link him thus with painters who flourished almost two centuries earlier. But the mere mention of their names at the date of Hazlitt's essay is a point of interest; for we may remark that the progress of taste in pictorial art for the last century has been steadily away from such showy, insincere and sentimental work as that of Guido, once so popular, and towards the primitive beauty and sincerity of such work as that of Giotto, once thought barbarous and ugly. With this progress of taste the name of Ruskin is specially associated; but that Hazlitt saw something of the truth is evident from passages in his *Notes of a Journey through France and Italy*. He is quite wrong, however, in attributing some of the Assisi frescoes to Ghirlandaio. He probably meant Cimabue. Ghirlandaio did paint scenes from the life of St Francis, but they are at Florence, and were painted not "within forty months" of the saint's death (as Hazlitt says), but two hundred and fifty years after. The remark, attributed to Lamb, about their having painted "when all was dark around them" is rather mysterious. It may mean that Giotto and Cimabue were initiators without the light of other men's experience to guide them, or it may be meant literally (as a sentence at the end of the essay seems to imply), in which case Lamb was probably alluding to the fact that much of their work was done in the dim light of church interiors.

p. 58, . 4. **Whose names,** etc. The history of this quotation is rather interesting. Writing to Bernard Barton (17 Feb. 1823), Lamb says: "I have quoted G. F. [i.e. George Fox, the founder of Quakerism] in my 'Quaker's Meeting' [*Essays of Elia*], as having said he was 'lifted up in spirit' (which I felt at the time to be not a Quaker phrase), 'and the Judge and Jury were as dead men under his feet.' I find no such words in his Journal, and I did not get them from Sewell, and the latter sentence I am sure I did not mean to invent. I must have put some other Quaker's words into his mouth. Is it a fatality in me, that everything I touch turns to a Lie? I once quoted two Lines from a translation of Dante, which Hazlitt very greatly admired, and quoted in a Book as proof of the stupendous power of that poet, but no such lines are to be found in the translation, which has been searched for the purpose. I must have dreamed them, for

I am quite certain I did not forge them knowingly.   What a misfortune to have a Lying memory."   The allusion is to the essay "On Posthumous Fame" (*Round Table*) where Hazlitt writes: "Dante has conveyed the finest image that can perhaps be conceived of the power of this principle over the human mind, when he describes the heroes and celebrated men of antiquity as 'serene and smiling,' though in the shades of death,

> "Because on earth their names
> In Fame's eternal volume shine for aye."

Much the same sentence and quotation occur in Hazlitt's article on Sismondi's *Literature of Southern Europe* in *The Edinburgh Review* for June, 1815.   The rendering (by Lamb's friend Cary) of a passage in *Inferno*, Canto IV, not unlike the quoted lines, reads thus:

> The renown of their great names
> That echoes through your world above acquires
> Favour in heaven.

Probably the form taken by the lines in Lamb's (or Hazlitt's) memory was influenced by the familiar strain from *The Faerie Queene*, Bk IV, Canto ii, Stan. 32:

> Dan Chaucer, well of English undifyled,
> On Fames eternal beadroll worthie to be fyled.

p. 58, l. 18.   **the Duchess of Newcastle.**   Margaret Lucas (1624?–1674), second wife of William Cavendish, Duke, Marquis and Earl of Newcastle (1592–1676), wrote a very sincere but rather "romancical" eulogy of her Cavalier lord (1667).   Her almost innumerable other works, including plays, poems and philosophical utterances, are very scarce and very little known, and would seem to afford a very interesting and practically untouched field of research for some future scholar.   Lamb was never tired of praising this most devout lover among wives.   "That princely woman the thrice noble Margaret Newcastle," he calls her, in *The Two Races of Men*; and again: "a dear favourite of mine, of the last century but one—the thrice noble, chaste, and virtuous,—but again, somewhat fantastical, and original-brained, generous Margaret Newcastle" (*Mackery End*); and again: "Such a book, for instance, as the Life of the Duke of Newcastle by his Duchess—no casket is rich enough, no casing sufficiently durable, to honour and keep safe such a jewel" (*Detached Thoughts on Books and Reading*).   Now hear another: "Thence home, and there, in favour to my eyes, stayed at home, reading the ridiculous History of my Lord Newcastle, wrote by his wife; which shows her to be a mad, conceited, ridiculous woman, and he an ass to suffer her to write what she writes to him and of him."   Thus Samuel Pepys.

p. 58, l. 18.   **Mrs Hutchinson**.   Lucy Apsley (1620–died some time after 1675), wife of Colonel John Hutchinson (1615–1664), wrote for her children's sake a life of her husband and their father.   It is a most admirable account of a Puritan gentleman in the best sense of both terms.   The book forms an excellent companion—and contrast—to the Duchess of Newcastle's panegyric   Mrs Hutchinson's book remained in manuscript till 1806 when it was first printed.

p. 58, l. 21.   **one in the room.**   Mary Lamb (1764–1847) was eleven years older than Charles.   The history of literature offers few

stories so tragic yet so consoling as the life-long association of this
famous brother and sister—the complete bachelor and the perfect old
maid.   Mary wrote verses which cannot be called important.   Her chief
contribution to literature is the larger part of the *Tales from Shakespeare*.
Mary wrote the Comedies and Charles the Tragedies.

p. 58, l. 24. **Ninon de Lenclos.** The celebrated courtly beauty,
friend of Molière, Racine and Boileau, beloved of a long line of noble
Frenchmen, including the Duc de La Rochefoucauld, author of the
famous *Maxims*, and the great Condé, victor of Rocroy.

p. 58, l. 27. **Voltaire.** François Marie Arouet (1694–1778),
among the greatest of French writers, was a most prolific author,
producing in rapid succession histories, tales, poems, tragedies,
pamphlets and innumerable letters, written with perfect ease of manner
and popular directness of appeal.   He assumed the name Voltaire
in 1718.   He spent some time in England where he made the acquaintance of Bolingbroke, Pope and other famous men of the time.   For
several years, too, he lived in close intimacy with Frederick the Great.
Voltaire assailed the political and religious abuses of the day with the
utmost fearlessness, and his penetrating satire helped to prepare the
way for the French Revolution.   In keenness of edge and perfection
of simplicity the prose of Voltaire is almost unsurpassed.   If, as Hazlitt
calls him, he is the "patriarch of levity," it should be added that his
levity of manner was joined with deep gravity of matter and purpose.

p. 58, l. 28. **Rabelais**. François Rabelais (1483–1553), born at
Chinon in Touraine, entered a monastery and passed his early years
in the study of languages and science.   He became disgusted with the
narrowness and ignorance of the Church and showed his sympathy
with "the New Learning" that we associate with the names of Erasmus,
Colet and More.   His great work, detailing the life and adventures of
the giant Gargantua and his son Pantagruel, is a wild medley of coarse
and riotous fun, biting satire and rich wisdom.   Three books of it
were translated by Sir Thomas Urquhart (1611–1660), a Scottish scholar,
and the rest by P. A. Motteux (1660–1718).

p. 58, l. 29. **Molière**. Jean-Baptiste Poquelin (1662–1673), who
took the name of Molière, was born in Paris and studied law; but in
1643 he formed a troupe of comedians, and, like the English actor-
manager William Shakespeare, wrote plays for his company to perform.
The comedies of Molière, embodying, as they do, enduring types of
human weakness and folly, are an important contribution to the
literature of the world and hold the stage as strongly now as when
they were written.   In recent years the great French actor Coquelin
scored his chief successes in the comedies of Molière, his Mascarille
(*Les Précieuses Ridicules*), Tartufe and Monsieur Jourdain (*Le
Bourgeois Gentilhomme*) being specially delightful interpretations.
Tartufe (in the play of that name) mentioned in Hazlitt's text is, like
the Pecksniff of Dickens, an example of roguery hypocritically masking
itself in morality.

p. 58, l. 30. **the print of that subject.** The picture of Molière
reading *Tartufe* at the house of Ninon was painted by Nicolas-André
Monsiau and exhibited at the Salon of 1802.   An engraving of this
picture was exhibited at the Salon of 1814 by Jean-Louis Anselin,
whose work is usually signed "Anselin, Bourgeois de Calais."

p. 58, l. 32.   **Racine**.   Jean Racine (1639–1699), the great French dramatist, wrote tragedies that still hold the highest rank in the theatre of France.   *Andromaque, Iphigénie, Les Plaideurs* (a serious comedy), *Phèdre, Athalie* and *Bajazet* may be named among his works. The part of the guilty Phèdre was one of Sarah Bernhardt's greatest impersonations.

p. 58, l. 32.   **Lafontaine**.   Jean de Lafontaine (1621–1695), the French poet, is remembered chiefly for his delightful *Fables choisies mises en Vers*, familiar to every student of French.

p. 58, l. 32.   **La Rochefoucauld**.   François, Duc de La Roche-foucauld (1613–1680), a French nobleman who played a prominent part at court in the days of Richelieu and Mazarin, wrote a collection of *Réflexions, ou Sentences et Maximes Morales*—a very masterly work both in matter and in style.   Hazlitt's volume called *Characteristics* (1823) was written in imitation of La Rochefoucauld.

p. 58, l. 32.   **Saint-Evremond**.   Charles Marguetel Saint-Denis, Seigneur de Saint-Evremond (1613–1703), was a courtier, scholar and soldier.   He is remembered now—at least by Englishmen—rather for his connection with Ninon and her brilliant circle than for any work of his own.

p. 58, l. 38.   **Tamerlane**.   Tamerlane or Timour (1336–1405), the great Mongol chieftain, overran and conquered most of western Asia. He is the subject of Marlowe's drama *Tamburlaine the Great*.   The most generally accessible account of the conquests of Timour is the excellent chapter (LXV) in Gibbon's *Decline and Fall of the Roman Empire*.

p. 58, l. 38.   **Genghis Khan**.   Chingiz, Genghis, Jenghis, or Zenghis Khan (1162–1227) was a Mongol chief who conquered and governed vast kingdoms and empires stretching from Poland to China, from the Black Sea to the Pacific Ocean.   His personal name was Temujin. Chingiz Khan is a title meaning The Most Mighty Ruler.   See Chapter LXIV of *The Decline and Fall* for an excellent account of his life and conquests.

p. 59, l. 4.   **Your most exquisite reason**.   *Twelfth Night*, Act II, Sc. iii, l. 155.

p. 59, l. 19.   **Leonardo's very fine one**.   The famous "Last Supper" by Leonardo da Vinci is in the refectory of Santa Maria delle Grazie at Milan.   The picture is painted on the wall and has almost entirely perished.   Elaborate restoration has left very little of the original work.

p. 59, l. 21.   **Oh! ever right, Menenius**.   *Coriolanus*, Act II, Sc. i, ll. 208–9.

p. 59, l. 24.   **If Shakespeare**, etc.   This remark here given to Hunt is assigned to Lamb by the report of other hearers.

p. 59, l. 33.   **overspread Europe**.   Hazlitt, the convinced Revolutionist and steady admirer of Napoleon, here refers to the break-up of the Congress of Vienna caused by the news of Napoleon's escape from Elba.   See the note on p. 174.   But the wonderful adventure of the Hundred Days came to nothing.   Napoleon was defeated, and "the night [of reaction] overspread Europe" once more.

ON READING OLD BOOKS

Essay xx in *The Plain Speaker*. First published in *The London Magazine*, Feb. 1821. The reader should compare this essay with Charles Lamb's "Detached Thoughts on Books and Reading" which appeared in *The London Magazine* a little more than a year later.

p. 60, l. 5. **Tales of My Landlord.** This was the general title under which certain of Scott's novels were first published. There were three series of *Tales*. *The Black Dwarf* and *Old Mortality* formed the first; *The Heart of Midlothian* the second; *The Bride of Lammermoor* and *A Legend of Montrose* the third. The authorship of the novels, though an increasingly open secret, was not formally disclosed till 1827.

p. 60, l. 7. **Lady Morgan's.** Sydney Owenson (1780–1859), born in Dublin, married Thomas Charles Morgan, M.D., afterwards knighted. Lady Morgan wrote novels, poems, memoirs and travels. Of her once popular stories, *St Clair*, *The Wild Irish Girl* and *O'Donnel*, only the second can be said to survive.

p. 60, l. 8. **Anastasius.** By Thomas Hope (1774–1831), a traveller in the East and a writer on artistic furniture, costumes, etc. His *Anastasius, or the Memoirs of a Modern Greek* (1819), was much admired in its day as a revelation of the East to general readers.

p. 60, l. 11. **Delphine.** A novel by Madame de Staël, published in 1802. The writer was the daughter of Necker, immortal as the rather mediocre finance minister who was to save France from bankruptcy, and whose dismissal by the Court in 1789 caused the popular outburst that culminated in the taking of the Bastille. His only daughter married the Swedish ambassador Baron de Staël-Holstein and became for some years a very prominent person in the world of European politics and literature. Her novels *Corinne*, and *Delphine*, and her *Dix années d'exil* and *De l'Allemagne*, have now an interest that is mainly historical.

p. 60, l. 13. **in their newest gloss.** *Macbeth*, Act i, Sc. vii, l. 34:

> And I have bought
> Golden opinions from all sorts of people,
> Which should be worn now in their newest gloss.

p. 60, l. 18. **black-letter.** Books of the fifteenth and early sixteenth century, printed in Gothic type, or "black letter" as it is called from the general appearance of the pages.

p. 60, l. 19. **Andrew Millar.** An eighteenth century publisher and bookseller immortalised in two passages of Boswell. Millar was the principal publisher concerned in the issue of the *Dictionary*. "When the messenger who carried the last sheet to Millar returned, Johnson asked him, 'Well, what did he say?' 'Sir' (answered the messenger), 'he said Thank God I have done with him.' 'I am glad,' (replied Johnson with a smile), 'that he thanks God for anything.'" Johnson paid him a very sincere tribute in another utterance, unusual from a hack-author about a publisher: "I respect Millar, Sir; he has raised the price of literature."

p. 60, l. 20.   **Thurloe's State Papers.**   John Thurloe (1616–1668), a secretary during the Protectorate of Cromwell, published a collection of State Papers in seven large volumes.

p. 60, l. 21.   **Sir William Temple's Essays.**   Sir William Temple (1628–1699) was the statesman and ambassador who negotiated the marriage between William Prince of Orange and Mary daughter of James II. His Essays were published under the title *Miscellanea*, and one of them, called *Upon the Ancient and Modern Learning*, gave rise to a vain dispute about the merits of ancient and modern literature, now only memorable from the fact that Temple's secretary, young Jonathan Swift, entered the lists with his *Battle of the Books* on behalf of his patron's views. For Temple generally see Macaulay's fine essay, and for his prose see Lamb's *The Genteel Style in Writing*.

p. 60, l. 22.   **Sir Godfrey Kneller.**   A German artist (1646–1723) who came to England and was appointed court painter. He is famous for the series of later Stewart portraits, many of which are at Hampton Court. He died at Twickenham, where his house is now a school of military music.

p. 61, l. 18.   **Rifacimentos.**   An Italian word (here with English plural) meaning something made a second time, and so, a recast.

p. 61, l. 40.   **for thoughts,** etc.   A combination of passages from Ophelia's flower scene, *Hamlet*, Act IV, Sc. v. l. 175, etc.: "There's rosemary, that's for remembrance; pray, love, remember; and there is pansies, that's for thoughts."

p. 62, l. 1.   **Fortunatus' Wishing Cap.**   In the old story, Fortunatus met the goddess of Fortune, who offered him a choice of six blessings, Wisdom, Strength, Health, Beauty, Long Life and Riches. Fortunatus chose Riches, and received a purse that should never be empty. He went to Cyprus where, by a trick, he gained the Sultan's chief treasure, the Wishing Cap, which gave instant realisation to the wearer's desire to be transported to any place in the world. Like most tales of the sort, this has a moral; for the wishing cap and inexhaustible purse brought disaster and death to Fortunatus and his sons. The order of events in this note follows *The Pleasant Comedy of Old Fortunatus*, a play by Thomas Dekker (1600).

p. 62, l. 5.   **My father Shandy.**   Hazlitt's father was the same good-hearted, simple, bookish and unworldly sort of person as Tristram's father in Sterne's ever delightful book.

p. 62, l. 5.   **Bruscambille.**   Bruscambille's prologue upon long noses was a volume that the elder Mr Shandy bought for three half-crowns and proceeded to solace himself with from morning to night as soon as he had brought it home. It is hardly necessary to add that Bruscambille and his prologue are both imaginary.

p. 62, l. 6.   **Peregrine Pickle.**   The famous novel by Tobias Smollett (1721–1771). Of Smollett's works, the most enduring are *Roderick Random* (1748), *Peregrine Pickle* (1751) and *Humphrey Clinker* (1771). The "Memoirs of Lady Vane" occur in *Peregrine Pickle*.

p. 62, l. 7.   **Tom Jones.**   This, probably the greatest of all English novels, was written by Henry Fielding (1707–1754). Fielding's chief works are *Joseph Andrews* (1742), *Tom Jones* (1749), *Amelia*

(1752) and *A Journal of a Voyage to Lisbon* (1755). It was at Lisbon, whither he had gone in search of health, that Fielding died. Lady Bellaston, Thwackum, Square, Molly Seagrim, Sophia Western and her deeply political aunt are all characters in *Tom Jones*. This novel has received the most magnificent compliment ever paid by one distinguished writer to another. Fielding was connected with the family of the Earls of Denbigh, and the Denbighs were supposed (quite erroneously) to be connected with the Imperial House of Habsburg. Thus writes Edward Gibbon, greatest of English historians, in his autobiography: "Far different have been the fortunes of the English and German divisions of the House of Habsburg; the former, the knights and sheriffs of Leicestershire, have slowly risen to the dignity of a peerage; the latter, the Emperors of Germany and Kings of Spain, have threatened the liberty of the old, and invaded the treasures of the new world. The successors of Charles the Fifth may disdain their brethren of England; but the romance of Tom Jones, that exquisite picture of human manners, will outlive the palace of the Escurial, and the imperial eagle of the house of Austria."

p. 62, l. 18. **the puppets dallying.** *Hamlet*, Act III, Sc. ii, l. 256: "I could interpret between you and your love, if I could see the puppets dallying."

p. 62, l. 29 **when 'ignorance was bliss.'** Gray, *Ode on a Distant Prospect of Eton College*:

> Yet ah, why should they know their fate,
> Since sorrow never comes too late,
> And happiness too quickly flies?
> No more! Where ignorance is bliss
> 'Tis folly to be wise.

p. 62, l. 30. **a raree-show.** A peep show; some curiosity shut in a portable box or case and looked at through a glass front.

p. 63, l. 3. **the Ballantyne press.** The printing firm of two brothers James and John Ballantyne, famous for producing certain of Scott's works. Scott was afterwards a partner in the concern, the bankruptcy of which was one of the great tragedies in his life.

p. 63, l. 4. **the Minerva press.** A publishing house remarkable for the melodramatic stories it issued.

p. 63, l. 10. **Cooke's pocket-edition.** *Tom Jones* occupied Vols. I–IV of Cooke's "Select Edition of British Novels."

p. 63, l. 12. **a tiresome ecclesiastical history.** Possibly the once popular *History of the Church* by Joseph and Isaac Milner.

p. 63, l. 13. **Mrs Radcliffe's Romance of the Forest.** Anne Radcliffe (1764–1823) was the most "thrilling" novelist of her time. Her chief tales, *The Romance of the Forest* (1791), *The Mysteries of Udolpho* (1794) and *The Italian* (1797), are full of mystery, ruins, cloaked villains and all the other apparatus of melodrama.

p. 63, l. 14. **sweet in the mouth.** The Revelation, x, 9: "And I went unto the angel, and said unto him, Give me the little book. And he said unto me, Take it, and eat it up; and it shall make thy belly bitter, but it shall be in thy mouth sweet as honey."

p. 63, l. 17. **gay creatures,** etc. See p. 185.

p. 63, l. 27. **Parson Adams.** Parson Adams and Mrs Slipslop are characters in Fielding's *Joseph Andrews*.

p. 63, l. 34. **It was just like,** etc. Some one of Hazlitt's several attachments, possibly Sarah Walker, whose acquaintance he had just made at the date of this essay.

p. 63, l. 38. **Major Bath and Commodore Trunnion.** The first in Fielding's *Amelia*, the second in Smollett's *Peregrine Pickle*. Major Bath is an honourable gentleman of straitened means who, to deceive the world, puts a bold front on his bearing, and swaggers like a man of consequence. The Commodore, anticipating Dickens's Wemmick, fortifies his house with moat and drawbridge, sleeps in a hammock and sets his "crew" of servants to keep naval watches. His epitaph, expressed in naval terms, is a very remarkable document.

p. 63, l. 38. **Trim and my Uncle Toby.** In Sterne's *Tristram Shandy*—two of the most delightful characters in English fiction.

p. 63, l. 39. **Gil Blas,** etc. The strange love affair between the elderly duenna Dame Lorença Sephora and the dashing Gil Blas is related in Book VII, Chapter 1 of Le Sage's famous story.

p. 63, l. 40. **Laura and the fair Lucretia.** Laura, formerly a fellow servant with Gil Blas, becomes a famous actress. In the latter part of the novel we meet her youthful daughter Lucretia whose beauty fascinates Philip IV of Spain.

p. 64, l. 14. **Chubb's Tracts.** Thomas Chubb (1679–1747) wrote many tracts or essays on theological subjects, taking a somewhat freer view of religion than was usual at the time. Chubb was born near Salisbury and received only the most elementary education. Hence the allusion in the text to Salisbury and the club of shoemakers.

p. 64, l. 23. **fate, free-will,** etc. See p. 161.

p. 64, l. 28. **never seen Wittenberg,** etc. For Marlowe, see p. 191. Of his tragedy *Dr Faustus*, the best part is the soliloquy of the sinful scholar on the night when his compact with the Evil One expires and his soul must pay the forfeit. In his last conversation with three scholars who visit him Faustus exclaims: "Faustus' offence can ne'er be pardoned. The serpent that tempted Eve may be saved, but not Faustus. O Gentlemen hear me with patience and tremble not at my speeches! Though my heart pants and quivers to remember that I have been a student here these thirty years, oh, would I had ne'er seen Wittenberg, never read book!"

p 64, l. 29. **Hartley.** David Hartley (1705–1757), a philosopher, author of *Observations on Man*. Hartley's doctrines of vibrations and the association of ideas form his chief contribution to thought. See *Biographia Literaria*, chapters 5–7. Hartley was much admired by Hazlitt's contemporaries. Indeed Coleridge named his eldest son after the philosopher. Hume, Berkeley, Locke and Hobbes have been dealt with in earlier notes.

p. 64, l. 38. **the New Eloise.** For Rousseau see p. 167. *Julie, ou La Nouvelle Héloïse,* is a long romance, written, like the novels of Richardson, in the form of letters. Saint-Preux and Julie are the hero and heroine of the story and their correspondence forms the bulk of the book. The description of the kiss occurs in Part I, Letter 14, the excursion on the water Part IV, Letter 17, Saint-Preux's description of their early love at the end of the same letter, and the account of Julie's death, Part VI, Letter 11.

p. 65, l. 10. **the Dedication to the Social Contract.** Rousseau's famous treatise was published in 1762. There is no "Dedication" to it. Possibly Hazlitt means one of Rousseau's anticipatory pieces, such as the *Discourse on Inequality* (1755).

p. 65, l. 12. **I have spoken elsewhere.** *The Round Table* essay *On the Character of Rousseau*.

p. 65, l. 13. **Sweet is the dew,** etc. This sentence occurs in the essay referred to above. However, in an earlier paper, that on Miss O'Neill's Juliet, Hazlitt writes: "To the tears formerly shed on such occasions, we may apply the words of a modern dashing orator, 'Sweet is the dew of their memory, and pleasant the balm of their recollection.'" This earliest use of the sentence seems to contradict the implication in the present essay that the words are his own.

p. 65, l. 15. **scattered like stray-gifts.** A reminiscence of Wordsworth's *Stray Pleasures*:

> They dance not for me,
> Yet mine is their glee!
> Thus pleasure is spread through the earth
> In stray gifts to be claimed by whoever shall find;
> Thus a rich loving-kindness, redundantly kind,
> Moves all nature to gladness and mirth.

p. 65, l. 17. **the Emilius.** Rousseau's *Émile, ou l'Éducation.* See note on p. 169.

p. 65, l. 33. **leurre de dupe.** A sham or decoy. Hazlitt got the phrase from Rousseau's *Confessions*: e.g. "et regardant, selon mon ancienne maxime, les objets lointains commes des leurres de dupe, etc." Book IX.

p. 65, l. 37, footnote. **a friend**. Charles Lamb. Hazlitt seems to be the only authority for this story.

p. 66, l. 1. **a load to sink a navy.** *Henry VIII*, Act III, Sc. ii, l. 382:

> The king has cured me;
> I humbly thank his grace; and from these shoulders,
> These ruined pillars, out of pity, taken
> A load would sink a navy: too much honour.

p. 66, l. 21. **Marcian Colonna.** An Italian tale in rimed verse by Barry Cornwall, the pen name of Bryan Waller Procter (1787–1874). The line is quoted from a Sonnet by Charles Lamb, *To the Author of Poems published under the name of Barry Cornwall.*

p. 66, l. 22. **Mr Keats's Eve of St Agnes.** This poem was first published in the volume of 1820 which contains Keats's greatest pieces. The allusions in the text are drawn from the famous 24th and 25th stanzas'

> A casement high and triple-arched there was,
> All garlanded with carven imag'ries
> Of fruits, and flowers, and bunches of knot-grass,
> And diamonded with panes of quaint device,
> Innumerable of stains and splendid dyes,
> As are the tiger-moth's deep damasked wings;
> And in the midst, 'mong thousand heraldries,
> A shielded scutcheon blushed with blood of queens and kings.

> Full on this casement shone the wintry moon,
> And threw warm gules on Madeline's fair breast,
> As down she knelt for heaven's grace and boon;
> Rose-bloom fell on her hands, together prest,
> And on her silver cross soft amethyst,
> And on her hair a glory, like a saint:
> She seemed a splendid angel, newly drest,
> Save wings, for heaven:—Porphyro grew faint:
> She knelt, so pure a thing, so free from mortal taint.

p. 66, l. 24. **come like shadows.** See p. 180.

p. 66, l. 33. **my Lord Hamlet.** A reference to Act II, Sc. ii:

Polonius. I'll speak to him again. What do you read, my lord?
Hamlet. Words, words, words.
Pol. What is the matter, my lord?
Ham. Between who?
Pol. I mean, the matter that you read, my lord?

p. 66, l. 39. **the great preacher.** Edward Irving (1792–1834), a Scottish preacher who created much sensation by his fervid eloquence and his alleged gift of prophecy. He was appointed preacher at the Caledonian Chapel, Hatton Garden, in 1822. He was afterwards accused of heresy, and, being dismissed from the ministry, founded a new religious body known as the Catholic Apostolic Church. See *The Spirit of the Age.*

p. 67, l. 3. **as the hart**. Psalm xlii, 1: "As the hart panteth after the water-brooks, so panteth my soul after thee, O God."

p. 67, l. 5. **Goethe's Sorrows of Werter.** Johann Wolfgang Goethe (1749–1832), the greatest of German writers. His tearfully sentimental romance *The Sorrows of Young Werther* (1774), the most popular book of its time, has lost much of its interest for the modern reader, who is more apt to remember it for the sake of Thackeray's delightful verses about Charlotte and the bread-and-butter than for its own.

p. 67, l. 6. **Schiller's Robbers.** Johann Christoph Friedrich Schiller (1759–1805), the great German poet, wrote in his youth *The Robbers*, a play, the violent and rather operatic romanticism of which came like a new note into the dry German literature of its time. Coleridge has translated two of his later and better plays, *Piccolomini* and *Wallenstein's Death.*

p. 67, l. 7. **Giving my stock,** etc. *As You Like It*, Act II, Sc. i, l. 47:

> First for his weeping into the needless stream:
> "Poor deer," quoth he, "thou mak'st a testament
> As worldlings do, giving thy sum of more
> To that which hath too much."

p. 67, l. 8. **Coleridge's fine Sonnet.** *To the Author of the Robbers* (1794). The present day reader will probably think this Sonnet less fine than Hazlitt found it. The "dark dungeon" and the "famished father's cry" are allusions to scenes in the play—the old Count de Moor having been imprisoned by his villainous son Francis de Moor in an old tower in a forest where he is left to starve. He is liberated by his outcast but noble-hearted son, Charles de Moor, captain of the robber band.

p. 67, l. 16. **the Lyrical Ballads**. This famous little volume published by Wordsworth and Coleridge in 1798 was the herald of a new movement in English poetry.

p. 67, l. 20. **Valentine, Tattle** and **Miss Prue**. Characters in the interesting prose comedy *Love for Love* by William Congreve (1670–1729). Valentine, the hero, feigns madness in order to circumvent his stingy father. Tattle is a foolish vainglorious fop. Prue is a young, silly, country-bred girl.

p. 67, l. 26. **know my cue**. *Othello*, Act I, Sc. ii, l. 84:
> Were it my cue to fight, I should have known it
> Without a prompter.

p. 67, l. 27. **Intus et in cute**. Persius, *Satires*, III, 30, "inside and out"; literally, "inwardly and in the skin." It is the motto of Rousseau's *Confessions*.

p. 67, l. 39. **The Periodical Essayists**. The most famous of these periodical issues of light essays and reflections were *The Tatler* (1709–1711) and *The Spectator* (1711–1712) written mainly by Steele and Addison. *The Rambler* (1749–1752) was written very largely by Johnson. *The Adventurer* (1752–53) was written chiefly by John Hawkesworth and partly by Johnson. *The World* (1753–1756) was written by various hands, none of great importance; and the same may be said of *The Connoisseur* (1754–1756).

p. 68, l. 11. **bright Clarissa**. Clarissa, the heroine of Richardson's fine novel bearing that name. Clementina appears in *Sir Charles Grandison* and Pamela in the novel of that name. Lovelace, mentioned in the footnote, is the heartless officer who causes the ruin and death of Clarissa. For Richardson generally, see p. 188.

p. 68, l. 12. **with every trick and line**, etc. A reminiscence of *All's Well that Ends Well*, Act I, Sc. i, ll. 105–7:
> 'Twas pretty, though a plague,
> To see him every hour; to sit and draw
> His arched brows, his hawking eye, his curls,
> In our heart's table; heart too capable
> Of every line and trick of his sweet favour.

p. 68, l. 14. **Mackenzie's Julia**. Henry Mackenzie (1745–1831), a once popular writer of sentimental fiction, but now little more than a name. His chief works are *The Man of Feeling* (1771), *The Man of the World* (1773) and *Julia de Roubigné* (1771).

p. 68, l. 19. **Miss ——**. Probably Miss Railton of Liverpool, daughter of the man who commissioned Hazlitt to make copies of certain pictures in the Louvre.

p. 68, l. 19. **that ligament**. The conclusion of the affecting story of Le Fever told in certain chapters of *Tristram Shandy*, Book VI: "The blood and spirits of Le Fever, which were waxing cold and slow within him, and were retreating to their last citadel, the heart—rallied back,—the film forsook his eyes for a moment—he looked up wishfully in my uncle Toby's face,—then cast a look upon his boy,—and that ligament, fine as it was,—was never broken."

p. 68, l. 25. **His story of the Hawk**. See p. 184.

p. 68, l. 29. **Farquhar.** George Farquhar (1678–1707), author of several comedies, the best of which are *The Beaux' Stratagem*, and *The Recruiting Officer.*

p. 68, l. 31. **at one proud swoop.** Doubtless a reference to *Macbeth*, Act IV, Sc. iii, l. 219, etc.:

> All my pretty ones?
> Did you say all? O hell-kite! All?
> What, all my pretty chickens and their dam
> At one fell swoop?

p. 69, l. 4. **with all its giddy raptures.** A reminiscence of Wordsworth's *Tintern Abbey* lines, 83–5:

> That time is past,
> And all its aching joys are now no more,
> And all its dizzy raptures.

p. 69, l. 5. **embalmed with odours.** *Paradise Lost*, II, 842–3:

> thou and Death
> Shall dwell at ease, and up and down unseen
> Wing silently the buxom air embalmed
> With odours.

p. 69, l. 15. **His form,** etc. *Paradise Lost*, I, 591–594.

p. 69, l. 19. **falls flat upon the grunsel edge.** *Paradise Lost*, I, 460, etc.:

> Next came one
> Who mourned in earnest, when the captive ark
> Maimed his brute image, head and hands lopt off
> In his own temple, on the grunsel-edge
> Where he fell flat, and shamed his worshippers:
> Dagon his name.

The story is told in I Samuel, v, 1–4.

p. 69, l. 29. **his Letter to a Noble Lord.** For his political services Burke had been granted a pension. This grant was opposed by the Duke of Bedford and the Earl of Lauderdale, Whig peers pretending to some sympathy with the French Revolution. Burke replied with his crushing and eloquent *Letter to a Noble Lord.* It is not correct to say that Burke calls the Earl "Citizen Lauderdale"; but early in the Letter there is a reference to "citizen Brissot and his friend Lauderdale."

p. 69, l. 40. **like an eagle.** *Coriolanus*, Act v, Sc. vi, l. 15:

> If you have writ your annals true, 'tis there,
> That, like an eagle in a dove-cote, I
> Fluttered your Volscians in Corioli:
> Alone I did it.

p. 70, l. 11. **an Essay on Marriage.** No such essay by Wordsworth is known to exist. Wordsworth had written in 1793 a prose apology for the French Revolution entitled *A Letter to the Bishop of Landaff*, and in 1809 a tract called *Concerning the Relations of Great Britain, Spain and Portugal to each other, etc.*—a tract known by its abbreviated title *The Convention of Cintra.* This Canning held to be the most eloquent political pamphlet since Burke's day. Whether either of these is meant; whether Hazlitt was confused; or (more likely) whether Coleridge was dreaming, must remain conjectures. In any case the matter is not important; for, in spite of Coleridge's assertion, Wordsworth's prose, at its strongest and most eloquent, bears no resemblance whatever to that of Burke.

p. 70, l. 34. **worthy of all acceptation.** 1 Timothy, i, 15.

p. 71, l. 6. **Lord Clarendon's History.** A dignified *History of the Rebellion in England* was written by Edward Hyde, Earl of Clarendon (1608–1674). Among the "well-penned characters" of Clarendon may be named the fine sketches of Falkland and Hampden.

p. 71, l. 12. **Froissart's Chronicles.** Jean Froissart (1333–1419) wrote Chronicles of the great war between England and France from 1326 to 1400. It was translated into picturesque Tudor English by Lord Berners (1523).

p. 71, l. 12. **Holinshed.** Raphael Holinshed (died about 1580) wrote *The Chronicles of England, Scotland and Ireland*, famous as the source from which Shakespeare drew the subject matter of his historical plays.

p. 71, l. 12. **Stow.** John Stow (1525–1605) wrote Chronicles; but his most important work is the *Survey of London and Westminster* (1598).

p. 71, l. 13. **Fuller's Worthies.** Thomas Fuller (1608–1661) was a voluminous author and one of the earliest of national biographers. His greatest work, the uncompleted *Worthies of England*, is a treasure of valuable biographical information expressed in quaint style.

p. 71, l. 18. **Thucydides.** The greatest of Greek historians; he flourished about 400 B.C. Of the many speeches in his history the most famous is that ascribed to Pericles in Book II.

p. 71, l. 18. **Guicciardini's History of Florence.** Francesco Guicciardini (1483–1540) wrote a valuable history of Italy from 1494 to 1532, not a specific history of Florence. Perhaps Hazlitt was thinking of the *History of Florence* written by the celebrated statesman and political philosopher Niccolò Machiavelli (1469–1527).

p. 71, l. 20. **Loves of Persiles and Sigismunda.** This was the last work of Cervantes (1547–1616), the immortal author of *Don Quixote. Galatea*, a pastoral romance, was his first work. A new English translation of the latter was published in 1903. It must be pronounced far less readable than the ever delightful *Don Quixote* and the interesting *Exemplary Novels*.

p. 71, l. 22. **Another Yarrow.** From Wordsworth's *Yarrow Unvisited*:

Be Yarrow stream unseen, unknown!
It must, or we shall rue it:
We have a vision of our own;
Ah! why should we undo it?
The treasured dreams of times long past,
We'll keep them, winsome Marrow!
For when we're there, although 'tis fair,
'Twill be another Yarrow!

ON ACTORS AND ACTING. I

The Round Table, Essay 38. First published in *The Examiner*, Jan. 5, 1817. The two essays should be compared with Lamb's *On Some of the Old Actors, On the Artificial Comedy of the Last Century, On the Acting of Munden, Stage Illusion* and *The Tragedies of Shakespeare*.

p. 72, l. 1. **the abstracts and brief chronicles.** *Hamlet*, Act II, Sc. ii, l. 548, etc.: "Good my lord, will you see the players well bestowed? Do you hear, let them be well used; for they are the abstract and brief chronicles of the time."

p. 72, l. 11. **hold a glass,** etc. Doubtless another reminiscence of *Hamlet*—the famous speech to the players (Act III, Sc. iii) in which it is said that the purpose of playing is "to hold, as 'twere, the mirror up to nature."

p. 72, l. 17. **we...imitate them.** For an amusing sketch of a man who loses his own personal identity through unconscious imitation of stage heroes see H. G. Wells's short story *The Obliterated Man*.

p. 73, l. 8. **the Beggar's Opera.** Gay's famous comedy interspersed with songs. The hero is a highwayman, the heroine the daughter of a dishonest informer and receiver, and the rest of the personages thieves and loose characters.

p. 73, l. 18. **George Barnwell.** A play by George Lillo (1693–1739) showing the influence of bad companionship upon the young employee of a London merchant. He yields to temptation and in the end is hanged for robbery and murder. This piece was for a long time performed every year in London as a piece of moral instruction to young men.

p. 73, l. 19. **the Ordinary's sermon.** By the "ordinary" here is meant the chaplain of Newgate. Compare Defoe's *Moll Flanders*: "All the while the poor condemned creatures were preparing for death, and the Ordinary, as they call him, was busy with them, disposing them to submit to their sentences."

p. 73, l. 26. **the Inconstant.** *The Inconstant, or The Way to Win Him*, is a comedy by George Farquhar. But the heroine's name is "Oriana," not "Orinda."

p. 74, l. 7. **Mr Liston.** John Liston (1776–1846), a popular comedian, whose performance in the familiar farce *Paul Pry* was specially famous. One of Lamb's minor essays is a mock biography of Liston.

p. 74, l. 19. **Etherege.** For Sir George Etherege, see p. 178.

p. 74, l. 32. **John Kemble.** See p. 178.

p. 74, l. 37. **Pierre,** etc. Pierre in Otway's *Venice Preserved*; Coriolanus in Shakespeare's play; Cato in Addison's tragedy of that name; Leontes in *The Winter's Tale*; the Stranger in the play of that name translated from the German of Kotzebue (1761–1819), a prolific writer whose works number about two hundred. *The Stranger* was a favourite lachrymose drama—the *East Lynne* of its time—the

part of Mrs Haller being in the repertory of all the leading emotional
actresses of the time.   Readers of *Pendennis* will remember that the
performance of Miss Fotheringay (known off the stage as Miss Emily
Costigan) in the part of Mrs Haller made havoc in the susceptible
heart of the youthful Pen.   Chapter IV of *Pendennis* will give as much
information about *The Stranger* as anyone, other than a commentator,
need have.

p. 75, l. 2. **Ossian's heroes**. James Macpherson (1736–1796)
published two epic poems, *Fingal* (1762) and *Temora* (1763) together
with some shorter pieces, alleged to have been translated from the
Gaelic of an ancient bard named Ossian.   The appearance of these
poems divided the reading world into two excited classes, those who
believed that the Ossianic poems were genuine, and those who believed
that Ossian and his epics were both invented by Macpherson.   The
vague and formless rhapsodies of the pseudo-Ossian find few admirers
now, but they had much influence in the dawning days of a new
Romantic period, when people had so far revolted from classical
formalism as to take *The Robbers* of Schiller for a great tragedy.   These
are the opening lines of *Fingal*, Book III: "Pleasant are the words of
the song," said Cuthullin, "lovely the tales of other times!   They are
like the calm dew of the morning on the hill of roes."

p. 75, l. 6. **Mr Bannister**. Jack Bannister (1760–1836) is
immortalised in Lamb's essay *On Some of the Old Actors*.   Hazlitt
praises his Autolycus, and says generally of him that "his gaiety,
good humour, cordial feeling, and natural spirits, shone through his
characters, and lighted them up like a transparency....Most of his
characters were exactly fitted for him...and no one else could do them
so well, because no one else could play Jack Bannister" (*Dramatic
Essays*; *Works*, Vol. VIII).

p. 75, l. 9. **the Prize**. By Prince Hoare (1755–1834), the writer
of many light pieces for the stage, especially the words of musical
comedies and operettas.   *My Grandmother*, mentioned lower down in
the text, is another of his pieces.   Prince Hoare wrote the words of
Shield's excellent song *The Arethusa* which every lover of the British
Navy knows or ought to know.

p. 75, l. 10. **Suett**. Dicky Suett (1755–1805), a famous comedian,
whose memory is preserved for ever in Lamb's *On Some of the Old
Actors*.   Suett had been a chorister at Westminster Abbey, and not
(as Lamb says) at St Paul's.   Hazlitt calls him "the delightful old
croaker, the everlasting Dicky Gossip of the stage."

p. 75, l. 10. **Madame Storace**. Anna Storace (1766–1817) was
a popular opera singer.   Her brother Stephen Storace (1763–1796)
wrote the music of *No Song No Supper*, a once popular operetta
with words by Prince Hoare.   The Storaces were Italians, and Madame
Storace never overcame the difficulties of pronunciation in her singing.

p. 75, l. 11. **the Son-in-Law**. A comic opera by John O'Keefe
(1747–1833), a prolific dramatic author.   His many pieces include
The Castle of Andalusia (once very popular), *The Wicklow Mountains*,
The Poor Soldier, *The Young Quaker* and *Wild Oats*, the last of which
is the only one that can be said to have survived.   The part of Rover
in it has been played by Sir Charles Wyndham.   In *Conversations of
Northcote* O'Keefe is referred to as the "English Molière"!

p. 75, l. 11. **Autolycus**. The humorous rascally pedlar in *The Winter's Tale*.

p. 75, l. 12. **Scrub**. A comic serving man in Farquhar's comedy *The Beaux' Stratagem*.

p. 75, l. 13. **King and Parsons,** etc. Thomas King (1730–1805), an actor specially famous as being the original performer of Sir Peter Teazle in Sheridan's play *The School for Scandal*. Hazlitt says of his acting that it "left a taste on the palate, sharp and sweet like a quince; with an old, hard, rough, withered face, like a John-apple, puckered up into a thousand wrinkles...the real amorous wheedling, or hasty, choleric, peremptory old gentleman in Sir Peter Teazle and Sir Anthony Absolute; and the true, that is, the pretended, clown in Touchstone, with wit sprouting from his head like a pair of ass's ears, and folly perched on his cap like the horned owl" (*Dramatic Essays*). William Parsons (1736–1795) is specially praised by Hazlitt for his performance of Foresight, the foolish astrologically-minded old man in Congreve's *Love for Love*. James Dodd (1740–1796) is immortalised in Lamb's *On Some of the Old Actors*, in which the most beautiful passage is devoted to him. Hazlitt specially praises his Bob Acres. John Quick (1748–1831) is described by Hazlitt as an actor "who made an excellent self-important, busy, strutting, money-getting citizen; or crusty old guardian, in a brown suit and a bob wig." John Edwin (1749–1790) is merely mentioned and not described in Hazlitt's *Dramatic Essays*, for the sufficient reason that Hazlitt was only twelve years old when Edwin died.

p. 75, l. 31. **all the world's a stage.** *As You Like It*, Act II, Sc. vii, l. 139, etc.

ON ACTORS AND ACTING. II

Essay 39 in *The Round Table*.

p. 76, l. 4. **leaving the world no copy.** *Twelfth Night*, Act I, Sc. v, l. 261, etc.:

> 'Tis beauty truly blent, whose red and white
> Nature's own sweet and cunning hand laid on:
> Lady, you are the cruellest she alive,
> If you will lead these graces to the grave
> And leave the world no copy.

p. 76, l. 14. **Colley Cibber's account.** Colley Cibber (1671–1757), famous as actor, manager and dramatist, and much less admirable as the adapter, that is, the mangler, of certain plays of Shakespeare. The familiar line,

> Off with his head! So much for Buckingham!

occurs in Cibber's version of *Richard III*. "Richard's himself again!" is another familiar Cibberism. He was the son of the sculptor who carved the large reliefs at the base of the Monument. His comedies, such as, *She Would and She Would Not, Love Makes the Man, The Careless Husband* and *The Double Gallant*, are of far less importance than his autobiography called the *Apology for the Life of Colley Cibber, Comedian,"* a very valuable view of the English stage in his day. It is this book to which Hazlitt refers in the present

essay. Cibber was appointed Poet Laureate in 1730. The curious
may turn to his *Ode for His Majesty's Birthday* and the *Ode to His
Majesty for the New Year* if they want delightful specimens of thoroughly
bad official verse. "Colley Cibber, Sir, (says Johnson), was by no
means a blockhead; but by arrogating to himself too much, he was in
danger of losing that degree of estimation to which he was entitled.
His friends gave out that he *intended* his birthday Odes should be
bad: but that was not the case, Sir; for he kept them many months
by him, and a few years before he died, he showed me one of them,
with great solicitude to render it as perfect as might be, and I made
some corrections, to which he was not very willing to submit."
Johnson expressed his opinion of Cibber and George II more briefly
in verse:

> Augustus still survives in Maro's strain,
> And Spenser's verse prolongs Eliza's reign;
> Great George's acts let tuneful Cibber sing,
> For Nature formed the Poet for the King.

Cibber, however, deserves gratitude for the firmness with which he
set his face against the disagreeable foulness that passed for fun on the
stage in the days of Lord Rake, Sir John Brute and Colonel Bully.

p. 76, l. 30. **Miss O'Neill.** A very famous emotional actress
(1791-1872) who retired from the stage in 1819 on her marriage to
William Wrixon Becher, M.P. (afterwards a baronet). Hazlitt refers
to her constantly, and nearly always in praise. One long essay of
his is devoted almost entirely to her. Here is a typical passage.
"With all the purity and simplicity, Miss O'Neill possessed the utmost
force of tragedy. Her soul was like the sea, calm, beautiful, smiling,
smooth, and yielding; but the storm of adversity lashed it into foam,
laid bare its centre, heaved its billows against the skies. She could
repose on gentleness, or dissolve in tenderness, and at the same time
give herself up to all the agonies of woe. She could express fond
affection, pity, rage, despair, madness." Perhaps the tribute of
another critic might be quoted: "I've seen the Siddons, sir, and the
O'Nale," said Captain Costigan of Costiganstown, "they were great,
but what were they compared to Miss Fotheringay?"

p. 76, l. 31. **Mrs Siddons.** Sarah Kemble (1775-1831) was the
daughter of Roger Kemble, the manager of a travelling theatrical
company. Her brother John Kemble is dealt with in an earlier note.
Like the "Infant Phenomenon" in the Crummles family, Sarah played
parts in her father's productions from her earliest childhood. She
married a fellow-actor, William Siddons, whose sole title to fame is
that he was the husband of so remarkable a woman. Garrick gave
Mrs Siddons her first London engagement, but she was not very
successful, and the engagement was not renewed. She continued to
work hard and earnestly at her art; and when, some years later, she
appeared again in London, she had so far improved in the technique
of interpretation, that her success was tremendous, and she reigned,
for the rest of her career, the great tragedy queen of the English stage.
It is worth noting that Mrs Siddons, who had spent practically all
her life on the stage, was twenty-seven before she was acclaimed as a
great actress—a sufficient rebuke to those who imagine that success
on the stage is easily won. All who have described the performances

of Mrs Siddons speak of her in terms of the highest admiration. Her striking features are familiar to everyone in Gainsborough's portrait (National Gallery) and in Reynolds's "Mrs Siddons as the Tragic Muse" (Duke of Wesminster's collection, replica at the Dulwich Gallery) It is said that when Reynolds signed his name on a border of drapery in the picture, he remarked, "Madam, I could not lose the honour this opportunity gives me of going down to posterity on the hem of your garment."   Hazlitt has almost countless references to her in the course of his essays.   There is a brief but very delightful account of an interview between Mrs Siddons and Johnson in Boswell under date 1783. The stern old moralist records that she behaved with great modesty and propriety, and that neither praise nor money, the two great corrupters of mankind, seemed to have depraved her.

p. 77, l. 7. **the British Gallery.** The British Institution was the precursor of the "Old Masters" exhibitions at the Burlington Fine Arts Club and the Royal Academy.   It was supported by numerous amateurs and collectors, and ceased about 1866.

p. 77, l. 13. **Betterton and Booth,** etc. Some of these stage favourites have been dealt with in preceding notes. Thomas Betterton (1635–1710) was an actor highly praised by such connoisseurs as Pepys, Dryden and Addison. "The best actor in the world," writes Pepys, a judge not disposed to give his praise easily. "Then straight to the Opera," he records in another place, "and there saw Hamlet, Prince of Denmark, done with scenes [i.e. scenery] very well, but above all, Betterton did the prince's part beyond imagination."   Barton Booth (1681–1733) played with Betterton. His greatest part was Cato, in Addison's tragedy. Samuel Sandford, James Nokes, Anthony Leigh, William Pinkethman, William Bullock, Robert Estcourt and Thomas Doggett were all famous actors of the Restoration and Queen Anne period. Of Sandford, Charles II said that he was "the best villain in the world"; though it is probable that the reference is to his performance of Malignii in *The Villain*, "a new play made by Tom Porter" which young Killigrew commended very highly to Mr Pepys, "as if there never had been any such play come upon the stage."   For Pinkethman (or Penkethman, the spelling is varied) see note below. Doggett is best known, not for his dramatic performances, but for his institution of the annual race between Thames watermen, the prize being "Doggett's Coat and Badge." Elizabeth Barry (1658–1713) is sufficiently described lower in the text. Susanna Mountfort was a daughter of William Mountfort the actor and dramatist who was murdered by Captain Hill and Lord Mohun in 1692—readers of *Esmond* will remember the villainous Mohun. Anne Oldfield (1683–1730) is familiar to everybody as the "Nance Oldfield" of a little play in which Ellen Terry acted delightfully. Anne Bracegirdle (1663–1748) was a fascinating actress specially famous in the plays of Congreve. Congreve and Rowe both loved her and wrote for her, and it was said that they put their own sentiments into the mouths of their lovesick characters and set them to plead their cause to her. She was the reigning beauty of the day, the tragic murder of Mountfort by Hill and Mohun being due to Hill's passion for Miss Bracegirdle and his jealousy of the actor. It is said that she was married to Congreve, but there is no proof of this. She played such Shakespearean parts as Isabella, Portia, Desdemona, Ophelia and Cordelia, but seems to have been at her best in the prose comedies of

Congreve and his contemporaries. If she was anything like Millamant she must have been a very delightful woman. Mrs Cibber (1714–1766) was Susannah Maria Arne, sister of Thomas Augustine Arne, the celebrated composer. She married Theophilus Cibber, the son of Colley. Mrs Cibber was famous both as a singer and as an actress. Charles Macklin (1697–1797), great alike in tragedy and comedy, was specially admired for his performance of Shylock. It was of Macklin's Shylock that Pope was alleged to have exclaimed "This is the Jew that Shakespeare drew." Frances Abington (1737–1815) is likely to be best remembered for the fine portraits of her painted by Sir Joshua Reynolds. She was successively flower-seller (hence her nickname "Nosegay Fan"), street-singer, cook, milliner and actress.

p. 77, l. 20. **gladdened life.** See p. 189.

p. 77, l. 23. **our hundred days.** A reference to Napoleon's dramatic "hundred days" in 1815. The period is usually reckoned from March 20 when Napoleon resumed the crown on his arrival in Paris, to June 28th when Louis XVIII was once again restored to his precarious throne.

p. 77, l. 25. **Booth's Cato.** Addison's play was produced in 1713 when the intrigues of Whigs and Tories at the end of Anne's reign caused political feeling to run very high. Addison was a writer on the Whig side, and his *Cato* (a sort of Roman Whig) was regarded as a political manifesto. "Some parts of the prologue, which were written by Mr Pope, a Tory and even a Papist, were hissed, being thought to favour of whiggism, but the clap got much the hiss. My Lord Harley, who sat in the next box to us, was observed to clap as loud as any in the house all the time of the play" (Berkeley to Percival, 16 Apr. 1713).

p. 77, l. 29. **Monimia** and **Belvidera.** Characters in Otway's *The Orphan* and *Venice Preserved.*

p. 77, l. 33. **Pinkethman's manner.** The reference is to *The Tatler* of June 22, 1710, No. 188. *The Tatler*, it may be noted, contains many interesting references to performances by the actors and actresses described in a preceding note. The 188th *Tatler* thus ends: "I shall conclude this paper with a note I have just received from the two ingenious friends, Mr Pinkethman and Mr Bullock:

'Sir,

'Finding by your Paper, No. 182, that you are drawing parallels between the greatest actors of the age; as you have already begun with Mr Wilks and Mr Cibber, we desire you would do the same justice to your humble servants,

'Wm. Bullock and Wm. Pinkethman.'

For the information of posterity, I shall comply with this letter, and set these two great men in such a light as Sallust has placed his Cato and Caesar.

"Mr William Bullock and Mr William Pinkethman are of the same age, profession and sex. They both distinguish themselves in a very particular manner under the discipline of the crab-tree, with this only difference, that Mr Bullock has the more agreeable squall, and Mr Pinkethman the more graceful shrug. Pinkethman devours a cold chick with great applause; Bullock's talent lies chiefly in asparagus.

Pinkethman is very dexterous at conveying himself under a table;
Bullock is no less active at jumping over a stick. Mr Pinkethman has
a great deal of money; but Mr Bullock is the taller man."

p. 77, l. 35. **Dowton**. A favourite actor (1764–1851), who played
all sorts of characters from Shylock to Lockitt in *The Beggar's Opera*.

p. 77, l. 39 (note). **Marriage à la Mode.** A comedy by Dryden.

p. 79, l. 9. **The web of our life**, etc. *All's Well That Ends
Well*, Act IV, Sc. iii, ll. 83–87; but the original passage has "crimes"
where Hazlitt puts "vices."

p. 79, l. 23. **like the giddy sailor**. *Richard III*, Act III, Sc. iv,
ll. 101–103:

> O momentary grace of mortal men,
> Which we more hunt for than the grace of God!
> Who builds his hopes in air of your good looks,
> Lives like a drunken sailor on a mast,
> Ready, with every nod, to tumble down
> Into the fatal bowels of the deep.

p. 79, l. 26. **hunks**. A miser. The origin of this odd word is
unknown.

p. 80, l. 6. **in a neighbouring country**. Probably Hazlitt is
alluding to Voltaire's poem on the death of Adrienne Lecouvreur, the
famous French actress (1692–1730). The poet scornfully points out
that, whereas in England Nance Oldfield was buried in Westminster
Abbey with Marlborough, Newton, Dryden and Addison, in France
Adrienne Lecouvreur was refused the last rites of religion and accorded
the burial of a dog.

p. 80, l. 8. **in our own.** It is perhaps necessary to remind
readers that the respectably high position of actors and actresses in
contemporary social life is quite a recent development. Until times
not very long ago the actor, and especially the actress, belonged to a
dubious half-world on the fringe of society. The character of the
stage-player, very low at the time of the Restoration, rose steadily
but imperceptibly to the days of Garrick. Kemble and Mrs Siddons
were respected. Macready (1793–1873) was perhaps the first actor who
entered without question into good circles. The Bancrofts made a still
further advance; and Henry Irving (1838–1905) by his genius and
personal qualities raised the status of the actor to the greatest possible
height. In the public mind no distinction was drawn between such
contemporary men of genius as Irving, Tennyson and Browning, and
that view received exalted confirmation in the knighthood conferred
upon Irving in 1895, a date that marks the first high official recognition
of the actor's art as one not necessarily disgraceful and socially disabling.

p. 80, l. 11. **ne plus ultra.** The limit beyond which there is
nothing to be desired.

p. 80, l. 11. **a consummation**, etc. *Hamlet*, Act III, Sc. i, l. 63:

> To die, to sleep:
> No more: and by a sleep to say we end
> The heartache and the thousand natural shocks
> That flesh is heir to, 'tis a consummation
> Devoutly to be wished.

p. 80, l. 17. **The wine of life,** etc.   No doubt a confused recollection of *Macbeth*, Act II, Sc. iii, l. 100–1 :

> The wine of life is drawn, and the mere lees
> Is left this vault to brag of.

p. 80, l. 20. **the vagabond.** In Elizabethan times an actor was a rogue and vagabond before the law, with the status of vagrant or sturdy beggar, unless he was licensed by a peer of the realm or personage of higher degree. It is frequently said that our greatest poet, being an actor, was therefore a rogue and vagabond. This is quite wrong. Shakespeare, like all the other actors of any note in his time, was a duly licensed player, and so, a legally respectable person.

p. 80, l. 26. **Hurried from fierce extremes**. *Paradise Lost*, II, 598, etc. :

> Thither, by harpy-footed Furies haled,
> At certain revolutions, all the damned
> Are brought; and feel by turns the bitter change
> Of fierce extremes, extremes by change more fierce,
> From beds of raging fire to starve in ice.

p. 80, l. 37. **in Gil Blas**. The first meeting of Gil Blas with the actor Melchior Zapata is related in Book II, Chapter viii.   The transitory life of the actor's art is very beautifully described in W. E. Henley's *Ballade of Dead Actors*.   Here are two of its stanzas:

> Where are the passions they essayed,
> And where the tears they made to flow?
> Where the wild humours they portrayed
> For laughing worlds to see and know?
> Othello's wrath and Juliet's woe?
> Sir Peter's whims and Timon's gall?
> And Millamant and Romeo?
> Into the night go one and all.
>
>   *   *   *   *   *   *
>
> The curtain falls, the play is played:
> The Beggar packs beside the Beau;
> The Monarch troops, and troops the Maid;
> The Thunder huddles with the Snow.
> Where are the revellers high and low?
> The clashing swords?   The lover's call?
> The dancers gleaming row on row?
> Into the night go one and all.

ON A LANDSCAPE OF NICOLAS POUSSIN

Essay XVII in *Table Talk*.   First published in *The New Monthly Magazine*, August, 1821.

Nicholas Poussin (1594–1665), perhaps the most scholarly of painters, was born near Les Andelys in Normandy.   After studying drawing and painting at home and in Paris, he went to Rome where he was specially attracted by the art of classical times, and where he was so happy and successful, that, with the exception of a three years' visit to France (1640–1643), he stayed there for the rest

of his life. Poussin's work is taken chiefly from sacred and
classical story. He is well represented in England, the National
Gallery having several fine examples. He must not be confused with
Gaspard Dughet who was a relative and pupil of Nicholas and assumed
his master's name. A little sixpenny volume containing sixty repro-
ductions of Poussin's pictures can be obtained (Gowans and Gray,
publishers), and should be used by the reader in illustration of this
essay. Unfortunately *Orion* is not there, nor is it reproduced in the
great work on Poussin by Emile Magne. The picture was painted
in 1658, and passed through several collections till it reached the
Sanford family, which still retains it, for it is at Corsham Court, Wilts,
the seat of Lord Methuen. Hazlitt saw it at the British Institution
in 1821 to which the Rev. J. Sanford had lent it.

p. 81, l. 1. **And blind Orion**. Keats, *Endymion*, II, 198:

> At this with maddened stare,
> And lifted hands, and trembling lips he stood,
> Like old Deucalion mountained o'er the flood,
> Or blind Orion hungry for the morn.

The *Endymion* of Keats had been published in 1817, three years before
this essay appeared. Orion was a magnificent giant and mighty
hunter. He fell in love with Merope, daughter of Oenopion, but so
shamefully used the maiden that her father blinded the giant as he
lay asleep. It was told Orion that his sight would be restored if he
let the light of the rising sun fall upon his eyes. Eos (Aurora), the
goddess of dawn, was smitten with instant love for him and carried
him away where he ranged the woods as a hunter with Artemis, the
goddess of the chase. He was afterwards placed among the constella-
tions. See below, note on the Pleiades.

p. 81, l. 2. **Nimrod**. See Genesis x, 8, 9: "And Cush begat
Nimrod: he began to be a mighty one in the earth. He was a mighty
hunter before the Lord."

p. 81, l. 2. **a hunter of shadows**. A reference to *Odyssey* XI,
in which Odysseus (Ulysses) describes his visit to the world of the
departed. There, among other wonders, he beheld the spirit of Orion
driving the beasts he had slain in life—the ghostly hunter driving the
ghostly herd.

p. 81, l. 14. **grey dawn**, etc. *Paradise Lost*, VII, 373, etc.:

> the grey
> Dawn and the Pleiades before him danced,
> Shedding sweet influence.

The Pleiades were seven sisters, daughters of Atlas, and companions
of Artemis in the chase. They were amorously pursued for several
years by Orion till Zeus, hearing their prayers for protection, placed
them and their pursuer among the stars. Orion is the most conspicuous
constellation in the winter and vernal sky. Near it is the huddled
little group of the Pleiades.

p. 81, l. 21. **shadowy sets off**. *Paradise Lost*, V, 43:

> now reigns
> Full-orbed the moon, and, with more pleasing light,
> Shadowy sets off the face of things.

p. 81, l. 27. **Sir Joshua has done him justice.** In the fifth of
the *Discourses on Art*. Here is the passage:

"Poussin lived and conversed with the ancient statues so long,
that he may be said to have been better acquainted with them than
with the people who were about him. I have often thought that he
carried his veneration for them so far as to wish to give his works the
air of ancient paintings. It is certain he copied some of the antique
paintings, particularly the Marriage in the Aldobrandini Palace at Rome,
which I believe to be the best relic of those remote ages that has yet
been found.

No works of any modern have so much of the air of antique painting
as those of Poussin. His best performances have a remarkable dryness
of manner, which, though by no means to be recommended for imitation,
yet seems perfectly correspondent to that ancient simplicity which
distinguishes his style. Like Polidoro, he studied the ancients so
much, that he acquired a habit of thinking in their way, and seemed
to know perfectly the actions and gestures they would use on every
occasion.

Poussin in the latter part of his life changed from his dry manner
to one much softer and richer, where there is a greater union between
the figures and ground; as in the Seven Sacraments in the Duke
of Orleans' collection; but neither these, nor any of his other pictures
in this manner, are at all comparable to many in his dry manner which
we have in England.

The favourite subjects of Poussin were ancient fables; and no
painter was ever better qualified to paint such subjects, not only from his
being eminently skilled in the knowledge of the ceremonies, customs and
habits of the ancients, but from his being so well acquainted with the
different characters which those who invented them gave to their
allegorical figures. Though Rubens has shown great fancy in his
Satyrs, Silenuses, and Fauns, yet they are not that distinct separate
class of beings, which is carefully exhibited by the ancients, and by
Poussin. Certainly when such subjects of antiquity are represented,
nothing in the picture ought to remind us of modern times. The
mind is thrown back into antiquity, and nothing ought to be introduced
that may tend to awaken it from the illusion.

Poussin seemed to think that the style and the language in which
such stories are told, is not the worse for preserving some relish of the
old way of painting, which seemed to give a general uniformity to
the whole, so that the mind was thrown back into antiquity not only
by the subject, but the execution.

If Poussin in imitation of the ancients represents Apollo driving
his chariot out of the sea by way of representing the sun rising, if he
personifies lakes and rivers, it is nowise offensive in him; but seems
perfectly of a piece with the general air of the picture. On the contrary,
if the figures which people his pictures had a modern air or countenance,
if they appeared like our countrymen, if the draperies were like cloth
or silk of our manufacture, if the landscape had the appearance of a
modern view, how ridiculous would Apollo appear instead of the
sun; an old man, or a nymph with an urn, to represent a river or a
lake!"

p. 82, l. 1. **denote a foregone conclusion.** *Othello,* Act III, Sc. iii, l. 428:

> But this denoted a foregone conclusion.

p. 82, l. 7. **take up the isles,** etc. Isaiah xl, 15: "Behold, the nations are as a drop of a bucket, and are counted as the small dust of the balance: behold, he taketh up the isles as a very little thing." The latter part of Hazlitt's quotation is doubtless a reminiscence of *v.* 12 in the same chapter: "and weighed the mountains in scales and the hills in a balance."

p. 82, l. 21. **To give us nature such as we have never seen.** Compare this passage with the oft-quoted lines from Wordsworth's *Peele Castle* stanzas:

> Ah! then, if mine had been the painter's hand,
> To express what then I saw, and add the gleam,
> The light that never was on sea or land,
> The consecration, and the poet's dream,
> I would have planted thee, thou hoary pile,
> Amid a world how different from this!

p. 82, l. 25. **high and palmy state.** *Hamlet,* Act I, Sc. i, l. 113:

> In the most high and palmy state of Rome,
> A little ere the mightiest Julius fell,
> The graves stood tenantless and the sheeted dead
> Did squeak and gibber in the Roman streets.

p. 82, l. 27. **so potent art.** *Tempest,* Act V, Sc. i, l. 50:

>   graves at my command
> Have waked their sleepers, oped, and let 'em forth
> By my so potent art.

p. 82, l. 34. **more than natural.** *Hamlet,* Act II, Sc. ii, l. 384: "There's something in this more than natural, if philosophy could find it out."

p. 82, l. 39. **gives to airy nothing,** etc. *A Midsummer Night's Dream,* Act V, Sc. i, l. 16:

> And as imagination bodies forth
> The forms of things unknown, the poet's pen
> Turns them to shapes, and gives to airy nothing
> A local habitation and a name.

p. 83, l. 14. **maudlin.** Tearfully sentimental—like exaggerated representations of the repentant Mary Magdalen.

p. 83, l. 26. **when Titan,** etc. Hyperion the Titan was ruler of the sun till those early gods were overthrown and dispossessed. The lordship of the Sun then passed to Apollo. See Keats's magnificent epic fragment *Hyperion.*

p. 84, l. 8. **His Giants.** This description would apply to two landscapes by Poussin in the Hermitage Gallery, Leningrad.

p. 84, l. 12. **An infant Bacchus or Jupiter.** There is an "Education of Bacchus" in the Louvre and another in the National Gallery. "The Childhood of Bacchus" is at the Musée Condé, Chantilly. Poussin painted two versions of "The Infancy of Jupiter"; one is at Dulwich, the other at the Royal Gallery, Berlin.

p. 84, l. 14. **His snakes**. There is, for instance, a large snake
on the rock to the left of his great picture, "The Deluge," and another
in "The Changing of Aaron's Rod into a Serpent"—both in the Louvre.

p. 84, l. 17. **his Plague of Athens.** The picture that Hazlitt
probably meant is not "The Plague of Athens," but "The Plague among
the Philistines at Ashdod," as described in 1 Samuel v. It is in the
Louvre, and there is a replica in the National Gallery. There is a
"Plague of Athens" by Poussin in the Cook collection at Richmond.

p. 84, l. 18. **His picture of the Deluge.** Known also as "Winter."
It is in the Louvre.

p. 84, l. 24. **o'er-informed**, etc. From the character of Shaftesbury
in Dryden's *Absalom and Achitophel*:

> A fiery soul, which working out its way,
> Fretted the pygmy body to decay,
> And o'er-informed the tenement of clay.

"O'er-informed" means "over-filled," so that the spirit was too strong
for the slight body.

p. 84, l. 31, footnote. **See his Life lately published.** *Memoirs of
the Life of Nicholas Poussin* (1820) by Mrs Graham, afterwards Lady
Callcott, whose best-known work, at least by name, is *Little Arthur's
History of England.*

p. 84, l. 35, footnote. **Mr West.** Benjamin West (1738–1820) was
born in Pennsylvania, and, after studying in Italy, settled in London
where he succeeded Sir Joshua Reynolds as President of the Royal
Academy. His work is mostly historical in subject and vast in size.
He is not now held in very great esteem. See *On the Old Age of Artists*
(*The Plain Speaker*) for an excellent character of West.

p. 85, l. 3. **the very stones**, etc. *Macbeth*, Act II, Sc. i, l. 58:

> Thou sure and firm-set earth,
> Hear not my steps which way they walk, for fear
> The very stones prate of my whereabout
> And take the present horror from the time
> Which now suits with it.

p. 85, l. 7. **a picture of Aurora**. Probably "Cephalus and
Aurora" now in the National Gallery. Aurora, or Eos (the Dawn),
loved the beautiful Tithonus and prayed the gods to grant him eternal
life. The prayer was answered; but as Aurora had forgotten to ask
for the necessary accompaniment of eternal youth, Tithonus withered
and shrank under the burden of unending years till, as one legend
says, he was changed into a cricket or grasshopper.

p. 85, l. 25. **his Nymphs and Fauns, are superior,** etc. It may
be urged that if the Fauns and Bacchantes of Poussin are more
"intellectual" than those of Rubens, they are, so far, inferior; as
these fabulous figures are intended to be personifications of the senses,
not of the mind.

p. 85, l. 32. **Leaping like wanton kids.** Spenser, *Faerie Queene,*
Bk 1, Canto vi, Stanza 14. A troop of Fauns and Satyrs surround Una:

> And all the way their merry pipes they sound
> That all the woods with doubled echo ring;
> And with their hornèd feet do wear the ground,
> Leaping like wanton kids in pleasant Spring.

p. 86, l. 1. **at Blenheim**. The great Duke of Marlborough was an admirer of Rubens, and the grateful cities of the Netherlands presented him with many fine examples, which, with his own purchases, went to form the best collection of Rubens in the possession of any one person. The pictures, some twenty in number, belonging for the most part to the master's best period, were mainly Scriptural in subject, only one, or perhaps two, being "Bacchanalian" in the sense of Hazlitt's remark. The great collection was dispersed at Christie's in 1886, with the rest of the Blenheim art treasures. Hazlitt refers elsewhere to these pictures, and gives them more detailed notice in his *Sketches of the Principal Picture Galleries in England*.

p. 86, l. 5. **his picture of Apollo.** "The Inspiration of Anacreon" at Dulwich, or "The Inspiration of the Poet" at the Louvre. Apollo is figured in both.

p. 86, l. 7. **the figure of a nymph**. The figure on the left of the picture "A Bacchanalian Dance" in the National Gallery.

p. 86, l. 10. **his picture of the shepherds**. "The Shepherds of Arcadia" in the Louvre—the most popular of Poussin's pictures.

p. 86, l. 11. **Vale of Tempe**. A romantic glen in Thessaly often celebrated by the Greek poets. "Et ego, etc."—"And I too have dwelt in Arcadia."

p. 86, l. 16. **the valleys low**, etc. *Lycidas*, 136, etc.:

> Ye valleys low where the mild whispers use
> Of shades and wanton winds and gushing brooks.

p. 86, l. 23. **within the book and volume**, etc. *Hamlet*, Act 1, Sc. v, l. 103:

> And thy commandment all alone shall live
> Within the book and volume of my brain,
> Unmixed with baser matter.

p. 86, l. 27. **the sober certainty**, etc. *Comus*, 263:

> But such a sacred and home-felt delight,
> Such sober certainty of waking bliss,
> I never heard till now.

p. 86, l. 30. **he who knows of these delights,** etc. Adapted from Milton's sonnet to "Lawrence, of virtuous father virtuous son":

> He who of these delights can judge, and spare
> To interpose them oft, is not unwise.

p. 86, l. 35. **embrowned the walls**. "Embrowned" because time has lent a sober darkening to the colours of many great pictures.

p. 86, l. 36. **Poussin has repeated this subject**. Another version is the "Shepherds of Arcadia" in the Duke of Devonshire's collection.

p. 87, l. 6. **the names the same**. Most of the painters here mentioned have been dealt with in earlier notes, which need not be repeated here. **The Carracci**. There were three painters of this name, forming a school. The founder was Ludovico (1555–1619), and he was assisted by two nephews, Agostino (1557–1602) and Annibale (1560–1609). Annibale was the most prolific of the three. The Carracci (like Naldo in George Eliot's *Stradivarius*) were painters of the "eclectic school," that is, they had no original vision or view of things, but selected for imitation all the most popular mannerisms of their famous predecessors. Their elaborate and showy works (mostly classical or Scriptural in subject), once highly praised, are now but slightly esteemed.

p. 87, l. 19. **Old Genius the porter,** etc. Spenser, *Faerie Queene*, Bk III, Cant. vi, stan. 31 and 32:

> Old Genius the porter of them was,
> Old Genius the which a double nature has.

> He letteth in, he letteth out to wend
> All that to come into the world desires.

p. 87, l. 27. **Pictures are scattered.** A reminiscence of Wordsworth's *Stray Pleasures*. See p. 206.

p. 87, l. 31. **the collections at Blenheim,** etc. All these are described in Hazlitt's *Sketches of the Principal Picture Galleries in England*. The collection of John Julius Angerstein is specially interesting, because, after his death, twenty-nine of his pictures were bought by the nation for £60,000, to form the nucleus of a National Gallery. The collection was opened to the public in 1824 at Angerstein's house in Pall Mall.

p. 87, l. 37. **since the Louvre is stripped.** Napoleon, in the course of his campaigns, especially the Italian campaign, had sedulously collected works of art and sent them to France. Many of these were restored after 1815. See the following essays. The "Iron Crown" is taken by Hazlitt as a symbol of Napoleon's career as a conqueror. The "Iron Crown" is the ancient regal emblem of Lombardy and is preserved at Monza, near Milan. Inside the gold circlet is a narrow band of iron said to have been beaten out of one of the nails used at the Crucifixion. According to legend, St Helena, mother of Constantine the Great, discovered the buried Cross at Jerusalem in 326 and gave one of the nails to her son. Queen Theudelinda, who converted the Lombards to Christianity in 600, is supposed to have incorporated the sacred relic into the Lombard crown. See George Meredith's fervid poem the *Song of Theodelinda*. Napoleon was crowned with this ancient circlet of the Lombard Kings in 1805. He died in 1821, shortly before the present essay was written, with his glory, as it seemed, in total eclipse.

ON THE PLEASURE OF PAINTING. I

Table Talk, Essay 1. First published in *The London Magazine*, December, 1820.

p. 88, l. 1. **There is a pleasure,** etc. The original source of this quotation is Dryden's *Spanish Friar*, Act II, Sc. i:

> There is a pleasure sure
> In being mad, which none but madmen know.

But Cowper's variation (*The Task*, Bk II) is better known:

> There is a pleasure in poetic pains
> Which only poets know.

p. 88, l. 11. **no juggling here**. This quotation is possibly a confused reminiscence of two passages in *Hamlet*:

> but 'tis not so above;
> There is no shuffling, there the action lies
> In his true nature   (III, iii, 61)

and,

> How came he dead?   I'll not be juggled with!
> (IV, v, 130).

Possibly a passage of *Troilus and Cressida* (II, iii, 77) may have contributed to the phrase:

"Here is such patchery, such juggling, and such knavery!"

p. 88, l. 16. **study with joy**, etc. Cowper, *The Task*, III, 227–228:

> The mind, indeed, enlightened from above,
> Views Him in all; ascribes to the grand cause
> The grand effect; acknowledges with joy
> His manner, and with rapture tastes His style.

p. 88, l. 19. **you learn something every moment.** Compare with this paragraph a passage in Browning's *Fra Lippo Lippi*:

> For, don't you mark, we're made so that we love
> First when we see them painted, things we have passed
> Perhaps a hundred times, nor cared to see;
> And so they are better, painted—better to us,
> Which is the same thing.   Art was given for that—
> God uses us to help each other so,
> Lending our minds out.   Have you noticed, now,
> Your cullion's hanging face?   A bit of chalk,
> And trust me but you should, though!   How much more,
> If I drew higher things with the same truth!

p. 89, l. 16. **more tedious**, etc. *King John*, Act III, Sc. iv, ll. 108–9:

> Life is as tedious as a twice-told tale
> Vexing the dull ear of a drowsy man.

p. 89, l. 20. **Werther**. Goethe's sentimental, not to say maudlin, story was published in 1774. The quoted passage is taken from Letter VIII.

p. 90, l. 8. **My mind to me**, etc. A poem by Sir Edward Dyer (1550?-1607):

> My mind to me a kingdom is,
>   Such present joys therein I find,
> That it excels all other bliss
>   That earth affords or grows by kind:
> Though much I want which most would have,
> Yet still my mind forbids to crave.

p. 90, l. 9. **to set a throne**, etc. Bacon, *Advancement of Learning*, Bk I: "But the commandment of knowledge is yet higher than the commandment over the will; for it is a commandment over the reason, belief, and understanding of man, which is the highest part of the mind, and giveth law to the will itself: for there is no power on earth which setteth up a throne, or chair of state, in the spirits or souls of men, and in their cogitations, imaginations, opinions, and beliefs, but knowledge and learning."

p. 90, l. 13. **Pure in the last recesses,** etc. Dryden's translation of the Second Satire of Persius:

> A soul, where laws both human and divine,
> In practice more than speculation shine:
> A genuine virtue, of a vigorous kind,
> Pure in the last recesses of the mind:
> When with such offerings to the Gods I come,
> A cake, thus given, is worth a hecatomb.

p. 91, l. 5. **palpable to feeling.** Perhaps from *Othello*, Act I, Sc.i i, l. 76:

> 'Tis probable and palpable to thinking. *See Addenda*, p. 251.

p. 91, l. 14. **this miracle of Rubens' pencil.** The landscapes of Rubens are a specially important part of his work. The National Gallery has two excellent examples. One famous "Rainbow Landscape" of Rubens is in the Pinakothek, Munich, and another in the Wallace Collection, London; but Hazlitt plainly refers to the one in the Louvre.

p. 91, l. 17. **Rembrandt's landscapes.** The landscapes of Rembrandt are among the greatest in that kind. A specially fine example is "The Mill," formerly at Bowood, in the possession of the Marquess of Lansdowne, but recently sold, and now in America. Other good examples are in the Northbrook and Westminster collections. A very impressive landscape by Rembrandt is the etching generally known as "The Three Trees."

p. 91, l. 19. **light thickened.** *Macbeth*, Act III, Sc. ii, l. 50:

> Light thickens; and the crow
> Makes wing to the rooky wood:
> Good things of day begin to droop and drowse;
> Whiles night's black agents to their preys do rouse.

p. 91, l. 24. **Wilson.** Richard Wilson (1714–1782), a great landscape painter, was born in Montgomeryshire, and studied in London. He began his career as a portrait painter, but during a visit to Italy, turned his attention to landscape. He was never successful in the worldly sense and passed most of his life in poverty. Circumstances brightened a little towards the end, when a legacy enabled him to retire to Llanberis, where he died. Wilson's admirable work has steadily increased in favour among capable judges. He is well represented in the National Gallery and South Kensington.

p. 91, l. 37. **Claude.** See p. 171. Claude was tireless in sketching the natural effects of form and light noticed in his rambles.

p. 92, l. 11. **an old woman.** This picture is in the museum at Maidstone.

p. 92, l. 26. **an old head by Rembrandt.** Possibly the portrait of the Countess of Desmond, still at Burghley House in the possession of the Marquess of Exeter. It should be noted that modern criticism does not accept as genuine any of the alleged Rembrandts at Burghley.

p. 92, l. 33. **with Sir Joshua.** In an essay contributed to *The Idler* (No. 82), the third of three excellent papers by him in that periodical, Reynolds had written thus: "If it has been proved that the painter, by attending to the invariable and general ideas of nature,

produces beauty, he must, by regarding minute particularities...
deviate from the universal rule, and pollute his canvas with deformity."
This was the concluding sentence, and it is said that the last six words
were added by Johnson. Hazlitt criticises the pronouncement very
elaborately in Essay xiv of *Table Talk*—the second of two papers
dealing with Sir Joshua's *Discourses on Art*, in which the *Idler* essays
were reprinted. The third and fourth discourses of Reynolds deal
specially with this question of the general and particular in art. Thus
in the fourth he writes: "The usual and most dangerous error is on
the side of minuteness; and therefore I think caution most necessary
where most have failed. The general idea constitutes real excellence.
All smaller things, however perfect in their way, are to be sacrificed
without mercy to the greater." On this point we might observe that
much depends on the painter's aim. An artist like Turner who, in
his later work, sought to reproduce luminosity of effect rather than to
represent objects, would plainly have no need to bother about
"minute particulars." But it is quite possible to combine perfection
of detail with all the breadth of a grand style. The Van Eycks are
triumphant examples of this. Nothing could be nobler in its general
effect than the great Ghent altarpiece "The Adoration of the Lamb";
yet the elaboration of detail extends to exquisitely painted little
blossoms almost hidden in the grass of the foreground, and even to the
exact rendering of lines and callosities on the upturned feet of the
group of kneeling pilgrims. The head of the donor in John van Eyck's
Virgin and Child (Bruges Museum) is very possibly the most wonderful
rendering in the world of an old man's face; yet what the eye first
sees is the deeply religious effect of the whole picture. The details
do not detract from the breadth of conception and force of style;
they give a separate and superadded pleasure.

p. 92, l. 40. **chiaro scuro.** An Italian word meaning literally the
"clear-obscure" or the "light-dark"; it is technically used to mean
the blending of light and shade in art—the rendering of light in darkness
and darkness in light. Rembrandt is the most obvious master of
chiaroscuro.

p. 93, l. 30. **as in a glass darkly.** 1 Corinthians, xiii, 12.

p. 93, l. 32. **sees into the life of things**. Wordsworth's, *Tintern
Abbey* lines, l. 49:

> While with an eye made quiet by the power
> Of harmony, and the deep power of joy,
> We see into the life of things.

p. 93, l. 39. **the perishable vehicle.** The "vehicle" in painting
is the liquid in which the pigments are mixed so that they can be brushed
on the canvas. The usual vehicle is oil—hence the term "oil painting."
In the old kind of painting called "tempera" the vehicle was white
of egg. The use of oil as a vehicle is traditionally supposed to have
been the invention of Hubert and John van Eyck (1370?–1426 and
1389–1440). How perishable some of the English vehicles (and pigments) have been may be seen in a comparison of the many ruined
pictures by Romney and Reynolds with the unfaded freshness of pictures
by Memlinc and the Van Eycks, painted three hundred and fifty years
earlier.

p. 94, l. 5. **Jan Steen**. Jan Steen (1626–1679), son of a Dutch brewer and himself in the same line of business, was appropriately the typical painter of jovial and carousing scenes. The National Gallery has several examples. Gerard Dow (1613–1675), another Dutch painter, is also famous for his "interiors."

p. 94, l. 6. **casuist**. A casuist is, so to speak, a lawyer of the conscience, one who determines the line of conduct to be followed in difficult cases where the claims of various obligations come into conflict. It will be easily understood that casuistry generally involved a great deal of hair-splitting.

p. 94, l. 8. **mist, the common gloss**, etc. *Paradise Lost*, v, 435, etc.:

> So down they sat,
> And to their viands fell; nor seemingly
> The Angel, nor in mist—the common gloss
> Of theologians—but with keen dispatch
> Of real hunger.

p. 94, l. 23. **Opie**. John Opie (1761–1807), a poor carpenter's son at Truro, where his talents were discovered by Peter Pindar (see p. 178) who helped him to become a successful painter. Opie's work is less admired than it was. He is one of the several painters to whom is attributed the famous reply to the question what he mixed his colours with—"With brains, Sir!"

p. 94, l. 31. **Richardson**. Jonathan Richardson (1665–1745) was famous both as a portrait painter and as a writer on art. His sound work as a portraitist can be studied in the National Portrait Gallery, which has some half dozen of his pictures, including portraits of Pope, Prior, Steele and himself. His literary works, *The Theory of Painting, The Connoisseur, an Essay on the whole Art of Criticism as it relates to Painting* and *An Account of some of the Statues, Bas-Reliefs, Drawings and Paintings in Italy*, are still deserving of attention by amateurs of art. Hazlitt quotes from him in the next essay. The original source of the story about Michael Angelo and Julius II is the famous *Lives of the Best Painters, Architects and Sculptors* written by Giorgio Vasari (1511–74).

p. 95, l. 33. **Andrea del Sarto**. A Florentine painter (1486–1531), whose "Portrait of a Sculptor" (erroneously called a portrait of himself) in the National Gallery is a well-known and popular picture. Hazlitt's choice of him as an example of "slow, patient, laborious execution" is not very happy, as Andrea was in fact a brilliant and rapid workman, whose mastery of technique earned him the title of "the faultless painter."

p. 95, l. 36. **That you might almost say,** etc. Donne, *The Second Anniversary*, l. 246:

> her pure and eloquent blood
> Spoke in her cheeks, and so distinctly wrought,
> That one might almost say, her body thought.

p. 96, l. 16. **Abraham Tucker**. Abraham Tucker (1705–1774), the author of *The Light of Nature Pursued*, lived near Dorking. His book extended to no less than seven volumes, four of which he published in 1768 under the pseudonym "Edward Search"; the other three, edited by his daughter, appeared posthumously in 1778. Tucker's book has an interest for students of Hazlitt, for he compiled an abridgement of it in a single volume (published 1807) and wrote a long preface which is one of the earliest pieces in which his characteristic qualities appear. The book itself may be described as a rambling philosophical treatise on things in general, written by a man of unusual common-sense and clear-headed understanding. Hazlitt says, "To the ingenuity and closeness of the metaphysician he unites the principal knowledge of the man of the world, and the utmost sprightliness, and even levity of imagination."

p. 96, l. 38. **rich impasting.** "Impasto" in painting is the laying on of colour very thickly.

p. 97, l. 2. **Shaftesbury's Characteristics.** Anthony Ashley Cooper, third Earl of Shaftesbury (1671–1713), a philosophical Whig peer, wrote several essays or disquisitions collected under the general title *Characteristics of Men, Manners, Opinions and Times.* Shaftes-bury had some free-thinking tendencies and drew upon himself many attacks, the most notable being the *Alciphron* of Berkeley. Lamb takes him as an extreme example of the "genteel style" in writing. Shaftesbury has been rather unfairly estimated, most people being content to take their view of him from his religious opponents. He was before his time, and, in fact, there is much in *Characteristics* that a modern reader may sincerely admire as anticipative of contemporary ideas. Some of the earlier editions of *Characteristics* have finely etched plates by Gribelin, for whom see p. 249.

p. 97, l. 5. **riches fineless.** "Infinite wealth," a phrase from *Othello,* Act III, Sc. iii, l. 173:

> Poor and content is rich and rich enough,
> But riches fineless is as poor as winter
> To him that ever fears he shall be poor.

p. 97, l. 16. **ever in the haunch,** etc. 2 *Henry IV,* Act IV, Sc. iv, l. 92:

> thou art a summer bird,
> Which ever in the haunch of winter sings
> The lifting up of day.

p. 97, l. 25. **with Correggio.** Many traditional stories exist about the poverty, timidity and modest self-distrust of Correggio. Modern research has tended to destroy these legends.

p. 97, l. 31. **to the Exhibition.** Hazlitt's portrait of his father was hung in the Royal Academy exhibition of 1806.

p. 97, l. 32. **Mr Skeffington.** Sir Lumley St George Skeffington (1771–1850), a "buck" of the Regency period, wrote several plays of no importance. He was a well known and much caricatured figure in the Society of his time, and is said to have been consulted by the Regent in important matters of dress.

p. 97, l. 37. **the battle of Austerlitz.** Dec. 2, 1805. Hazlitt, the ardent Napoleonist, was naturally as uplifted by his hero's victory over the Austrians and Russians as he was afterwards saddened by Waterloo and St Helena.

p. 98, l. 1. **the great Platonic year.** Plato's year is the mythical period in which the heavenly bodies will have completed as many revolutions as will bring them all back to the same relative positions that they held at the beginning of time. To use a simple explanation, it is the "least common multiple" of all the different planetary and celestial "years," and it was estimated at anything from 12,000 to 365,000 terrestrial years. The new era begun when this "year of years" was completed would reproduce the past in every particular. See Plato's *Timaeus*, 38, for the passage describing this "year" (Jowett's translation, Vol. III, p. 457).

p. 98, l. 6. **full of years.** Hazlitt's father died in 1820 aged 83. His mother was over 90 at her death.

ON THE PLEASURE OF PAINTING. II

Essay II of *Table-Talk*.

p. 99, l. 4. **Whate'er Lorraine,** etc. Thomson, *The Castle of Indolence*, Canto 1, Stanza 38. "Savage Rosa" is Salvator Rosa (1615–1673), a painter whose melodramatic representations of wild landscapes were much admired in the "Romantic" period of Hazlitt's youth. Salvator was a man of many accomplishments, and won fame as poet and musician.

p. 99, l. 8. **Lord Radnor's park,** etc. Longford Castle, Wiltshire, where there is an admirable collection of paintings. The Radnor Claudes are a pair. One represents the landing of Aeneas in Italy at sunrise, and is an allegory of Rome in its uprising. The other shows a ruined arch and aqueduct in a pastoral landscape, and is an allegory of Rome decayed and fallen. They were shown a few years ago at an "Old Masters" exhibition at the Royal Academy. Van Dyck's portrait of the Herbert family hangs in the Great Room at Wilton for which it was painted and from which it has never been moved. For the Blenheim Rubens see p. 223. The Van Dyck there was a portrait of the Duchess of Buckingham with her three children looking at a miniature—presumably of the assassinated Duke. Rembrandt's "Belshazzar's Feast" is still in the possession of Lord Derby at Knowsley. It was shown at the Rembrandt "Old Masters" exhibition of 1899. Burghley House, near Stamford, the famous residence of Lord Exeter, still has its large collection of Guido's sentimental saints.

p. 99, l. 17. **bosomed high**, etc. *L'Allegro*, l. 78:

> Towers and battlements he sees
> Bosomed high in tufted trees.

p. 100, l. 2. **the Orleans Gallery.** Philippe, Duke of Orleans (1674–1723), the Regent of France on the death of Louis XIV, amassed a vast and wonderful collection of important pictures, in number nearly five hundred, including, for instance, 27 assigned to Titian, 19 to Rubens, 12 to Van Dyck and 7 to Rembrandt. Even with the deductions made for too optimistic attributions, the Orleans collection was by far the greatest in the possession of any one person. The strange adventures of the collection began with the death of the founder. His son Louis was a fanatic, and, disapproving of some Correggios, he cut off their heads, and burned them. The son of Louis was the notorious Philippe Égalité of the Revolution (1747–1793). The Orleans collection did not interest him and he sold the pictures in 1792 for a mere fraction of their value. The best of them were bought by a Belgian banker, and a large number by an English collector, Mr Thomas Moor Slade. A patriotic Frenchman, angry at seeing the pictures lost to France, bought back the Belgian purchase; but during the Terror, he fled to England and carried the pictures with him. Finding himself without means, he sold his Orleans purchase to an English dealer. From him they were bought by three English noblemen acting in concert, the Duke of Bridgewater, the Marquis of Stafford and the Earl of Carlisle. The pictures were catalogued and exhibited for public sale from December, 1798, to August, 1799. It was then that Hazlitt saw them. In the end, the best of the pictures were kept by the noble purchasers who, however, got for the rest at least as much as they had paid for the original collection.

p. 100, l. 8. **hands that the rod,** etc. Gray's *Elegy*.

p. 100, l. 9. **a forked mountain.** *Antony and Cleopatra*, Act IV, Sc. xiv, l. 5, etc.:

> Sometime we see a cloud that's dragonish;
> A vapour sometimes like a bear or lion,
> A towered citadel, a pendent rock,
> A forkèd mountain, or blue promontory
> With trees upon't, that nod unto the world,
> And mock our eyes with air.

p. 100, l. 20. **signifying nothing.** *Macbeth*, Act V, Sc. v, l. 28:

> Life's but a walking shadow, a poor player
> That struts and frets his hour upon the stage
> And then is heard no more: it is a tale
> Told by an idiot, full of sound and fury,
> Signifying nothing.

p. 100, l. 25. **the Provoked Husband.** A comedy by Vanbrugh left incomplete, and finished by Colley Cibber.

p. 100, l. 27. **Ruysdael and Hobbima.** Two admirable Dutch landscape artists. Jacob van Ruisdael (1628 or 9-1682) is well represented in the National Gallery, where his peaceful landscape scenes with their characteristic silvery tones are general favourites. Meindert Hobbema (1638-1709) painted excellent landscapes during a very short period of his life. His "Avenue of Middelharnis" in the National Gallery is one of the most popular, as it is one of the most delightful, among landscape pictures.

p. 100, l. 33. **when I went to the Louvre.** In October, 1802.

p. 100, l. 38. **Titian's Mistress,** etc. See p. 197. In this picture the beautiful Laura is seen twisting a tress of golden hair before a mirror. Alfonso is dimly descried in the background. "A Young Nobleman with a Glove" is the familiar and splendid "L'homme au gant," one of Titian's finest portrait pictures. The "companion to it" is Titian's portrait of Aretino, generally described as "Homme Inconnu." Both hang in the "Grande Galerie" of the Louvre.

p. 101, l. 8. **the Transfiguration.** By Raphael. This great picture, Raphael's last work, was part of the loot gathered by Napoleon in his Italian campaign. It was brought to Paris in 1797 and returned to Rome in 1815. It is now in the Vatican.

p. 101, l. 19. **where Rubens hung out,** etc. Marie de' Medici, widow of Henri IV, ordered eighteen large paintings from Rubens to decorate the Luxembourg Palace. They were planned by the master, and largely executed by his pupils, with finishing touches from his own hands. They now hang in a hall of the Louvre specially arranged for them.

p. 101, l. 23. **un beau jour.** Doubtless a reference to the famous description by Bailly of the 6th October, 1789, when, after what is known as the "insurrection of women," Louis XVI was brought by compulsion from Versailles to Paris where he would be under the eye of the National Assembly. Burke is very indignant about Bailly's "beau jour."

p. 101, l. 29. **the Transfiguration, the St Peter,** etc. For the "Transfiguration" see note above. Titian's "St Peter Martyr," another of Napoleon's captures, was given back to Venice in 1815. It was destroyed by fire in 1867. His portrait of Cardinal Ippolito de' Medici is now in Florence whence Napoleon had taken it. Domenichino's "Communion of St Jerome," one of his best works, was given back to Rome and is now in the Vatican.

p. 101, l. 38. **if thou hast not seen the Louvre,** etc. A reminiscence of *As You Like It*, Act III, Sc. ii, l. 35, etc.:

Touchstone. Wast ever in court, shepherd?
Corin. No, truly.
T. Then thou art damned.
C. Nay, I hope.
T. Truly, thou art damned like an ill-roasted egg, all on one side.

p. 102, l. 3. **the Elgin marbles.** Many sculptures, architectural fragments and casts of the highest value from Athens, Mycaenae and elsewhere, brought from Greece in 1812 by Lord Elgin (1766–1841), the British Ambassador to the Porte. These irreplaceable works of art were gradually being destroyed, and, to save them, Lord Elgin obtained permission from the indifferent Turks for their removal. In 1816 the British government bought the collection, which is now housed in the British Museum. There, such great works as "The Dew Maidens" (or "Three Fates") and the "Ilyssus," have long been familiar and admired figures. The purchase aroused great controversy, in which the experts were utterly in the wrong. One of Hazlitt's essays deals with the Elgin marbles.

p. 102, l. 5. **Quatre heures,** etc. "Past four o'clock; it is closing time, citizens."

p. 102, l. 9. **hard money.** Doubtless a reminiscence of Farquhar's *The Recruiting Officer*, Act IV, Sc. iii: "Your mother has a hundred pound in hard money lying at this minute in the hands of a mercer not forty yards from this place." "Hard money" is cash, as distinguished from paper money. "Hard cash" is a familiar modern phrase.

p. 102, l. 10. **thou tenantless mansion.** Tenantless, through the restoration of many famous pictures.

p. 102, l. 16. **experimentum crucis.** A crucial or decisive experiment.

p. 102, l. 17. **number numberless**. *Paradise Regained*, III, 310:
He looked, and saw what numbers numberless
The city gates outpoured.

"Numbers numberless" visited France after the Peace of Amiens in 1802, the first real breathing space since the outbreak of war in 1793.

p. 102, l. 27. **casual fruition.** *Paradise Lost*, Bk IV, l. 766.

p. 102, l. 38. **Knowledge is pleasure as well as power.** Hazlitt has the same sentence in his *Round Table* essay *On Imitation.* Compare Newman, *University Teaching*, Discourse V, par. 6: "Knowledge, indeed, when thus exalted into a scientific form, is also power.... Doubtless;...I only say that, prior to its being a power, it is a good; that it is, not only an instrument, but an end."

p. 103, l. 25. **W.** Richard Wilson, or possibly Sir David Wilkie.

p. 103, l. 26. **Dutch cabinet picture.** A cabinet picture is so called because it is intended to be hung in a private room, and not in a Church or public institution. The Dutch were among the first to produce paintings for domestic use.

p. 104, l. 11. **a friend of mine.** Northcote, for whom see p. 176. The important work was no doubt his *Memoirs of Sir Joshua Reynolds*, published in 1813 and praised in *The Edinburgh Review.*

p. 104, l. 29. **A friend had bought.** It is suggested that this was Haydon. It might have been Lamb.

p. 105, l. 36. **Richardson.** See p. 228. The instances he quotes are drawn mainly from Vasari.

p. 106, l. 18. **who restored Painting.** This high view of Annibale Carracci is not now held. See p. 223.

p. 107, l. 3. **missed a Cardinal's hat.** Vasari is the authority for the statement that Pope Leo X intended to bestow a Red Hat on Raphael.

p. 107, l. 9. **Parmigiano.** Francesco Maria Mazzola, called Parmigiano from Parma, his birthplace.

p. 108, l. 10. **Gandy.** William Gandy, portrait painter, was born in the latter half of the seventeenth century. He was the son of James Gandy, a portrait painter of Exeter, who was said to have been a pupil of Van Dyck. William Gandy lived at Exeter and seems to have spent the whole of his life in Devonshire. He died in 1715. Reynolds was also a Devon man.

p. 108, l. 21. **Dan Stringer.** Daniel Stringer studied in the Royal Academy about 1770. He has been praised for his portrait heads and comic sketches; but he lacked application, and seems gradually to have abandoned art. For further references to Gandy and Stringer see *Conversations of Northcote.*

p. 108, l. 29. **swallowing the tailor's news.** *King John*, Act IV, Sc. ii, l. 195:

> I saw a smith stand with his hammer, thus,
> The whilst his iron did on the anvil cool,
> With open mouth swallowing a tailor's news.

p. 108, l. 29. **bastards of his genius.** Perhaps a reminiscence of Shakespeare's *A Lover's Complaint*, 174—5, lines descriptive of one who

> Thought characters and words merely but art,
> And bastards of his foul adulterate heart.

THE FIGHT

Published in *The New Monthly Magazine*, 1822, and not included by Hazlitt in any collection of his essays. It was republished in *Literary Remains* and *Winterslow*. So many heroes of the Ring are referred to in the piece that a general note covering all of them may be given at once. Quotations not otherwise described are taken from Pierce Egan's *Boxiana*.

JACK RANDALL, "the Prime Irish Lad otherwise the Nonpareil," was the best light-weight of his day. In one of his combats, that with "West-country Dick" in 1817, he fought twenty-nine rounds and left the ring without a mark on his face. One of his severest battles was fought with Ned Turner, another light-weight, a London Welshman, as Randall was a London Irishman. After thirty-five rounds the Welshman failed to come up. Randall retired in the height of his fame and took "The Hole in the Wall" public house in Chancery Lane, which thereafter became a regular place of call for the Fancy. NED TURNER, though defeated by Randall, was an accomplished fighter. His most terrible "mill" was that with Curtis in 1816, which lasted for sixty-eight rounds and terminated fatally, for the defeated Curtis died after leaving the Ring. Turner received many compliments at his trial, though he was found technically guilty of manslaughter and sentenced to imprisonment for two months. He was also prominent in another fight, that with the "All-conquering Scroggins." JACK SCROGGINS, whose real name was John Palmer, had served in the Royal Navy, and apparently had spent his time in fighting, not the enemy, but his own shipmates. His success in these friendly combats led him to the Prize Ring where "little Scroggy," in spite of an unorthodox style, soon gained much renown among amateurs of the Fancy. For a long time he was unbeaten; but a quarrel having arisen between him and Turner, the matter went to the Ring. The first fight (March, 1817) was interrupted, but in the second, a few weeks later, "the invincible Scroggy," the "little Napoleon of the Ring," met his Waterloo. A third contest confirmed the supremacy of Turner. Scroggins, it may be observed, had taken to drink and refused to train. Hence his downfall. TOM BELCHER, brother of the more celebrated Jem, was victor in eight out of twelve big contests in the Ring. "As a sparrer Tom is truly distinguished, and exhibits all the various traits of the art with the utmost elegance and perfection; and who has turned out a number of very expert and scientific pupils. In several of the principal towns of the kingdom TOM has pourtrayed the utility of the Science of Self Defence with considerable respectability and attention; and is in height about five feet nine inches, weight near eleven stone —his appearance much of the gentleman, and his manners and deportment are of that mild and inoffensive nature well calculated to prepossess the stranger much in his favour." JACK MARTIN, "the Baker," was an active fighter of light to middle weight. He was called "The Master of the Rolls" in allusion to his trade. BILL RICHMOND was a "gentleman of colour" born in America. He was about five feet ten and fought at fourteen stone. He was discovered by General Earl Percy (afterwards Duke of Northumberland) during the American

War of Independence, and brought to England, where he presently took to the Ring. Unlike certain other coloured pugilists, Richmond was "intelligent, communicative and well-behaved." BILL MATTHEWS, a bookbinder, distinguished himself in a big drawn fight with another coloured pugilist "Black George." TOM CRIBB, the Champion of England, was a Gloucester man. His fight with Jem Belcher took place at Epsom on Feb. 1, 1809. Belcher had been Champion, but was defeated after thirty-one rounds, and "resigned the palm of Victory to Cribb, never more to enter the field of honour." Cribb was an ornament to the Ring and was highly esteemed by all noble and gentle sportsmen of the day. "He left the field of glory covered with honour and renown to pass the remainder of his days in tranquillity and peace, by paying attention to his business as a coal-merchant"—though later he declined upon that inevitable last refuge of the retired professional, the public-house. Tom, it seems, was "placid, condescending, and obliging, possessing great forbearance of temper." HENRY PEARCE, "scientifically denominated the Game Chicken...the Broughton of his time and one of the most heroic and humane Champions of England, who not only added fresh laurels to that title but never lost that distinguished appellation till it was wrested from him by that Conqueror of Conquerors—Death!"—thus the epic strain of *Boxiana*. The Chicken gained much glory by his heroic rescue of a woman from a burning house. JOHN GULLEY, Champion of England in succession to the Chicken, was a tall man and heavy weight, a very notable fighter on scientific lines. "With a knowledge of the world he unites the manners of a well-bred man. Unassuming and intelligent upon all occasions, this conduct has gained him respect and attention in the circles in which he moves; and which are by no means of an inferior class. Thus proving, in himself, a lively instance, that ALL PUGILISTS are not excluded from polite society." JOHN JACKSON, "Gentleman Jackson," "one of the best made men in the kingdom...wisely endeavoured to unite with the above expression that of being one of the best behaved men also." He seems to have made a great impression, not only by his strength and science in the Ring, but by what Mr Turveydrop would have called his deportment. A cast of his arm was taken and preserved as a model of anatomical perfection. BILL NEAT, "a butcher by trade and a stout hearty blade," one of the heroes of Hazlitt's first fight, was a Bristol man of very respectable connections. He stood half an inch short of six feet and turned the scale at thirteen stone seven. His first big fight was in 1818 with Oliver, whom he defeated in twenty-eight rounds. His hits from the shoulder had astonishing and peculiar force. There was some ill-feeling between Neat and the great Cribb, but it does not appear that they ever met in the Ring. TOM HICKMAN, "better known as the Gas-Light Man," is described almost lyrically by *Boxiana* as "a second Hotspur—impatient—fiery —daring—hardy—impetuous—laughing to naught all his opponents." "This tremendous hero of the 'Fives' first opened his *peepers* in search of chivalrous adventures in Ken Lane, Dudley, in Worcestershire, on the 28th of January, 1785." He seems to have been a fighter from his cradle, and his name (like that of another fighter, Cromwell) was used as a word of fear to frighten small evil-doers into virtue. He stood 5 ft. 9½ in. and fought at 11 st. 11 lbs. Many of his victories were gained in extremely short times, fifteen minutes being enough for some of his opponents. "The Gas" seems to have had a regrettable tendency towards boasting. *Boxiana* concludes his biography with a significant sentence. "No boxer ever had a higher opinion of his own powers than HICK. It should seem that he almost flatters himself he is INVULNERABLE." However, he met his fate at the hands of Bill Neat on December 11th, 1821, in the battle described by Hazlitt. Eighteen rounds settled the matter, but the Gas was really beaten by the ninth. As in the case of other great victories, a medal was struck to celebrate the event, but it is sad to relate that numismatic art failed to attain the ideal of pugilistic accuracy, for the combatants are represented as fighting on boards instead of on the grass, and are placed in attitudes that would give any fighting man a fit of hilarious contempt. The fourth volume of *Boxiana* devotes many pages to this fight. The Muse, too, was not silent. Perhaps we may quote the last stanza of one song:

> In eighteen rounds *the Gas* was spent,
>   His pipes lay undefended,
> When Gas-light shares fell cent. per cent.,
>   And thus the battle ended.
> The Cockney's tune was altered soon,
>   In purse and spirits undone,
> As on the rack they toddled back
>   With empty clies to London.
>   Come Bristol boys, let's claim the *bays*,
>   Come Daffies, spruce and clever,
>   With loud HUZZAS proclaim his praise,
>   Sing CHAMPION NEAT for ever.

Clies, we might observe, are pockets.

Three other literary "fights" may be named, those in Borrow's *Lavengro*, George Meredith's *Amazing Marriage* and Conan Doyle's *Rodney Stone*. Borrow's hymn of praise to the "bruisers of England" is noticeably in the key of Hazlitt's essay. See Chapter XXVI in *Lavengro*.

p. 109, l. 1. **the fight's the thing.** Adapted from *Hamlet*, Act II, Sc. ii, ll. 633–4:

> the play's the thing
> Wherein I'll catch the conscience of the king.

p. 109, l. 6. **'the proverb' nothing 'musty.'** Adapted from *Hamlet*, Act III, Sc. ii, ll. 359, etc.: "Ay sir, but, 'while the grass grows'—the proverb is something musty."

p. 109, l. 18. **the Fancy.** "Fancy" means, among other things, "preference" or "inclination." Those who have a "fancy" for dogs are called "dog-fanciers," for pigeons, "pigeon-fanciers," and so on. But chief of all the sporting "fancies" is "*The* Fancy," meaning the patrons of pugilism.

p. 109, l. 22. **the author of Waverley.** Not yet publicly known as Scott. "To ask at" is a Scotticism, that is, an expression that might be used by any Scot, including "the Author of Waverley"; but I cannot recall an instance of Sir Walter's actually using it in any of the novels.

p. 109, l. 24. **with the authenticity,** etc. Randall being the champion light-weight, his lady, Mrs Randall, would probably have authentic information about the fight.

p. 109, l. 31. **blue ruin.** Gin.

p. 110, l. 9. **Jo. Toms**. Identified as Hazlitt's friend Joseph Parkes, a lawyer, later well known as a Radical politician.

p. 110, l. 22. **fleet the time**. Adapted from *As You Like It*, Act I, Sc. i: "They say he is already in the forest of Arden;...they say many young gentlemen flock to him every day, and fleet the time carelessly as they did in the golden world"—the golden world being the fabled "golden age" or "age of Saturn," in the childhood of the world, when life knew nothing of sin and pain.

p. 110, l. 25. **Jack Pigott**. Identified as Hazlitt's friend P. G. Patmore, for whom see p. 174.

p. 110, l. 30. **What more felicity,** etc. From Spenser's *Muiopotmos, or the Fate of the Butterflie*, Stanza 27. The lines are famous through their appearance as a sort of motto on the title page of Keats's first published volume, the *Poems* of 1817.

p. 111, l. 5. **we meet at Philippi**. Adapted from *Julius Caesar*, Act IV, Sc. iii.

p. 111, l. 6. **to Piccadilly**. The Bath and Bristol mails started from the White Horse Cellars, Piccadilly—now a restaurant. It was from the White Horse Cellars that Mr Pickwick and his friends started on their memorable visit to Bath.

p. 111, l. 15. **my Rubicon**. The Rubicon was a small stream that flowed into the Adriatic where the modern town of Rimini stands. Its importance was that in the days of Caesar it formed part of the boundary between Cisalpine Gaul and Italia proper. To cross the Rubicon southwards was therefore to pass from a province into the actual territory of Rome. Julius Caesar governed in Cisalpine Gaul, and when in 53 B.C., as a result of Pompey's enmity, the Senate ordered Caesar to disband his forces and resign his power, the great leader's reply was to cross the Rubicon with his army and thus to become the invader of his own country and the originator of civil war. "To cross the Rubicon" means therefore to take a decisive, irrevocable step. Hazlitt calls Hyde Park Corner his Rubicon because to pass it meant a resolution to continue his journey westwards out of London. Hyde Park Corner was regarded as the beginning of London, a popular name for the Duke of Wellington's residence, Apsley House, which stands just to the east of the Park gate, being "Number One, London."

p. 111, l. 37. **I follow fate**. Dryden, *The Indian Emperor*, Act IV, a song at the beginning of Sc. iii:

> Ah, fading Joy, how quickly art thou past?
>   Yet we thy ruin haste.
> As if the cares of human life were few,
>   We seek out new,
> And follow Fate which would too fast pursue.

p. 112, l. 10. **the Brentford Jehu**. Jehu, a slang name for a driver; the reference being to 2 Kings ix, 20, "and the driving is like the driving of Jehu the son of Nimshi, for he driveth furiously."

p. 112, l. 18. **Tom Turtle**. Identified as John Thurtell (1794–1824), a Norwich man, who figured largely in the sporting world, and became later notorious as the murderer of a gambling companion named Weare. He was hanged at Hertford. It was Thurtell who first taught boxing to the author of *The Bible in Spain*; and readers of *Lavengro* will remember the sinister entry of Thurtell into that story and the forecast of his fate made in the storm by Jasper Petulengro. Thurtell arranged many fights and was so interested in his sport that shortly before his execution he desired to read Pierce Egan's account of the fight between Spring and Langan which had just taken place.

p. 112, l. 38. **quite chap-fallen.** From Hamlet's speech about the skull of Yorick—Act v, Sc. i: "Where be your gibes now? your gambols? your songs? your flashes of merriment that were wont to set the table on a roar? Not one now, to mock your own grinning? quite chap-fallen?" "Chap-fallen" means "dejected," "dispirited," or literally "down in the mouth," as Yorick's skull was, the chaps or cheeks having disappeared and the lower jaw fallen.

p. 113, l. 11. **under the rose.** "Secretly"—familiar, too, in its Latin form "sub rosa." A legend relates that Cupid gave a rose to Harpocrates, or Horus, the god of silence, to bribe him not to betray certain inconvenient secrets.

p. 113, l. 23. **where good digestion,** etc. Adapted from *Macbeth*, Act III, Sc. iv, l. 38.

p. 113, l. 28. **Follows so,** etc. See p. 167.

p. 113, l. 33. **coloquintida,** etc. Colocynth is the dried and powdered medicinal herb known as "bitter apple." Aconite is the poisonous extract derived from the plant monkshood or wolf's bane. Compare *Othello*, Act I, Sc. iii, l. 355: "The food that to him now is as luscious as locusts, shall be to him shortly as bitter as coloquintida." Hazlitt's bitterness has reference, no doubt, to the failure of his marriage. At the date of this essay divorce proceedings were being taken against him in the Scottish courts by his wife.

p. 113, l. 36. **more figures.** See p. 155.

p. 114, l. 2. **an indigestion.** In Hazlitt's case the result of excessive tea-drinking.

p. 114, l. 16. **a foregone conclusion.** See p. 221.

p. 114, l. 19. **seriously inclined.** *Othello*, Act I, Sc. iii, l. 145:
> This to hear
> Would Desdemona seriously incline.

p. 114, l. 20. **un beau jour.** See p. 232.

p. 115, l. 2. **the vein of Gilpin.** There is nothing in Cowper's delightful ballad exactly like this answer. In spirit it may be likened, perhaps, to the following stanza, with its witty equivocation:
> I came because your horse would come,
>   And, if I well forbode,
> My hat and wig will soon be here,
>   They are upon the road.

p. 115, l. 11. **mum's the word.** See p. 165.

p. 115, l. 29. **A lusty man,** etc. From Chaucer, *Prologue to the Canterbury Tales*, l. 167:
> A monk ther was, fair for the maistrie,
> An outridere that lovéde venerie;
> A manly man, to been an abbot able.

p. 116, l. 5. **oaken towel.** An old slang name for a cudgel. The word "towelling" for a thrashing may still be heard.

p. 116, l. 7. **he moralized**, etc. From *As You Like It*, Act II, Sc. i, l. 44:

> *Duke.* But what said Jaques,
> Did he not moralize this spectacle?
> *Lord.* O, yes, into a thousand similes.

p. 116, l. 8. **like Bardolph's.** 1 *Henry IV*, Act III, Sc. iii, l. 29, etc.:

Bard. Why, you are so fat, Sir John, that you must needs be out of all compass,—out of all reasonable compass, Sir John.

Fal. Do thou amend thy face, and I'll amend my life. Thou art our admiral, thou bearest the lantern in the poop,—but 't is in the nose of thee; thou art the Knight of the Burning Lamp.

Bard. Why, Sir John, my face does you no harm.

Fal. No, I'll be sworn, I make as good use of it as many a man doth of a death's-head or a *memento mori*. I never see thy face but I think upon hell-fire, and Dives that lived in purple; for there he is in his robes, burning, burning. If thou wert any way given to virtue, I would swear by thy face; my oath should be, "By this fire, that's God's angel." But thou art altogether given over, and wert indeed, but for the light in thy face, the son of utter darkness. When thou rann'st up Gadshill in the night to catch my horse, if I did not think thou hadst been an *ignis fatuus* or a ball of wild-fire, there's no purchase in money. O, thou art a perpetual triumph, an everlasting bonfire-light. Thou hast saved me a thousand marks in links and torches, walking with thee in the night betwixt tavern and tavern: but the sack that thou hast drunk me would have bought me lights as good cheap at the dearest chandler's in Europe. I have maintained that salamander of yours with fire any time this two-and-thirty years; God reward me for it!

There is a further reference in *Henry V*, Act II, Sc. iii.

p. 116, l. 21. **loud and furious fun.** A reminiscence of Burns, *Tam o' Shanter*:

> As Tammie glowered, amazed and curious,
> The mirth and fun grew fast and furious.

p. 117, l. 31. **the old maxim.** The most famous form of this saying is Danton's great utterance in 1792 when the safety of the young Republic of France was threatened by powerful Austrian and German forces: "De l'audace, encore de l'audace, toujours de l'audace, et la France est sauvée."

p. 117, l. 37. **Alas, the Bristol man,** etc. Cowper, *The Task*, II, 322:

> Alas! Leviathan is not so tamed:
> Laughed at, he laughs again; and stricken hard,
> Turns to the stroke his adamantine scales,
> That feel no discipline of human hands.

p. 118, l. 9. **Achilles surveyed Hector.** The great fight between Achilles and Hector is told in *Iliad* XXII.

p. 118, l. 30. **man was made to mourn.** The title and refrain of a poem by Burns.

p. 119, l. 25. **Between the acting**, etc. *Julius Caesar*, Act II, Sc. i, 63–65.

p. 120, l. 9. **Ajax.** Ajax or Aias, one of the Greek heroes at the siege of Troy, second only to Achilles in prowess.

p. 120, l. 13. **with Atlantean shoulders.** *Paradise Lost*, II, 306, part of the description of Beelzebub:

> sage he stood
> With Atlantean shoulders fit to bear
> The weight of mightiest monarchies

—Atlas being one of the Titans, who, as Homer says, "knows the depth of every sea and himself upholds the tall pillars which keep earth and sky asunder."

p. 120, l. 14. **Diomed.** Another of the Greek heroes at the siege of Troy.

p. 121, l. 11. **grinned horrible.** *Paradise Lost*, II, 846:

> He ceased, for both seemed highly pleased, and Death
> Grinned horrible a ghastly smile, to hear
> His famine should be filled.

p. 121, l. 35. **like two clouds.** *Paradise Lost*, II, 714–6.

> As when two black clouds
> With Heaven's artillery fraught, come rattling on
> Over the Caspian, then stand front to front
> Hovering a space, till winds the signal blow
> To join their dark encounter in mid air:
> So frowned the mighty combatants, that Hell
> Grew darker at their frown.

p. 122, l. 38. **In doleful dumps.** From the ballad *Chevy Chase*.

p. 123, l. 4. **Sir Fopling Flutter.** See p. 178. Sir Fopling is a foolish beau fond of dragging in French phrases on all possible occasions.

p. 124, l. 5. **O procul.** Vergil, *Aeneid*, VI, 258:

> "Procul. O procul este, profani,"
> Conclamat vates, "totoque absistite luco."

"Away, be ye gone, ye unhallowed ones," the prophetess cries, "and withdraw from all this sacred grove."

p. 124, l. 5. **flash-men.** Rogues—coiners, thieves, etc.

p. 124, l. 6. **Tothill Fields.** A part of Westminster.

p. 124, l. 9. **a cross.** That is, not a straight fight, but one in which the beaten man is bribed to lose.

p. 124, l. 12. **sans intermission.** A reminiscence of *As You Like It*, Act II, Sc. vii, l. 32:

> And I did laugh sans intermission
> An hour by his dial.

p. 124, l. 29. **Mr Windham.** William Windham (1750–1810), a statesman, friend of Burke, Johnson, etc., much admired in his day.

p. 124, l. 37. **Broughton and George Stevenson.** Jack Broughton (1704–1789), the father of English pugilism. Broughton was very famous in his day as a scientific fighter, and taught the noble art in his ring at

Hanway Street. Broughton held his own for many years, but was defeated at last by Slack, to the great disgust of his noble patron the Duke of Cumberland, hero of Culloden, who lost heavily over the fight. George Stevenson, the Coachman, fought Broughton when the latter was out of condition, but Broughton was nevertheless the victor. Hazlitt's nice old gentleman seems to have been the kind of nice old gentleman often found at race meetings and similar gatherings; for as the fight between Broughton and "Coachee" took place in 1741 and Hazlitt was writing of 1821, it is hard to see how even the nicest old gentleman in the best state of preservation could have any clear personal recollections of a fight that had taken place eighty years before! The date 1770 is quite wrong. In that year Broughton would have been sixty-six, hardly the age at which a man goes in the Ring.

THE INDIAN JUGGLERS

Essay IX in *Table Talk*.

p. 126, l. 13. **past finding out.** A reminiscence of Romans xi, 33: "O the depth of the riches both of the wisdom and knowledge of God! how unsearchable are his judgments, and his ways past finding out."

p. 128 l. 26. **Sadler's Wells.** A once famous theatre in the north of London, made fashionable in later years by the excellent acting of Samuel Phelps (1804–1878) in a repertory of standard plays. After his time the house rapidly declined, and now no longer exists as a theatre.

p. 128, l. 31. **Peter Pindar.** See p. 178. For Opie, see p. 228.

p. 129, l. 31. **In argument,** etc. Goldsmith, *The Deserted Village*.

p. 130, l. 4. **Jaggernaut.** Juggernaut or Jaggernaut (Jagannath, meaning "lord of the world") was a Hindu god whose image was worshipped at Puri in Orissa. On a certain day of the year, the car of the image made a triumphal procession, and it is said that fanatical devotees used to throw themselves under the vehicle in the belief that, dying thus, they would at once gain entrance to paradise.

p. 131, l. 3. **human face divine.** *Paradise Lost*, Bk III, l. 44, etc., part of the poet's beautiful lament for his blindness:

> Thus with the year
> Seasons return; but not to me returns
> Day, or the sweet approach of even or morn,
> Or sight of vernal bloom, or summer's rose,
> Or flocks, or herds, or human face divine;
> But cloud instead, and ever-during dark
> Surrounds me.

p. 131, l. 18. **H——s and H——s.** One of these is probably Benjamin Haydon, for whom see p. 162. The other may be John Hoppner (1758–1810), a portrait painter of much merit, for whom, however, Hazlitt seems to have had little admiration.

p. 131, l. 21. **in tones and gestures hit.** A reminiscence of *Paradise Regained*, IV, 255:

> There thou shalt hear and learn the secret power
> Of harmony, in tones and numbers hit
> By voice or hand.

p. 131, l. 22. **To snatch this grace.** Pope, *Essay on Criticism*:

> Thus Pegasus, a nearer way to take,
> May boldly deviate from the common track;
> From vulgar bounds with brave disorder part,
> And snatch a grace beyond the reach of art.

p. 131, l. 25. **commercing with the skies.** *Il Penseroso*, from the beautiful passage in which Melancholy is personified as a "pensive nun, devout and pure":

> With even step and musing gait,
> And looks commercing with the skies,
> Thy rapt soul sitting in thine eyes.

p. 132, l. 10. **And visions,** etc. The immediate source of this quotation is a letter from Gray to Walpole (September 1737) describing Burnham Beeches—a beauty spot of which Gray may be called the discoverer: "My comfort amidst all this is, that I have at the distance of half-a-mile, through a green lane, a forest (the vulgar call it a common) all my own, at least as good as so, for I spy no human thing in it but myself. It is a little chaos of mountains and precipices; mountains, it is true, that do not ascend much above the clouds, nor are the declivities quite so amazing as Dover cliff; but just such hills as people who love their necks as well as I do may venture to climb, and crags that give the eye as much pleasure as if they were more dangerous. Both vale and hill are covered with most venerable beeches, and other very reverend vegetables, that, like most other ancient people, are always dreaming out their old stories to the winds,

> And as they bow their hoary tops relate,
> In murm'ring sounds, the dark decrees of fate;
> While visions, as poetic eyes avow,
> Cling to each leaf, and swarm on every bough.

At the foot of one of these, squats ME I (il penseroso), and there grow to the trunk for a whole morning. The timorous hare and sportive squirrel gambol around me like Adam in Paradise, before he had an Eve; but I think he did not use to read Vergil as I commonly do there." The verses seem to be adapted by Gray from *Aeneid*, VI, 282–284 which William Morris thus translates:

> But in the midst a mighty elm, dusk as the night, outspread
> Its immemorial boughs and limbs, where lying dreams there lurk,
> As tells the tale, still clinging close 'neath every leaf-side mirk.

p. 132, l. 20. **Thrills in each nerve.** Possibly a reminiscence of Addison's poem *Milton's Style imitated in a Translation of a Story out of the Aeneid*—the story of Polyphemus:

> we stood
> Amazed, be sure; a sudden horror chill
> Ran through each nerve, and thrilled in every vein,
> Till, using all the force of winds and oars,
> We sped away.

p. 132, l. 38. **half flying, half on foot.** *Paradise Lost*, II, 941–2:

> nigh-foundered, on he fares,
> Treading the rude consistence, half on foot,
> Half flying.

p. 133, l. 13. **I know an individual.** Leigh Hunt.

p. 133, l. 22. nugæ canoræ. "Tuneful trifles," quoted from Horace *On the Art of Poetry*.

p. 133, l. 23. Rochester. John Wilmot, Earl of Rochester (1647–1680), a courtier of Charles II's reign. Rochester wrote many love poems and satires in verse, but possibly his best remembered piece is the witty epitaph on Charles II:

> Here lies our Sovereign Lord the King,
> Whose word no man relies on,
> Who never said a foolish thing
> Nor ever did a wise one.

To which the "merry" monarch was said to have replied that his words were certainly his own, but his deeds were the work of his Ministers.

p. 133, l. 23. Surrey. Henry Howard, Earl of Surrey (1517–1547), a brave and gifted member of a noble family, was executed by Henry VIII on a ridiculous charge of high treason. He wrote many pleasant poems and was the first to use blank verse and the sonnet in English.

p. 133, l. 37. Themistocles said. Themistocles (525–459 B.C.), the famous statesman and soldier of Athens, whose belief in sea power was justified by the great victory over the Persian fleet at Salamis (480). Plutarch's life of Themistocles records that, "when in company where people engaged themselves in what are commonly thought the liberal and elegant amusements, he was obliged to defend himself against the observations of those who considered themselves highly accomplished, by the somewhat arrogant retort, that he certainly could not make use of any stringed instrument, his only accomplishment being the ability so to govern a small and obscure city as to make it great and glorious."

p. 135, l. 2. Jedidiah Buxton. Buxton (1707–1772), the son of a Derbyshire schoolmaster, possessed an altogether abnormal power of mental calculation, but was otherwise illiterate and unteachable. He is said to have worked out the value of a farthing continuously doubled for 139 times and then to have squared the number of pounds in this product. The results, tested by logarithms, appeared to be correct. He was taken to see Garrick in *Richard III* and paid no attention to the piece, his mind being occupied in counting the number of words spoken by the actors. See *Table Talk: On Genius and Common-sense (II)* for a much fuller reference to Jedidiah Buxton.

p. 135, l. 3. Napier's bones. John Napier of Merchiston (1550–1617), a Scottish baron and a wise investigator in many branches of human knowledge, is most famous as the inventor of logarithms. "Napier's bones" was a piece of apparatus for calculations—not unlike the modern slide-rule. Hazlitt's sentence took its form, no doubt, as a reminiscence of Ezekiel xxxvii, 3: "Son of man, can these bones live?"

p. 135, l. 14. A great chess-player. Probably Hazlitt was thinking of Sarratt whom he describes in the essay *On Coffee-House Politicians (Table Talk)*.

p. 135, l. 20. he dies, etc. *Twelfth Night*, Act I, Sc. 5:

> Lady, you are the cruellest she alive
> If you will lead these graces to the grave
> And leave the world no copy.

p. 135, l. 27. **John Hunter.** A very famous surgeon (1728–1793). His great collection of specimens was purchased after his death and forms the nucleus of the museum at the Royal College of Surgeons in Lincoln's Inn Fields.

p. 135, l. 34. **Sir Humphry Davy.** Davy (1778–1829) was born at Penzance and showed early his bent for science. He became famous for his researches in chemistry and electricity, his discoveries including the isolation of such important elements as sodium, potassium and calcium. He is most widely known, however, for his investigations into fire-damp in coal mines and the consequent invention of the Davy safety-lamp. Davy was famous as a lecturer, and in his youth was one of the early admirers of Wordsworth and Coleridge, whom he assisted by supervising the proof-sheets of *Lyrical Ballads*, Vol. II. Hazlitt's disparagement of Davy sounds rather foolish now.

p. 136, l. 5. **a 'great scholar's memory,'** etc. A reminiscence of *Hamlet* III, ii: "O heavens! die two months ago and not forgotten yet? Then there's hope a great man's memory may outlive his life half-a-year."

p. 137, l. 7. **The Roman poet said.** Horace, *Odes* III, 1, l. 40. The original Latin is, "Post equitem sedet atra cura."

p. 137, l. 12. **domestic treason,** etc. *Macbeth*, Act III, Sc. ii, l. 25.
Duncan is in his grave;
After life's fitful fever he sleeps well;
Treason has done his worst: nor steel, nor poison,
Malice domestic, foreign levy, nothing
Can touch him further.

"in the instant," a line above, is another echo of *Macbeth*:
Thy letters have transported me beyond
This ignorant present, and I feel now
The future in the instant.   (Act I, Sc. v. l. 59.)

p. 137, l. 30. **a great orator.** Possibly Pitt.

p. 138, l. 5. **Mr Brougham's speeches.** Henry Brougham, afterwards Lord Brougham and Vaux (1778–1868), was once very famous as a Whig statesman, orator and writer. He undoubtedly did much good in advancing the cause of popular education, but he concerned himself with so many things and wrote so much on all sorts of subjects, that his genuine force was dissipated rather than wisely used. He became Lord Chancellor in 1830, a promotion that provoked O'Connell's gibe, "It's a pity Brougham doesn't know a little law, for then he would know a little of everything." Brougham's restless activities are constantly satirised by Peacock, who calls him "the learned friend," or, more openly, "Sir Guy de Vaux." See *Crotchet Castle* and *Gryll Grange*. A vivacious account of him will be found in Bagehot's *Biographical Studies* and another in Hazlitt's *The Spirit of the Age*.

p. 138, l. 5. **Mr Canning's wit.** George Canning (1770–1827) showed his brilliant gifts very early in his contributions to *The Microcosm*, an Eton periodical of the moment, and later in pieces written for *The Anti-Jacobin*, a famous sheet that attacked the French Revolution and its defenders with the weapons of humour and satire. The delightful *Needy Knife-Grinder* is the best known of his lighter verses, a more serious piece being the address to Pitt as "The Pilot who weathered the Storm." Canning imported his brilliance into Parliamentary speeches. He supported Pitt's war policy and served in that statesman's ministries. He was an efficient Minister for Foreign Affairs during many critical years of the Napoleonic wars, as well as at a later period. He died shortly after becoming Prime Minister. A statesman of this sort was naturally not very acceptable to a Revolutionist like Hazlitt. See however the "Character of Canning" contributed to *The Examiner* and reprinted in some editions of *The Spirit of the Age*.

p. 138, l. 6. **Foul like the Quarterly.** *The Quarterly Review*, a Tory periodical founded in 1809 in opposition to the Whig *Edinburgh*, gained a very unsavoury reputation for the foulness of its attacks on many famous writers during the editorship of William Gifford (1757–1826), successively cabin-boy, shoemaker's apprentice and man of letters. Keats, Hunt, Hazlitt and Lamb were among the notable victims of *The Quarterly*, the attack on Keats being specially disgraceful. See Hazlitt's *A Letter to William Gifford, Esq.* and the sketch of Gifford in *The Spirit of the Age*.

p. 138, l. 6. **the Edinburgh Review.** This famous Whig periodical was started in 1802 with a brilliant band of contributors including Brougham, Sydney Smith, Francis Jeffrey and Francis Horner. Scott was among the early contributors, Hazlitt and Macaulay among the later ones. See Bagehot's essay *The First Edinburgh Reviewers*. A "let" ball is a hindered or obstructed ball—e.g. in lawn tennis, one that touches the top of the net in passing over and has to be served again. Hazlitt seems to imply that *The Edinburgh Review* was not direct and decided enough. For Hazlitt on Jeffrey, see *The Spirit of the Age*.

p. 138, l. 27. **the Rosemary Branch.** Once a well-known pleasure resort and music hall in Southampton Street, Camberwell, and now an ordinary public house. Copenhagen House mentioned lower down was a very famous resort in North London. It was pulled down about 1851–55. The Metropolitan Cattle Market (The Caledonian Market) stands on its site.

p. 139, l. 11. **Goldsmith.** Hazlitt refers to this more explicitly in his eassy "On Envy" (*Plain Speaker*). "Goldsmith was jealous even of beauty in the other sex. When the people at Amsterdam gathered round the balcony to look at the Miss Hornecks, he grew impatient, and said peevishly, 'There are places where I also am admired,'" There is still another reference in the essay "On Living to One's-self" (*Table Talk*). Boswell tells the story under date 1763 of his *Johnson*, and no doubt the general currency of the anecdote derives from Boswell as its source. It is very obvious, however, that Boswell the Scotsman utterly misunderstood and depreciated the Irishman Goldsmith in almost every respect, and certainly in this particular instance; for Mrs Gwyn, "the Jessamy Bride" herself, declared that Goldsmith's remark was merely a playful jest and that she was shocked at seeing it adduced as a proof of his envious disposition.

p. 139, l. 22. **Lord Castlereagh's face.** Robert Stewart, Viscount Castlereagh (1769–1822), was the Tory Foreign Minister during part of the Napoleonic war. He stood in the popular mind for harsh and repressive government and was therefore greatly hated. Lord Castlereagh was a man of handsome appearance, and Hazlitt admits more than once, with almost unwilling admiration, the detested minister's good looks. Castlereagh committed suicide.

p. 139, l. 23. **Mr Croker.** John Wilson Croker (1780–1857), Tory secretary to the Admiralty for many years, and prolific writer in *The Quarterly Review*. He is now familiar as the object of Macaulay's dislike and as the original of Rigby, the venal politician in Disraeli's *Coningsby*.

p. 139, l. 27. **Mr Murray.** John Murray (1778–1843), head of the famous publishing house in Albemarle Street, lives in literary history for his connection with *The Quarterly Review* and his long association with Byron.

p. 139, l. 29. **Hungerford Stairs.** Where Charing Cross Railway Bridge (north end) now stands.

p. 140, l. 8. **the Fleet or King's Bench.** Two famous debtors' prisons, the King's Bench in the Borough, Southwark, and the Fleet in Farringdon Street, where the Memorial Hall now stands. Both prisons have been immortalised by Dickens—the King's Bench in *David Copperfield* as the home of Mr Micawber during a period of financial embarrassment more acute than usual, and the Fleet as the scene of Mr Pickwick's incarceration at the instance of Messrs Dodson and Fogg after the case of Bardell *v.* Pickwick. Games like fives and racquets were almost the only out-door exercises possible for the prisoners or "Collegians" as Mr Dorrit preferred to call them.

p. 140, l. 20. **Mr Manners Sutton.** He became Speaker in 1817.

p, 140, l. 25. **Let no rude hand,** etc. Adapted from Wordsworth's *Ellen Irwin*:

> By Ellen's side the Bruce is laid;
> And, for the stone upon his head,
> May no rude hand deface it,
> And its forlorn "Hic jacet."

"Hic jacet" means "here lies."

ON GOING A JOURNEY

From *Table Talk*, Essay XIX. First published in *The New Monthly Magazine*, 1822.

p. 141, l. 4. **never less alone.** Quoted in Cicero, *De Officiis*, Bk III, 1, as a saying attributed to Scipio Africanus: "P. Scipionem, ...eum, qui primus Africanus appellatus est, dicere solitum scripsit Cato...'Nunquam se minus otiosum esse quam quum otiosus, nec minus solum quam quum solus esset'"—"It is related by Cato that P. Scipio—he who was first distinguished by the title of Africanus—was accustomed to say that he was never less at leisure than in his leisure and never less alone than when alone." Swift, in his *Essay on the Faculties of Mankind*, writes "A wise man is never less alone than when alone." Compare, too, Byron, *Childe Harold*, Canto III, St. xc.:

> Then stirs the feeling infinite, so felt
> In solitude, when we are least alone.

p. 141, l. 5. **The fields his study.** Bloomfield (1766–1823), *The Farmer's Boy, Spring,* l. 31:

> Strange to the world, he wore a bashful look,
> The fields his study, Nature was his book.

p. 141, l. 15. **a friend in my retreat.** Cowper, *Retirement*:

> I praise the Frenchman—his remark was shrewd—
> How sweet, how passing sweet, is solitude!
> But grant me still a friend in my retreat
> Whom I may whisper solitude is sweet.

"The Frenchman" is La Bruyère (1645–96), famous author of *Characters*.

p. 141, l. 23. **May plume her feathers,** etc.   Milton, *Comus*, 378–80:

> And Wisdom's self
> Oft seeks to sweet retired solitude;
> Where, with her best nurse, Contemplation,
> She plumes her feathers, and lets grow her wings,
> That in the various bustle of resort
> Were all to-ruffled and sometimes impaired.

p. 148, l. 28. **a Tilbury.** A kind of gig holding two persons; like the "hansom" it was named from the maker or designer.

p. 142, l. 7. **sunken wrack.** *Henry V*, Act I, Sc. ii, l. 165:

> And make her chronicle as rich with praise
> As is the ooze and bottom of the sea
> With sunken wrack and sumless treasuries.

p. 142, l. 14. **Leave, oh, leave me to my repose.** The closing line of certain stanzas in Gray's *Descent of Odin*—a conversation between Odin and the Earth-Spirit, exactly like the conversation between Wotan and Erda in Act III of Wagner's *Siegfried*. The goddess, questioned by Odin, murmurs her answer, and adds:

> Unwilling I my lips unclose:
> Leave me, leave me to repose.

p. 142, l. 16. **very stuff of the conscience.** *Othello*, Act I, Sc. ii, l. 2:

> Though in the trade of war I have slain men,
> Yet do I hold it very stuff o' the conscience
> To do no contrived murder.

p. 142, l. 28. **Out upon such half-faced fellowship.** 1 *Henry IV*, Act I, Sc. iii, l. 208.

p. 142, l. 32. **an observation of Mr Cobbett's.** For Cobbett see p. 165.

p. 143, l. 36. **give it an understanding.** *Hamlet*, Act I, Sc. ii, l. 250:

> If you have hitherto concealed the sight
> Let it be tenable in your silence still;
> And whatsoever else shall hap to-night,
> Give it an understanding, but no tongue.

p. 143, l. 37. **My old friend C——.** Coleridge. See the essay *My First Acquaintance with Poets*.

p. 143, l. 40. **far above singing.** Beaumont and Fletcher, *Philaster*, Act v, Sc. v:

> You left a kiss
> Upon these lips then, which I mean to keep
> From you for ever. I did hear you talk
> Far above singing!

p. 144, l. 4. **Allfoxden.** See p. 160.

p. 144, l. 5. **that fine madness.** A reminiscence of Drayton's Elegy *To my dearly loved friend Henry Reynolds, Esqr., Of Poets and Posey*:

> Neat Marlowe bathéd in the Thespian springs
> Had in him those brave translunary things
> That the first poets had; his raptures were
> All air and fire which made his verses clear,
> For that fine madness still he did retain
> Which rightly should possess a poet's brain.

p. 144, l. 19. **the boy Endymion.** The reader will perhaps hardly need to be reminded that the story of "pale Phoebe's" love for the Latmian shepherd Endymion has been told for all time by Keats in the first of his longer poems. The pictures of Endymion and Diana by Watts will be familiar to many.

p. 144, l. 26. **The Faithful Shepherdess.** A delightful pastoral play by John Fletcher (1579–1625), the surviving dramatist of the famous partnership.

p. 144, l. 33. **L——.** Lamb.

p. 145, l. 3. **to 'take one's ease,'** etc. 1 *Henry IV*, Act III, Sc. iii, l. 92, etc.: "What, shall I not take mine ease in mine inn but I shall have my pocket picked?"

p. 145, l. 10. **The cups that cheer.** Cowper, *The Task*, Bk IV:

> Now stir the fire and close the shutters fast,
> Let fall the curtains, wheel the sofa round,
> And while the bubbling and loud hissing urn
> Throws up a steamy column, and the cups,
> That cheer but not inebriate, wait on each,
> So let us welcome peaceful evening in.

Cowper's *Task* was published in 1784. Forty years earlier had appeared Berkeley's *Siris*, a remarkable little book recommending tap water as a cure for all diseases. Readers of *Great Expectations* will remember the famous occasion when Pip mixed this household remedy with the brandy. In section 217 of *Siris*, Berkeley contrasts the beneficent action of tar-water with that of fermented spirits, and says that the nature of tar is "so mild and benign and proportioned to the human constitution, as to warm without heating, to cheer but not inebriate, and to produce a calm and steady joy like the effect of good news."

p. 145, l. 13. **Sancho...once fixed upon cow-heel.** See *Don Quixote*, Part II, Chapter XLIX; but the circumstances were not the same. Sancho was not at an inn; he was exercising his governorship of Barataria, and had undergone some trying disappointments in the matter of food.

p. 145, l. 16. **Shandean contemplation.** A reference to Sterne's ever delightful *Tristram Shandy*; but it is not clear in what sense Hazlitt uses the word. He may mean "genial" with reference to the prevailing geniality of the book, or "informal," with reference to the rapid flitting from topic to topic characteristic of Sterne's apparently artless art.

p. 145, l. 37. **unhoused free condition.** *Othello*, Act I, Sc. ii, l. 26:

For know, Iago,
But that I love the gentle Desdemona,
I would not my unhousèd free condition
Put into circumspection and confine
For the sea's worth.

p. 145, l. 39. **lord of one's self.** Dryden, *Epistle to my Honour'd Kinsman, John Driden*:

Promoting Concord, and composing Strife,
Lord of yourself, uncumber'd with a wife.

p. 146, l. 19. **as once at Witham Common.** Witham Common is in Somerset. Hazlitt's philosophical problem is referred to more fully in the first essay (p. 19).

p. 146, l. 23. **Gribelin's engravings of the Cartoons.** Simon Gribelin (1611–1733), a French engraver who lived in England for many years, engraved the Cartoons of Raphael (see p. 171) but on a very small scale. The set of prints was published in 1707.

p. 146, l. 25. **Westall's drawings.** Richard Westall, R.A. (1765–1836), an artist of the English School, was much admired for his illustrations to the works of several poets. The National Gallery, The Wallace Collection and South Kensington Museum all possess examples of his art. There are many references to this once popular painter in Hazlitt's works, especially in *Conversations of Northcote*. Hazlitt did not admire him and posterity has confirmed that judgment.

p. 146, l. 32. **at Bridgwater.** See the essay *My First Acquaintance with Poets*, where the reading of *Paul and Virginia* is placed at Tewkesbury.

p. 146, l. 34. **Madame D'Arblay's Camilla.** See p. 160.

p. 146, l. 36. **the New Eloise.** See p. 167. It should be noted that Rousseau was one of the first to dwell in literature upon the sublime beauty of mountain scenery, which, up to his time, had been regarded by all polite people with sentiments of disgust and horror. The reference in the text is to one such passage—the letter describing the excursion on the water, Part IV, Letter 17, St Preux to Milord Edouard. The 10th of April was Hazlitt's birthday.

p. 146, l. 40. **bonne bouche.** Hazlitt incorrectly wrote *bon bouche.*

p. 147, l. 7. **green upland swells,** etc. For this passage see p. 160.

p. 147, l. 18. **the light of common day.** Wordsworth, *Ode on the Intimations of Immortality, etc.*:

> The Youth, who daily farther from the east
> Must travel, still is Nature's Priest,
>   And by the vision splendid
>   Is on his way attended;
> At length the Man perceives it die away,
> And fade into the light of common day.

p. 147, l. 20. **The beautiful is vanished and returns not.** Coleridge, *Death of Wallenstein* (translated from Schiller), Act v, Sc. i, l. 68:

> The bloom is vanished from my life.
> For O! he stood beside me, like my youth,
> Transformed for me the real to a dream,
> Clothing the palpable and the familiar
> With golden exhalations of the dawn.
> Whatever fortunes wait my future toil,
> The beautiful is vanished—and returns not.

p. 147, l. 31. **O sylvan Dee.** A reminiscence of Wordsworth's *Tintern Abbey* lines, l. 56:

> How oft in spirit have I turned to thee
> O sylvan Wye! thou wanderer through the woods.

The rest of the sentence is, no doubt, a mingled reminiscence of Revelation xxii, 1, and xxi, 6: "And he shewed me a pure river of water of life, clear as crystal, proceeding out of the throne of God and the Lamb"; and, "I will give unto him that is athirst of the fountain of the water of life freely."

p. 148, l. 6. **The landscape bares its bosom.** A reminiscence of Wordsworth's sonnet *The world is too much with us*:

> This Sea that bares her bosom to the moon;
> The winds that will be howling at all hours,
> And are up-gathered now like sleeping flowers;
> For this, for everything, we are out of tune;
> It moves us not.

p. 148, l. 15. **Beyond Hyde Park,** etc. For Etherege and his plays see p. 178. The sentiment, however, is not uttered by Sir Fopling Flutter himself:

Dorimant. To be with you I could live there [i.e. in the country] and never send one thought to London.

Harriet. Whate'er you say, I know all beyond Hyde Park's a desert to you, and that no gallantry can draw you further.

p. 149, l. 14. **The mind is its own place.** *Paradise Lost*, I, 254:

> The mind is its own place, and in itself
> Can make a Heaven of Hell, a Hell of Heaven.

p. 149, l. 17. **I once took a party to Oxford.** Charles and Mary Lamb. See the second essay *On the Conversation of Authors*.

p. 149, l. 19. **With glistering spires.** *Paradise Lost*, II, 550:

> or some renown'd metropolis
> With glistering spires and pinnacles adorned.

p. 149, l. 22. **at Blenheim.** See p. 223.

p. 149, l. 23. **powdered Cicerone.** A footman. A *cicerone* (Italian, pronounced in four syllables with the c's like ch, pl. *ciceroni*) is a guide who accompanies travellers to show them the beauties or antiquities of a place.

p. 150, l. 2. **when I first set my foot,** etc. Hazlitt first visited France in 1802 when his idol, Napoleon, was governing as First Consul. In 1822, the date of this essay, Napoleon was dead in exile, and the French people bore contentedly the yoke of the Bourbons whom they had once dethroned. Hence Hazlitt's scornful allusions lower down.

p. 150, l. 26. **Dr Johnson remarked.** See Boswell, under date 1778: "How little does travelling supply to the conversation of any man who has travelled." Modern readers may possibly dissent from Johnson's pronouncement on this point. "Travellers' tales" have now become proverbial for unveracity—and dullness.

ADDENDA

p. 91, l. 5. **palpable to feeling.** Most probably a reminiscence of *Macbeth*, Act ii, Sc. i, ll. 36–37:

> Art thou not, fatal vision, sensible
> To feeling as to sight?

The "air-drawn visions" of l. 2 no doubt came from Act iii, Sc. iv, ll. 62–63 of the same play:

> This is the air-drawn dagger which, you said,
> Led you to Duncan.

p. 128, l. 26. **Sadler's Wells.** The note on p. 241 happily needs amplification. The old theatre has been rebuilt and was reopened in 1931. It is now, in the north of London, what the Old Vic is in the south, a popular home of drama, opera and ballet.

p. 132, l. 20. **Thrills in each nerve.** This is an ingeniously blended quotation. One ingredient is indicated in the note on p. 242. Another, clearly, is Pope, *Essay on Man*, i. 217–8:

> The spider's touch, how exquisitely fine!
> Feels at each thread, and lives along the line.

p. 150, l. 8. **the vine-covered hills,** etc. A line from a song by William Roscoe, the famous Liverpool writer. It was parodied in *The Anti-Jacobin* (No. 4, Dec. 4, 1797) as "the blood bedew'd valleys and mountains of France." (*La Sainte Guillotine; a New Song attempted from the French.*)

p. 150, l. 24. **jump.** Quoted from *Macbeth*, Act i, Sc. vii, l. 7:

> We'ld jump the life to come.